D1740020

Corporate Disclosure and Corporate Governance in China

KLUWER LAW INTERNATIONAL

1 1 APR 2012

£100·00

Corporate Disclosure and Corporate Governance in China

Jane Fu

Reference Only

I Φ D

INSTITUTE OF DIRECTORS

Information Centre

Tel: 020 7451 3100

Wolters Kluwer

Law & Business

AUSTIN   BOSTON   CHICAGO   NEW YORK   THE NETHERLANDS

Published by:
Kluwer Law International
PO Box 316
2400 AH Alphen aan den Rijn
The Netherlands
Website: www.kluwerlaw.com

Sold and distributed in North, Central and South America by:
Aspen Publishers, Inc.
7201 McKinney Circle
Frederick, MD 21704
United States of America
Email: customer.service@aspenpublishers.com

Sold and distributed in all other countries by:
Turpin Distribution Services Ltd.
Stratton Business Park
Pegasus Drive, Biggleswade
Bedfordshire SG18 8TQ
United Kingdom
Email: kluwerlaw@turpin-distribution.com

STANDARD NUMBER	9789041126696
ACCESSION NUMBER	019701
CLASS MARK	ASIA PACIFIC. CHINA.FU
LOCATION	INTERNAT

Printed on acid-free paper.

ISBN 978-90-411-2669-6

© 2010, Kluwer Law International BV, The Netherlands

All rights reserved. No part of this publication may be reproduced, stored in a retrieval system, or transmitted in any form or by any means, electronic, mechanical, photocopying, recording, or otherwise, without prior written permission of the publisher.

Permission to use this content must be obtained from the copyright owner. Please apply to: Permissions Department, Wolters Kluwer Legal, 76 Ninth Avenue, 7th Floor, New York, NY 10011-5201, USA.
E-mail: permissions@kluwerlaw.com

Printed in Great Britain.

Table of Contents

About the Author

Jane (Jian) Fu, LLB (Beijing), LLM (Canberra) and PhD (UNSW), worked for eight years as a draftsperson for the Legislative Affairs Commission of the Standing Committee of the PRC National People's Congress in Beijing. During this period, she was a Judge at the People's Court in Beijing, as a researcher at School of Law, City University of Hong Kong and as an associate in the office of an international law firm in Hong Kong. Ms Fu worked at four Australian law schools as an academician. She is currently a Senior Lecturer in Law in the School of Law, Deakin University, Australia. She also held visiting positions at Oxford University in 2006, and University of California at Berkeley in 2006 and 2007. Ms Fu publishes her work extensively in China, Australia and elsewhere. Her publications focus on Chinese commercial law, Chinese civil law, comparative study of China's company and securities law and the Australian corporations law.

Foreword

Dr Jane Fu's book reviews the development of China's securities market and seeks to convey an in-depth understanding of its corporate disclosure laws and rules by examining their origins and functions. This is the first book, as far as I know, that particularly focuses on China's lawmaking process and the manner in which foreign experiences have been drawn upon in this process. Through a comparative study, this book persuasively argues that the inefficiency of China's current disclosure regulations have, to a great extent, resulted from the lack of empirical studies of foreign corporate disclosure laws and the mistakes made by the drafters of Chinese laws and regulations in the process of transplanting foreign laws into China. This book also recommends Australia as a model for incorporating foreign laws into China's unique environment.

Dr Fu was educated at law schools in both China and Australia. She has drawn upon her work experience as a draftsperson for the Legislative Affairs Commission of the People's Republic of China's Standing Committee of the National People's Congress and as a legal academic in Australia to undertake her research on corporate disclosure issues under both Chinese law and Australian law. Her book casts a much-needed light upon features of the background of Chinese corporate disclosure law that are not often discussed and debated by legal academics. It also reviews the unique history of the development of the Australian corporate disclosure system that spans more than a century. Dr Fu's empirical research supports her detailed descriptions, discussions, and evaluations of corporate disclosure laws in both China and Australia.

Dr Fu's work is an important source for further study and research on Chinese securities law, not only for legal academics, legal researchers, legal practitioners, and members of the business community, but also for Chinese lawmakers and policy makers. With the development of globalization and internationalization, it is necessary for all countries in the world to examine their lawmaking methods and processes from a comparative perspective. This is especially important for emerging and transitional countries such as China. It is equally important for other countries to understand Chinese law from a comparative perspective.

For these reasons, I commend this book of my former colleague, Dr Jane Fu, to scholars, legal practitioners, and students, as well as to lawmakers and policy makers who are concerned with China's securities laws and policy issues.

Li Fei
Vice Chairman
Legislative Affairs Commission
Standing Committee of the National People's Congress
The People's Republic of China

Preface

Information disclosure is a fundamental technique in securities regulation and corporate governance. Most countries with securities markets have developed securities regulatory regimes that strongly focus on corporate disclosure. The modern securities market in the People's Republic of China re-emerged in the late 1980s and developed extremely quickly thereafter. This market has been modelled on Western markets, especially the United States model. Chinese securities regulation reformers advocated the establishment of United States-style securities regulation, which includes a detailed corporate disclosure regime.

After the establishment of the Chinese securities market, the improvement and further reform of China's corporate disclosure regime continued to follow the United States model. Further research on Chinese securities markets has tended to be focused upon segmented areas of regulation without regard to the overall context of disclosure in China. There has been little, if any, in-depth research on the historical development of China's securities market and the formation and reform of its corporate disclosure laws and regulations. This book is intended to fill these gaps.

I have been following the development of the Chinese securities market since the mid-1990s, when I left my position as a draftsperson for the Legislative Affairs Commission of the Standing Committee of the People's Republic of China's National People's Congress so as to pursue postgraduate studies in Australia. The lack of a wide understanding of the Chinese securities market from a historical and comparative perspective prompted my interest in researching this area. My interest in this research continued after I finished my postgraduate studies. This book reports on my decade-long research efforts, and I hope it will be of interest to legal researchers, policy makers, and legal practitioners. It provides a detailed picture of the Chinese corporate disclosure regime that has emerged during the period of China's economic transition since the 1990s.

Preface

This book could not have been completed without strong support from a number of people. I wish to thank Professors Roman Tomasic, Angus Corbett, Ian Ramsay, Paul Redmond, Wang Baoshu, Wang Weiguo, Zhao Xudong, Gu Gongyun, and Jiang Ping for their kind encouragement, valuable direction, and the comments that they provided as Australian or Chinese company law authorities. I would also like to express my special gratitude to my former colleagues at the Legislative Affairs Commission of the National People's Congress for their friendly support and help. Finally, I wish to thank the anonymous interviewees who assisted me with this research, as well as Dr Hu Ruyin, Mr Yuan Xiuguo, and Mr Ouyang Danian of the Shanghai Stock Exchange, and Mr Zhang Yujun, formerly of the Shenzhen Stock Exchange, for sharing their views and insights. I should add that any errors or omissions that may exist in this book are entirely my own.

I am greatly indebted to Mr Simon Bellamy and his editorial team at Kluwer Law International for their patience and professional support of this project.

This book is dedicated to my parents. Without their unselfish support, I could not have achieved what I have in my life. During the writing of this book, my children have sustained me and have given me great joy, comfort, and support.

Jane Fu
Melbourne
January 2010

Chapter 1

Corporate Disclosure, Corporate Governance, and Law Reform in the People's Republic of China

1.1.   WHY HAS THE STUDY OF CORPORATE
            GOVERNANCE IN THE PEOPLE'S REPUBLIC OF
            CHINA BECOME IMPORTANT?

On 1 October 2009, the People's Republic of China (hereinafter PRC) held the sixtieth anniversary celebration of its founding in 1949. For the Chinese people, sixty years traditionally constitute a cycle. The PRC government organized a grand and lavish event, celebrating its many significant achievements. In his National Day Speech, PRC President Hu Jintao, wearing a Sun Yatsen suit, as Chairman Mao Zedong did on the founding day of the PRC on 1 October 1949, proudly announced that, 'today a socialist China has stood straight in the East of the world, facing modernization, facing the world and facing the future'.[1]

Rapid economic development has attracted attention from around the world upon China's corporate governance developments. There is no doubt that China can be proud of its achievements since the commencement of the economic reform effort some thirty years ago. According to the World Bank, by 2007, China had become the third-largest economy in the world.[2] In the past few years, some of China's companies, mainly large state-owned companies (usually known as SOEs), have been aggressively buying foreign businesses overseas. The failed bid

---

1. <http://cpc.people.com.cn/GB/64093/64094/10152026.html>, 2 Oct. 2009.
2. 'Li Rongrong Encourages Takeover Overseas', <www.caijing.com.cn/2009-07-04/110193145.html>, 5 Jul. 2009.

of China National Offshore Oil Corporation Ltd (CNOOC),[3] which is 70% owned by the Chinese government, to buy Unocal in the United States of America (USA) in 2005[4] caused political uproar in the USA and raised the alarm for many other countries that are China's trading partners. China Steel bought Midwest in Australia and held five seats on Midwest's board of directors in September 2008.[5] In 2009, China Minmentals' investment in Oz Minerals in Australia was finalized.[6] China Hunan Valin's investment in Fortescue is proceeding. Chinalco's failure to acquire a further shareholding in the dually listed Australian – United Kingdom company Rio Tino in early 2009 raised concern and anxiety among China's Western business partners and their various governments.

The large scale of China's capital injection and aggressive investments in countries that are rich in natural resources has raised increasing and deep concerns among these countries' governments, their business communities, and the public. While it is very important for the PRC to improve its corporate governance law and practice, it is equally important for the PRC's business-partner countries, such as Australia, to understand corporate governance issues within Chinese companies, especially state-owned companies. Only after having acquired substantial knowledge and understanding of corporate governance in the PRC can foreign governments and their business communities, such as those in Australia, deal effectively and efficiently with the Sino-Australian relationship. Unfortunately, up until now, limited comprehensive research on corporate governance in China has been done from a comparative perspective. This book aims to fill this vacuum.

The concept of corporate governance did not come into use in the PRC until the mid-1990s.[7] The lack of understanding of corporate governance in the first decade of the twenty-first century by the senior management of listed Chinese companies was confirmed by some senior executives of these companies.[8] China's great economic achievements do not compare well with the poor corporate governance practices of many Chinese companies. If we take corporate disclosure as

---

3. 'Unocal Shareholders Approve Chevron Takeover', *All Business: A D&B Company*, <www.allbusiness.com/retail-trade/food-stores/4486656-1.html>, 2 Oct. 2009.
4. Unocal was the ninth-largest oil company in the world at the time. CNOOC withdrew its bid in early August 2005 for 'unprecedented political opposition' after a flurry of legislation was introduced in both Houses of Congress of the United States aiming to derail the deal, *ibid*.
5. 'China Steel Finalises Buying Midwest by Mid September', <www.caijing.com.cn/2008-09-11/110011795.html>, 13 Jul. 2009.
6. ABC, 'Minmetals Launches Oz Minerals Takeover Bid', <www.abc.net.au/lateline/business/items/200902/s2493057.htm>, September 2009.
7. Tu, Guangshao & Zhu Congjiu (eds), *Corporate Governance: International Experience and China Practice* (Beijing: People's Press, 2001), 1.
8. The author and her colleagues' interviews of an Australian Research Council-funded Discovery Project on Corporate Governance of China's Top 100 Listed Companies, which finished at the end of 2005. Also, Mary Ma's unpublished speech at the Ninth Annual Conference of the Asia Corporate Governance Association entitled Asia Business Dialogue on Corporate Governance, which was held in Beijing from 11–12 Nov. 2009. Ma is the Managing Director of TPG (Hong Kong) and a non-executive director and former Chief Finance Officer of Lenovo Ltd, which bought the PC business from IBM. She acknowledged that even in 2007, when she was the CFO of Lenovo, she did not know much about corporate governance.

an example, since the establishment of the Shanghai and Shenzhen Stock Exchanges in 1990, there have been numerous false disclosure scandals.[9] The most recent of these was made public only days before China's grand 60th anniversary celebrations. According to an announcement made by the pivotal regulatory institution for corporate governance in the PRC, the China Securities Regulatory Commission (hereinafter CSRC) on 23 September 2009, Wuliangye Corporation Group, one of China's best-known and largest brewery companies, had been involved in breaching disclosure laws and regulatory rules. One of the breaches was the falsification of business profits of Yuan Renmibi (CNY) 8.251 billion, which was claimed to have been made by one of Wuliangye's subsidiary companies; these profits were disclosed in the 2007 annual report of Wuliangye Corporation Group. According to the CSRC, the real profits for that year were CNY 7.251 billion.[10] A huge discrepancy of CNY 1 billion appeared in the annual report, and this made investors doubt the explanation of the 'recording error' that had been given by Wuliangye Corporation Group.[11] The strong economic achievement of many Chinese SOEs and their relatively poor corporate governance have also made it important to look more closely at this area by researching China's corporate governance theory and practice. The corporate disclosure regime, as one of the fundamental systems of corporate governance, plays a critical role in this regard, and it has therefore been selected as the core area of attention of this book.

1.2.   AN OVERVIEW OF CORPORATE DISCLOSURE AND
             CORPORATE GOVERNANCE IN CHINA

1.2.1.   THE CONCEPT OF CORPORATE GOVERNANCE USED IN CHINA

Like its economic achievements, the PRC has also made significant progress in law reform since 1978. The Chairman of the National People's Congress of the PRC, Wu Bangguo, proudly declared on 8 March 2009 that the socialist legal system with Chinese characteristics was 'basically formed'. According to him, by January 2009, China had made 231 Laws, more than 600 Administrative Regulations, more than 7,000 Local Regulations, and more than 600 Autonomous Regional regulations.[12]

Among China's numerous laws, regulations, and rules, those with a direct impact on corporate governance were mainly made during the last decade, as corporate governance is a relatively new term, only recently introduced into China. Around the world, there is no universally accepted concept of corporate

---

9.   More disclosure cases will be discussed in Ch. 6.
10. <http://finance.people.com.cn/GB/10144385.html>, 30 Sep. 2009.
11. *Wuliangye Announcing Recording Error Leading to the Extra RMB 10 Billion in Profits*, <http://finance.people.com.cn/GB/10144385.html>, 30 Sep. 2009.
12. <http://society.people.com.cn/GB/8217/165799/165802/9975961.html>, 3 Oct. 2009. China's legal system is discussed in Ch. 3.

governance. However, Sir Adrian Cadbury's use of the concept in the 1992 Cadbury Report of UK[13] is widely accepted. In the Cadbury Report, 'corporate governance is the system by which companies are directed and controlled'. Generally speaking, corporate governance involves a broad range of issues regarding the management of corporations. An important underlying philosophy drawn from the economic literature in this area is concerned with the agency relationship between shareholders (who are seen as principals) and managers (who are seen as their agents). However, common law courts have not adopted this view and do not see directors as being the agents of the shareholders, but prevailing theoretical models of corporate governance do rely upon this philosophy. Corporate governance was discussed by Berle and Means in the 1930s, when they examined the separation of ownership and control in companies.[14] However, 'corporate governance' did not become a hot topic and an often-used expression in the Western world until the early 1990s. It was not until late 1994 when it was used and discussed in the PRC,[15] and it was not until 22 September 1999 when the term 'corporate governance' was for the first time formally written into the Central Committee of the Communist Party of China's (hereinafter CCCCP) Resolution on Important Issues Regarding Reform and Development of State-Owned Enterprises at the Fourth Plenary Session of the Communist Party of China's (hereinafter CPC) Fifteenth National Congress.[16]

It is well-known that China has a unitary system of government, while most Western countries have a system that promotes some degree of separation of powers; some (such as the USA, Canada, Germany, and Australia) are even structured as federal systems. The controlling and dominant status of the CPC is made clear in China's Constitution.[17] The fact that the Chinese State is under the 'leadership' of the CPC means that major changes in this society are either initiated or approved by the CPC. This has been true with regard to economic reform of China.

---

13. The Committee on the Financial Aspects of Corporate Governance and Gee and Co. Ltd, *Report of the Committee on the Financial Aspects of Corporate Governance*, 1992. As Sir Adrian Cadbury is the Chairman of this Committee, this Report is also known as the Cadbury Report.
14. This model was presented in the context of the strident legal debate between lawyers A.A. Berle and E.M. Dodd in the pages of the *Harvard Law Review* (1932), where each presented contrasting visions of the legal responsibilities of directors and of corporate governance; see further, A.A. Berle, 'Corporate Powers as Powers in Trust', *Harvard Law Review* 44 (1931): 1049; E.M. Dodd, 'For Whom Are Corporate Managers Trustees?', *Harvard Law Review* 45 (1932): 1145; and A.A. Berle, 'For Whom Corporate Managers Are Trustees: A Note', *Harvard Law Review* 45 (1935): 1365.
15. Tu, Guangshao & Zhu Congjiu (eds), *Corporate Governance: International Experience and China Practice*, 1.
16. <http://cpc.people.com.cn/GB/64162/64168/64568/65403/4429273.html>, 3 Oct. 2009. The Resolution stated that the CPC held the view that SOEs were the foundation of the state economy and China should standardize corporatization of medium-sized and large SOEs, and establish and improve corporate governance schemes in these SOEs so as to transform the management to meet the needs of the market.
17. Preamble.

In the first two decades or so after 1978, the economic reform in China was not focused on improving corporate governance, although there had been discussions about the separation of ownership and management. This served to focus motivation for China's economic reform. When the CPC decided in 1978 to conduct the economic reform, there were few private enterprises, and those that did exist were not seen as a major business form by the CPC; in contrast, the majority of China's enterprises were state-owned enterprises and township and rural collectives.[18] The term 'corporate governance' was unheard of in China at that time. On 22 December 1978, the Third Plenary Session of the CPC Eleventh National Congress published its Public Announcement *(Huiyi Gonggao)* in Beijing. It was declared in this Announcement that 'the focus of the Party's work will be switched to the building of a socialist modernization from 1979'.[19] It was also pointed out that the central government should give more self-management powers and rights to local governments and to industrial and agricultural enterprises under 'the state's uniform plan' so as to ease the over-centralization of China's economic system;[20] it was also decided that 'the number of government departments should be reduced' and that, in the case of those that ceased to be government departments, 'most of their powers and responsibilities should be transferred to specialized companies or joint companies'.[21] It is worth noting that the Third Plenary Session of the CPC Eleventh National Congress did not change the nature of the planned economic system of China.[22]

In China, the concept and origin of corporate governance were first researched and discussed in detail by the staff of the Research and Development Centre of the Shanghai Stock Exchange (hereinafter SSE) in 1997. Since then, their research on corporate governance has continued.[23] The SSE's early corporate governance research was mainly influenced by the corporate governance movements in the USA and the Organization for Economic Co-operation and Development's (hereinafter OECD) 1999 Principles of Corporate Governance.[24] In the view of the SSE, the term 'corporate governance' has been used in both the broad sense and the narrow sense. In the narrow sense, corporate governance is a system of directing and controlling companies. It is about the structure and functions of the board of directors of a company, the powers and responsibilities of the chairman of the board of directors and the managers of the company, and the related systems of

---

18.   See Fu, Jian, 'The Enterprise Concept in Chinese Law and Its Application in PRC Company Law', *Australian Journal of Corporate Law* 8, no. 3 (1998): 266–299.
19.   The Public Announcement of the Third Plenary Session of the CPC Eleventh National Congress, s. 1, <http://cpc.people.com.cn/GB/64162/64168/64563/65371/4441902.html>, 2 Oct. 2009.
20.   *Ibid.*, s. 2.
21.   *Ibid.*
22.   *Ibid.*
23.   Since 2003, the SSE has released its corporate governance report annually.
24.   Hu, Ruyin, 'The Concept and Importance of Corporate Governance', in *Corporate Governance: International Experience and China Practice*, ed. Tu Guangshao & Zhu Congjiu (Beijing: People's Press, 2001), 15–18.

incentives and supervision.[25] In the broad sense, corporate governance includes the narrow sense, as well as the systems and methods of corporate management and control for the interests of all stakeholders, and the corporate disclosure system.[26] From the sources that the SSE drew upon, it is evident that their research had been greatly influenced by the theories of corporate governance developed and/or used in the USA, the OECD, and the World Bank.[27]

1.2.2.　　　　IS CORPORATE GOVERNANCE IN CHINA IMPROVED BY THE ADOPTION
　　　　　　　OF A TOP-DOWN OR BOTTOM-UP APPROACH?

Corporate governance in China was developed by a combination of top-down and bottom-up approaches. The top-down approach was implemented by the CPC, which started the economic reform effort in late 1978 as China's sole controlling political party. In this approach, every major corporate governance plan had to be first endorsed by the CPC before it could be written into law by the National People's Congress (hereinafter NPC) or its Standing Committee (hereinafter NPCSC).[28] The bottom-up approach is the natural choice of any market economy. In this approach, corporate governance plans that are mainly borrowed from Western countries can be tried and implanted into the Chinese corporate landscape until they are clearly banned by the CPC.[29] In this combination, the top-down approach has been dominant over the bottom-up approach. This outcome is a natural result of the CPC's absolute leadership in China and its determined desire to build a socialist market economy.

The late development of corporate governance in China was consistent with its economic movement. The CPC decides and leads the economic reform in China. The development of corporate governance in China is only a by-product of such reform. Many major steps of corporate governance are adopted by the central government from the top. The following part reviews the CPC's Resolutions and Reports made during the past three decades of the economic reform, aiming at disclosing how the top-down approach has impacted on the corporate governance development in China.

For a long time after the CPC decided to begin the reform of its economic system in late 1978, the notion of a market economy was not accepted or adopted in China. As a result, there had been no discussion of the separation of ownership and the control or management of companies. By the end of 1978, China still had a centrally planned and controlled economy that was modelled on the experiences of

---

25. *Ibid.*
26. Above n. 24, Hu, 16.
27. In SSE's research, they had referred to C. Michael Jensen and William Meckling's work, the OECD Corporate Governance Principles, and the view of then President of the World Bank James D. Wolfson; see above n. 19.
28. The establishment of a modern corporate system within state-owned companies was first written into the CPC's Resolution before it was written into the PRC Company Law of 1993.
29. The adoption of an executive remuneration scheme is such an example.

the former Soviet Union. There were only a few pieces of national legislation then. It was at the Third Plenary Session of the CPC's Eleventh National Congress on 12 December 1978 that lawmaking by the PRC National People's Congress and its Standing Committee was set as a high priority;[30] it was also made clear for the first time that China would apply four rules regarding its socialist legal system, namely, 'there are laws to follow, laws must be followed, laws must be strictly enforced, and breaches of laws must be punished'.[31]

To reflect and implement the spirit of the Third Plenary Session of the CPC's Eleventh National Congress, the NPCSC enacted the PRC Sino-Foreign Equity Joint Venture Enterprises Law of 1979 (hereinafter the PRC SFEJVEL 1979) on 1 July 1979. This Law was one of the first made by China's National Parliament after China started its economic reform and open-door policy; it was also the first national law in China requiring equity joint ventures to be set up as limited liability companies[32] and to form a board of directors.[33] The purpose of the PRC SFEJVEL 1979 was to 'expand international economic cooperation and technological exchange'.[34] In other words, the term 'company' was first used then in law as a business form to accommodate the need for China's open-door policy. Domestic companies had been operating without national laws or regulations until 1992, when the State Council issued two Opinions on standardizing companies in the form of Administrative Regulations.[35]

The economic reform process in China has been gradual. The Twelfth CPC National Congress was held in Beijing from 1–11 September 1982,[36] and it created the theory of 'building a socialism with Chinese characteristics' and declared that the core task of China was 'economic construction'.[37] The Third Plenary Session of the Twelfth CPC National Congress passed the Resolution on Reforming the Economic System, in which a planned commodity economy became China's new economic system. Thus, on 12 October 1992, President Jiang Zemin pointed out that 'reform and open door started from the Eleventh CPC National Congress and expanded comprehensively after the Twelfth CPC National Congress'.[38] However, after 1982, the Chinese economy was still 'based on the plan and assisted

---

30. The Public Announcement of the Third Plenary Session of the CPC Eleventh National Congress, s. 1, <http://cpc.people.com.cn/GB/64162/64168/64563/65371/4441902.html>, 2 Oct. 2009.
31. *Ibid.*, s. 3.
32. Article 4.
33. Article 6.
34. Article 1.
35. These were the Opinion on Standardizing Limited Liability Companies and Opinion on Standardizing Joint Stock Limited Liability Companies. These two Opinions formed the basis for the drafting of the first Company Law of the PRC.
36. <http://cpc.people.com.cn/GB/64162/64168/64565/index.html>, 3 Oct. 2009.
37. The 'Architect' of China's economic reform, Deng Xiaoping, made the opening speech, pointing out that China must 'go its own way and build a socialism with Chinese characteristics', <http://cpc.people.com.cn/GB/64162/64168/64565/65448/4429495.html>, 3 Oct. 2009.
38. Jiang, Zemin, *To Speed Reform and Modernisation So as to Make Greater Achievements in the Course of Building a Socialism with Chinese Characteristics: Report to the Fourteenth CPC*

with markets'.[39] In addition, the 1982 Resolution made it clear that the economic reform was undertaken under the 'leadership of the CPC and the government' with plans, steps, and orders.[40]

However, a major breakthrough was made by the Third Plenary Session of the Twelfth CPC National Congress held on 20 October 1984 in Beijing.[41] For the first time, it was recognized that 'the ownership and management of enterprises can be separated to some extent' and that enterprises should be made 'legal persons with relevant rights and responsibilities'.[42] It was declared at this Plenary Session that the 'commodity economy is a stage which cannot be skipped in the process of development'.[43] However, the separation adopted then was focused on the separation of the government from enterprises, not of the ownership from management.

Incorporation stopped from 1989 to 1992 as a result of the decision of the CPC to 'clear up companies for three years'.[44] On the other hand, during this period of time, securities markets were opened in both Shanghai and Shenzhen.[45]

In February 1992, Deng Xiaoping made a historical speech after his tour to southern China (known as *nanxu jianghua*). He pointed out that China must observe its economic reform principles and strengthen this process.[46] This speech soon became the directive for further economic reform.

In October 1992, the CPC declared in President Jiang Zemin's Report to the Fourteenth CPC National Congress that the purpose of the economic reform was to 'establish and perfect a socialist market economy'.[47] Jiang's Report touched on a number of issues, which are corporate governance issues in a broad sense. It was pointed out that China must improve several areas in the process of building a socialist market economy, including changing the management scheme of SOEs, especially large and medium-sized SOEs. It was also pointed out that the shareholding system was beneficial for separating the government from enterprises and for changing the management plan of enterprises. It was accepted that enterprises

National Congress, <http://cpc.people.gov.cn/GB/64612/64168/64567/65446/4526308.html>, 3 Oct. 2009.

39. Hu, Yaobang, then CPC Party Chief, *Open a Brand New Situation for Construction of Socialist Modernisation: Report to the Twelfth CPC National Congress*, 1 Sept. 1982, <http://cpc.people.com.cn/GB/64162/64168/64565/65448/4429495.html>, 3 Oct. 2009.

40. The CPC Resolution on Reforming the Economic System, <http://cpc.people.com.cn/GB/64162/64168/64565/65378/4429522.html>, 3 Oct. 2009.

41. <http://cpc.people.com.cn/GB/64162/64168/64565/65378/4429527.html>, 3 Oct. 2009.

42. <http://cpc.people.com.cn/GB/64162/64168/64565/65378/4429522.html>, 3 Oct. 2009.

43. *Ibid.*

44. *The Announcement of the Fifth Plenary Session of the Thirteenth CPC National Congress*, <http://cpc.people.com.cn/GB/64162/64168/65388/444185/html>, 3 Oct. 2009.

45. Both the Shanghai and Shenzhen Stock Exchanges were set up by local governments in 1990.

46. Jiang, Zemin, *To Speed Reform and Modernisation So as to Make Greater Achievements in the Course of building a Socialism with Chinese Characteristics: Report to the Fourteenth CPC National Congress*, <http://cpc.people.gov.cn/GB/64612/64168/64567/65446/4526308.html>, 3 Oct. 2009.

47. *Ibid.*

should be made separate legal entities and participants in the market.[48] The CPC also for the first time advocated a market scheme that included a financial market of shares and debentures, a technical market, a service market, an information market, a real estate property market, etc.[49]

The Third Plenary Session of the Fourteenth CPC National Congress was held from 11–14 November 1993 in Beijing.[50] It passed a CPC Central Committee Resolution on Several Issues Regarding Building a Socialist Market Economy, which had ten parts with fifty articles. Part 4 was entitled 'Changing Management Mechanism of SOEs and Building a Modern Enterprise System'. The modern enterprise system requires clear ownership, clear rights and responsibilities, the separation of government and enterprises, and scientific management.[51]

Based on the Decision of the CPC, the NPCSC passed the first Company Law of the PRC in 1993. This Law was a product of China's then economic reform and the learning experiences that had been drawn from overseas corporate legislation.[52] The purpose of this Law was to help SOEs build a modern enterprise system.[53] From then on, SOEs began the process of the large-scale transformation into business forms of companies.

During the Fifteenth CPC National Congress, held from 12–18 September 1997, the then CPC Party Chief, Jiang Zemin, for the first time used the term 'Deng Xiaoping theory' in his Report entitled 'Holding the Big Flag of Deng Xiaoping Theory and Taking the Course of Building a Socialism with Chinese Characteristics into the 21st Century'.[54] Since then, the Deng Xiaoping theory has become one of the directing theories in the CPC's further policy making and in 1999 was written into the PRC Constitution.

The Fourth Plenary Session of the Fifteenth CPC National Congress was held during 19–22 September 1999. It marked another cornerstone of corporate governance development in China. For the first time, the term 'corporate governance' was used in the CPC Central Committee's Resolution on Major Issues Regarding SOEs Reform and Development.[55] The shareholding system was further encouraged to be used in SOEs. It advocated 'effective management of state-owned assets', 'incorporatisation of large and medium size SOEs', as well as 'building and improving their corporate governance structure'.[56] A year later, at the Fifth Plenary Session of the Fifteenth National Congress, the CPC announced that China

---

48. *Ibid.*
49. *Ibid.*
50. *The Announcement of the Third Plenary Session of the Fourteenth CPC National Congress*, <http://cpc.people.com.cn/GB/64162/64168/64567/65395/4441750.html>, 3 Oct. 2009.
51. *Ibid.*
52. Details will be discussed in Ch. 4.
53. Article 1.
54. <http://cpc.people.com.cn/GB/64162/64168/64568/65445/4429243.html>, 3 Oct. 2009.
55. *The Announcement of the Fourth Plenary Session of the Fifteenth CPC National Congress*, <http://cpc.people.com.cn/GB/64162/64168/64568/65403/4429273.html>, 3 Oct. 2009.
56. *Ibid.*

had made major achievements in building a modern enterprise system in its SOEs.[57]

The Sixteenth CPC National Congress was held in Beijing from 8–14 November 2002. The then Party Chief, Jiang Zeming, presented a Report entitled 'Building a Comprehensively Affluent Society and Opening a New Situation of a Socialism with Chinese Characteristics'.[58] According to this Report, the foundations of China's socialist market economic system had been laid, the reform of SOEs had been moving steadily, and China's living standards had reached an affluent status. This Report also set a target to build a comprehensive affluent society. To achieve this target, a number of measures were to be implemented. One of them was to authorize the central government and local governments to represent the state's shareholdings in SOEs at the central and local levels so as to deepen the reform of state assets management.[59] The CPC also required the separation of governments from SOEs and the separation of ownership from management.

The Third Plenary Session of the Sixteenth CPC National Congress was held in Beijing from 11–14 October 2003.[60] It passed the CPC Central Committee Resolution Dealing with Several Issues with Regards to Improving the Socialist Market Economic System. In this Resolution, it was pointed out that China should encourage multiple forms of ownership and construct a shareholding system as the main form of public ownership; that China should establish and improve its state assets management and supervision; that China should deepen reform of SOEs and improve its corporate governance structure; and that non-public enterprises should be given equal treatment in the areas of investment, taxation, use of land, and foreign trade.[61] The Resolution also set out the measures for improving corporate governance.[62] These were to clarify the rights and responsibilities of the shareholders' congress (or meeting), the board of directors, the supervisory board, and the managers; the CPC was to support the shareholders' congress, the board of directors, the supervisory board, and the managers of an enterprise, and to participate in the major decision-making of the enterprise; and the CPC was to focus on the role of managing its cadres who served as officers of the enterprise.[63]

The Sixth Plenary Session of the Sixteenth CPC National Congress was held in Beijing from 8–11 October 2006. This Congress passed the Resolution on Several

---

57. *The Announcement of the Fifth Plenary Session of the Fifteenth CPC National Congress*, <http://cpc.people.com.cn/GB/64162/64168/64568/65404/4429268.html>, 3 Oct. 2009.
58. <http://cpc.people.com.cn/GB/64162/64168/64569/65444/4429125.html>, 3 Oct. 2009.
59. *Ibid.*, Report entitled *Building a Comprehensive Affluent Society and Opening a New Situation of a Socialism with Chinese Characteristics*, s. 3(4).
60. <http://cpc.people.com.cn/GB/64162/64168/64569/65411/4429167.html>, 3 Oct. 2009.
61. *Ibid.*
62. Section 2(8), <http://cpc.people.com.cn/GB/64162/64168/64569/65411/4429165.html>, 3 Oct. 2009.
63. *Ibid.*

Major Issues Regarding Building a Socialist Harmonious Society.[64] It was also emphasized that opening up and reform were the only road to the development of a socialist market with Chinese characteristics and to achieving the goal of a renaissance of the great Chinese people.[65]

The Seventeenth CPC National Congress was held in Beijing from 15–21 October 2007. In his Report, the new Party Chief, Hu Jintao, pointed out that, to develop the economy, China must implement a number of measures, including preserving multiple forms of ownership; equally protecting all kinds of property rights; deepening the shareholding system reform of SOEs; adopting fair and just capital-raising requirements so as to encourage the development of individual, private, and medium and small enterprises; and building and improving the credit system in the whole society.[66]

While the Chinese government under the leadership of the CPC has been constantly reviewing its policies and plans for economic reform and enterprise reform, the theory and practice of corporate governance in Western countries have gradually had a greater impact on China in a bottom-up approach.

The Research Centre of the SSE is the one of the earliest institutions that pioneered systematic research on corporate governance theory and practice in China. Since 1997, the Centre has set up corporate governance research projects, and has attended and participated in the Asian Corporate Governance Roundtable.[67] One of the empirical studies that it did was conducting a survey of all the companies listed on the Shanghai Stock Exchange. Based on this research, the SSE released the first Directive Document on corporate governance in China – Shanghai Stock Exchange Guidelines for Corporate Governance of Listed Companies – in October 2000.

This Directive Document has seven parts, with fifty-three articles. The seven parts are entitled 'Objectives and Principles'; 'Shareholders and Annual General Meeting'; 'Directors and the Board of Directors'; 'Supervisors and the Board of Supervisors'; 'Managers'; 'Remuneration Policies'; and 'Disclosure'. The content of this Document shows that the SSE had undertaken research on all the major issues of corporate governance in a broad sense of the term. Since then, the SSE has been focused on corporate governance research and practices. Since 2003, the SSE has been publishing its Annual Corporate Governance Report, which includes the research results of its Research Centre. Sometimes, the SSE publishes interim research reports on corporate governance issues. The continuing research of the SSE has apparently guided and is still driving corporate governance lawmaking in China.

---

64. *The Announcement of the Sixth Plenary Session of the Sixteenth CPC National Congress*, <http://cpc.people.com.cn/GB/64162/64168/64569/72347/4912748.html>, 3 Oct. 2009.
65. *Ibid.*
66. Hu, Jintao's Report at the Seventeenth CPC National Congress, <http://cpc.people.com.cn/GB/64093/67507/6429847.html>, 3 Oct. 2009.
67. Zhu, Congjiu, Preface to the SSE *China Corporate Governance Report 2003* (Shanghai: Fudan University Press, 2003), 3.

Based on the research and practices of the SSE and combined with the needs of regulating both the SSE and the Shenzhen Stock Exchange (SZSE), the CSRC and the former State Economic and Trade Commission,[68] on 7 January 2001, jointly issued an administrative rule dealing with corporate governance issues in listed companies: the Code of Corporate Governance for Listed Companies in China (hereinafter CCG 2001). Relevant staff members of the SSE were involved in drafting this Code.[69] The CCG 2001 has a preface and eight chapters with ninety-five articles in total; the Code is divided into sections dealing with shareholders and shareholders' meetings; listed companies and their controlling shareholders; directors and boards of directors; supervisors and supervisory boards; performance assessments and incentive and disciplinary systems; stakeholders; information disclosure and transparency; and supplementary articles. This Code is the first set of national corporate governance regulatory rules in China.

1.2.3. STAGES OF CORPORATE GOVERNANCE DEVELOPMENT IN THE PRC

The state of corporate governance in the PRC has been consistent with its economic reform movement, especially with its capital market development. As Yao Gang, a Deputy Chairman of the CSRC emphasized on 3 November 2009, 'China's capital market is still an emerging and transitional market' with imperfect market regulatory mechanisms, immature investors, and unique shareholding structures.[70] In such a market, the corporate disclosure framework and corporate governance are accordingly undergoing constant changes. The SSE divided the development of corporate governance in China into three phases: the system of administrative governance before 1978; the planned and market-based two-track governance system that existed from 1978 to 1992; and the evolving modern corporate governance practice that has arisen since 1992.[71]

This book accepts these phases as proposed by the SSE. However, it suggests that since 1992, more phases should and could have been added to them. This book further divides the period after 1992 as, firstly, the period from 1992–1999, which focused on incorporatization and securitization reform; secondly, the period from 2000–2003, which focused on the development of a capital market; and finally, the period from 2004 to date, which has focused on implementing universal corporate governance practices.

---

68. Now part of the Ministry of Finance.
69. Shanghai Stock Exchange, *China Corporate Governance Report 2003* (Shanghai: Fudan University Press, 2003), 34.
70. 'International Symposium on Securities Investors Protection Opened in Beijing', <www.csrc.gov.cn/pub/newsite/bgt/xwdd/200911/t20091105_167227.htm>, 29 Nov. 2009.
71. Shanghai Stock Exchange, *China Corporate Governance Report 2003* (Shanghai: Fudan University Press, 2003), 33.

1.2.4.   Major Corporate Governance Issues in China

Some of the major corporate governance achievements summarized by the SSE are set out below:[72]

- *The role of the government in the management of SOEs has been redefined.* With the gradual separation of ownership and management, the state has minimized its management role in company operations. The State-Owned Assets Supervision and Administration Commission (hereinafter SASAC), which was established on 6 April 2003, was made the representative of the state's shareholding in state-owned companies and state-invested shareholding companies. The government is no longer directly involved in the operations of SOEs.
- *The legal and regulatory environment has constantly improved.* The PRC Company Law, the PRC Securities Law, amendments to the Criminal Law, and the CCG 2001 and other administrative regulations all have provided bases for the enforcement of corporate governance laws.
- *Majority shareholders' infringement upon listed companies' interests are under control.* To deal with and prevent further infringement upon the interests of listed companies, the Ministry of Finance issued Accounting Principles for Related Party Transactions and Disclosure in 1999. These Principles need to be read together with the CCG 2001 and the CSRC Circular on Issues regarding Listed Companies' Guarantee to Others.[73] Because most listed companies in China were once SOEs, the biggest problem in corporate governance is the agency problem, which is very different from the manner in which this problem arises in regard to companies in the USA. The agency problem in China was first caused by the non-tradable state-owned shares,[74] and then by the lack of responsible agents of the state-owned assets in listed companies in which tradable state-owned shares were the majority shares. Majority shareholders or insiders dominate the governance of large listed companies.[75]
- *The increasing independence of the boards of directors has boosted the boards' role.* The CSRC issued Guiding Opinions about Establishing the System of Independent Directors in Listed Companies in August 2001. Under this Administrative Rule, one-third of the directors of listed companies should have been independent directors by 30 June 2003. Independent directors have increasingly ensured the independency of the boards of

---

72. *Ibid.,* 34–45.
73. Released in June 2000 to prohibit listed companies from providing guarantees to its shareholders and the other related parties.
74. Shanghai Stock Exchange, *China Corporate Governance Report 2004: Independence and Effectiveness of Boards of Directors* (in Chinese) (Shanghai: Fudan University Press, 2004), 1.
75. Shanghai Stock Exchange, *China Corporate Governance Report 2006: Corporate Governance of State Holding Listed Companies* (in Chinese) (Shanghai: Fudan University Press, 2006), 1.

directors, although many independent directors have not been seen as being independent enough.[76]

- *Institutional investors have grown rapidly.* Institutional investors in China include mutual funds, pension funds, insurance companies, securities companies, and investment companies. They experienced substantial development only after the policy support given by the government. To fulfil its promises for accession to the World Trade Organization in November 2001, a year later, the CSRC and the People's Bank of China jointly issued the Tentative Procedures for Qualified Foreign Institutional Investors (hereinafter QFII) Investing in Domestic Securities Markets. Under this Administrative Rule, QFIIs are allowed to invest in the A-share market, which was only accessible to Chinese nationals and companies.

- *The corporate disclosure system has been improved dramatically.* Since the early 1990s, the regulators of securities markets have focused on corporate disclosure, as it is the core of a functioning securities market. China established a multi-dimensional and multi-layered disclosure regulatory system consisting of laws, administrative regulations, and administrative rules.[77] In addition, the uniform listing rules of stock exchanges, which are approved by the CSRC, also play a vital part in ensuring good corporate governance. The internationally accepted disclosure standards – accuracy, truthfulness, completeness, timeliness, and effectiveness – have all been incorporated into the Securities Law of the NPCSC and the disclosure regulations of the State Council, the disclosure rules of the CSRC, and the listing rules of the SSE and the SZSE. In 2006, China adopted the international accounting standards and rules.

Nevertheless, fundamental problems and major shortcomings in corporate governance still exist in China. According to the SSE, there are seven major problems of corporate governance in listed companies:

(1) *The shareholding structure is inappropriate.* A prominent characteristic of Chinese listed companies is an overwhelmingly large percentage of non-tradable shares.[78] The Chinese government has realized the seriousness of this problem, which was caused by the transitional nature of the economy. The Measures on Division of State-Owned Shares, which were released by the State Council in 2005, were aimed at dealing with this problem. In the near future, all the shares will become tradable on the markets.

(2) *The role of the government has been misplaced.*[79] To date, the development of the market economy is a result of the government's policy. The government has often acted as both regulator and owner of SOEs.

---

76. Shanghai Stock Exchange, *China Corporate Governance Report 2003*, (Shanghai: Fudan University Press, 2006), 39.
77. *Ibid.*, 44.
78. *Ibid.*, 46.
79. *Ibid.*, 48.

(3) *Law enforcement is inadequate, and shareholders face difficult obstacles when seeking legal actions.*[80] Although the rights of shareholders were broadened in the Securities Law of 2005, the procedures for exercising these rights are unclear, especially in regard to the bringing of shareholder representative actions; these procedures diminish the significance of the protection mechanisms in practice. Civil compensation is still minimal and discourages their use.

(4) *Insiders' control in corporate affairs without monitoring created 'poor companies and rich insiders'.*[81]

(5) *The external governance structure is far from perfect.* The market function in governance is still very weak, as the current system provides loopholes for market manipulation and insider trading;[82] institutional shareholders play an insignificant role, as the market is dominated by individual shareholders who are mainly interested in short-term profits and exhibit herding behaviours.[83]

(6) *The quality of disclosure is not guaranteed.* 'New regulations concerning disclosure are drafted and enacted with impressive speed, but the practice of disclosure lags behind'.[84]

(7) *Fiduciary duties have not been imposed on directors, supervisors, or managers of listed companies.*[85]

1.3. ESTABLISHING THE CORPORATE DISCLOSURE REGIME AS A TOOL FOR IMPROVING CORPORATE GOVERNANCE IN CHINA

Corporate disclosure, an idea often associated with the famous expression, 'Sunshine is said to be the best of disinfectants; electronic light the most efficient policeman,' by American Judge Louis Brandeis,[86] has been a priority from the beginning of establishing securities markets in China. Disclosure rules have been frequently added and updated since the first disclosure rule was issued in 1993. However, in the first decade of the development of the Chinese securities market, the disclosure regime was not connected to corporate governance. The corporate disclosure regime was not seen as an important aspect of corporate governance until 2000, when the SSE first issued the Guidelines for Corporate Governance to regulate the companies listed on its market.

---

80. *Ibid.*, 50.
81. *Ibid.*, 52.
82. *Ibid.*, 53.
83. *Ibid.*, 54.
84. *Ibid.*, 55.
85. *Ibid.*, 57.
86. L.D. Brandeis, *Other People's Money and How the Bankers Use It* (Chevy Chase: National Home Library Foundation, 1933), 62.

1.4.   TRANSPLANTING FOREIGN CORPORATE
          DISCLOSURE LAWS INTO CHINA

There is an old Chinese saying that, 'When mandarins are planted in the south of the Huai River, they will become zhi'[87] *(ju sheng huai nan ze wei zhi)*. In the same vein, any transplantation of foreign law must fit into the cultural, legal, and political environment of China.

Corporate practices in China have demonstrated that China's disclosure laws that have been borrowed heavily from Western securities markets often lose their functions in practice. The lack of knowledge about how best to transplant foreign laws into China is one of the most fundamental reasons for the widespread breaches of disclosure laws and rules. The seriousness and prevalence of these breaches of disclosure laws and rules in the two decades or so of the history of China's securities market have provided the impetus for undertaking the research reported in this book on corporate disclosure in China.

1.5.   IMPROVING THE APPROACH OF TRANSPLANTING
          FOREIGN LAWS USING THE AUSTRALIAN
          TRANSPLANTATION EXPERIENCE

Although the Australian approach to transplanting foreign laws is far from perfect, it provides a valuable experience for China. Among Western countries, the Australian securities market emerged relatively late. Its first national market was not formed until 1987;[88] however, this market has been operating quite efficiently and effectively. It avoided the negative impacts of the 1997 Asian financial crisis and performed much better than its Western counterparts during the global financial crisis that started in late 2008. It did not fall as badly as the New York Stock Exchange or the London Stock Exchange during the global financial crisis of 2008.

The fundamental reason for Australia's success is that its government and market regulators updated their laws and rules in a timely manner so as to meet the needs that arose in practice. For instance, Australian corporate disclosure laws are among the most detailed and strict in the world. Although Australia has a relatively new national securities market, its corporate governance practices are much better than those in many other Western countries. Australia has had less corporate scandals than many other Western countries, although it has not been immune to corporate scandals. It is in this sense that this book advocates the Australian approach to China's adoption of foreign laws; it is neither the intention nor the purpose of this book to advocate the adoption of Australian disclosure laws as such. Although the Australian approach is not perfect, it provides a valuable experience for China's lawmakers, who have been keen to learn from foreign laws.

---

87. *Zhi* is a kind of fruit that looks like mandarins but tastes bitter.
88. The emergence and development of the Australian securities markets will be discussed in Ch. 7.

Chapter 2
Introduction

2.1.   BACKGROUND OF THE FORMATION OF THE
     CORPORATE DISCLOSURE REGIME IN THE PRC

The current securities market of the PRC emerged very late in the history of the development of modern securities markets. Although securities had been issued in the late 1970s and the early 1980s after a long absence dating from the mid-1950s, the first national securities market, the Shanghai Stock Exchange, did not begin to operate until 19 December 1990.[1] Compared with securities markets in Western countries, the PRC market emerged for quite different reasons. To meet the needs for capital of PRC enterprises, the issuing of shares was first used by small collective enterprises in the countryside from 1979 to 1983,[2] when the PRC was still a planned economy.[3] At that time, private ownership had not been recognized by the Constitution[4] of the PRC and companies had not been formally recognized as business associations.[5] However, with the deepening of economic reforms, including the reform of the banking system, the state could no longer order the banks to provide all the funds needed by state-owned enterprises.

  Thus, the issuing of shares became a major mechanism for SOEs to meet their capital needs. The government not only allowed this to occur, but also encouraged some large SOEs (which were already in financial difficulty) to issue shares so that the State could ease its financial burdens. In contrast, share issuing in

---

1. Li, Zhangzhe, *Finally Successful: The Report on the Chinese Securities Market Development* (in Chinese) (Beijing: World Knowledge Press, 2001), 151.
2. *Ibid.*, 61.
3. Under Article 15 of the Constitution of 1982, 'The state practises a planned economy on the basis of socialist public ownership'.
4. Under Article 11 of the Constitution of 1982, 'The individual economy is a complement to the socialist public economy'.
5. The term 'company' had not been used in the national laws passed during this period of time.

Western countries is an important means for most companies to raise capital from the public, and the government is not usually involved in such fund raising by companies. From the establishment of the London Stock Exchange in 1773 until the market crash of the late 1920s, Western securities markets developed largely free of government intervention; this reflected the laissez-faire environment that existed up until that time.[6] In comparison, the formation and development of the PRC's securities market were affected by government policies from an early stage of its emergence. Strong governmental interference in the PRC's securities market is fundamentally different from the situation that is found in Western securities markets, which largely emerged and developed in a free-market context.

The PRC's securities market is often described as an emerging and transitional market[7] with unique features that are substantially different from those of mature and complex securities markets, such as those in the USA, the UK, and Australia. The PRC's securities market emerged soon after the commencement of economic reforms in the late 1970s. This signalled that the Chinese government realized that the planned economy had to be changed. However, some four decades of experience with a planned economy had already had a deep influence on the development of the Chinese economy. The state continued to embrace the planned economy when the securities market started to emerge in the early 1980s.[8] The government did not constitutionally adopt a market economy until 1993,[9] but even then, the PRC distinguished its economy from that of most Western countries by labelling it as 'a socialist market economy'.[10] During the 1980s, the PRC's economy experienced a transition from a planned economy to a planned commodity economy.[11] The PRC's economy is still in a transitional stage of development, now moving from a planned commodity economy to the so-called socialist market economy. The PRC's securities market is still experiencing many changes as a result of this ongoing transition.

The development of the PRC's securities markets has followed a pattern that is very different from that of most Western securities markets. The two securities

---

6. Hong, Weili, *Securities Regulation: Theory and Practice* (in Chinese) (Shanghai: Shanghai University of Finance and Economics, 2000), 104–105.
7. Hong, Weili, *Preface* in *Securities Regulation: Theory and Practice*; Zhou, Daojiong, *Promote the Standardisation and Development of China's Securities Market by Attaining Perfection of Securities Legislation: Opening Remarks for the International Symposium on the Securities Law Bill* (Beijing: Law Press, 1997), 3; the China Securities Regulatory Commission, *China Capital Markets Development Report* (in Chinese) (Beijing: China Finance Press, 2009), 3.
8. Article 15 of the PRC Constitution of 1982 provides that, 'The state practises a planned economy on the basis of socialist public ownership'.
9. Article 15, the PRC Constitution of 1993.
10. Under this economic system, public ownership is still the dominant part of the whole economy.
11. The Twelfth National Congress of the Chinese Communist Party (hereinafter the CCP) held its Third Plenary Meeting in Beijing in 1984. This Meeting passed the Resolution of the Central Committee of the Chinese Communist Party on Economic Reform. This Resolution points out that the socialist economy of China is a planned commodity economy based on public ownership. See fn. 35 of vol. 3 of *Select Article Collections of Deng Xiaoping* (in Chinese) (Beijing: People's Press, 1993).

exchanges of the PRC were first established by local governments with the approval of the central government.[12] They began to move from the control of their local governments to the direct control of the central government, when the State Securities Commission and its operational arm, the CSRC, both were established at the end of 1992.[13] The enactment of the PRC's first Securities Law in 1998 set the regulatory role of the CSRC.[14] Under this Law, the articles of association of each stock exchange have to be approved by the CSRC;[15] the general manager of each stock exchange is also appointed by the CSRC.[16] In addition, each stock exchange adopted the same Listing Rules that were approved by the CSRC,[17] and more than 90% of listed PRC companies are former SOEs.[18] However, the supremacy of the CSRC's securities market regulatory role was not finalized until August 1997. This will be discussed in detail in Chapter 4. In 2005, the PRC made substantial amendments to the Securities Law, which, however, maintained the CSRC's control of the two stock exchanges.[19] These led to the unique features that are evident in the PRC securities market. To understand this market, it is necessary to review these unique features and to identify the common features that are shared with the markets in other countries.

The PRC's economic reform was one of the results of its open-door policy. The formation of its securities market has, however, been greatly influenced by ideas drawn from securities markets in other countries. With more and more knowledge of the practices of Western countries, the PRC learned a great deal from major Western countries and regions. However, it faced a major problem in choosing an appropriate model that would be used to establish a regulatory framework for its own market. As the USA was viewed as having the most developed economy, the American model was always treated as the ideal model by the Chinese.[20] Moreover, the American experience has always been studied and adopted first because the senior staff of the CSRC, from an early stage, had been

---

12. The Shanghai Stock Exchange was established by the Shanghai municipal government with the approval of the Central Committee of the CCP; see Li, Zhangzhe, *Finally Successful: The Report on the Chinese Securities Market Development*, 129; The Shenzhen Stock Exchange was established by the Shenzhen municipal government with the approval of the central government; see Li, Zhangzhe, *Finally Successful: The Report on the Chinese Securities Market Development*, 177.
13. C. Walter & F.J.T. Howie, *Privatizing China: The Stock Markets and Their Role in Corporate Reform* (Singapore: John Wiley & Sons (Asia) Pte Ltd, 2003), 59.
14. Article 7.
15. Article 96.
16. Article 100.
17. Before 1997, each stock exchange had its own listing rules. From 1997 to 2000, both the Shanghai and the Shenzhen Stock Exchanges had similar listing rules, in which there were only two Articles that were different. Since 2001, both stock exchanges have adopted standard listing rules, which were approved by the CSRC.
18. Tu, Guangshao & Zhu Congjiu (eds), *Corporate Governance: International Experience and Chinese Practice* (in Chinese) (Beijing: People's Press, 2001), 103.
19. Articles 103, 107, and 118.
20. Zhou, Yousu (ed.), *General Theories on Securities Law* (in Chinese) (Chengdu: Sichuan People's Press, 1999), 12.

educated in and had worked in the USA.[21] In the meantime, the Hong Kong experience was viewed as being similar to other Western models (especially the United Kingdom [UK] model), because it had been a colony of the UK from 1842 to 1997. Geographically and culturally, because Hong Kong is so close to mainland China, it was convenient for mainland China to learn from the Hong Kong experience. As has been mentioned, many PRC lawmakers and securities-market regulators had been educated in and had worked in the USA,[22] or they had worked at the Hong Kong Securities and Futures Commission.[23] For these reasons, the securities regulatory experiences of the USA and Hong Kong became the main models for the PRC to rely upon as it sought to establish its own regulatory regime.[24] The drafting of the Company Law of 1993 and the Securities Law of 1998, as well as the drafting of the Listing Rules of the stock exchanges, saw the experiences of the USA and Hong Kong being closely studied by PRC policy-makers and reformers.[25]

However, if we look at the development of the PRC securities market in the past decade or so, we can find that this market has always been quite vulnerable. For example, in October 2007, the Shanghai Composite Index jumped to more than 6,000 points. Beginning in November 2007, share prices began to fall. At the end of January 2008, the Shanghai Composite Index fell below 5,000 points, and on 28 February 2008, both the Shanghai and Shenzhen Stock Exchanges experienced a significant 'black Monday' fall for no apparent reason. The Shanghai market fell by 342 points or 7.19%, while the Shenzhen market fell by 1,116.18 points or 6.45%.[26] On 18 June, the Shanghai market fell to 2,748.87 points and the Shenzhen market fell to 9,161.56 points.[27] In September, the Shanghai market fell to 1,680 points. On 8 September 2009, the Shanghai market closed at 2,930

21. Walter, Carol E. & Fraser J.T. Howie, *Privatizing China: The Stock Markets and Their Role in Corporate Reform* (Singapore: John Wiley & Sons (Asia) Pte Ltd, 9.

22. A former executive deputy chairman of the CSRC, Gao Xiqing was educated at Duke Law School in the USA and had about five years' of work experience on Wall Street before he was appointed as the first Chief Council of the CSRC.

23. One of the former deputy chairpersons of the CSRC, Laura Cha worked as a deputy chairperson of the Hong Kong Securities and Futures Commission; a former special counsel of the CSRC, Anthony Neoh was former Chairman of the Hong Kong Securities and Futures Commission (HKSFC).

24. Among the foreign experts on drafting the Securities Law invited by the CSRC in 1997, most of them came from the USA and Hong Kong, even though there were a few from Japan and the UK; see the CSRC (ed), *Collection of Essays and Articles from the International Symposium on the Securities Law Bill* (in Chinese and English) (Beijing: Law Press, 1997).

25. According to the author's experience when working for the legislature in the PRC, the drafters especially visited Japan, the UK, the USA, and Hong Kong during the process of drafting the Company Law of 1993. According to the CSRC (ed.), *Collection of Essays and Articles from the International Symposium on the Securities Law* (in English and Chinese) (Beijing: The Law Press, 1997), the foreign securities law experts were from the USA, the UK, Japan, and Hong Kong.

26. <www.caijing.com.cn.todayspecx/finance/2008-01-28/46781.shtml>, 29 Jan. 2008.

27. <http://business.sohu.com/20080619/n257609252.shtml>, 19 Jun. 2008.

points.[28] Over the past two decades, contraventions of the Securities Law and the Listing Rules have occurred from time to time. Among these breaches, one of the most serious problems was that of false corporate disclosure; from the 1993 case of Beihai Zhengda Co. acquiring shares in Suzhou Sanshan Co., to the *Qiongminyuan Co.* case of 1996, to the *Hongguang Industrial Co.* case of 1998, to the *Dongfang Guolu Co.* case of 1999, to the *Daqing Lianyi Co.* case of 2004, to the *Kelong Electrics* case of 2005 and the *Hangxiao Ganggou* case of 2007, it seemed that false and misleading disclosure had become a widespread phenomenon in the PRC securities market. Not surprisingly, the CSRC designated 2001 as the 'Year of Supervision' and focused on the investigation and punishment of false disclosure and fraudulent conduct in the securities market. According to a government newspaper, *The China Securities Daily*, the CSRC found that cases of false and misleading disclosure occurred every month in 2001. On 3 August 2001, the influential *Caijing* magazine revealed that a listed company – the Yinguangxia Corporation – fabricated an operating result of CNY 745 million so as to achieve its listing.[29] This has been the largest PRC case thus far involving false disclosure. Lack of transparency is the major weakness of the PRC's securities market. Why? This book aims to identify and explain the principal reasons for false corporate disclosure practices in the PRC. Based upon the analysis of PRC disclosure practices, it also makes suggestions for the improvement of PRC securities regulation and the building of a strong and effective securities market in China, especially from the perspective of how foreign laws should be transplanted into the PRC.

How can a strong securities market be built? Professor Bernard Black has proposed that there are two essential prerequisites for strong public securities markets. In his opinion, a country's securities law and related institutions must give minority shareholders the following: (1) good information about the value of a company's business; and (2) the confidence that the company's insiders (its managers and controlling shareholders) will not cheat investors out of most or all of the value of their investments through self-dealing. Only if these two requirements are achieved will a country have the potential to develop a vibrant securities market that can provide capital to growing firms.[30]

The PRC's securities market has been vulnerable since the early 1990s. It is still a very weak market if we evaluate it in reference to the criteria proposed by Professor Black: first, investors cannot acquire accurate information about PRC listed companies under the current law; and second, investors cannot improve their confidence in this market because they have often been cheated by both company insiders and the government that controls the market.

As the PRC attempts to build an efficient and effective securities market, it must solve the problem of finding the best way to deal with the two fundamental

---

28. <http://finance.people.com.cn/GB/67815/68059/10013576.html>, 8 Sep. 2009.
29. Walter, Carol E. & Fraser J.T.Howie, *Privatizing China: The stock Markets and Their Role in Corporate Reform* (Singapore: John Wiley & Sons (Asia) Pte Ltd), xxxvi.
30. B. Black, 'The Legal and Institutional Preconditions for Strong Securities Markets', *UCLA Law Review* 48 (2001): 781–858 at 783.

prerequisites for a strong securities market as proposed by Professor Black. When one looks at the design and formation of the PRC's securities market, it can be seen that there has been much regulatory activity in the PRC; this is evident when the nature of US and Hong Kong securities regulation is compared with that of the PRC. However, this book instead looks at Chinese securities regulation from a perspective different from that which most PRC reformers have relied upon to date. This book reviews Chinese securities regulation, especially its disclosure regime, from the perspective of the Australian securities regulation experience.

One important reason for this line of analysis is that Hong Kong's regulatory framework was greatly influenced by the Australian experience through the involvement of Australians who worked or continue to work for the Hong Kong Securities and Futures Commission.[31] This suggests that the Australian model of securities regulation has indirectly influenced the development of the PRC's securities regulation, which justifies a more systematic comparison with Australian securities market experience than has hitherto been available. With the signing of a Memorandum of Understanding between the Chinese stock exchanges and the Australian Stock Exchange, Australian securities regulation ideas will have a more direct impact on PRC's securities regulation. This foreign influence is reflected in the PRC's securities regulatory regime, as can be seen in the drafting of the national Securities Law, securities regulations, and administrative rules.[32] Another reason for choosing the Australian model to study is that, after the collapse of Enron and WorldCom in the USA, some Chinese regulators began to doubt the appropriateness of choosing the USA as the ideal model.[33]

A further reason for the PRC to study foreign experiences is its need to solve the problems that it has been facing since its accession to the World Trade Organization (WTO). The PRC formally became the 143rd member of the WTO on 11 December 2001. In its agreements with the WTO, the PRC promised to open its securities industry to foreign brokers.[34] This process had begun when it adopted the system of Qualified Foreign Institutional Investors in December 2002 to allow some approved foreign institutional investors to invest in the Chinese securities markets.[35] To regulate new participants in the Chinese securities market, the PRC again had to look at the experiences of other countries. Opening its securities markets, on one hand, requires the PRC to review its approach to the inception of foreign laws and practices. On the other hand, countries that wish to see their firms enter into the Chinese securities industry have to study the PRC securities

---

31. An Australian had been appointed as the first Chairman of the HKSFC. According to an interview, a former HKSFC Chairman, Anthony Neoh, many Australians had worked at the HKSFC.
32. Several Australian academic and professionals were involved in the drafting.
33. Zhou, Xiaochuan, then Chairman of the CSRC, Speech at the International Symposium on Development of China Securities Investment Funds 2002, <www.peopledaily.com.cn>, 19 Jun. 2002.
34. 'CSRC Publishes the Main Concessions on the Securities Market Access in China's WTO Accession' (in Chinese), *The Chinese Weekly*, Melbourne, 14 Dec. 2001, 21.
35. The CSRC, *China Capital Markets Development Report*, 32.

market because of its fundamental differences from their own markets. Foreign investors also need to study this market because of its great potential for profit, while realizing that it also has potential risks.

2.2. THE SIGNIFICANCE OF THIS BOOK

Because Australian securities regulation has had an indirect influence on PRC's securities regulation and continues to have an impact on this market by the direct contacts that exist between the securities regulators of these two countries, a book examining comparative corporate disclosure regulations in China and Australia is likely to generate important insights. Since its establishment, the Australian securities market has been relatively stable.[36] This is especially true when compared with the American securities market following the shock caused by the collapses of high-profile American companies such as Enron and WorldCom. Even during the global financial crisis that started in 2008, the Australian securities market did not suffer as badly as its other Western counterparts did because Australia was one of the very few developed countries that just barely avoided the economic recession. The practices of the Australian securities market, as well as the way in which Australia has adopted foreign experiences in securities regulation, have become important for the PRC to learn from, if it wants to improve its regulatory regime to suit the development of its domestic market.

The unique features of the PRC's transitional securities market and its regulations, as well as the lack of empirical study of Chinese securities regulation, call for an examination of the issues developed in this book, particularly in regard to the information disclosure regime in the PRC's securities market. The significance of using a securities market as a major means of raising capital by SOEs, the opening of the securities market to foreign investors following the PRC's WTO commitments, and the ongoing negotiations on a free trade agreement between the PRC and Australia[37] have made a sustained study of PRC's securities market regulation both meaningful and important.

There are a number of reasons why corporate disclosure is important in this analysis: first, disclosure is the most important common means of ensuring the implementation of the principles of fairness, openness, and justice. An American jurist, Justice Louis Brandeis, first emphasized the importance of high-quality disclosure by making the analogy that, 'Sunshine is said to be the best of disinfectants; electronic light the most efficient policeman'.[38] This sentiment has often

---

36. However, this should not be overstated; see further T. Sykes, *Two Centuries of Panic: A History of Corporate Collapses in Australia* (Sydney: Allen & Unwin Australia, 1988).
37. The FTA negotiations officially started on 23 May 2005; see 'Wu Bangguo Opens FTA Forum with High Ranking Goodwill', *Australia: China Connections*, June/July 2005, 14.
38. L.D. Brandeis, *Other People's Money and How the Bankers Use It* (Chevy Chase: National Home Library Foundation, 1933), 62.

been subsequently applied to securities market regulation around the world. In other words, disclosure makes the securities market more transparent, which is crucial in maintaining investor confidence in securities markets because investors trade on the basis of securities information. From this point of view, securities law is fundamentally about disclosure regulation. All securities markets, whether developed or developing, are concerned with this fundamental issue.[39]

Second, disclosure is a key tool in raising governance standards.[40] Disclosure is as much an opportunity for corporations to establish their business aims and principles as it is a means of enhancing their accountability.[41] The PRC formally started a move towards good corporate governance when the CSRC released the Code of Corporate Governance for Listed Companies in January 2002. This move was well in step with corporate governance developments occurring elsewhere around the world.

Third, it is argued here that the PRC's securities market emerged for reasons that were different from those that led to the establishment of securities markets in Western countries. The PRC government had strong control of the market, and disclosure was not one of the key issues that concerned the government at the time of the establishment of the market. In most Western countries, the corporate system had been established at least since the mid-nineteenth century. Companies were viewed as having the legal status of separate legal entities at least since the decision in the UK case *Salomon v. Salomon & Co.* Ltd [1897] AC 22 in 1897.

Issuing securities is one of the many ways that companies can raise capital. Companies themselves can decide whether they should raise capital by issuing securities, and they can decide how many securities they should issue. A free-market economy is the foundation for companies to raise capital successfully by issuing securities, but in the PRC, issuing stocks has been used for different reasons. As mentioned above, in the late 1970s and the early 1980s, share issuing was used by collective enterprises in the countryside to raise capital,[42] and in the mid-1980s, small non-state-owned companies started raising capital by issuing shares.[43] The shares issued then were really more like company bonds, as they were not freely transferable and there was no market for the trading of these shares. The so-called shareholders were guaranteed the repayment of capital. In addition, they were paid 'interest' rather than dividends. During the period from 1984[44] to 1992,

---

39. Developing markets such as the PRC have been disturbed by the existence of false and deceptive disclosure from the beginning of the emergence of the market. Developed markets such as those in the USA and Australia have been greatly damaged by non-compliance with disclosure rules. The collapses of Enron and WorldCom in the USA and HIH and One.Tel in Australia are widely discussed cases of false and deceptive disclosure.
40. A. Cadbury & I.M. Millstein, *The New Agenda for ICGN*, Discussion Paper No. 1 for the ICGN Tenth Anniversary Conference, London, July 2005, 13.
41. *Ibid.*
42. Li, Zhangzhe, *Finally Successful: The Report on the Chinese Securities Market Development* (in Chinese) (Beijing: World Knowledge Press, 2001), 151.
43. *Ibid.*
44. The first joint stock company – Beijing Tianqiao Shareholding Company – was established in July 1984. See Wang, Yuming & An Jiang, *The Economic Legal Perspective of State-Owned*

the PRC gradually began to experiment with establishing a modern enterprise system. However, the joint stock companies established during this period of time did not clarify the property rights of the companies and did not establish systems of corporate governance. As a famous Chinese economist has argued, 'The newly established securities market was born disabled' because of the lack of normal forms of companies.[45] With the reform of SOEs, the state could not continue to fund many SOEs that kept losing money. In 1992, the State Council issued the Regulation Concerning Change of Management of SOEs, which aimed to direct SOEs to establish a modern enterprise system. According to the government, a modern enterprise system was intended to recognize that companies were separate legal entities and were not subjects of the government.

The NPCSC passed the PRC's first Company Law in 1993, seeking to encourage the transformation of SOEs into companies. Under this Law, some SOEs were transformed into joint stock companies and raised funds by issuing shares to the public. At that time, many SOEs were losing money and the government therefore urged them to try to solve their financial problems by resorting to the issuing of shares.[46] Thus, it can be seen that the establishment of securities markets in the PRC was planned by the government. This is very different from the explanations for the issuing of shares by companies in Western countries.

Fourth, the PRC had adopted a quota system for share issuing for a decade or so after the establishment of its Shanghai and Shenzhen Stock Exchanges; this had made share issuing a privilege for some enterprises, especially SOEs. This system encouraged many enterprises to ignore the improvement of their performance, focusing instead on changing their names and seeking to gain profits from share issuing.[47] To some extent, the quota system prevented the PRC from building transparency in its securities market. The quota system for stock issuing was adopted in the PRC before 1999.[48] Under this system, each year, the central government made a plan to allow a certain number of companies to issue certain kinds of stocks, and it set the amount of securities that could be issued. The central and local governments jointly decided which companies could issue shares and how many shares they could issue. Most share-issuing companies were SOEs; some of the loss-making SOEs were encouraged by the government to issue shares so as to use up the quota. To meet the Shanghai and Shenzhen Stock Exchanges' requirements of share issuing, SOEs and their provincial government supporters often made false disclosures about the operations of these SOEs.[49]

    Enterprises Reform (in Chinese) (Beijing: China People's Public Security University Press, 2001), 16.

45. Wu, Jinglian, *Ten Years of Development of the Securities Market* (in Chinese) (Shanghai: Shanghai Far East Press, 2001), 60.
46. Wang & Jiang, *The Economic Legal Perspective*, 19.
47. *Ibid.*
48. Liu, Shuqiang, *Annotation of the Securities Law* (in Chinese) (Beijing: The People's Court Press, 1999), 46.
49. For example, the listing of Yinguangxia was encouraged and approved by the local government even though it had not made much profit.

Fifth, another unique feature of the PRC's securities market is that this market is often described as a 'policy market' by the Chinese people.[50] This is because the PRC's securities market is controlled by the central government. The rise and fall of share prices does not depend so much on the performance of the companies as on changing government policies. Pressure from investors has often forced the government to adopt policies that have pushed up share prices. This practice has led to a failure to appreciate the importance of disclosure. For example, the CSRC once had to adopt four so-called market-saving policies so as to raise share prices that were affected under pressure from investors.[51] Influential economists have also affected changes of official policies. In early 1994, when securities prices fell dramatically, several influential economists argued that the 'securities market is a result of the economic reform and if we want to save the reform we must save the securities market'.[52] Up until that time, economists in the PRC had not developed a theory regarding how to best build a market economy.

Although the Securities Law enacted at the end of 1998 tried to diminish the government's interference in the market by adopting a registration system of issuing shares in place of the quota system, the government retained strong control over the securities market. One example of this is the change of policy on sale of non-tradable state-owned shares. In June 2001, the State Commission of Economics and Trade[53] released the Measures for the Reduction of State-Owned Shares. This Administrative Rule caused a sharp fall in the securities market.[54] Consequently, the CSRC had to release another Administrative Rule in August 2001 to urgently suspend the implementation of the Administrative Rule issued by the State Commission of Economics and Trade on state-owned share reductions.[55] The problem with the non-tradable state-owned shares was not solved until 2005, when Measures for the Division of State-Owned Shareholding were released by The Ministry of Commerce and the CSRC. It can therefore be seen that the PRC's securities market is not based on a free-market economy and that this market is still under the strict control of the government. From the mid-1980s until the present, the influence of the government can be seen in many areas of the process of economic development.

Although Chinese legislators and securities regulators have adopted a number of disclosure laws and rules that are mainly based on experiences from Western countries,[56] whether or not these rules work effectively in a different market situation remains unclear. The reasons for this are included among the issues that this book will examine.

---

50. Securities Daily, *Essays on Securities Economy* (Beijing: China Economy Press, 1997), 21.
51. *Ibid.*
52. Hong, Weili, *Securities Regulation: Theory and Practice* (in Chinese) above n. 6, 71.
53. This Commission had been merged with the Ministry of Foreign Trade and Cooperation as the Ministry of Commerce in March 1998.
54. <www.peopledaily.com.cn>, 15 Jun. 2001.
55. *Ibid.*
56. The CSRC (ed.), *Disclosure Requirements of China Securities Market 2001* (Beijing: China Finance and Economics Press, 2001), 1.

The evolution of securities regulation in the world makes this book especially meaningful as China seeks to determine how best to adopt Western practices in this area. From time to time, lawmakers and securities regulators in Western countries learn lessons from the effects of a bubble economy caused by false and misleading disclosure: in such cases, they implement clear, mandatory, and timely disclosure requirements for public companies. Corporate disclosure regulatory regimes in these countries have been seen as relatively comprehensive. Unfortunately, this has not stopped some companies' misconduct of giving false or misleading information to securities markets, which demonstrates the limited effectiveness of disclosure regimes. Following corporate collapses, such as Enron and WorldCom in the USA, as well as HIH and One. Tel in Australia, in 2001, the issue of reforming disclosure regulations and enhancing corporate governance were once again put on the agenda of lawmakers and regulators in many countries, including the PRC.[57] Since then, determining how to reform disclosure regimes so as to make them more effective and preventive has become a common challenge facing both complicated securities markets, such as those of the USA and Australia, and transitional markets, such as that of the PRC.

| 2.3. | THREE HYPOTHESES EXPLORED IN THIS BOOK[58] |

Professors Pistor and Wellons propose three relevant hypotheses that test the role of law in economic development in six Asian countries: the convergence hypothesis, the divergence hypothesis, and the differentiation hypothesis.[59] The convergence hypothesis suggests that laws converge as a result of economic convergence,[60] the divergence hypothesis suggests that legal developments in each country are idiosyncratic,[61] and the differentiation hypothesis suggests that some areas of law may converge with economic development while others may persistently diverge.[62] Pistor and Wellons found evidence that favoured the differentiation hypothesis when they looked at legal developments in Asia. Their research also found that laws had not fully converged, despite the existence of strong signs of economic convergence.[63]

---

57. The collapse of Enron and WorldCom in the USA led to the enactment of the Sarbanes-Oxley Act of 2002, the collapse of One.Tel and HIH in Australia led to the HIH Inquiry and the enactment of Corporate Law Economic Reform Program 9 (Audit Reform and Corporate Disclosure) Act of 2004.
58. The concept of 'hypothesis' used in this book is in the sense of legal analysis and should not be seen as that used in scientific testing.
59. K. Pistor & P.A. Wellons, *The Role of Law and Legal Institutions in Asian Economic Development 1960–1995* (Oxford: Oxford University Press, 1998), 263.
60. *Ibid.*
61. *Ibid.*
62. *Ibid.*
63. *Ibid.*

This book will assess the applicability of these three hypotheses in regard to the development of the PRC's securities market and securities regulation. After an examination of China's legal history and securities market development, this book will show that neither the convergence hypothesis nor the divergence hypothesis alone can fully explain what has happened in the PRC's securities market and securities regulation. Instead, this book will show that the legal system of China has long been dramatically different from both the civil law systems and the common law systems that exist in most Western countries. The development of the PRC's securities market also demonstrates some unique features of PRC securities regulation. As will be pointed out, because the current PRC securities market is in a transitional period of development, the regulation of this market is therefore also characterized by transitional features. The development of this market demonstrates that the forces of divergence have been stronger in the PRC's approach to securities regulation,[64] although the forces of convergence have also been strong.[65] However, this book will show that the differentiation hypothesis reflects the trend of legal development around the world more appropriately than do the other two hypotheses. With regard to the development of the corporate disclosure framework in the PRC, this book explains how the PRC securities market has become what it is today; it also demonstrates that both the convergence and divergence hypotheses have impacted upon the PRC, and that its corporate disclosure regulatory regime is the product of the mutual influence of both hypotheses.

It will be shown that the PRC government, legal academics, and legal practitioners have strongly advocated borrowing from foreign experiences to develop China's securities market and securities regulation; this is particularly true in the area of corporate disclosure regulation. However, there has been little study of how foreign experiences have been borrowed and how they should be borrowed. Simply copying foreign laws has taught the PRC many lessons in the process of developing its securities market and related regulations; corporate disclosure is a typical illustration of this practice.

This book aims to find better ways of learning lessons from foreign experiences so as to improve the PRC corporate disclosure regime and tackle the endemic problem of false and deceptive disclosure in the securities market. By examining the ways in which Australia has learned from foreign experiences, this book argues that relevant lessons can be learned by the PRC. It proposes that Australia is a good model from which the PRC can learn from foreign experiences. Because China is culturally, historically, economically, and politically quite different from Western

---

64. The divergence theory in this book is comparable with the theory of path dependence. The theory of path dependency in corporate law was developed mainly by Professors Bebchuk and Roe. They argue that corporate ownership and governance differ among advanced economies in the world because of path dependence, although economies and business practices have converged in many countries in the world.

65. The theory of convergence developed by Hansmann and Kraakman opines that at the beginning of the twenty-first century, there was rapid convergence on the standard shareholder-oriented model as a normative view of corporate structure, and this normative convergence produced substantial convergence as well in the practices of corporate governance and in corporate law.

countries, it should first undertake an empirical study of foreign laws and focus on their applications to China's domestic situation, while drawing on experiences from developed and complicated securities markets. Simply borrowing disclosure rules from developed markets has not produced the results that might have been expected. PRC legislators have to move away from their simplistic guideline for lawmaking set forth by the late Deng Xiaoping that, 'A bad law is better than no law,'[66] because, in China, a bad law can be worse than no law.

2.4. THE OUTLINE OF THIS BOOK

Because this book is a comparative study focused on the disclosure regulatory regime of the PRC, it undertakes substantial discussion and analysis of PRC laws and characteristics of the PRC's securities market. Because the PRC had been an isolated country for a long period of time, Western countries began to study this country and its ancient civilization in depth only after it adopted an open-door policy in the late 1970s. Being a country that has traditionally respected authority rather than law,[67] it has been extremely hard for the PRC to establish a modern legal system. In the process of moving towards the rule of law, traditional legal concepts and rules still affect the lawmaking of the PRC. The lack of the doctrine of separation of powers has produced a poor record of law enforcement. The Chinese Communist Party's unchallengeable authority has determined the pace of the movement towards the rule of law in China. As a result, the pace of change in this regard has been slow.

Nevertheless, the PRC's economy has developed very quickly. In many respects, its securities market is rapidly catching up with markets in Western countries. It has adopted many features of Western countries. PRC securities regulation can be seen as a mixture of Western experiences and domestic practices. To understand the PRC securities disclosure regime, it is pivotal to have a basic knowledge of the PRC's legal system. This is the purpose of Chapter 3, which briefly looks at the legal history of China and attempts to identify how this history has affected lawmaking and the enforcement of law in the PRC. Understanding the approach to lawmaking and the enforcement of law in ancient China can help lead to an understanding of lawmaking and the enforcement of law in the PRC today; this includes an understanding of the regulation of the PRC's securities market and the making of rules for regulating such a market, in particular, the making of corporate disclosure laws and the functions of these laws.

After a brief introduction to ancient Chinese legal history, Chapter 3 provides a review of the process of lawmaking and the effects of the enforcement of law in the PRC. An analysis of the sources of law in the PRC provides a rough sketch of

---

66. Deng, Xiaoping, 'Liberalise Our Mind, Seek Truth from Facts, and Unite to Look Forward', *Collections of Deng Xiaoping's Articles*, vol. II (Beijing: People's Press, 1983), 147.
67. Zhang, Wenxian, *Jurisprudence* (in Chinese) (Beijing: Higher Education Press and Peking University Press, 1999), 144.

Chinese law; examining the procedures of law and rule making in the PRC makes it easier to effectively trace the path of PRC disclosure rules, which are discussed in Chapter 4. Examining the poor record of the enforcement of law helps lead to an understanding of why there have been so many cases involving the violation of disclosure laws and why cases of breach of disclosure laws constantly occur in the PRC's securities market.

Chapter 4 examines the various types of participants involved in PRC securities regulation. By reviewing their roles and functions in the securities market, this chapter seeks to identify the difficulties in maintaining consistency among disclosure rules made by different governmental departments. The structure and functions of the CSRC, as the most prominent regulator, shows the strong influence of convergence of economic development. This chapter also demonstrates that the strong governmental control in the PRC has created an inflexible market and that the existence of multiple regulatory bodies had caused inefficient market regulation.

Chapter 5 analyses PRC securities regulatory laws and rules. An overview of the securities regulatory regime is provided in this chapter. The discussion of the process of disclosure rule making demonstrates the existence of a stronger influence of convergence than that of divergence. The major problems evident in PRC corporate disclosure practices, which are identified in this chapter, demonstrate that the PRC's corporate disclosure regime does not properly reflect the impact of divergence in its securities market development practice.

Chapter 6 first provides an introduction the development of the Chinese securities market and then discusses some classic disclosure cases that have arisen in this market. This chapter also identifies the driving forces behind the market. The development of the PRC securities market demonstrates stronger divergence than convergence. This chapter makes an assessment of the level of information available in the PRC's securities market. It also identifies problems with the remedies available to investors who suffer losses caused by a breach of disclosure rules and shows the existence of a large gap between disclosure rules and disclosure practices. This chapter concludes that the PRC's securities market is still in a stage of transition because listed companies, securities companies, securities investors, and market regulators are not sufficiently experienced and securities regulatory rules are not sophisticated enough as a result of how the securities market was formed and developed and how the regulatory rules are formed. It warns that the PRC in this transitional period has to be extremely cautious while transplanting corporate disclosure laws from developed and complicated securities markets.

Chapter 7 provides a comparative study of the Australian corporate disclosure regime; this is relevant and important because it allows a better understanding of problems with the PRC's corporate disclosure regulatory regime from a comparative perspective. It examines the history of the Australian securities markets and the development of the corporate disclosure regime in Australia. In particular, it reviews the assumptions underlying the Australian corporate disclosure framework. It traces the process of the establishment of the corporate disclosure framework in Australia and identifies unique features that are not found in the USA securities market, which has been the most important foreign model in forming the PRC's corporate disclosure framework thus far. By examining the establishment and the continuous improvement of the Australian corporate disclosure regime, this chapter draws the conclusion that the approach by which Australia adopted foreign experiences in disclosure regulation provides a more useful model for the PRC than those that have been relied upon to date.

The final chapter of this book demonstrates that the legal system of a country is closely connected with the country's own culture, history, economy, and politics. When transplanting foreign corporate disclosure experiences into the PRC, it is essential to focus on the country's domestic situation, because the development of the PRC's securities market tends to follow the differentiation hypothesis. The simple copying of foreign experiences is one of the most fundamental reasons why the PRC's corporate disclosure regulation constantly fails. It is suggested that the approach that Australia adopted from foreign experiences provides appropriate lessons for the PRC.

2.5.   METHODOLOGY

Because securities disclosure involves both theoretical debates and practices, the following methodology is used in this book. First, through a comparison of the history of securities markets development and the adoption of foreign experiences of Australia and the PRC, this book intends to demonstrate the utility of the convergence theory and the path dependence theory in shaping an appropriate corporate disclosure regime. Through a review of the history of the development of the PRC's securities market, it demonstrates that this history affects the making of disclosure rules in the PRC, thereby providing an understanding of the current approach that has been adopted in regard to PRC securities regulation.

In the process of reviewing the functions of the PRC and Australian corporate disclosure regulatory regimes, face-to-face interviews and telephone interviews were conducted in Beijing, Shanghai, Hong Kong, Sydney, and Melbourne at different times from 1998 to 2008. Different questions were asked of different interviewees, depending on the issues raised at the time and the expertise of the interviewees. Interviewees included legislators of the NPC and its Standing Committee, drafters of the PRC Company Law and Securities Law Bills, rule makers of the State Council, regulatory officials of the CSRC, policy researchers at the Shanghai, Shenzhen, and Hong Kong Stock Exchanges, prominent corporate and securities law academics and practitioners in China, and regulators of the Hong Kong Securities and Futures Commission. Several Australian securities law academics and Australian advisers to the Australian government's corporate law reform were also among these interviewees.

As noted above, to provide a better understanding of the PRC's securities regulatory regime, one chapter of this book discusses Chinese legal history and its legal system. Only after understanding the PRC legal system can one properly understand the regulatory rules of the PRC's securities market and how they work in practice. In this way, it is possible to appropriately assess the PRC's corporate disclosure regime.

To support the arguments and to provide a clearer picture of the development of the PRC's securities market, a number of classic cases are analysed and discussed, even though the PRC does not have a doctrine of precedent as such. The discussion of these cases is, however, important, as they are well-known and are frequently referred to in debates in China and abroad about transparency in the PRC's listed companies. The sources for this discussion of classic disclosure cases in the PRC are mainly the official securities newspapers, journals, and the official bulletins of the CSRC.

2.6.   THE CUT-OFF DATE

The laws and materials referenced in this book are current as of 30 November 2009.

Chapter 3

An Introduction to the Chinese Legal System: Setting the Context for Securities Law Reform

3.1.   INTRODUCTION

Traditionally, as a civil law country, China has had a legal system that is fundamentally different from those in common law countries, such as Australia. Because China has a unique history of more than five thousand years, its legal system also has significant differences from those of other civil law countries, such as Germany and France. Before discussing the corporate disclosure regime in the PRC, it is necessary to briefly review the major features of the Chinese legal system.

The law has played a significant role in Chinese history. Although the concept of the rule of law in Western countries has never been fully adopted in China, the term 'law' *(fa)* has been used in China for a long time. The present Chinese legal system is being developed through battles between traditional ideas and modern concepts. As the concept of law in China is moving towards the Western concept, it is very important for the Chinese to look at their legal history and examine how they should reform their legal system in the transition from a planned economy[1] to a market economy.[2] It is also fundamental for them to study legal sources so as to better understand the Chinese legal system. Only after acquiring basic knowledge about the Chinese legal system is it possible to further understand the development of the Chinese securities market and the formation of its regulatory regime. After that, it will be possible for China to identify and solve the problems associated with transplanting foreign corporate disclosure laws.

---

1. Under this economic system, everything was planned by the state.
2. Under this economic system, the state is not actively involved in the development of the economy. The development of the economy to a large degree is decided by the market.

This chapter argues that the formation and development of the Chinese legal system has been greatly influenced by its own history, by its political situation, and by the traditions of both civil and common law systems. As a result, law in the PRC cannot be strictly enforced because of its legal environment. This is the fundamental reason why there have been so many cases involving breaches of disclosure rules in the securities market.

Arguments to this effect include the following aspects. First, a brief discussion of Chinese legal history provides fundamental knowledge for an understanding of the PRC's securities regulatory regime. Then, this chapter investigates the sources of law, the forms of law, the lawmaking bodies, the lawmaking procedures at different levels, and the enforcement of law in the PRC. Comparisons with the relevant aspects of Australian law are made whenever necessary.

PRC law will be reviewed at both the national level and provincial levels. However, as the PRC adopts a unitary system, national law plays a dominant role in managing the whole country. National legislation of the PRC includes the Constitution and Laws; national regulations are referred to as Administrative Regulations. Within the State Council, ministries and commissions have the power to make Departmental Administrative Rules.[3] At the local government level, there are Local Administrative Regulations and Local Administrative Rules. These forms of law have different types of authority: Laws have the highest supremacy but are very general and slow to be amended; Administrative Regulations in practice play a more important role than Laws to a great degree, as they are ranked between Laws and Departmental Administrative Rules; and Departmental Administrative Rules are the most detailed and effective form of laws. However, their characteristics of a low level of authority, frequent changes, and sometimes a lack of transparency have tarnished the function of Departmental Administrative Rules.

Currently, in the PRC securities market, Departmental Administrative rules in fact play a far more important role than do Laws and Administrative Regulations. To understand the Chinese legal system, and in particular, to understand the securities regulatory regime, one must have insight into the formation of rules in the Chinese context. This chapter provides such insight. In particular, it highlights the importance of Departmental Administrative Rules.

3.2.   LEGAL HISTORY OF THE PRC

3.2.1.   THE IMPORTANCE OF REVIEWING CHINESE LEGAL HISTORY

The PRC has been in a transitional period since the Chinese Communist Party announced in late 1993 that it would adopt a 'socialist market economy'.[4] As a

---

3. The PRC Law on Law-Making 2000, Art. 2.
4. On 14 Nov. 1993, the Third Plenary Meeting of the Fourteenth CPC Congress passed the Resolution on Several Issues Concerning the Establishment of a Socialist Market Economy. See Wang, Yuming & An Jian, *The Economic Law Perspective of the Reform of State-Owned Enterprises* (Beijing: China University of People's Public Security, 2003), 56.

necessity for this transition, the PRC has been building a legal system for the socialist market economy. Since 1993, China's legislatures – the National People's Congress and its Standing Committee – have enacted several hundred pieces of national legislation, in particular, in the area of commercial law. In 2006, the NPC and its Standing Committee passed fourteen laws.[5] The PRC is moving faster towards the rule of law than ever before.

Nevertheless, the PRC has a long history that is very different from most Western countries. Before it adopted the open-door policy in the late 1970s, the PRC had existed in a self-isolated environment, in which it was separated from the developments of law and society in Europe, the USA, and other Western countries. This self-isolation was a result of China being a self-centred 'middle kingdom' (the literal meaning of 'China') and the rule by man that developed during some two thousand years of feudalism, and it presents difficulties for the inception of Western ideas of the rule of law. Because the Chinese legal system is being developed through clashes between traditional ideas and modern concepts of law, it is important to first review Chinese legal history to understand the transitional features of the Chinese legal system.

3.2.2. A BRIEF REVIEW OF CHINESE LEGAL HISTORY

The current legal system of the PRC is a mixture of civil law, common law, so-called socialist law, and traditional Chinese law, with civil law being the most significant.[6] This conclusion can be drawn from China's complex legal history, beginning with the primitive society that existed about five thousand years ago.

Because China has a very long history, many ideas that are thousands of years old have been passed on from generation to generation. These ideas still have an impact on lawmaking in the PRC today. The first stage of Chinese history is classified as a primitive society. It started during the Xia Dynasty, then continued with the Shang Dynasty, and then the Western Zhou Dynasty (1100 BC to 771 BC). Some of the ideas of these times were incorporated into law by the rulers of the country at various times. The first recorded dynasty in China was the Xia Dynasty, which existed more than four thousand years ago. According to the ancient history book *Zuozhuan,* 'Due to political disorders in Xia, *Yu Xing (Law of Yu)* was formulated'.[7] During the first period of its history, China was ruled mainly by customary law, with the statutory law *Yu Xing* as its supplement. *Li* (a set of ritual rules) was developed from Chinese customs for the ruling of the country. It focused on people's status in society and required people to behave according to *li.*

---

5. Wu Bangguo, the Chairman of the NPC Standing Committee, *The 2006 Work Report of the Standing Committee.*
6. In the history of Chinese legal reform, China has been influenced by Japanese law, German law, the law of the former Soviet Union, as well as common law.
7. Zeng, Xianyi (ed.), *The Legal History of China* (in Chinese) (Beijing: Beijing University Press and High Education Press, 2000), 25. Yu was a king of the Xia Dynasty.

During the Xia Dynasty, China had established rules on the ownership of land, the tax system, judicature, and even prisons.[8]

The period from 770 BC to 476 BC was called the Spring–Autumn Period. There were several kingdoms with slavery systems during this period. Each kingdom had its own laws, but Legalism and Confucianism became the two dominant legal schools. Legalism emphasized equality before the law and severe punishment by law, while Confucianism focused on the order of the nation and the order of families as set forth in a set of rules made by the king.[9]

In 475 BC, China entered into the Period of Warring States (475 BC to 221 BC). During this period, the slavery systems were replaced by feudalism. To establish feudalism and strengthen the rules of the landlords, the state kingdoms undertook legal reforms.[10]

In 221 BC, the king of Qin Kingdom, Yingzheng, defeated the other six kingdoms and unified China. He became the first emperor of the Qin Dynasty. The emperors in following dynasties tried to establish a set of rules to control and run the Middle Kingdom. Most dynasties had their own *lu* (also called *fa,* meaning 'law'). Thus, the Qin Dynasty had *Qin Lu*, the Han Dynasty had *Han Lu*, the Tang Dynasty had *Tang Lu,* the Qing Dynasty had *Great Qing Lu*, etc. [11]

As these *Lu* were made to ensure the stability of control by the emperors, they were virtually criminal regulations. Before the Qin Dynasty, the famous philosopher and political figure Confucius created Confucianism, which focused on the rule by the king in a country, the rule by the father in a family, and the rule by the husband between spouses. One emperor of the Han Dynasty, following the suggestion of one of his officials, Dong Zhongshu (179 BC to 104 BC), elevated Confucianism to the position of the official orthodoxy of the country. Other emperors of the following dynasties continued this practice. For about two thousand years, Confucianism was treated as the dominant set of legal rules in China. The theory and ideas of Confucianism were deeply rooted in Chinese society until about a century ago.

The dominance of Confucianism continued until the beginning of the nineteenth century, when a Qing emperor decided to introduce Western law into China. Shen Jiaben (1840–1913), the Minister in charge of legal reform in the late Qing Dynasty, invited Japanese jurists to assist in the legal reform process.[12] The late Qing Dynasty also sent some Chinese officials to Japan to study Japanese law and invited some Japanese law experts to help with the drafting of laws in China.[13] Because Japanese law at that time had drawn many concepts from German law, the legal reforms of the late Qing Dynasty featured German legal theories.[14] In the

---

8. *Ibid.*
9. *Ibid.,* 60.
10. *Ibid.,* 66.
11. See generally Zeng, Xianyi, *The Legal History of China.*
12. Wang, Chenguang, 'Introduction: An Emerging Legal System', in *Introduction to the Chinese Law,* ed. Wang Chenguang & Zhang Xianchu (Hong Kong: Sweet & Maxwell, 1997), 8.
13. Zeng, Xianyi, *The Legal History of China*, 258.
14. J.M. Otto & M.V. Polak, 'Preface', in *Law-Making in the People's Republic of China,* ed. J.M. Otto et al. (The Hague: Kluwer Law International, 2000), 23.

drafting of some bills, several civil law countries had a direct influence on the late Qing Dynasty. For example, the first three parts of the Great Qing Civil Code was modelled on the Japanese Civil Code and used the structure of the German Civil Code of 1900, with some contents from the Austrian Civil Code.[15] Thus, the law of the late Qing Dynasty was a mixture of Chinese feudalist law and civil law. The *Current Great Qing Lu*, edited by Shen Jiaben, reflected this mixture.[16]

With the fall of the Qing Dynasty, the acts made under the directorship of Shen Jiaben ended in invalidation. However, the Kuomintang (Nationalist) government retained some of Shen Jiaben's legal reforms. Thus, Western legal ideas started to be adopted in China. Based on the Confucian tradition and mixed with some Western legal ideas (mainly Japanese law and German law), the Nationalist government enacted the so-called Six Laws, which laid the foundation for the Kuomintang legal system. The Six Laws are still used today in Taiwan.

From the time when the CPC established the first Soviet Congress in Ruijin County of Jiangxi Province[17] until it took control of the western region of China in 1931 after the Long March,[18] the Soviet Union law that supported a planned economy was implemented in this region.[19] The CPC called its legal system Law for the Liberated Areas.[20] It spread this legal system to every corner it took from the hands of the Nationalist government.

Officially, the CPC claimed that it had established a new legal system in the PRC after its founding in 1949, but, in fact, many features of the post-1949 legal system of the PRC can be traced back to 1927.[21] In 1927, Chiang Kai-shek turned against and prosecuted the communists. The CPC tried to set up 'revolutionary bases' under its control and to develop its own government and laws in these bases. It established the Chinese Soviet Republic in 1931 in the west of China and enacted a number of laws effective within the Chinese Soviet Republic. These laws were modelled on legislation of the Soviet Union. A system of 'people's courts' was also established, and a 'people's democratic legal system' developed.[22] From 1927 to 1949, the CPC went through three periods, namely the Second Revolutionary Civil War (1927–1936), the War of Resistance against Japan (1937–1945), and the Third Revolutionary Civil War (1946–1949). The laws of the Chinese Soviet Republic were later adopted in the areas taken over by the CPC from the hands of the

---

15. *Ibid.*, 264.
16. *Ibid.*, 266.
17. *Ibid.*, 345.
18. The CPC and its Red Army, headed by Mao Zedong, started the guerilla war between the CPC and the Kuomingtang (Chinese Nationalist Party) via the Long March, which lasted for about 10,000 *li* (approximately 5,000 miles or 8,000 kilometers) and finally won this war against the Kuomingtang.
19. Cited by Jianfu Chen in *Chinese Law: Towards an Understanding of Chinese Law, Its Nature and Development* (The Hague: Kluwer Law International, 1999), 33.
20. These areas were taken over from the Nationalist government.
21. Chen, Albert HY, *An Introduction to the Legal System of the People's Republic of China* (Hong Kong: Butterworths, 1993), 23.
22. Wu, Jianfan, 'Building New China's Legal System', *Columbia Journal of Transnational Law* 22, no. 1 (1983): 1.

Japanese and the Nationalist government. With the defeat and escape of Chiang Kai-shek to Taiwan, the CPC founded the PRC, which completely abolished the Nationalist legal system and developed a new socialist legal system based on the system that had been adopted in CPC-controlled areas.

The first stage of the construction of a new legal system in China can be viewed as the period from 1949, after the founding of the PRC, to the enactment of the first Constitution of the PRC in 1954. The CPC issued instructions on 31 March 1949 to abolish all laws of the Kuomintang governments, mainly the Collection of Six Laws.[23] During this first stage, the National Political Consultative Congress, as the interim legislature, enacted some basic legislation, such as laws relating to land reform, marriage, labour, and the organization of courts. In 1949, this Congress also adopted a Common Program, which served as a provisional Constitution until 1954, when the first Constitution of the PRC was enacted.

In the meantime, the CPC started several mass movements, such as the 1950 Movement to Suppress Counter-Revolutionaries, the 1952 Three-Anti Movement (anti-corruption, anti-waste, and anti-bureaucratism), and the Five-Anti Movement (anti-bribery, anti-tax evasion, anti-embezzlement of state property, anti-cheating on government contracts, and anti-stealing of state economic information).[24] These mass movements involved all the ordinary Chinese people. According to the Chinese government, the main purpose of these movements was to break the old social order and establish a new revolutionary order. However, these mass campaigns were guided by the CPC's policies rather than by legal institutions.[25]

During these campaigns, ad hoc 'people's tribunals' and so-called 'revolutionary courts' were set up, and mass trials[26] were held all over the country. In fact, this period was without a legal system; instead, all matters were completely decided upon by the CPC under the leadership of Mao Zedong, Chairman of the CPC and of the PRC.

Scholars of Chinese history described the period of 1954–1956 as the 'new democracy' period. During this time, the PRC's legal system was established and experienced rapid growth. However, what the PRC developed was a Soviet-style legal system, as the Soviet Union's legal experts were invited to assist with law-making. A significant step in this development was the enactment of the first Constitution of the PRC by the First Plenary Meeting of the first National People's Congress – China's parliament – in 1954. This Constitution, drawing upon the

---

23. Li, Buyun (ed.), *Chinese Jurisprudence: Past, Present and Future* (Nanjing: Nanjing University Press, 1988), 370; Ren, Zili, *The Chinese Securities Law: An Analysis of Theories and Classic Cases (zhong guozheng quan fa: cao zuo yuan li, jing dian an li ping xi)* (China Procuratorate Press, 2000), 27; Chen, Jianfu, 'Coming Full Circle: Law-Making in the PRC from a Historical Perspective', in *Law-Making in the People's Republic of China*, ed. J.M. Motto et al. (The Hague: Kluwer Law International, 2000), 28.
24. Chen, Albert HY, *An Introduction to the Legal System of the People's Republic of China*, 23–26.
25. *Ibid.*, 24.
26. The trials were conducted by the ordinary people – the masses. This was a result of the campaign to abolish the old legal system. Under this campaign, the judges trained by the Kuomintang government were discharged.

experience of other socialist countries, according to then-President of the PRC, Liu Shaoqi,[27] included characteristics of the socialist law of the Soviet Union. One of the great contributions made by this Constitution was the doctrine of equality.[28]

After the enactment of the 1954 Constitution, the same NPC passed five other basic laws relating to the structure of the state: the Organic Law of the NPC, the Organic Law of the State Council,[29] the Organic Law of the People's Courts, the Organic Law of the People's Procuratorates, and the Organic Law of the Local People's Congresses and Local People's Governments. Thus, the framework of the PRC's legal system was primarily established. The laws enacted during this period mainly focused on the establishment of the state structure and the stability of the power of the CPC.

Following these pieces of legislation, other laws and regulations in the economic field were also made. Work on the drafting of the Criminal Law, the Civil Law, and the Criminal Procedure Law also began.

However, this period of active lawmaking did not last long. In early 1956, Chairman Mao Zedong announced a new policy that encouraged all people to 'correct the Party' by expressing their thoughts and criticism freely. This was the movement called 'letting a hundred flowers bloom and a hundred schools contend' *(bai hua qi fang bai jia zheng ming,* which could be seen as a preliminary form of freedom of speech. Unfortunately, as this movement raised strong criticism about the CPC, Mao Zedong launched another movement called 'Anti-rightists' in 1957 to purge critics both inside and outside the CPC.[30]

The Anti-rightists Movement was really a result of Mao Zedong's concern about his rule over China. Thousands of critics of the Party were labelled as 'rightists' and sent to farms for 're-education through labour' without the benefit of any judicial procedures. Many jurists, lawyers, judges, and procurators, who were among these critics, were accused of 'using the law to oppose the CPC', or 'attempting to reject the Party's leadership by stressing the independence of justice'.[31] The doctrine of equality was criticized as encouraging the growth of a 'super class' and was omitted from the Constitution of 1975 and the Constitution of 1978.

The 'Anti-rightists Movement' was the beginning of the destruction of the newly established and far-from-improved socialist legal system. Beginning in 1957, legal institutions began to be destroyed. Lawyers were stopped from practising, the publication of legal materials declined, and law schools were forced

---

27. Liu said in his speech on the draft constitution: 'When the Constitution Drafting Committee worked on the draft, it used as reference materials the earlier and later constitutions of the Soviet Union and the constitutions of other people's democracies. Obviously, the experience of the advanced socialist countries headed by the Soviet Union has been of great assistance to us'.
28. Chen, Albert HY, *An Introduction to the Legal System of the People's Republic of China,* 26.
29. The executive government of the PRC.
30. Chen, Jianfu, *Chinese Law,* 39.
31. Liao, KS, '"Independent Administration of Justice" and the PRC Legal System', *Chinese Law and Government* 16 (1983): 123.

to teach the politics and policies of the CPC.[32] Many courts, especially those at lower levels, were merged with the public security departments or the procuratorates at the same level.[33] In 1959, even the Ministry of Justice was abolished.[34] All the important and basic legal principles were denounced as being bourgeois and were abolished. These included judicial independence, procuratorial independence, and procuratorial supervision over legal trials, equality of citizens before the law, defence lawyers' appearance in criminal trials, the presumption of innocence of the accused before the end of a trial, etc.[35] The Chinese legal system was almost destroyed, except for a few remaining laws.

The Cultural Revolution that started in 1966 stopped the re-drafting of criminal law and criminal procedural law, which had begun in 1962 and 1963, respectively. By 1976, when the Cultural Revolution was ended, the legal system was completely destroyed as a result of the Movement to Smash the Public Security, the Courts and the Procuratorates *(za lan gong jian fa yun dong)*. During this period of time, most disputes were settled by 'struggling meetings,' where Mao Zedong's instructions took the place of law. Although the court system was reinstated in 1972, there were still no normal judicial trials. The procuratorates[36] were formally abolished in 1969 and were not reinstated until 1978.[37]

After the Gang of Four,[38] who mainly directed the Cultural Revolution, were arrested and tried in 1976, the First Plenary Session of the Fifth National People's Congress enacted the third Constitution in 1978. Both the then-Chairman of the PRC and the CPC and the then-Chairman of the NPC spoke of the need to strengthen the socialist legal system.[39]

Deng Xiaoping delivered a speech at the preparatory meeting for the Third Plenary Session of the Eleventh Central Committee of the CPC held in December 1978. He made a famous comment on democracy and the legal system:

> In order to safeguard the people's democracy, the legal system must be strengthened. Democracy needs to be institutionalised and legalised so that such a system and such laws would not be changed merely because of a change of leadership or a change of the leaders' views and attention. The current problem is that the laws are not complete; many laws have not yet

---

32. Li, VH, 'The Evolution and Development of the Chinese Legal System', *China Quarterly* 44 (1971): 66.
33. Zhao, ZJ, *Forty Years of the Chinese Legal System* (Beijing: Peking University Press, 1990), 116.
34. *Ibid.*
35. *Ibid.*, 348.
36. Their functions are similar to those of the Directors of Public Prosecutions (DPPs) in Australia.
37. Chen, Albert HY, *An Introduction to the Legal System of the People's Republic of China,* 33.
38. The widow of the late Chairman Mao Zedong, Jiang Qing, formed a group within the highest bureaucracy of the CPC with Zhang Chunqiao, Yao Wenyuan, and Wang Hongwen, to control the political powers of the PRC after Mao's death. This group was arrested and put on trial by the CPC, headed by Deng Xiaoping.
39. *Collection of the Documents of the First Session of the Fifth NPC of the PRC* (Beijing: People's Press, 1978), 55, 132–133.

been enacted; the leaders' words are often taken as 'law', and if one disagrees with what the leader says, it will be called 'unlawful'.[40]

The Communiqué of the Eleventh Central Committee of the CPC followed this famous comment and declared that the socialist democracy and a socialist legal system ought to be developed. Because China is a country controlled by only one political party, the CPC not only controls the people's daily lives, but also set the guidelines and principles of legislation for the Chinese national parliament – the NPC. The 1978 Communiqué of the CPC set forth the basic legal principles and legislative tasks for China, which were to be followed by the NPC and the Chinese people:

> In order to safeguard the people's democracy, it is imperative to strengthen the socialist legal system so that democracy is systematised and written into law in such a way to ensure the stability, continuity and full authority of this democratic system and these laws; there must be laws for people to follow, the laws must be observed, the enforcement of law must be strict and law breakers must be punished. From now on, legislative work should have an important place on the agenda of the NPC and its Standing Committee. Procuratorial and judicial organs must maintain their independence; they must faithfully abide by the laws, regulations and rules; they must serve the interests of the people, keep to the facts, and guarantee the equality of all people before the law; they must not give any one the privilege of being above the law.

The control and influence of the CPC on legislation is reflected not only in the setting forth of legal principles, but also in the insertion of the CPC's policies into sections of Chinese law. There are many such examples. In March 1979, Deng Xiaoping pointed out on behalf of the CPC that the four basic principles of observance must be carried out by all Party members.[41] These four basic principles of observance refer to the observance of the leadership of the CPC, the observance of the guidance of Marxism-Leninism and Mao Zedong's thoughts, the observance of socialism, and the observance of the people's democratic dictatorship.[42] Upon Deng's insistence,[43] these four principles of the CPC were incorporated in the Constitution of 1982.[44] The then PRC President Jiang Zemin proposed that 'Deng Xiaoping Theory' be another guidance for the Chinese people and the CPC. This guidance was added to the Preamble of the Constitution in 1999 and was later adopted as the guidelines for lawmaking in the PRC Law on Lawmaking of 2000.[45] The 'one country two systems' policy was proposed by the CPC, and it was

---

40. Deng, Xiaoping, cited by Chen, Albert HY in *An Introduction to the legal System of the People's Republic of China*, 136, 137.
41. Deng Xiaoping, *Selected Works of Deng Xiaoping (1975–1982)* (Beijing: People's Press, 1983), 172.
42. *Ibid.*
43. Chen, Jianfu, *Chinese Law*, 71.
44. Preamble of the PRC Constitution of 1982, para. 6.
45. Article 3.

incorporated into Article 31 of the PRC Constitution in 1982. This article allows the state to establish special administrative regions when necessary.

Following Deng's comments in 1979, a new Constitution was enacted in 1982. A new legislative system was established to speed up China's lawmaking process: firstly, the PRC Constitution of 1982 provides the NPC and the Standing Committee of the NPC with lawmaking power;[46] secondly, it provides the State Council with the power to make administrative regulations and provides the ministries and commissions under the State Council with the power to make departmental administrative rules; and thirdly, it provides the People's Congresses of provinces, minority autonomous regions, and municipalities directly under the control of the central government with the power to make local regulations.

With the enactment of the PRC Constitution of 1982, China formally began a new stage to improve its lawmaking. It is worth pointing out that from 1979 to 1982, the key laws that were enacted focused on the state administration apart from the laws on foreign investments (such as the Joint Venture Laws). The Constitution of 1982 reflected the 'one centre two basic points' of the Third Plenary Meeting of the Eleventh Central Committee of the CPC. From then on, the PRC's legislation included not only lawmaking regarding the state's political structure, but also the enactment of laws regarding the economic system. It was around 1983 when China's securities market started to emerge. Following the development of the securities market, local regulations on securities were first adopted.[47]

From 1982 to 1989, China enacted a number of basic laws to improve its legal system. However, most of them were public laws, and the guidelines for legislation were still Marxism-Leninism and Mao Zedong's thoughts.[48] Few of them were commercial laws, including the General Principles of the Civil Law of 1986, the Customs Law of 1987, the Technology Contract Law of 1987, the Law of Industrial Enterprises Owned by the Whole People of 1988, and the Chinese-Foreign Contractual Joint Venture Law of 1988. However, the pace of legislation slowed down after the crackdown on the 1989 students' movement.

It was after Deng Xiaoping's speech in his famous tour of southern China in early 1992 that China furthered its economic reform, including developing its securities market.[49] It was the CPC that first created the term 'socialist market economy' in the Third Plenary Meeting of the Fourteenth CPC Congress. The CPC declared that:

> The establishment and improvement of a socialist market economic structure must be regulated and protected by a comprehensive legal system. We must pay due attention to the construction of legal system, to ensure the co-ordination of reform and opening up to the outside world with legal construction, and to learn to manage the economy with legal mechanisms. The goals of establishing

---

46. The PRC Constitution of 1982, Arts 62 and 67.
47. This first piece of law on securities may be the Interim Rules on Securities Issue by the People's Bank of China in 1983.
48. The Constitution of 1982, Preamble.
49. See above Li, Zhangzhe, 191.

a legal system are: first, following the principles prescribed in the Constitution, to speed up the economic lawmaking so as to further improve the civil, commercial and criminal laws and to basically build a legal system appropriate for a socialist market economy by the end of this century; second, to reform and improve the judicial system and the administrative law-enforcement mechanism; third, to establish a sound supervisory mechanism of law enforcement and legal service institutions for the deepening and promotion of legal education, so as to enhance legal consciousness throughout the whole society.[50]

This policy of the CPC was later incorporated into the Amendments to the Constitution in March 1993. The establishment of a socialist market economy and a legal system serving such an economy was an ideological breakthrough in China. Under the leadership of Deng Xiaoping, the Chinese government had become very pragmatic.[51] The focus of the country moved to economic development. With the PRC in need of this development, the legislative task moved to another focus – the construction of a legal system serving its socialist market economy.

The NPC set economic legislation as the most important work for itself and its Standing Committee at the First Plenary Session of the Eighth NPC in March 1993. The then-Chairman of the NPC, Qiao Shi, said that, 'This Standing Committee shall set the economic legislation as the first task to fulfil, and shall enact a number of laws on the socialist market economy'.[52] From then on, the main task of the legislature was to enact a set of commercial laws that suited the development of economic reform. The Company Law of 1993 was one such law. It included many basic provisions on fundraising, which laid the foundation for further regulation of the Chinese securities market. This Law was a product of the mixture of the experiences of common law countries such as the USA, the UK, and Hong Kong, and civil law countries such as Japan, Germany, and Taiwan.[53] Following the Company Law of 1993, a number of commercial laws were enacted: the revised Economic Contract Law, the Arbitration Law, the Consumer Protection Law, the Law of Negotiable Instruments, the Maritime Law, the Foreign Trade Law, the Advertisement Law, etc. Meanwhile, the drafting of the Securities Law had also begun. The legislative plan for 1992 to 1997 was to enact 125 laws, of which fifty-four were related to the 'socialist market economy'.[54] The lawmaking during this period demonstrated that the development of the Chinese legal system had been driven by the deepening of China's economic reform. The fact that many articles in the Laws are inadequate by today's standards is a reflection of the process of gradual development.

---

50. *The Resolution of the Central Committee of the CPC Concerning the Establishment of a Socialist Market Economy 1993*, para. 44.
51. Chen. Jianfu, *Chinese Law*, 43.
52. Qiao, Shi, *The Work Report of the First Plenary Session of the Eighth NPC*, 1993.
53. The legislators either toured these countries and regions or studied with law professors specialized in the laws of these countries and regions.
54. Author's copy of the NPC Legislative Plan 1992–1997.

Following this brief introduction to Chinese legal history, this chapter will go on to examine the sources of law in China and thus allow the characteristics of lawmaking in the PRC to be identified.

3.3. SOURCES OF LAW IN THE PRC AND THEIR IMPORTANCE

3.3.1. INTRODUCTION

To understand a legal system, it is necessary to start with its sources of law. To examine the sources of law in the PRC, a preliminary question to be answered is whether or not the concept of sources of law in common law countries, such as Australia, is the same as that in China. In common law systems, there are two sources of law: primary sources and secondary sources. Primary sources consist of legislation, that is, the statutes passed by the legislature or by those to whom the legislature has delegated legislative authority, and common law, which contains legal rules and principles developed by the courts in the course of adjudicating disputes. Both statutes and case law are the primary legal sources. The courts enjoy judicial independence in upholding the rule of law. Secondary sources include comments on law by legal academics, legal journal articles, and, in Australia, the legal reports of the Australian Law Reform Commission and Parliamentary reports. These secondary sources may be used by the courts when there is a need to interpret the purposes of legislation because of a lack of clear rules.

The states of Australia developed from the colonies of Great Britain, and therefore, the Australian legal system was shaped by the principles of the imperial country until 1986.[55] Because Australia has a federal system, the federal Constitution[56] separates the powers of the states and the Commonwealth, as well as the powers of the federal Parliament, the federal government, and the judiciary.[57] At the state level, each state has a state constitution[58] that regulates the functions of state parliament, state government, and state courts. Thus, Australia has two sets of law: federal law and state law. The states enjoy general legislative power while the Commonwealth enjoys specific legislative power.[59] Case law is one of the basic features of the common law system in many countries, including Australia. In Australia, case law predates legislation as a

---

55. In 1986, the federal Parliament of Australia and the Parliament of the United Kingdom passed identical legislation – the Australia Acts – to terminate the application of British law to Australia.
56. The Commonwealth of Australia Constitution Act was enacted by the UK Parliament on 9 Jul. 1900.
57. Chapters 1, 2, 3, and 5.
58. Section 106 of the Commonwealth of Australia Constitution Act of 1900.
59. *Ibid.*, ss 107 and 108.

principal source of law, although much legislation pre-supposes case law and builds upon it.[60]

In contrast, the PRC, as a civil law country from its legal traditions, has very different sources of law from those of common law countries such as Australia. There are two main reasons for this feature of the PRC's legal system. First, contemporary Chinese law originated in the late Qing Dynasty, which drew upon experiences from Japan.[61] Because the modern Japanese legal system originated from German law, the PRC has consequently been influenced by German civil law, and civil law concepts deeply influenced the legal theorists of China in the early twentieth century. Second, the civil law tradition was succeeded by the Kuomintang (Nationalist) government. For example, the Company Code of the Kuomintang was modelled on the Qing Company *Lu*.[62] The current Taiwanese government continues to adhere to the civil law system. Although the PRC completely abolished the Collection of Six Laws of the Nationalist government in early 1949, the old legislative practices and some legal ideas continued to be used by PRC legislators,[63] who, after the 1980s, started to learn from Taiwan. Many Taiwanese legal experts visited the PRC and introduced Taiwanese law,[64] while many PRC legal experts also visited Taiwan.[65] More interestingly, the current Collection of Six Laws of Taiwan is being used as an important reference by the drafters of the Legislative Affairs Commission[66] of the Standing Committee of the NPC.[67] Thus, the civil law tradition as adopted by the PRC has been influenced by the study of and borrowings from Japanese law, German law, and Taiwanese law.

The PRC's civil law tradition means that the main source of its law is statutory law, which is easily understood by ordinary Chinese people as well as by lawyers and judges. Statutory law suits the situation in the PRC, which has more 1.3 billion people, of whom 80% are farmers. Many of these farmers are illiterate and at most

---

60. E. Campbell, P.Y. Lee, & J. Tooher, *Legal Research Materials and Methods*, 4th edn. (Sydney: Law Book Company, 1996), 63.
61. P.C.C. Huang, *Code, Custom, and Legal Practice in China: The Qing and the Republic Compared* (Palo Alto: Stanford University Press, 2001), 39.
62. Zeng, Xianyi, *The Legal History of China*, 305.
63. Taiwanese law is one of the main references used by the PRC legislators.
64. For instance, the late Zhang Xiaoci, a law professor and President of Soochow University in Taiwan and son of former Taiwan President Jiang Jingguo, visited the PRC twice.
65. For instance, Jiang Ping, a well-known law professor at China University of Politics and Law and a former legislator at the NPC, also visited Taiwan. He is an admirer and good friend of Taiwan law professor Wang Zejian. The legal exchange between them has had a great impact on the drafters through PRC legal experts.
66. This is a working committee of the Standing Committee of the NPC of the PRC. It finalizes the law drafts for the bimonthly meeting of the Standing Committee of the NPC or the Annual Plenary Meeting of the NPC.
67. The Collection of Six Laws of Taiwan is shown on the bookshelf in the Legislative Affairs Commission's library. The drafting reports of the Legislative Affairs Commission include relevant provisions of Taiwan's six laws on many pieces of commercial legislation. For the PRC drafters, Taiwanese law not only has similar legal traditions, but also is easy to understand as it is written in Chinese.

have had only nine years of compulsory education.[68] In addition, the qualifications for Chinese lawyers is very different from those of lawyers in Western countries. Under the PRC Lawyers Law of 1996, a person who holds a non-law bachelor's degree may take the national lawyer's qualification exam.[69] This means that a university graduate without a law degree can practice as a lawyer if he or she passes the national lawyer's qualification exam. Under the same Law, a person who has not studied at a university but earns a law diploma after three years of legal studies (an undergraduate bachelor of laws takes four years in the PRC) can take the national lawyer's qualification exam. If the person passes the exam and meets the good-character requirement, he or she can be admitted as a practicing lawyer. The Lawyers Law of 2007 did not make any changes in this regard. However, the first type of lawyer does not have sound legal knowledge, while the second type of lawyer does not have enough social experience. This situation demonstrates that Chinese law is not as complicated and sophisticated as Western law is. Compared with Western law, Chinese law is too general and lacks detail. Many Chinese laws are more like state declarations than legal rules.[70]

It is worth mentioning that people's courts do not have the power to interpret laws; this power belongs to the NPC's Standing Committee. Under Article 67 of the Constitution, the NPC's Standing Committee interprets the Constitution and laws. The concept of 'laws' used in the Constitution is a narrow one, including only those enacted by the NPC or its Standing Committee. Although the NPC's Standing Committee has the power to interpret laws, the status and function of such interpretation remained unclear for a long time. The Law on Lawmaking for the first time clarified this issue. It prescribes that the NPC's Standing Committee's interpretation of laws has the same authority as do the laws themselves.[71] In this sense, the NPC Standing Committee's interpretation of laws can be seen as another source of law.

As in Australia, sources of law in the PRC can be classified into two types: primary sources and secondary sources. However, the PRC does not have case law, as do common law countries such as Australia. The doctrine of precedent has not been recognized in the PRC. The function of Chinese courts is to enforce laws, but not to make them.[72] In the process of dealing with cases, the Supreme People's Court has the power to interpret questions concerning specific applications of laws and rules.[73] This is called judicial interpretation in the PRC. It is different from interpretation by the legislature, which is called legislative interpretation. Although legislative interpretation and judicial interpretation are enforceable, the

---

68. See Art. 18 of the PRC Education Law of 1995.
69. The PRC Lawyers Law of 1996, Art. 6.
70. Some examples are that the Company Law of 1993 only has 230 articles; the Securities Law of 1998 has 214 articles; and the Product Liability Law of 1993 only has 46 articles. In contrast, the Australian Corporations Act of 2001(Cth) has more than 3,000 sections.
71. *Ibid.*, Art. 47.
72. The PRC Constitution of 1982, Art. 123.
73. The Organic Law of People's Courts of 1983, Art. 33.

legislature and the Supreme People's Court rarely exercise this power.[74] In China, this situation is described in the following way: 'The courts have no interpretation power of legislation but have the power to interpret the implementation of legislation'.[75]

The legal traditions of China are one of the important reasons for this situation, but there are many other reasons. For instance, the standards of Chinese judges is a factor. During the Cultural Revolution, with the movement to 'smash *gong* (public security departments), *jian* (procuratorates) and *fa* (courts),' the PRC became a country without the rule of law or any legal institutions. Although *gong, jian,* and *fa* started to be re-established beginning in the early 1970s, the lack of legal professionals had affected the standards of the appointment of judges. For more than ten years, judges were mainly appointed from the ranks of retirees of the People's Liberation Army (hereinafter the PLA), most of whom had no university education or legal instruction but were deemed to have good character.[76] At the beginning of China's economic reform, there were few national laws,[77] and thus Chinese leaders believed that retired PLA officers and soldiers with good character could acquire legal knowledge quickly and hear cases impartially.

With the development of economic reform, the limited legal knowledge of judges became one of the main reasons for the poor enforcement of laws. The PRC recognized the urgent need to improve the quality of its judges, and so the NPC's Standing Committee enacted the Judges Law of 1995. Disappointingly, this Law legalized the status of judges who did not have any legal background. While this Law did not fulfil the major purpose of the legislation – to raise the standard of judges – it did set up a ranking system[78] and an appraisal system[79] for judges so as to prevent incompetent people from being appointed. In practice, it has failed to solve the problem of corruption within the judiciary.

The second reason for the poor enforcement of law in the PRC is that the people's courts do not have the same independent status under the Constitution as do the courts in common law countries. An example of this is that the President (the equivalent of the Chief Justice) of the Supreme People's Court of the PRC is a far less important position than that of the Prime Minister (as a result of the officials-ranking system): under the PRC's bureaucratic structure, the importance of this position is basically equivalent to that of a Deputy Prime Minister.

A third reason for poor law enforcement is that the courts are financially dependent on the government. This is because the budget of the courts is decided upon by the Ministry of Finance according to the budget system of the PRC.

---

74. Zhang, Wenxian, *Jurisprudence* (Beijing: Higher Education Press and Peking University Press, 2001), 328.
75. *Ibid.*, 327.
76. S. Lubman, *Bird in a Cage: Legal Reform in China after Mao* (Palo Alto: Stanford University Press, 1999), 253.
77. For instance, there were only thirteen pieces of national legislation enacted in 1980.
78. Chapter VII.
79. Chapter VIII.

Financial dependence also affects the independent judgment of the courts. In contrast to the PRC, the Australian judicial system is independent of the executive government under the Constitution.[80] The Australian legal system generally subscribes to the doctrine of the separation of judicial power from the other branches of government.[81]

The CPC's dominant leadership[82] in the PRC also shows that the people's courts are not independent. The judiciary bodies have to follow the instructions of the CPC and even abide by the decisions of the State Council. The judiciary's dependence on the CPC and the State Council is the most apparent reflection of the lack of the rule of law.

Why are the PRC courts not independent? First, the CPC controls the appointment of the President of the highest court in China – the Supreme People's Court. Although the Constitution gives the NPC the power to elect the President of the Supreme People's Court,[83] in practice, the NPC has to elect the only nominee recommended by the CPC. Thus, the NPC simply rubber-stamps the nominee of the CPC. The seven- or nine-member Standing Committee of the CPC's Central Political Bureau is in fact the most powerful body in the PRC. For a long time, the Prime Minister was the second-most important person in that Standing Committee, while the Chairman of the NPC was usually the third-most important person. The President of the Supreme Court has never been a member of that Committee.

Under the officials-ranking system, the top-ranked person in the PRC is the Secretary-General of the CPC, currently Hu Jintao. The Prime Minister, currently Wen Jiabao, is second in rank, and the Chairman of the NPC, at present Wu Bangguo, is third. Based on this ranking, it is unlikely that the people's courts in the PRC can play the same role as its Western counterparts do.

A second factor that contributes to the courts' dependence is their source of financing. Under the Budget Law of 1994, the Ministry of Finance determines the budgets of all the governmental departments, including the budgets of the NPC and the Supreme People's Court.[84] At the local government level, the Bureaus of Finance of local governments determine the budgets of the local People's Congresses and local People's Courts. As a result, the courts at local levels are very often subject to pressure from local governments in hearing cases.

Third, the existence of judicial committees prevent judges from exercising judicial independence. Article 11 of the Organic Law of Peoples' Courts of 1983 stipulates that, 'The task of the judicial committees is to sum up judicial experience and to discuss import or difficult cases and other issues relating to the judicial work'. In practice, when deciding complicated or influential cases, a judge or panel

---

80. Chapter I vests legislative power with the legislature, Ch. II vests executive power with the executive government, and Ch. III vests judicial power with the courts.
81. M. Castan & S. Joseph, *Federal Constitutional Law: A Contemporary View* (Law Book Co., 2001), 10.
82. This is clearly provided for in the Preamble of the PRC Constitution of 1982.
83. Article 62(7).
84. Article 2.

of judges often has to consult with the judicial committee of the court.[85] The decisions of the judicial committees often take the place of decisions of the judges. This form of judicial dependence is the internal dependence that exists inside the court system itself.

The legal tradition, the quality of judges, and the lack of judicial independence all contribute to the fact that that case law cannot be used as a source of law in the PRC.

However, China has no case law does not mean that lower-level courts do not have to abide by the decisions on similar cases of upper-level courts. In fact, the decisions of upper-level courts, especially of the Supreme People's Court, are often used as guidelines or models for the lower-level courts in dealing with similar cases.[86] However, because the PRC does not recognize case law, the doctrine of precedent does not exist in the PRC. Lower-level courts do not have a legal obligation to follow the decisions of upper-level courts. Under this system, if there is no statute regarding a particular issue, the decision will be made at the discretion of the judge or panel of judges. Consequently, similar cases could be dealt with differently in different courts or by different judges.

The practice of the application of previous judicial decisions on similar cases existed in ancient China. During the Spring–Autumn Period, a legalist named Xunzi said that, 'If there is law, law should be applied; if there is no law, precedent should be applied. This trial is perfect'.[87] From then on to the Qin Dynasty, the Han Dynasty, the Tang Dynasty, the Ming Dynasty, the Qing Dynasty, and even the Kuomintang government, the application of previous decisions always existed.[88] The current situation is that case law has not been formally treated as a source of law in the PRC in theory, but, in practice, previous decisions by the upper-level courts on cases of similar facts are often followed by the lower-level courts. Of course, this practice is optional, not mandatory. As one Chinese legal scholar observed:

> Among the decisions by the direct upper level court, there is a difference between the first instance decisions and the second instance decisions. Among the second instance decisions, some of them were originally made by the same court but some were made by another court ... The decision of the direct upper level court has a strong influence on the direct lower level court.[89]

As mentioned above, statutory law is the most important source of law in the PRC. Apart from statutory law, there are secondary sources of law in the PRC, but these

---

85. This practice was witnessed by the author while she was working as an assistant judge in the Intermediate Court of Beijing, the PRC.
86. The Supreme People's Court publishes its case citations in its official monthly *Gazette* and gives instructions to the lower level courts on their difficult cases.
87. Xunzi, *Xunzi-jundao*, cited in Wang, Liming, 'On the Creation of Case Law in the PRC' (2000):11.
88. Wang, Liming, 'On the Creation of Case Law in the PRC', *Case and Interpretation Study* (in Chinese) (2000): 11 and 12.
89. H. Dong, *On Judicial Interpretation* (in Chinese) (Beijing: China University of Politics and Law Press, 1999), 361.

are different from those in Australia and play a different role. In the PRC, not all the debates over proposed bills in the NPC or its Standing Committee are open to the public, and therefore, they are not a source of law. The explanatory reports of the legislative bodies, the comments and suggestions of legal experts and legislators, and law journal articles can be used by the courts only as references but not as secondary sources of law. Although the PRC Law on Lawmaking of 2000 requires explanatory memoranda and other background materials to be attached to a bill, it does not clarify the function of explanatory memoranda and other background materials.[90] To date, explanatory memoranda have rarely been published or made available to the public.

The courts in the PRC are independent from any other individuals and institutions under the Constitution.[91] As was briefly discussed previously, in practice, the courts in the PRC are influenced to a great degree by the policies of the government when implementing the law. They also do not have the power to interpret legislation. Legislative interpretive power *(li fa jie shi quan)* belongs to the legislature itself[92] and has the same effect as legislation.[93] The Supreme People's Court has the power to make interpretations of questions concerning specific applications of laws and rules in judicial proceedings.[94] This power is called judicial interpretative power *(si fa jie shi quan),* which applies to the courts only while they are dealing with cases. It is not accepted as a source of law.

Common law countries have a very different approach to the interpretation of legislation. For example, under the Constitution of Australia, the courts exercise the power to interpret laws, while Parliament exercises the power to make laws. Judges make laws in the process of dealing with cases, and the courts follow the doctrine of precedent. Case law, as a source of law, is of the same importance as statutory law. If there is any conflict between case law and statutory law, statutory law prevails over case law. A secondary source of law is usually used by judges if neither statutory law nor case law can resolve the problem under Section 15AB of the Acts Interpretation Act of 1901.

The above-mentioned fundamental differences in the legal systems of the PRC and Australia mean that the corporate disclosure regimes in these two countries are also very different. This book will later demonstrate that Australia can be a model for the PRC in transplanting foreign laws for reforming its securities regulation.

3.3.2.   FORMS OF LEGAL SOURCES IN THE PRC

According to the PRC Constitution of 1982 and the PRC Law on Lawmaking of 2000, statutory laws can be classified into two tiers at the national level and the

---

90. *Ibid.,* Art. 48.
91. Article 126.
92. *Ibid.,* Art. 42.
93. *Ibid.,* Art. 47.
94. The PRC Organic Law of People's Courts (Amended) of 1983, Art. 33.

local provincial level according to the hierarchy of their authority. At the national level, there are the Constitution and laws. Laws include basic laws *(ji ben fa)* and departmental laws *(bu men fa).*[95] Basic laws are enacted by the National People's Congress. There are two types of basic laws: one type is concerned with the basic systems in civil, economic, political, and criminal law;[96] while the other type includes laws enacted by the NPC for the special administrative regions. The latter are only applied within the administrative regions and serve as 'mini-constitutions' for these regions.[97] A law may take the form of a 'law', 'regulation', 'rule', 'measures', 'decision,' or 'resolution'. Among these, a law is the most commonly used form.

The NPC may also enact departmental laws, which are concerned with particular areas, such as the Environmental Protection Law. The Constitution can only be amended by the NPC with special procedures.[98] When the NPC is not in session, its Standing Committee may enact and amend all laws except the Constitution.[99] When the Standing Committee amends basic laws enacted by the NPC, it must comply with the basic principles contained in the original laws.[100] According to the hierarchy of their authority, the Constitution and laws are ranked from top to bottom as follows: the Constitution, then basic laws, and then departmental laws. Departmental laws are usually enacted and amended by the Standing Committee of the NPC at its bimonthly plenary meeting.[101]

Below the Constitution and laws are administrative regulations *(xing zheng fa gui),*[102] which are made and amended by the State Council (the equivalent of the Australian executive branch of government).[103] The State Council's power to make administrative regulations comes from two sources: the Constitution and the delegation from the NPC or its Standing Committee. Article 89 of the Constitution lists the administrative powers of the State Council. Administrative regulations may be made for two purposes: to implement laws enacted by the NPC or its Standing Committee, or to exercise the administrative power given by Article 89 of the Constitution.[104] An important and problematic characteristic of laws is that they are too general and lack enough details. Very often, people find that the laws of the PRC are too ambiguous to follow. The main purpose of legislators' enacting

---

95. Zhang, Wenxian, *Jurisprudence*, 60.
96. Such as the Criminal Law, the Criminal Procedure Law, and the General Principles of the Civil Law.
97. The Basic Law for Maucao Special Administration of 1988 and the Basic Law for Hong Kong Special Administration of 1984 are two such examples.
98. Usually, the NPC makes a proposal for an amendment of the Constitution to the CPC. If the CPC approves the proposal it will also make recommendations to the NPC. The NPC amends the Constitution based on the recommendations of the CPC. The amendments to the Constitution can only be made by the NPC. The Standing Committee does not have such power.
99. The PRC Constitution of 1982, Art. 67.
100. *Ibid.*
101. *Ibid.*
102. The PRC Law on Lawmaking of 2000, Art. 2.
103. The PRC Constitution of 1982, Art. 89.
104. *Ibid.*, Art. 56.

such general laws is to avoid the inappropriateness of detailed laws caused by the rapid development of practice. To meet the needs of practice, legislators give the State Council the power to make administrative regulations so as to implement laws, because the making and revising of administrative regulations is relatively easier and quicker than is making amendments to laws. Under this system, once a law is enacted, it is very common for the State Council to soon pass detailed implementation measures or rules. Because the executive branch of government makes decisions about the day-to-day management of the country, administrative regulations are more useful for society than laws are. Administrative regulations may take the form of 'measures', 'rules', 'regulations', 'decisions,' or 'orders'.[105]

One question to consider is what happens when the implementing rules do not comply with the law. Under the Constitution, administrative regulations must comply with the Constitution and laws.[106] Article 67 provides that the Standing Committee of the NPC has the power to annul administrative regulations that contravene the Constitution or laws. In fact, the Standing Committee has never used this power because of the fact that the State Council is more powerful than the NPC and its Standing Committee, and the NPC and its Standing Committee still act as a 'rubber stamp' for the State Council. Thus, it is not uncommon for administrative regulations to contain articles that are inconsistent with laws.

There are two functions of administrative regulations. First, when the NPC and its Standing Committee do not have enough resources and time to meet the legislative requirements, the State Council often releases administrative regulations before the relevant laws are made. For example, after the CPC announced in late 1993 that China would adopt a socialist market economy, the PRC started the reform of SOEs. Most SOEs began to transform into modern companies by adopting a shareholding system. Because there were no laws to follow, the State Council passed the Interim Regulations Concerning Share Issue and Trading (hereinafter the 1993 Interim Regulation) in April 1993. Although the first Company Law was enacted in December 1993, like other laws, it is very general and only contains one chapter on the issue and transfer of shares of joint stock limited liability companies.[107] This chapter simply copies the main articles of the 1993 Interim Regulation. Because the 1993 Interim Regulation is more detailed than the Company Law with respect to share issuing and trading,[108] it is still being used by companies, courts, and legal practitioners. This is an example of why administrative regulations are more important than laws in practice because they are more detailed. Sometimes, administrative regulations can be used as the bases for the drafting of laws. For example, the Company Law was first based on two Standard Opinions of the State Council.

---

105. The PRC Constitution of 1982, Art. 62.
106. *Ibid.*
107. The PRC Company Law of 1993, Ch. IV.
108. There are eighty-four articles in the 1993 Interim Regulation, but only twenty-two articles in this aspect in the Company Law.

Another function of administrative regulations is to supplement and implement laws. For instance, the Company Law of 1993 has 230 articles, among which there are only four articles on the registration of companies.[109] Obviously, these four articles are not enough for practical purposes. To implement the Company Law of 1993, the State Council passed the Administrative Regulation on Company Registration on 24 June 1994. This Regulation clearly states that the Administration Departments for Industries and Commerce at all levels are the bodies in charge of the registration of companies. It also prescribes the procedures for company registration in detail and contains seventy-six articles dealing with company registration. From these examples, it is clear that, in practice, administrative regulations in the PRC play a more important role than laws do.

Below administrative regulations are departmental administrative rules *(bu men xing zheng gui zhang)*, which are made by the ministries and commissions of the State Council on the issues concerned with their respective departments.[110] Departmental administrative rules may take the form of orders, directives, or regulations.[111] Departmental administrative rules must comply with the Constitution, laws, and administrative regulations.

Although the Constitution gives the ministries and commissions of the State Council the power to make departmental administrative rules, these rules are not binding on PRC courts. Unlike the situation for the Constitution, laws, and administrative regulations, the PRC courts only use administrative rules (including departmental administrative rules and local administrative rules) as references.[112] If there are no relevant provisions in the Constitution, laws, or administrative regulations, judges may choose whether or not to apply administrative rules. In other words, the courts have discretion over the application of administrative rules. The reason for this is that a judicial review system has not been adopted in the PRC and the courts cannot review the validity of laws, administrative regulations, or administrative rules. In practice, because judges often lack experience in many aspects of administration, they are very reluctant to ignore administrative rules and therefore usually make judgments according to administrative rules if there is no other legal source to refer to. This is one of many reasons why administrative rules outnumber administrative regulations on particular issues in the PRC. Corporate disclosure is one such issue.

An example of this is the function of the No. 1–19 Rules on Content and Format of Disclosure by Listed Companies released by the China Securities Regulatory Commission. The Company Law of 1993 and the Securities Law of 1998 both contain basic principles of information disclosure for share issuing and trading. The 1993 Interim Regulation has similar articles on information disclosure by listed companies, but these articles are far from detailed enough for implementation. The implementation of these principles mainly depends on administrative

---

109. The Company Law of 1993, Arts 8–11.
110. The PRC Constitution of 1982, Art. 90; the PRC Law on Lawmaking of 2000, Art. 71.
111. *Ibid.*
112. The PRC Administrative Procedures Law of 1989, Art. 158.

rules issued by the CSRC from time to time after it formally became a national securities regulator in August 1997. In fact, the CSRC deals with violations of information disclosure rules in the securities market according to its rules. This practice has been accepted by listed companies, shareholders, and the courts.[113] In the PRC's securities market, the administrative rules of the CSRC play the most important role. This will be further discussed in detail in the following chapters.

PRC laws at the second tier are local regulations *(di fang fa gui),*[114] which include all the regulations made by the People's Congresses or their Standing Committees of twenty-three provinces and four municipalities directly under the control of the central government.[115] Local regulations must not be in conflict with the Constitution, laws, or administrative regulations. Once they are passed by local legislatures, they must be reported to the Standing Committee of the NPC for the record.[116] The People's Congresses and their Standing Committees of the five Minority Autonomous Regions[117] may make autonomous regulations *(zi zhi tiao li)* and specific regulations *(dan xing diao li).*[118] Autonomous regulations must be made within the autonomous power provided by the Constitution and must be approved by the Standing Committee of the NPC before they take effect.[119] Although autonomous regulations may be different from laws, their making is under the strict control of the central government. The authority of autonomous regulations and autonomous specific regulations is the same as that of local regulations.

Below local regulations are local administrative rules *(di fang gui zhang).* Local rules are made by the executive local governments of the thirty provinces, autonomous regions, and municipalities directly under the control of the central government, as well as some big cities.[120]

The last type of statute laws is local regulations of some Special Economic Zones (SEZs). In some SEZs, the local People's Congresses and their Standing Committees may formulate regulations enforced in these SEZs. This type of law-making is called delegated legislation. It is worth noting that not all the SEZs have the power to enact delegated legislation. The delegation of such power is made when there is a need in practice, often depending on the CPC's policies. In the PRC, only the NPC and its Standing Committee have the power to delegate legislative power to a particular SEZ. Usually, this legislative power is delegated through

---

113. The typical cases of violations of disclosure rules were dealt with by the CSRC, such as those of the Hongguang Industrial Company and the Qiongminyuan Company.
114. The PRC Constitution of 1982, Art. 100.
115. They are Beijing, Shanghai, Tianjin, and Chongqing.
116. The PRC Law on Lawmaking of 2000, Art. 3.
117. They are the Xinjiang Uyghur Minority Autonomous Region, Tibetan Minority Autonomous Region, Ningxia Muslim Minority Autonomous Region, and Guangxi Zhuang Minority Autonomous Region.
118. The PRC Constitution of 1982, Art. 116. The difference between an autonomous regulation and a specific regulation is that a specific regulation is concerned with a particular matter in an autonomous Region.
119. *Ibid.*
120. *Ibid.,* Art. 73.

special legislation of the NPC or its Standing Committee. For instance, the First Plenary Meeting of the Seventh National People's Congress of the PRC passed the Resolution of the NPC on the Establishment of the Hainan Special Economic Zone on 13 April 1988. Under this Resolution, the Hainan Province was established as the Hainan SEZ. The People's Congress of Hainan Province is empowered to formulate regulations for the enforcement of laws in the Hainan SEZ and for the needs of development of the Hainan SEZ. In July 1992, the Standing Committee of the Seventh NPC passed a resolution delegating to the People's Congress of Shenzhen and the government of Shenzhen the power to make local regulations and local administrative rules, respectively. Later, the Shantou and Xiamen SEZs were also delegated the same lawmaking power. The regulations and rules made in this way are only applicable within the respective SEZs. The authority of SEZ regulations and rules is the same as those of local regulations and local administrative rules, respectively.

In addition, international conventions and agreements may become another source of law once the PRC becomes a party to them. If there is any conflict between domestic law and international law, the latter prevails unless the PRC has announced reservations. This rule has not been written into the Constitution, but is briefly mentioned in the General Principles of the Civil Law of 1986.[121] However, some people argue that this rule only applies in the area of commercial law.[122]

In summary, the hierarchy of authority of various forms of law in the PRC, from top to bottom is, as further illustrated in Figure 3.1: the Constitution, laws, administrative regulations, local regulations (including autonomous regulations and autonomous separate regulations) and departmental administrative rules, and local administrative rules.[123] Local regulations have higher authority than do local administrative rules.[124] The authority of administrative rules is the same as that of local regulations.[125] However, the hierarchy of authority regarding local regulations and departmental administrative rules, and regarding departmental administrative rules and local administrative rules, has not been clarified. Any dispute in this regard is decided by the State Council.[126] This practice causes uncertainty in enforcement.

Laws and administrative regulations are usually too general for implementation, even if the latter are relatively more detailed. To a great extent, laws and administrative regulations need to be supplemented by departmental administrative rules or local administrative rules. However, courts are not legally bound by these rules, although they often follow them. PRC courts are very reluctant to hear cases of securities disputes because securities law is a very complicated area and PRC courts are not confident in their ability to hear such cases when the law has no

---

121. Article 142.
122. Author's interview with a senior draftsperson of the LAC in September 1999.
123. *Ibid.*, Arts 78–81.
124. The Law on Lawmaking of 2000, Art. 80.
125. *Ibid.*, Art. 82.
126. *Ibid.*, Art. 86(2) and (3).

Figure 3.1   Hierarchy of the Authority of the Forms of Law in the PRC

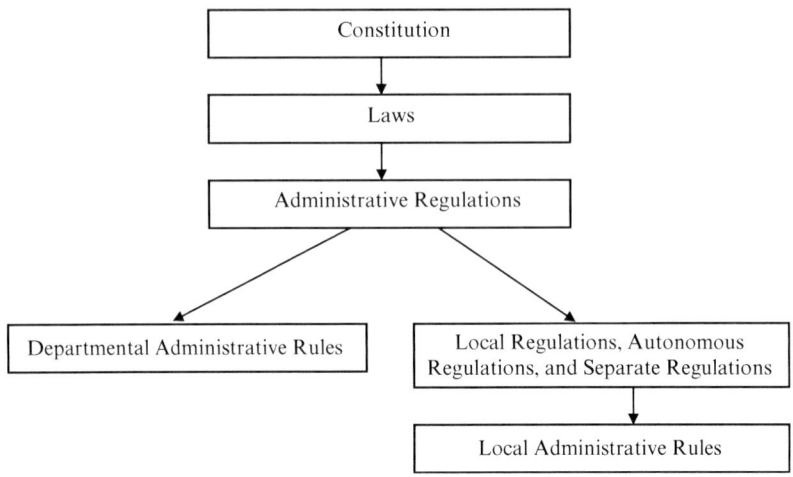

clear provisions.[127] This situation is one of the reasons why there have been very few court cases regarding securities disputes in the PRC.

Unlike Australia, the PRC is a unitary country.[128] The central government has absolute power over state administration and it decides the most important issues for local governments. In other words, the power of local governments comes from the delegation of the central government. Laws and administrative regulations play the most important role in theory, because they have the highest authority. However, as discussed above, in practice, administrative regulations are more useful to lawyers and judges in dealing with cases. Yet, like laws, administrative regulations are still usually general, simple, and lacking in details. Thus, they are also frequently supplemented by the departmental administrative rules of a respective ministry or commission, which are more comprehensive. Consequently, in some areas, such as securities regulation, the departmental administrative rules of the CSRC are most useful in practice.

3.4.   LAWMAKING BODIES IN THE PRC

In the PRC, there are a number of institutions that have different lawmaking powers. The laws at different levels constitute the entire legal system. The problem with this system is that the lawmaking powers of each institution are not very clear.[129] As a result, it is not uncommon for some bodies to exceed or even abuse

---

127. The PRC courts did not hear securities compensation cases involving false disclosure until 15 Jan. 2002.
128. The PRC Constitution of 1982, Arts 57–59.
129. Chen, Jianfu, *Chinese Law*, 115.

their lawmaking powers. Consequently, conflicts among laws, administrative regulations, local regulations, and administrative rules are commonplace.[130] The inconsistencies among the different forms of laws will no doubt affect the application of the rule of law. The problem of inconsistency exists in a number of areas, including the regulation of the securities market, which will be analysed in the following chapters.

As mentioned previously, lawmaking bodies are identified in the Constitution. First, the NPC is the supreme legislative body of the PRC.[131] It enacted and amends the Constitution and some basic laws.[132] Second, the Standing Committee of the NPC enacts other national laws, except those that should be enacted by the NPC.[133] It may amend the national laws enacted by the NPC when the NPC is not in session.[134] The NPC and its Standing Committee are the two bodies that make laws in China.

Because Australia has both statutes and case law, its lawmaking bodies include a wider range of categories. The Commonwealth Parliament is the body that enacts legislation for the Commonwealth. The parliaments in each state are the bodies that enact state legislation. The judges at all levels are able to make laws in the process of exercising their judicial power without interference from any level of government.[135]

In the PRC, the courts are not lawmaking bodies because of the lack of a case law system. Statutory law is the main source of law. The lawmaking bodies of the PRC discussed herein make the above-mentioned forms of statutory law.

Like the hierarchy of authority among various forms of law in the PRC, some degree of a hierarchy of authority among the lawmaking bodies exists. As discussed previously, at the central government level, the NPC is the highest lawmaking body. When the NPC is not in session, its Standing Committee may exercise part of the NPC's lawmaking function. At the same time, the Standing Committee has its own legislative power. It makes other basic laws and departmental laws apart from the Constitution. It also exercises another lawmaking function – interpreting law. The State Council has less authority than the NPC's Standing Committee, which allows it to make administrative regulations.[136] The ministries and commissions of the State Council have less power than the State Council, which allows them to make departmental administrative rules.

At the provincial government level (including minority autonomous regions and municipalities under the direct control of the central government), their People's Congresses and Standing Committees make local regulations; the executive governments at the provincial level and of some big cities have

---

130. *Ibid.*, 119.
131. The PRC Constitution of 1982, Arts 58 and 62; the PRC Law on Lawmaking of 2000, Art. 7.
132. The PRC Constitution of 1982, Art. 62(1) and (3); the PRC Law on Legislation of 2000, Art. 7.
133. The PRC Constitution of 1982, Art. 67(2).
134. *Ibid.*, Art. 67(3).
135. See above Castan & Joseph, *Federal Constitutional Law: A Contemporary View*, 10.
136. The PRC Constitution of 1982, Art. 89; the PRC Law on Lawmaking of 2000, Art. 56.

the power to make local administrative rules. The People's Congresses and executive governments of SEZs have the power to make SEZ regulations and SEZ rules.

3.5.   LAWMAKING PROCESSES IN THE PRC

Because there are different forms of law in the PRC, the lawmaking processes are very complex. This part provides a brief introduction to the lawmaking processes by following the hierarchy of the authority of different forms of law.

3.5.1.   LAWMAKING PROCESS OF THE NPC

Lawmaking procedures of the NPC are governed by the Constitution of 1982, the Law on Lawmaking of 2000, the Rules of Working Procedures for the NPC of 1989, and the Organic Law of the NPC of 1982. Among these, the Law on Lawmaking was based on the other three pieces of legislation and contains more-detailed procedures. Currently, the enactment of a piece of legislation by the NPC usually has to go through five stages: the proposal and presentation of a bill, the examination of the bill, the revision of the bill, the passage of the bill, and the publication of the enacted law.[137] It should be noted that a proposed bill may be examined more than once.

The processes of lawmaking of the NPC are relatively formal and detailed because there are four national laws that govern this matter. As pointed out previously, the NPC only conducts one meeting each year, and therefore it only passes Constitutional amendments and basic laws. As discussed above, the function of lawmaking is mainly performed by the NPC's Standing Committee.

Under the Law on Lawmaking, the proposal of a bill may be made in two ways. First, it may be made by state institutions, including the Presidium of the NPC, the Standing Committee of the NPC, the State Council, the Supreme People's Court, the Supreme People's Procuratorate, and the Committees of the NPC.[138] Second, it may be made by a delegation of the NPC[139] or by thirty delegates of the NPC.[140] In practice, most proposals of bills are initiated by the Standing Committee of the NPC or the State Council.[141] The proposed bills from the State Council are usually drafted by its relevant ministries or commissions.[142]

---

137. The PRC Law on Lawmaking of 2000, Art. 2 of Ch. 2.
138. *Ibid.*, Art. 12.
139. The delegates from the same province form a delegation.
140. The PRC Law on Lawmaking of 2000, Art. 13. These thirty deputies do not have to be from the same delegation.
141. According to the author's experience while working for the LAC, the Standing Committee of the NPC mainly initiated basic law bills, while the State Council usually initiated departmental law bills. However, there is no clarification about the power to initiate a bill.
142. For example, the bill of the Lawyers Law was introduced by the Ministry of Justice.

Once the proposal of a bill is made, a decision on whether the proposed bill will be presented to the NPC will be decided by the Presidium of the NPC.[143] Once a proposed bill is presented to the NPC, it will be examined by all the delegates of the NPC[144] and then by the relevant special committee of the NPC.[145] Before the examination, either the person responsible for the proposal of the bill or the Standing Committee of the NPC must make a legislative explanation to the NPC.[146]

If the bill is accepted after examination by the delegations and the relevant special committee, the Law Committee of the NPC will conduct a final examination and then revise the bill according to the comments of the delegations and the relevant special committee of the NPC. It will then submit an examination report to the Presidium of the NPC.[147] If the proposed bill is not accepted by either the delegation from a province or the relevant special committee of the NPC, it will not be presented to the NPC.

The final draft of the bill will be presented to the General Assembly of the delegates of the NPC for a vote. If a simple majority votes for the bill, it will be enacted.[148] After enactment, the bill will be signed by the President of the PRC and become a law.[149] The law will be published in the major national newspapers and the *Gazette* of the NPC.

One point that needs to be made here is that, although the delegates and the relevant committee(s) of the NPC have the power to examine a bill, the drafting of the bill and the revision of the bill according to the comments and suggestions of the examining bodies are the responsibilities of a working body of the Standing Committee of the NPC,[150] the Legislative Affairs Commission (hereinafter the LAC). The LAC consists of about 100 lawyers. Its working procedures are clarified by legislation; however, through the legislative practices over the last two and a half decades, the LAC has developed very detailed working procedures.

The first responsibility of the LAC is the drafting of bills. Once a proposed bill is accepted by the NPC, its Standing Committee will name a drafting group to draft a trial bill. The members of the drafting group include legal experts in the relevant area,[151] the representatives from the relevant ministries and commission of the State Council, and the representatives from the relevant special committee of the NPC.

Once the trial bill is finalized, it will be sent to the LAC, which then will conduct research and investigation for the drafting of the bill. These are the most important procedures of the LAC. First, it will organize many seminars that will be attended by members of the relevant ministries and commissions of the State

---

143. The PRC Law on Lawmaking of 2000, Arts 12 and 13.
144. *Ibid.*, Art. 16.
145. *Ibid.*, Art. 17.
146. *Ibid.*, Art. 14.
147. *Ibid.*, Art. 18.
148. *Ibid.*, Art. 22.
149. *Ibid.*
150. *Ibid.*, Arts 34–36.
151. Chen, Jianfu, *Chinese Law,* 120.

Council, the representatives from local People's Congresses, the representatives from local governments, the legal experts from universities and law firms, and, sometimes, individual citizens. Second, the LAC will study and summarize the relevant provisions from the current laws, administrative regulations, administrative rules, local regulations, local administrative rules, and sometimes government policies at all levels. Third, the LAC will look at the current practice in different provinces and regions. Fourth, it will do a comparative study on the relevant laws in other countries. Fifth, members of the LAC will travel to some other countries to conduct research on the practices in these countries. Obviously, the laws in the countries that the LAC visits will have a great influence on China's legislation.[152]

Based on the research and investigation of the above-mentioned five procedures, the LAC will draft its own trial bill. There will be many discussions on this trial bill among the LAC and the relevant ministries and commissions of the State Council, the legal experts and lawyers, the local People's Congresses and local governments, as well as individual citizens. Based on their opinions and comments, a final version of the trial bill will be drafted. This will become the formal bill to be sent to the NPC for debate.

After each debate by the delegates of the NPC, the LAC will revise the bill. How many debates the delegates will have is decided by the Presidium of the NPC. The three-reading rule, widely used in Western countries, does not exist in the PRC. During the debates of the delegates, the LAC will organize seminars and conferences of the representatives of the relevant departments, universities, and law firms to comment on the revised bill. Afterwards, the LAC will report these comments to the delegates. Based on further debate, the LAC will revise the bill again until all the delegations approve the bill. The final bill then will be sent to the General Assembly for a vote. When the vote is in favour of the final bill, it becomes a law.

3.5.2.   Lawmaking Process of the Standing Committee of the NPC

The procedures for lawmaking in the PRC are similar to those in many Western countries, but there are still some major differences between them. For example, the three-reading system in Western countries is different from the three-examination system in the PRC.

The lawmaking power of the NPC's Standing Committee was not prescribed in the 1954 Constitution – the first Constitution of the PRC. The NPC was then the only institution that exercised national legislative power. The NPC's Standing Committee only had the power to interpret law. In 1955, the NPC delegated to its Standing Committee the power to make separate regulations (*dan xing fa gui*).[153] In 1959, the NPC authorized its Standing Committee to amend laws when

---

152. The understanding of these internal working processes of the LAC came from the author's work experience with the LAC.
153. Chen, Albert HY, *An Introduction to the Legal System of the PRC* (Hong Kong: Butterworths, 1992), 82.

the NPC was not in session.[154] Under the 1982 Constitution, the NPC's Standing Committee has the power to make laws that are not within the NPC's legislative power.[155] Hence, the NPC's Standing Committee also acquired some national legislative power. The Constitution also provides that the NPC's Standing Committee has the power to interpret the Constitution and laws. From the time of the adoption of the 1982 Constitution, the NPC's Standing Committee has acquired a wide range of powers. Because the NPC is only in session once a year, national legislative power is usually exercised by its Standing Committee. According to the statistics of the NPC's Standing Committee, about 370 Laws were enacted from 1979 to 2000, among which 330 were made by the NPC's Standing Committee.[156]

The bodies authorized to make proposals of bills to the NPC's Standing Committee are similar to those that can make proposals of bills to the NPC, except that only the members of the NPC's Standing Committee, not the delegates of the NPC, have the power to propose a bill to the NPC's Standing Committee. The members of the NPC's Standing Committee must be the delegates of the NPC. However, the delegates of the NPC are elected, while the members of the NPC's Standing Committee are appointed from among the delegates. Only ten or more members of the NPC's Standing Committee can jointly propose a bill.[157]

No matter who makes the proposal of a bill, the Chairman of the NPC's Standing Committee makes the decision about whether this proposal will be accepted into the agenda of the NPC's Standing Committee.[158] If the proposal is not accepted, the reasons should be given to the person who proposed the bill.[159] It is hard to say whether or not the decision of the Chairman of the NPC's Standing Committee is always fair.

The LAC plays the same role in the lawmaking of the NPC's Standing Committee as that of the NPC, because it serves both the NPC and its Standing Committee. All the members of the Standing Committee have the power to examine bills. The Law on Lawmaking drew on experiences from Western countries and provides that the bills accepted into the NPC's Standing Committee's agenda usually should be debated three times before it is voted upon.[160] At the first examination of a bill, the person proposing the bill should present an explanation, including the reasons for the proposal and major issues of the proposal.[161] After the explanation, the members of the Standing Committee will examine the bill in the form of a group meeting.[162]

---

154. *Ibid.*
155. Article 67.
156. Qiao, Xiaoyang (ed.), *Lectures on the Law on Lawmaking* (Beijing: China Democracy and Legal System Press, 2000), 131.
157. The PRC Law on Lawmaking of 2000, Art. 25.
158. The Meeting of Chairmen consists of the Chairman and more than ten deputy chairmen of the NPC Standing Committee.
159. The PRC Law on Lawmaking of 2000, Art. 25.
160. *Ibid.*, Art. 27.
161. *Ibid.*
162. *Ibid.*

According to the opinions and comments of the first examination, the LAC will revise the bill and then submit it to the Law Committee of the NPC. After being reviewed and passed by the Law Committee of the NPC, the revised bill will be sent back to the members of the NPC's Standing Committee for the second examination in the form of a group meeting.[163]

The LAC will revise the bill again according to the comments and opinions from the second examination and send the revised bill to the Law Committee. The Law Committee will report the changes made by the LAC to the members of the Standing Committee and submit the revised bill for the third examination.[164] After the third examination, the Law Committee and the other relevant bodies, such as the LAC or other relevant special committees of the NPC, will revise the bill again and submit it to the plenary meeting of the members of the NPC's Standing Committee for a vote. When a simple majority vote is gained, the bill will be enacted and become law.[165] The enacted law will be signed by the President of the PRC and then be published in state-owned national newspapers and the *Gazette* of the NPC's Standing Committee.[166]

The interpretation of laws by the NPC's Standing Committee has the same effect as the laws themselves. Thus, such interpretation is a kind of lawmaking process. The Law on Lawmaking has several articles on the procedures for the interpretation of law.[167]

In the PRC, there are two kinds of formal interpretations: legislative interpretation and implementing interpretation. The former is about the literal meaning of articles and the purposes of the law. Implementing interpretation is made by the Supreme People's Court and concerns the application of ambiguous articles with regard to cases.[168] This division of legislative interpretation and implementing interpretation is not clear, because in many situations, the interpretation of how to apply the articles in a law is in fact about how to understand the literal meaning of the articles of the law.

Every institution at the central-government level and the Standing Committees of the provincial People's Congresses may request the NPC's Standing Committee to interpret laws.[169] The LAC is in charge of drafting interpretations for the NPC's Standing Committee. The Chairmen's Meeting of the NPC's Standing Committee decides whether an interpretation should be put on the NPC's Standing Committee's agenda. The draft interpretation must be examined by the members of the NPC's Standing Committee and revised by the LAC.[170] The final version of the draft interpretation must be submitted to all the members of the NPC's Standing

---

163. *Ibid.*
164. *Ibid.*
165. *Ibid.*, Art. 40.
166. *Ibid.*, Art. 41.
167. *Ibid.*, Arts 42–47.
168. *Ibid.*, Art. 42; Qiao, Xiaoyang (ed.), *Lectures on the Law on Lawmaking* (Beijing: China Democracy and Legal System Press, 2000), 172; Chen, Jianfu, *Chinese Law,* 94.
169. *Ibid.*, Art. 43.
170. *Ibid.*, Art. 44.

Committee for a vote.[171] It can be seen from the articles in the Law on Lawmaking that the process for the interpretation of law is very similar to the lawmaking of the NPC's Standing Committee. These procedures are too formal and time-consuming, and, as a consequence, legislative interpretation by the NPC's Standing Committee is not frequent. Because of the generality of PRC laws, either the State Council has to make implementation regulations or the courts in the PRC have to exercise a great degree of discretion in dealing with cases.

Although lawmaking procedures at the national level in the PRC are similar to those in many Western countries, there are significant differences with regard to the examination of bills and the quality of legislators. If a bill is very simple and there are no significantly different opinions from the members of the NPC's Standing Committee, it may be passed after one meeting of the members. However, if a bill is very important or complicated, the NPC's Standing Committee may make more examinations. Thus, the process of passing such a bill may take a very long time. For instance, the first Securities Law bill was written in 1992 and was examined five times before it became a Law in 1998. This means that the rule of three examinations by the NPC's Standing Committee is not compulsory, but optional. To this extent, the processes of the NPC's Standing Committee are less formal than those of the NPC.

3.5.3.   PROCESS FOR MAKING ADMINISTRATIVE REGULATIONS BY
          THE STATE COUNCIL

The making of administrative regulations by the State Council is governed by the Constitution of 1982 and the Law on Lawmaking of 2000. The Constitution gives the State Council the power to make administrative regulations.[172] The Law on Lawmaking of 2000 contains the articles regarding the processes for the making of administrative regulations.[173] These articles mainly came from the State Council's Provisional Regulations on the Procedures for the Enactment of Administrative Regulations of 1987 (hereinafter PRPEAR), which contain detailed procedures for the making of administrative regulations.

A ministry or commission of the State Council is generally responsible for drafting an administrative regulation regarding a matter within its jurisdiction. However, in the case of a matter involving different ministries or commissions, a drafting group consisting of representatives from these ministries or commission will be set up.[174] This drafting group is organized by the State Council[175] through

---

171. *Ibid.*, Art. 45.
172. Article 89(1).
173. Chapter III.
174. PRPEAR, Art. 5.
175. The PRC Law on Lawmaking of 2000, Art. 57.

the work of the Legislative Affairs Office (called the Legislative Affairs Bureau before 1998) of the State Council.[176]

From a practical point of view, administrative regulations of the State Council always play an important role in the management of the state. Their function can be clearly seen from the Law on Lawmaking of 2000. Administrative regulations have two purposes: to implement laws and to exercise the State Council's administrative responsibilities.[177] The NPC and its Standing Committee may delegate their legislative power to the State Council to make administrative regulations regarding matters that should be governed by the laws made by the NPC or its Standing Committee.[178] After a period of the application of an administrative regulation, the State Council could request the NPC or its Standing Committee to upgrade this administrative regulation to a law.[179]

This practice reflects the facts that administrative regulations are widely used in the PRC and that the State Council has become the most powerful de facto lawmaking body.[180] Administrative regulations govern the day-to-day management of the country and provide the base and experience for national legislation. On the other hand, national legislation often lags behind practical needs and repeats administrative regulations. Laws often seem to be more like political declarations.[181]

The Law on Lawmaking of 2000 leaves room for debate on how the drafting of an administrative regulation should be governed by the Organic Law of the State Council.[182] Thus, the State Council indirectly has been delegated the power to make regulations for itself. This kind of delegation is not uncommon in the PRC. The reason for this might be that the NPC Standing Committee thinks that the working procedures of the State Council is the business of the State Council. This ambiguous delegation and lack of supervision of such delegated lawmaking can easily lead to the abuse of power by the State Council and often results in conflicts between laws and administrative regulations.

After the passage of an administrative regulation, the State Council should publish it in the *Gazette* of the State Council. This was first required by the PRPEAR of 1987[183] and reiterated by the Law on Lawmaking of 2000.[184] Thus, currently in the PRC, laws and administrative regulations must be published and made available to the public. The PRC has adopted the principle of transparency to some degree.

---

176. The PRC Law on Lawmaking of 2000, Art. 79.
177. Article 56.
178. *Ibid.*
179. *Ibid.*
180. Chen, Jianfu, *Chinese Law,* 103.
181. Some laws have less than fifty articles.
182. The PRC Law on Lawmaking of 2000, Art. 60.
183. *Ibid.*
184. Article 62.

3.5.4.   THE MAKING OF LOCAL REGULATIONS BY LOCAL PEOPLE'S
            CONGRESSES[185]

The procedures for the making of local regulations are to be decided by the local provincial governments.[186] Because local regulations have very few provisions on corporate disclosure, they are not discussed in this book.

3.5.5.   THE MAKING OF DEPARTMENTAL ADMINISTRATIVE RULES BY THE
            MINISTRIES AND COMMISSIONS OF THE STATE COUNCIL AND THE
            MAKING OF LOCAL ADMINISTRATIVE RULES BY THE
            PROVINCIAL GOVERNMENTS

As discussed above, departmental administrative rules in practice often play an even more important role than do laws and administrative regulations. This is true with regard to securities regulation. Hence, it is meaningful to discuss the procedures dealing with the making of departmental administrative rules. In addition, at the beginning of the formation of securities markets, local governments formed and supervised these markets. Up to the present time, local governments still have some indirect influence on share issuing and trading of enterprises owned by the local governments.[187] Therefore, it is also worth discussing the procedures of the making of local administrative rules.

The Constitution of 1982 provides that ministries and commissions of the State Council have the power to issue orders, directives, and rules within their respective jurisdictions.[188] This power is again clarified in the Law on Lawmaking of 2000.[189] The State Council is given the power to alter or annul departmental administrative rules and local administrative rules.[190] The Organic Law of the State Council of 1982 also clearly states this power.[191] However, there are no clear statutory definitions for departmental administrative rules and local administrative rules.

Under the Organic Law of People's Congresses and People's Governments at all Local Levels of 1986, people's governments at the provincial level and in some designated big cities may issue local administrative rules.[192] In the PRC, departmental administrative rules and local administrative rules are the most practical rules. They not only contain the details required for the implementation of laws and

---

185. The making of autonomous region regulations and separate regulations follows the same procedure and therefore they are not discussed separately.
186. The PRC Law on Lawmaking of 2000, Art. 68.
187. mainly by deciding on the state-owned companies' development strategies in share issuing and trading.
188. Article 90.
189. Article 71.
190. Article 89(13) and (14).
191. Article 10.
192. Articles 7 and 38.

administrative regulations,[193] but they also supplement laws and administrative regulations.[194] The content of departmental administrative rules and local administrative rules is about how to implement laws and administrative regulations so as to protect people's rights and interests, but not to create new rights and duties for people. The power to make local administrative rules and administrative rules is only to be exercised within the administrative power given by the central government.[195]

The PRC Law on Lawmaking vests the power to set the procedures for making departmental administrative rules and local administrative rules in the State Council and local governments.[196] There are two unofficial reasons for this: first, the NPC Standing Committee is politically weaker than the State Council, and it simply does not want to get into trouble by contesting the State Council or its ministries or commissions; and second, the NPC Standing Committee simply does not have enough resources to deal with this issue because of its own busy legislative schedule.[197] However, up until now, neither the State Council nor local governments have set formal procedures. In practice, departmental administrative rules and local administrative rules are made in different ways at different times, depending on who makes them. Consequently, in this practice, senior officials of the ministries and commissions, as well as local governments, have influential power over rule making. This is why many departmental administrative rules and local administrative rules contain provisions that conflict with laws or administrative regulations.

Because there are no clear rules on procedures for the making of local regulations and local administrative rules, the courts are not required to use them as legal bases in hearing cases. However, in fact, because the governments at all levels are managing the day-to-day issues of the country, judges are very reluctant to ignore the relevant local regulations and local administrative rules. Because national law clarifies neither the priority of departmental administrative rules and local administrative rules nor that of administrative regulations and departmental administrative rules, the courts often have no detailed rules to follow in hearing cases, which causes difficulties for judges, who have no power to make law.

3.6.   ENFORCEMENT OF LAW IN THE PRC

The process of the enforcement of law is to apply laws and rules to the management of the state's affairs. Law functions only if it is enforced. The poor enforcement of law in the PRC has been acknowledged by Chinese scholars and government

---

193. Articles 64(1) and 71.
194. Although this function is not clearly defined in the legislation, the making of administrative rules when no relevant laws or administrative regulations are available has in fact led to this result.
195. The PRC Law on Lawmaking of 2000, Art. 71.
196. Article 73.
197. Based on the author's previous work experience at the LAC.

officials.[198] The problem with the enforcement of law is probably worse than the problem of lawmaking in the PRC. It greatly undermines the PRC's goal of building a country with the rule of law.

In the PRC, the people's courts are the judicial bodies[199] that implement law. There are four levels of courts. According to the hierarchy, they are the Supreme Court of the PRC; the High Courts at the provincial level; the Intermediate Courts of the capital cities of the provinces, minority autonomous regions, and municipalities directly under the control of the Central Government; and the Basic Courts at the county or district level. In dealing with cases, courts apply and enforce the law.

Unlike Western countries, the PRC has not adopted the doctrine of separation of power. Thus, there is no separation of powers among the legislature, the executive government, and the judiciary. Because the CPC is the only controlling political party[200] in China, its status is strengthened in the Constitution. The political structure in China is that the CPC is the controlling party of China,[201] the NPC is the highest body of state power,[202] the President and Vice-President are elected by the National People's Congress,[203] the State Council is the highest executive body of state power,[204] and the people's courts are the judicial bodies of the state.[205] This structure provides the government departments with opportunities to abuse their powers and makes the courts to a large extent dependent upon the executive government. This dependency has affected the enforcement of law.

Under the Constitution, the NPC is the supreme body in China. The NPC and its Standing Committee exercise legislative power.[206] The Chairman and other senior members of the NPC and its Standing Committee, such as the Vice-Chairmen and the Secretary-General, are elected by the delegates of the NPC.[207] The President of the PRC is elected by the NPC.[208] The State Council is accountable to the NPC and its Standing Committee. It is accountable to the NPC Standing Committee when the NPC is not in session,[209] as it is the executive body of state power. The Prime Minister (hereinafter PM) is appointed by the President in pursuance of the decisions of the NPC or its Standing Committee.[210] As has been

---

198. Chen, Jianfu, *Chinese Law*, 95.
199. The PRC Consitution of 1982, Art. 123.
200. Eight so-called democratic parties existing in the PRC are under the leadership of the CPC.
201. Preamble of the Constitution.
202. Article 57 of the Constitution.
203. Article 79 of the Constitution.
204. Article 85.
205. Article 123.
206. Article 58.
207. Article 65.
208. Article 79.
209. Article 91.
210. Article 80.

discussed, the Supreme People's Court is the highest judicial body in China[211] and is accountable to the NPC and its Standing Committee.[212]

However, in fact, the NPC and its Standing Committee are mere puppets of the CPC. All the nominees of the most senior positions of the State Council and the Supreme People's Court are recommended by the Central Committee of the CPC. To date, in all cases, there has been only one nominee for each position. The NPC and its Standing Committee have no other choice but to appoint the CPC's nominees. This again shows that the NPC and its Standing Committee are still simply 'rubber-stamps' of the CPC. Thus, the CPC has both direct and indirect control of lawmaking.[213]

Although the PRC does not subscribe to the doctrine of separation of powers,[214] it claims that there is a division of functions among the legislature, the executive body, and the judiciary. The power division is decided upon by the CPC and is written in the Constitution. The CPC clearly refuses to initiate the doctrine of separation of powers, which is widely used in democratic countries because it is based on the concept of democracy. A movement toward democracy inevitably leads to a multi-party system, but this is the last thing that the CPC wants.

The result of the division of functions is that the executive body often acts above the legislature and judicature. The judiciary has to follow the decisions of the CPC and even the decisions of the State Council. There are three reasons for this situation. First, the CPC controls the appointment of the President of the Supreme People's Court. The seven or nine member Political Bureau of the Central Committee of the CPC is in fact the most powerful body in the PRC, which, as discussed above, has an officials-ranking system. In practice, the Supreme Courts may have an lower even status than the State Council's ministries and commissions.[215] Under this ranking system, it is clear that the courts in China are not independent.

A second factor that contributes to the courts' dependence on the executive government is its financial budget. According to the Budget Law of the PRC, the Ministry of Finance determines the budgets of all the government departments, including the budgets of the NPC and the Supreme People's Court. At the local government level, the Bureaux of Finance of the local governments determine the

---

211. Article 127.
212. Article 128.
213. The CPC is directly responsible for the drafting of Constitutional bills and indirectly supervises the drafting of the NPC and its Standing Committee through the Leading Group of Politico-Legal Groups of the Central Committee of the CPC. See Chen, Jianfu, *Chinese Law,* 114.
214. The Chinese government believes that the doctrine of separation of powers belongs to capitalism and will only bring chaos for the government.
215. This is a result of the fact that the budget of the Supreme Court is decided the Ministry of Finance.

budgets of the local people's congresses and local people's courts. The courts at the local level very often have to give in to the pressure of the local governments because they are financed by the local governments.

Third, the judicial committees within the courts prevent judges from exercising judicial independence. This dependence is the internal dependence that exists within the court system and it has been discussed previously.

The personnel appointment system, the budget system, and the internal judicial committees system in China mean that the courts in China cannot be independent from the CPC and the State Council. Legislators are clear about the lack of judicial independence in China. A former Deputy Chairman of the Law Committee of the NPC, Qiao Xiaoyang, pointed out, 'Currently some local courts have become the courts of the local governments and this is inconsistent with the rules of the WTO'.[216] Legislators have realized the importance of judicial justice and have recognized that judicial justice has to be accomplished through judicial reform. As Qiao Xiaoyang pointed out, the independence of the judiciary has to be ensured by legislative means.[217]

The executive body of the PRC also has some functions in the enforcement of law. First of all, the State Council has the power to pass administrative regulations so as to enforce laws passed by the NPC and its Standing Committee.[218] Secondly, the State Council may alter or annul inappropriate directives and decrees of its ministries and commission.[219] This function of the State Council is called the administrative enforcement of law.

Lawyers also have some role to play in the enforcement of law. After the PRC was founded in 1949, the CPC abolished the legal system of the previous government. During the Cultural Revolution, from 1966 to 1976, there was virtually no law in the PRC. Until the late 1970s, there were no lawyers in the PRC. As a result of the PRC's open-door policy, which was adopted in 1978, the legal system was re-instated. The Fifth Standing Committee passed the first law of lawyers – The Interim Regulations on Lawyers of the PRC – in 1980. However, under this Regulation, the functions of lawyers in the PRC were completely different from those enjoyed by lawyers in Western countries. Article 1 of the 1980 Regulation reads: 'Lawyers are state legal workers whose task is to give legal assistance to state organs, enterprises, public organizations and citizens in order to ensure the correct implementation of the law and protect the interests of the state and collectives as well as the lawful rights and interests of citizens'. Under this Article, the status of lawyers was that of public servants. As government employees, lawyers could not protect the rights and interests of citizens because these were not always

---

216.   <www.npcnews.com.cn/gb/paper8/14/class000800007/hwz212014.htm>, 26 Jun. 2002.
217.   *Ibid.*
218.   The PRC Constitution of 1982, Art. 89(1).
219.   *Ibid.*, Art. 89(14).

the same as the interests of the state. The role of lawyers in corporate life started changing in 1992 as a result of the deepening of economic reform and the increased need for legal services. Lawyers in the PRC now have roles similar to those of their counterparts in democratic countries. A lawyer is now defined as 'a practitioner who has acquired a lawyer's practicing certificate pursuant to law and provides legal service to the public'. The significant change of the roles of lawyers was confirmed with the enactment of the Lawyers' Law of 1996.[220] The definition of 'lawyer' was revised to 'a practitioner who has acquired a lawyer's practicing certificate, and is engaged or appointed to provide legal service to their clients so as to protect their client's legal interest, ensure the enforcement of law and maintain social justice' by the Lawyers' Law of 2007.[221] However, a Chinese lawyer, while practising, is required to 'base himself on facts and take law as the criterion'.[222] Because there is no interpretation of 'taking law as the criterion', lawyers' roles are still not completely clear.

3.6.1.   THE ENACTMENT OF THE COMPANY LAW OF 1993 AND THE
           SECURITIES LAW OF 1998 AND THEIR AMENDMENTS IN 2005, AS
           WELL AS RELEVANT ADMINISTRATIVE REGULATIONS AND
           ADMINISTRATIVE RULES

It should be clear from previous discussions that, in the PRC, the process of making and amending national laws takes a long time, that national laws usually are very short and general, and that the drafters' knowledge of law has an important impact on the content of bills. Thus, a national law often emerges as summary of a long period of practice. Laws have to be supplemented by administrative regulations and even departmental administrative rules. PRC laws are either particularly influenced by civil law countries or common law countries, or both, while they are still founded on the development of the PRC's economic reform process. The Company Law of 1993 and the Securities Law of 1998 are two such examples.

This section briefly reviews the drafting process of the first Company Law and Securities Law. It demonstrates how the drafting of these two Laws were influenced by foreign experiences. It also discusses why administrative regulations, and especially departmental administrative rules, play a more important role in securities regulation. The purpose of this section is to provide a comprehensive understanding of the securities regulatory rules of the PRC based on knowledge of the PRC's legal system.

---

220. The PRC Lawyers Law of 1996, Art. 2.
221. The PRC Lawyers Law of 2007, Art. 2.
222. *Ibid.*, Art. 3.

3.6.2.   How Did the PRC Start Regulating the Securities Market?

The Chinese securities market existed before the founding of the PRC in 1949.[223] It continued to exist for a short period of time before it was abolished by the central government as a result of the movement of 'socialist industrial and commercial reform', which ended in 1957. After that time, for almost three decades, there was no securities market because the PRC adopted a planned economy. Private enterprises were converted into state-owned enterprises. SOEs carried out the state plan of production, and their products were sold according to the state plan. They became subordinates of state bodies. Individual SOEs did not have the power to manage their business. All the capital needed by SOEs came from the state budget. There was no need to raise capital by issuing shares.

The re-emergence of the securities market started with the issuing of shares and bonds in the collective enterprises in the countryside beginning in 1979[224] and of state treasury bonds in 1981.[225] When SOEs were first allowed to issue shares in 1984, the securities market started to re-emerge.[226]

The re-emergence of the Chinese securities market was not planned, but instead a result of economic reform. The securities market has gone through a process from free development, to local regulation, and then to central regulation. Beginning in 1984, some enterprises started issuing enterprise bonds to the public and/or to their employees to raise capital. Because there were no relevant laws or regulations, the issuing of these bonds was made under the enterprises' rules, which were unclear and confusing. In that same year, the State Council issued the Provisional Administrative Regulation on Enterprise Bonds to standardize the issuance of enterprise bonds.

Since around the mid-1980s, issuing shares became a way to raise capital in the cities. The Beijing Tianqiao Joint Stock Limited Liability Co. was formed in 1984 as the first shareholding company.[227] Its first shares were issued to its employees. In the same year, Shanghai Feile Stereo Co. became the first company to issue shares to the public.[228] Since then, companies in other big cities followed by issuing their own shares.

Before a national securities market was formed, the central government did not adopt any national laws or regulations to standardize the shares market. From the mid-1980s to the early 1990s, the regulation of securities markets was

---

223.   The first Stock Exchanges law was enacted in 1914, Zheng, Zhenlong (ed.), *The Concise History of Chinese Securities Development)* (Beijing: Economic Science Press, 2006), 126.
224.   The State Council released Several Interim Provisions on Development of Country Collective Enterprises on 3 Jul. 1979 to allow the country enterprises to issue shares to its members so as to raise the capital for the development of such enterprises.
225.   Zheng, Zhenlong (ed.), *The Concise History of Chinese Securities Development*, 321.
226.   *Ibid.*
227.   Zheng, Zhenlong (ed.), *The Concise History of Chinese Securities Development*, 69.
228.   *Ibid.*, 73.

conducted by local governments and the People's Bank of China. In 1986, the branches of the People's Bank of China in Xiamen City of Fujian Province and in Beijing released their local Provisional Administrative Measures on Enterprise Bonds and Shares. The Shanghai government issued Shanghai Administrative Measures on Securities Trade in 1990, Shanghai Administrative Measures on Special RMB (CNY) Shares in 1991, and Shanghai Provisional Regulations on Joint Stock Limited Liability Companies in 1992. The Shenzhen government issued Shenzhen Provisional Measures on Share Issue and Trade in 1991 and Shenzhen Provisional Measures on Special RMB (CNY) Shares in 1991.

The PRC securities market developed mainly with the reform of SOEs. With the economic reform, a planned economy was no longer appropriate. The Western rule of the separation of ownership and control was introduced to SOEs in China.[229] Gradually, the central government realized that SOEs should adopt the modern enterprise system, namely, the company system. As a result of this reform, legislation regarding companies was put on the legislative agenda.

3.6.3.   HOW WERE THE FIRST COMPANY LAW AND SECURITIES
              LAW ENACTED?

The first PRC Company Law was not enacted until 1993. It was a result of the PRC's economic reform. The process of its enactment may be divided into several distinct stages.[230] The first proposal for a company law was submitted in February 1982 by the Economic Law Research Centre of the State Council in its 1982–1986 Five Year Legislative Plan. In August 1985, the State Council set up a drafting group, headed by the State Economics Commission, to draft company regulations. However, the draft company regulations were set aside. In 1988, the State Council's Legislative Affairs Bureau and the State Commission on Reform of the Economic System (SCRES) drafted and submitted the draft of the Limited Liability Company Law, which was approved by the State Council.

Because many legal issues regarding SOEs were not clear, the State Council decided to issue two necessary relevant administrative regulations and submitted the draft Limited Liability Company Law to the NPC Standing Committee for enactment of a national law.

The Limited Liability Company Bill was inserted into the legislative plan of the Standing Committee of the NPC in 1992. On 28 August 1992, the Twenty-Seventh Plenary Session of the Seventh NPC Standing Committee was convened, at which the Limited Liability Company Bill was first debated and investigated.

---

229. *Ibid.*, 94.
230. The discussion of the process of drafting of the Company Law draws upon the work of Song, Yanni & Shuqiang Liu, *Textbook on China's Company Law* (in Chinese) (Beijing: University Press of the Central Committee of the Chinese Communist Party, 1994).

Most of the members of the Standing Committee thought that the draft was too narrow to meet the practical needs. A meeting of the Chairmen of the Monetary Policy Committee (MPC) Standing Committee decided to ask the LAC to draft a broader Company Law based on the draft of the State Council's Limited Liability Company Law.

On 6 November 1992, the LAC finished the first draft of the Company Law. The draft became a Law at the end of 1993. In the process of drafting, the LAC drew upon the experiences of foreign laws, domestic regulations and decrees related to companies, and domestic development of companies. The PRC's Company Law was influenced by the Company Laws in Japan, Germany, the UK, the USA, and Hong Kong, among others. However, the influences of Germany and Japan perhaps were the greatest because of the similarity of their legal traditions.[231] Insights were also gained from two Administrative Regulations and Local Administrative Rules: Standard Opinions on Limited Liability Companies and Standard Opinions on Joint Stock Limited Liability Companies of the State Council, the Interim Regulation on Joint Stock Limited Liability Company of the Shanghai Municipal Government and the Company Regulation Draft of the Shenzhen Special Economic Zone, which was drafted by the Guangdong Provincial Government and the State Council's 1991 and 1992 versions of the draft Limited Liability Company Law.[232] From November 1992 to January 1993, about twenty seminars and conferences were held to discuss and revise the draft Company Law by the State Council. On 22 June 1993, the Second Plenary Session of the Eighth NPC Standing Committee investigated and examined the revised draft Company Law for the second time.

The LAC afterwards held more than thirty seminars on the Company Law draft from April to May in 1993.[233] From 20–29 December 1993, the Fifth Plenary Session of the Eighth NPC Standing Committee conducted the third examination of the revised draft Company Law. Based on the opinions and suggestions of this Session, the LAC made further revisions of the draft. On 29 December 1993, the PRC's first Company Law was eventually enacted by the Fifth Plenary Session of the Eighth NPC Standing Committee. It came into effect on 1 July 1994. It needs to be pointed out that, even if there had been a number of seminars and investigations conducted in the process of drafting, the contents of those meetings, the relevant reports of those seminars, and investigations had never been made public. Such lack of transparency is one of the big problems in the Chinese lawmaking process.

When the Company Law was being drafted, the regulation of the securities market had moved to the combination of regulation by the central and local governments. Because it takes time to enact a national law in the PRC, the State Council issued the Standard Opinions on Limited Liability Companies and Standard Opinions on Joint Stock Limited Liability Companies in 1992 as a

---

231. Song Yanni & ShuqiangLiu, *Textbook on China's Company Law,* 54.
232. *Ibid.*
233. Ibid., 56.

temporary solution to meet practical needs. Both Administrative Regulations contain several articles on share issuing. They can be seen as the first national rules on share issuing. From then on, the central regulation of the securities market started. The first step of the State Council was to set up the State Council Securities Commission (SCSC) and the CSRC in October 1992.[234] Soon after the establishment of these two commissions, the State Council issued the Circular on Further Strengthening Micro-management of the Securities Market. Under this Administrative Regulation, the State Council clarified the division of the administrative powers among its ministries and commissions. The departments involved in the regulation and supervision of the securities market and their powers will be discussed in detail in the following chapters.

While the SCSC and the CSRC were the national government departments to regulate the securities market and make administrative rules on securities regulation, the other ministries and commissions could also supervise the securities market and make relevant administrative decrees with their respective jurisdiction.[235] There were more than ten ministries and commissions that were involved in the regulation of the securities market. Most of the laws regulating the securities market were very detailed departmental administrative rules. They were released either by the ministry or commission in charge of the relevant issue or by the ministries and commissions in charge jointly. For example, the SCSC and the State Commission of Restructuring the Economic System (hereinafter SCERS) jointly released the Prerequisite Provisions in the Articles of Association of Companies Seeking Listing Overseas in August 1994.

The Company Law of 1993 has one chapter that includes thirty articles on share issuing and transfer, as well as on listed companies. However, most of these articles are general principles. To implement these principles, the Securities Law was needed. Another reason to enact the Securities Law of 1998 was that the articles about the securities in the Company Law only covered the issuing and transfer of shares. There were no provisions on the regulation of the market as a whole. The articles in the Company Law of 1993 were far from meeting the needs of the development of the securities market. Thus, the Securities Law of 1998 (which was first drafted in 1992) was once again put on the agenda of the NPC Standing Committee.

The Securities Law of 1998 was the first law that was drafted by a drafting group organized by a special committee of the NPC. The drafting group was set up in mid-1992 at the suggestion of the then Chairman of the NPC, Wan Li.[236] The members of the drafting group included experts from Beijing University, China University of Politics and Law, The University of International Business and Trade, and the members of the Finance and Economics Committee of the NPC, as well as experts in the securities industry.

---

234. *Ibid.*, 205.
235. *Ibid.*, 326.
236. The NPC Drafting Group of the Securities Law, *Annotation of the PRC Securities Law* (Beijing: China Financial Press, 1999), Preface.

The first draft was finished in August 1993 and was submitted to the Third Session of the Eighth NPC Standing Committee for its first examination. In December, the revised draft was submitted to the Fifth Session of the Eighth NPC Standing Committee for a second examination. In June 1994, the Eighth Session of the Eighth NPC Standing Committee examined the revised draft for the third time. After that, the legislative process stopped because of the occurring of a number of securities and futures cases.[237]

Beginning in October 1998, the Fifth Plenary Session of the Ninth NPC Standing Committee again examined the draft Securities Law that was submitted by the LAC. This draft was different from the 1993 draft in many aspects. There were many reasons for these differences: first, the LAC drafters were more focused on the domestic situation; second, they lacked a good understanding of the regulation of securities markets in Western countries; third, the leaders of the drafters were very conservative CPC members and they did not like the 1993 draft, which was mainly written by scholars who had been educated in the USA and had several years of work experience on Wall Street. Although the draft provided by the LAC was very disappointing to the hard line reformists, it was basically accepted by the members of the NPC Standing Committee, who had little knowledge of securities. The NPC Standing Committee and the NPC special committees had conducted further study and investigation at home and abroad. These committees draw upon the experiences from the USA, Hong Kong, Japan, and Australia.[238] The then Chairman of the NPC, Li Peng, specifically flew to Shenzhen to investigate the main issues raised by the members of the NPC Standing Committee.[239] In December 1998, the Sixth Session of the Ninth NPC Standing Committee examined the draft for the fifth time and passed it on 29 December 1998.

Before the Securities Law of 1998 was enacted, the PRC securities market had moved to a new stage. The combination of regulation by both the central government and local governments caused many inconsistence in policies and practice. The central government decided to unify regulation of the securities market. The State Council minimized the ministries' and commissions' involvement in the securities market by dissolving the State Council's Securities Commission and delegating the highest rule-making power to the CSRC.[240] From then on, the CSRC released a large number of administrative decrees to regulate the securities market. From its establishment in October 1992 until the end of 1999, the CSRC passed about 200 departmental administrative rules. Many of them are about disclosure, which is a major problem in the securities market. Because there was no law or regulation on the procedure for the making of departmental administrative rules,

---

237. Song Yanni & Shuqiang Liu, *Textbook on China's Company Law,* 58.
238. Law professors, lawyers, and securities regulators from these countries were invited to China to introduce their home countries' experience.
239. Song Yanni & Shuqiang Liu, *Textbook on China's Company Law,* 59.
240. In March 1998, the State Council Securities Commission was dissolved. The CSRC was given the regulative powers over the securities market that used to be enjoyed by the State Securities Commission. In July, the CSRC took over the Securities Regulative Offices from the local governments with the release of a circular by the General Office of the State Council.

ministries and commissions usually copied the State Council's main procedures in passing administrative regulations. However, the procedures for the making of administrative rules in practice are much simpler and more informal. Thus, they can be changed frequently without much consideration. This may also lead to conflicts between laws and administrative regulations.

Only a limited number of provisions of the Company Law of 1993 were amended in 1999 and 2004, and the minimal amendments to the Securities Law of 1998 were made in 2004. Substantial amendments to both the Company Law of 1993 and the Securities Law of 1998 were made in October 2005. The Company Law of 2005 and the Securities Law of 2005 include some changes to the disclosure rules. These changes will be discussed in Chapter 4.

In sum, the PRC has formed a set of securities regulatory rules, consisting of laws, administrative regulations, and local administrative regulations, departmental administrative rules and local administrative rules. Among these, departmental administrative rules are most useful and practical. In the area of corporate disclosure, the Rules of the CSRC are the most important ones.

3.7. CONCLUSION

From the analysis in the previous sections, it can be seen that the PRC's legal system is based on the traditions of a long history of feudalism, which were greatly influenced by Confucianism. The PRC is still a country with rule by man rather than the rule of law. Thus, the leaders of the country have supremacy in influencing lawmaking. The CPC as the ruling party decides upon the most important matters of the country.[241] Ordinary people and entities are not allowed to challenge the decisions of the CPC.

The Chinese legal system has also incorporated experiences from both civil law systems and common law systems, with more aspects of civil law systems because of the civil law tradition adopted in the late Qing Dynasty and its economic reform, which started in the late 1970s. The law of the former Soviet Union also had a great impact on the PRC's legal system before the economic reform. The experience of the Soviet Union contributed to the planned economy and centralization. All these put together have formed the main features of the PRC's legal system: the country is very highly centralized; the most general and highest legislative power belongs to the NPC and its Standing Committee; and the local legislative bodies have specific lawmaking powers. However, because the executive body is practically more important than the legislature, conflicts between national legislation and regulation making are not rare. This situation is one of the contributories to the poor enforcement of law. The courts widely use their discretion to choose applicable laws. Because there is no doctrine of precedent in China, similar cases may be dealt with very differently.

---

241. For instance, the adoption of a socialist market economy was decided by the CPC first and then was inserted into the Constitution.

During the economic reform, the legislative institutions of China have also paid special attention to drawing upon experiences from the common law system. For instance, during the drafting and amending of the Company Law and the Securities Law, Chinese legislators learned a lot from common law countries such as the USA, the UK, and Hong Kong. However, because the economic system and the legal system of the PRC were and are fundamentally different from those of common law countries, many foreign concepts and procedures simply cannot be transplanted into the PRC. The drafters of the Company Law and the Securities Law lacked knowledge of common law,[242] and this prevented them from absorbing the substance of common law. Recent Chinese commercial lawmaking has copied many sections of statutes from common law countries, but the functioning of these sections still remains to be tested. The Chinese legal system is a mixture of many different legal systems, but it may not necessarily be the appropriate combination.

How the PRC should draw upon foreign experiences has never been seriously studied. Many pieces of legislation are like a monk's *bai na yi*, consisting of little pieces from other people's old clothes.[243] This characteristic obviously causes confusion. For instance, the copying of corporate disclosure sections from both common law countries and other civil law countries often confuse people about the real meanings of some provisions in the laws.

Moreover, the powerful ministries and commissions of the State Council often interfere with the enforcement of law by the courts. The ambiguity of the authority of different forms of law causes conflicts among them and leaves the courts having to resort to departmental administrative rules and even local administrative rules, even when they are inconsistent with national law. All these problems demonstrate that, currently, the CSRC is the most powerful regulatory body of the securities market. The CSRC's administrative rules even play a role that should be played by national law.

Although the courts at different levels theoretically should be cooperative, the actual practice turns out to very different. Judgments of one court are not always enforced by another court in another province, even if that is a lower-level court. Local protectionism is a serious problem in law enforcement. Because the financial budget of local courts is made by the local governments and the judges of local courts are appointed by the local legislative bodies, local protectionism often takes priority over the consistency of law. This situation was one of the reasons why the State Council gave the CSRC the supreme power to regulate the national securities market. It is well-known that the enforcement of law in the PRC has a bad record. There are systematic, historical, political, and practical reasons for that. The problem with the enforcement of law will be further discussed in the following

---

242. For example, the approximately 100 drafting staff members of the Legislative Affairs Commission did not have a person who had a sound common law education; Chen, Jianfu, 'Coming Full Circle: Lawmaking in the PRC from a Historical Perspective', in *Lawmaking in the PRC,* ed. J.M. Otto et al. (The Hague: Kluwer Law International, 2000), 23.
243. This kind of Buddhist monk's dress, usually made of different pieces of cloth, looks very haphazard.

chapters with regard to the enforcement of information disclosure articles provided for in laws, administrative regulations, and administrative rules. The poor enforcement of law is also one of the reasons for the frequent occurrence of cases involving false disclosure.

Chinese legal history, the development of the lawmaking process in the PRC, and the poor enforcement of law have caused the PRC to have a legal system that is quite different from those of Western countries. There is a strongly persistent divergence in its economic development and legal system. Although further economic reform and the influence of globalization have caused the PRC's laws to move in the direction of convergence, its history, culture, and legal tradition still continue to influence it as it finds its path.

Chapter 4

Gatekeepers in the Chinese Securities Market[1]

4.1.   INTRODUCTION

The previous chapter provided a brief introduction to the Chinese legal system. With this broad picture of the legal system in mind, it is possible to develop a deeper understanding of the unique features of Chinese securities regulation, especially those of corporate disclosure regulation.

To evaluate the corporate disclosure regime of the PRC, it is first important to look at the functions of the regulators in its securities market, which are the focus of this chapter. In contrast to Western countries, the PRC has a very bureaucratic governmental structure, with many governmental departments involved in securities regulation. An examination of the roles of the 'players' in these departments is essential to an understanding of the regulatory structure of the PRC's securities market and how it works. This chapter will explain the roles of the different departments, at both the central government and provincial government levels, involved in securities rule making and enforcement. It will further explain that this multi-departmental regulatory structure had led to the inefficiency of the PRC's securities market. Although the situation has improved since the CSRC was made the sole regulatory body of the securities market, this market still does not function well because the CPC and others continue to improperly interfere with securities regulation. This will be explained in the following chapter.

This chapter is structured as follows: it first reviews the re-emergence of the issuance of securities and then explains the roles of the CPC and the governmental

---

1. Neil Gunningham used the metaphor 'goalpost' in his article 'Moving the Goalposts: Financial Market Regulation in Hong Kong and the Crash of October 1987', *Law & Social Inquiry* 15, no. 1 (1990): 1–47 at 1.

departments in securities regulation and corporate governance. It further demonstrates that the driving forces for the development of the Chinese securities market are the PRC's economic reform and the need to ease the government's financial burden caused by the inefficiency of SOEs. In contrast, making the securities market transparent for shareholders and other investors seems less important for the PRC government. This general historical characteristic of a lack of transparency of the PRC has caused the fundamental difference between Chinese securities regulation and other securities regulatory regimes, such as that in Australia. This chapter will go on to examine the functions of different players in the PRC's securities markets and analyse how the multi-departmental regulatory regime is structured, as well as to identify the problems with the multi-departmental regulatory framework. The goal is to illustrate why a single regulatory regime should be formed and how it should be formed. It will be shown that foreign securities regulatory regimes have had a significant influence on the PRC, in particular in the area of corporate disclosure. Finally, this chapter critically evaluates the functions of the sole regulator of the PRC's securities markets – the CSRC.

In conclusion, the unique features of the Chinese securities market are a reflection of the divergence hypothesis, while the similarities between the PRC's securities market and some securities markets in developed countries demonstrate the influence of the convergence hypothesis. In the end, however, the development of the PRC's securities market is a result of the differentiation hypothesis, with a stronger influence of divergence.

4.1.1. RE-EMERGENCE OF SECURITIES ISSUE AND REGULATION

As discussed in Chapter 3, the PRC's securities market was not formed until the early 1990s, although the issuing of securities had been used as a way of capital raising years ago. The regulation of the securities market in the PRC started much later than the formation of the market. The re-emergence of the securities market in the PRC is one of the results of its economic reform, which started in the late 1970s. Government departments were heavily involved in the re-emergence of the issuing of shares.

China's economic reform first began in the countryside. With the development of this reform, the shareholding system was first used in the countryside in southern China in the late 1970s. At that time, some villages and groups started raising capital by issuing shares and paying interest on shares.[2] Because the shareholding system was used in few industries, there were no laws, administrative regulations, or administrative rules governing the issuance of shares.

The activity of issuing shares was first officially recognized by the central government in The State Council's *Several Regulations on Development of*

---

2. Li, Zhangzhe, *Finally Successful: Development Report of Chinese Shares Market* (in Chinese) (Beijing: World Knowledge Press, 2000), 61.

Villages and Groups (for trial) on 3 July 1979.[3] In 1982, then Chairman of the NPC, Wan Li, pointed out that some household businesses that wanted to expand their production scales should adopt joint operation by issuing shares.[4] In 1983, the CPC made it clear in its Several Issues on Current Countryside Economic Policies that 'Co-operation does not only mean pay by work without pay by shareholding.'[5] Number One document released by the CPC in 1984 clearly stated that 'Farmers are encouraged to invest in all types of enterprises by holding shares.'[6] The policy contained in this document further stimulated the development of a shareholding system in the countryside. The wide use of this system in the countryside initiated the adoption of shareholding in the cities. The shareholding system was strongly supported by the ruling party and the central government through their policies. Such strong government involvement was and continues to be one of the major differences between the PRC's securities regulation and other regulatory regimes.

While the practice of the shareholding system was developing, theoretical debates did not come until later. A leading economist at Peking University, Professor Li Yining, was the first person who advocated for the adoption of the shareholding system in SOEs. He later became a member of the Standing Committee of the NPC. As a key legislator, he lobbied for the enactment of the first Company Law and the Securities Law. His suggestion on the adoption of the shareholding system was first made at a symposium on Labour and Payment organized by the Secretariat of the CPC and the State Labour Bureau (later changed to the Ministry of Labour) in April 1980.[7] However, at that time, the government had not realized the importance of regulation, given that the securities market had yet to be formed.

At the beginning of the issuing of shares, local governments were involved in developing policy guidelines, and people did not have a clear idea about the nature of shares. Fushun City of Liaoning Province was the first city to raise capital by issuing shares. On 1 January 1980, Liaoning Fushun No. 1 Red Bricks Factory in that city issued shares to the public. By January 28, more than 200 enterprises had purchased its shares. The shares, worth a total CNY 28 million, were sold to enterprises and individual investors.[8]

On 2 April 1980, the CPC branch of Chengdu City, the capital of Sichuan Province, approved an application to establish Chengdu Industrial Products Trading Shareholding Company, which came up with the idea to raise capital by issuing shares from a movie. On June 11, the Chengdu municipal government issued a document to support the Company's issuing of shares issue. At that time, no one in the company had even seen shares before. Several employees drew a picture of a

---

3. *Ibid.*
4. *Ibid.*
5. *Ibid.*
6. *Ibid.*
7. *Ibid.*, 62.
8. *Ibid.*, 63.

share and sent it for printing. Because Chinese people had limited knowledge of the nature of shares, the following was stated on the back of each share certificate: 'Shares are securities with value. They are not allowed to be traded on the market or for speculation . . . Shares belong to the buyers who can enjoy the interests on their holding shares.'[9]

Guangdong Province was the one of the first provinces to adopt the share-holding system. Its shareholding practice started in Shenzhen. In 1982, the Bao'an County government of Shenzhen approved the establishment of the Guangdong Bao'an Joint Investment Company. Because of a lack of capital, the Company observed how capital was raised in the Hong Kong securities market and followed its example. On 8 July 1983, the Company was formally incorporated. On July 25, the *Shenzhen SEZ Weekly* published the company's prospectus. This was the first company in the PRC to issue shares through the newspapers. However, this issuance was not standard. The Company did not have 'shareholding' in its name, and its shareholders were paid only interest on their shareholdings. The Company later changed its name to Shenzhen Bao'an Investment Shareholding Group and became a formal shareholding company on 9 September 1990.[10]

Another classic case involving the issuing of shares was Beijing Tianqiao Department Store. On 26 July 1984, the Beijing municipal government decided to change Beijing Tianqiao Department Store into Beijing Tianqiao Department Store Joint Stock Company Ltd. It also decided that the Company would have three allotments of shares, which would be worth CNY 10 million. It further decided that the issuance of these shares would not be advertised. Even so, many people heard the news and bought shares of the Company.[11]

In Shanghai, Shanghai Feile Stereo Facilities Joint Stock Company Ltd (Feile Co.) was established on 18 November 1984. From the beginning of the preparation of the issuance of shares, it gained strong support from the Shanghai municipal government.[12] The news of the issuance of shares was published in a local newspaper, *Xinmin Evening News*. Again, because at that time, people had limited knowledge of shares and were not very interested in buying them, Feile Co. guaranteed the payment of a fixed interest rate and the principal capital to its shareholders, demonstrating that Feile's share issuance was at a primitive stage. Even government officials and the issuer itself had no clear idea about the nature and function of shares – let alone the investors.[13] At that time, the benefit of buying shares was to get a higher return than that earned by depositing savings in banks. This was very different from the purpose of investing in shares in Western countries. However, Feile Co. allowed its shareholders to sell the shares freely, gave its shareholders the rights to attend shareholders meetings and make

---

9. *Ibid.*, 64.
10. *Ibid.*, 66.
11. *Ibid.*, 69.
12. *Ibid.*, 74.
13. *Ibid.*, 73.

proposals, and paid its shareholders dividends.[14] In effect, Feile Co. was moving to a more standard form of share issuance.

Thus, at the time of the re-emergence of share issuance in the early 1980s, most people in China had limited knowledge of shares, with senior officials even having no clear idea about the functions of shareholding. As China had for a long time had a socialist system, shares were thought of as a product of capitalism. Most government officials were afraid of approving share-issuing applications, and most ordinary people were afraid of buying shares.

In the early 1980s, a story appeared in a newspaper about the fact that Shenyang Jinbei Co.,[15] which, although it was issuing shares in the office building of the State Council, sold few shares. This story again demonstrates that not only the general public in China, but also government officials and bankers, did not clearly understand the function of shares.

Another example of the lack of understanding of the function of shares is that the economic reform leader of the PRC, Deng Xiaoping gave a share as a gift to the Chairman of the New York Stock Exchange in 1986.[16] On 14 November, the Chairman of the New York Stock Exchange visited China, and Deng Xiaoping gave him a share of Shanghai Feile Co., which had a face value of CNY 50, via the Governor of the People's Bank of China (hereinafter PBOC), Chen Muhua. The Chairman was both excited and surprised when he received this share: he was excited that China had begun to issue shares, but he was surprised that the name on the share was not his, but rather the name of a deputy governor of the PBOC's Shanghai Branch. The Chairman of the New York Stock Exchange insisted that because the share was his, it should have his name on it. On November 23, he specifically went to the first share-trading site in China – the Shanghai Jing'an Branch of the PBOC – to have the name on the share that he held changed.[17] This story demonstrates that even senior officials of the central government did not understand the nature of shares as personal property. Thus, the securities rules were made for the purpose of market regulation rather than for the purpose of protection of property rights of securities holders. This purpose led to the persistence of divergence in the development of the PRC's securities market and fundamentally distinguished this market from Western markets.

The first companies that issued shares in China were not real shareholding companies such as those that exist today. Although Liaoning Fushun Red Bricks Factory was the first enterprise to issue shares, Sichuan Chengdu Industrial Exhibition Co. was the first to use a prospectus for share issuing, Shenzhen Bao'an Joint Investment Co. was the first to publish a prospectus in a newspaper, Beijing Tianqiao Department Store Joint Stock Co. was the first state-owned enterprise that adopted a shareholding system, none of them was a real joint stock company. First, before the issuance of stock, all the companies promised to pay back the

---

14. *Ibid.*
15. *Ibid.*, 104–109.
16. *Ibid.*, 76.
17. *Ibid.*

capital and the fixed interest rate, which was higher than the interest rate of banks. Second, the shares were mainly issued to the companies' employees, who did not have a choice of whether or not to buy shares but were forced to buy them with their salaries. Third, public offerings were rarely used. Fourth, the prospectuses were incomplete because they did not contain basic information, such as the use of the raised capital and accounting records. Lastly, shares were not transferable in the market but were transferred internally or secretly.[18]

In the early 1980s, when some SOEs started issuing shares to meet the shortage of capital, there were no clear policies or regulations on how to raise capital by issuing shares. Approval by the local government was the only way to legally issue shares. For instance, Liaoning Fushun No. 1 Red Bricks Factory got approval from Shenyang municipal government and[19] Chendu Industrial Exhibition Co. got approval from Chengdu municipal government.[20]

Because issuing shares is a way of raising capital and raising capital had been one of the objects of the business of the PBOC, it and other banks first started issuing regulatory documents in the early 1980s. The first measures on share trading were released by the Jing'an Branch of Shanghai Trust and Investment Co., which belonged to Shanghai Industry and Commerce Bank in 1983. This document, the Interim Measures on Trading Shares as Agents, was really an internal business management document. Wuhan Financial Investment Co. issued Measures for Share Issue of Wuhan Financial Trust and Investment and Interim Measures for Share Trading as the Agent of Wuhan Financial Investment Co. on 1 July 1987. From the release of these measures, it can be seen that because the government did not make relevant regulations, the participants in the securities market had to make rules for themselves. This was another symptom of the irregularities that existed at the first stage of the development of the Chinese securities market.

In July 1984, the Shanghai Branch of the PBOC released the Interim Administrative Measures on Share Issue. This was the first local administrative document on share issuance. It described the types of shares, the scope of share issuance, the interest rate and bonus of shares, the transfer of shares, and the term of issue. However, because it was not a local administrative regulation or a local administrative rule, it had very limited application.

As a result of the wide adoption of the shareholding system in the mid-1980s, local governments started regulating the market by releasing regulatory documents. The Shanghai municipal government approved the Interim Measures on Share Issue released by the Shanghai Branch of the PBOC in August 1984. This was the first local regulatory document on securities. The Shanghai municipal government also became the first local government to pass the first local administrative rule, entitled Shanghai Interim Administrative Measures for Share Issue, on 23 May 1987. The Shenzhen municipal government released its first local administrative rule on securities administration, Interim Regulations on the

---

18. *Ibid.*, 60–80.
19. *Ibid.*, 63.
20. *Ibid.*

Experiment of a Shareholding System in State-Operated Enterprises in the Shenzhen Special Economic Zone, in July 1986. This was also the first local administrative rule aimed at adopting shareholding in SOEs.

From the re-emergence of the securities market, capital raising by share issuance was first used in the countryside, was later adopted by small enterprises in the cities, and later experimented with in some large SOEs designated by the central government. There were no regulatory rules at the beginning of capital raising by share issuance, and there were no national rules on securities in the 1980s, as there were still theoretical debates on whether China, as a socialist country, should adopt a shareholding system, which was seen as a product of a capitalist system.

However, with more and more enterprises raising capital by share issuance, the government had to deal with the problems arising out of the operation of this market. Because the securities market was treated as a capital market, its regulation fell within the regulatory scope of the PBOC first. The local governments, along with the PBOC, issued several joint documents concerning the securities market. For instance, the Shanghai government and Shanghai branch of the PBOC jointly released the Interim Regulation on Securities Trading over the Counter in 1985, the Administrative Measures on Securities Trading in 1990, the Shanghai Administrative Measures on B Shares in 1991, and the Shanghai Interim Regulations on Joint Stock Companies in 1992.

Regulation of the securities market started with regulation by local governments and the local branches of the central government's PBOC. The Shanghai and Shenzhen municipal governments were the first two local governments to release documents governing the shareholding issue. The PBOC and its branches in Shanghai and Shenzhen were the first central government departments involved in securities regulation.

Direct policy support for shareholding from the central government did not occur until April 1984. As the department in charge of the economic reform under the State Council at that time, the SCRES held a Symposium on the Trial of Municipal Economic Reform. It was clearly stated in the Symposium minutes that China should further loosen the control of municipal collective enterprises and small SOEs, and the measures to be applied was to allow employees to invest in company shares and receive bonuses (which, at that time, were not bonus shares but rather the interest on their investment) at the end of each year.[21] This was the first clear support for a shareholding system from the central government. The term 'shareholding system' was first used in an administrative directive released jointly by the SCRES and the Ministry of Commerce in the Circular on Several Issues on Commercial System Reform in 1986. In December 1986, the State Council for the first time allowed several SOEs to conduct a shareholding experiment based on the Administrative Regulation entitled Several Rules on Further Deepening Enterprises Reform. Since then, the regulation of the securities market by the central government has been strengthened.

---

21. *Ibid.*, 63.

The State Council released the Circular on Further Strengthening Administration of Shares and Debentures in March 1987. This was the first administrative regulation concerning securities regulation. In September 1987, the CPC's Thirteenth Plenary Meeting stated that shareholding was a type of property and should be allowed a trial period.[22] This was the first time that the ruling party of China formally gave its direct support to the shareholding system.

With the encouragement of the central government, local governments continued to adopt local regulations and local administrative rules. For instance, Fujian Province issued the Interim Measures on Shareholding Enterprises (Fujian Province) and the Interim Measures on Administration of Shares (Fujian Province) in 1987. The Shenzhen municipal government released the Shenzhen Interim Measures on the Printing of Shares in 1988, the Administrative Rules on Examination and Approval of Enterprises Share Issue in 1989, and the Shenzhen Interim Measures on Securities Business Fee Charges in 1989. The making of local rules was a result of a lack of national rules and practical needs.

There was no single regulatory body of the securities market, and few uniform policies on securities were established until the early 1990s. The development of the securities market was affected by a number of factors, such as the economic need for the development of further reform, the government's support of SOEs, which were in desperate need of financial support,[23] and its intervention in over-speculation in the securities market. For example, at the beginning of 1989, the Shenzhen Development Bank started paying dividends that were as high as 50% of the issuing price. It then started allocating shares to its shareholders. Each shareholder was allocated a free share for every two shares held. This practice encouraged public speculation in the securities market. Novice shareholders thought that share trading was a way to make a fortune overnight. They did not realize that they could also lose a large amount of money overnight. Over-speculation in the securities market drove share prices to an unrealistically high level. For instance, the trading price of shares of the Shenzhen Development Bank went up to 140 times its face value in the black market in May 1989.[24] Over-speculation also made many companies raise large sums of capital in a very short period of time. It also encouraged illegal share issuing. For instance, several companies issued and transferred shares without approval from the government.

Facing the abnormal development of the securities market, local governments were forced to adopt a number of measures to prevent people's over-speculation in the securities market. The Shenzhen government released the Combined Measures on Maintaining Order in the Securities Market on 1 January 1990. This document stated that all shares that were allowed to be transferred by the PBOC must be transferred through designated securities trading companies.

---

22. *Ibid.*, 109.
23. Leng, Jing, *Corporate Governance and Financial Reform in China's Transition Economy* (Hong Kong: Hong Kong University Press, 2009), 127.
24. Above n. 2, 121.

To control the irregularities in the trial of the shareholding system, the SCRES was delegated the power by the State Council to release regulatory rules on share issuing because it was in charge of making policies on economic reform. On 11 February 1989, the SCRES drafted the Circular on the Adoption of the Shareholding System for the State Council. On the same day, it also drafted the Experimental Measures for Adoption of the Shareholding System in Enterprises and the Interpretation on Several Issues of the Circular on the Experimental Measures for Adoption of the Shareholding System in Enterprises. These Administrative Regulations were passed by the State Council to direct the reform of SOEs.

Before the Shanghai and Shenzhen Stock Exchanges were established in 1990, the shareholding system was adopted for a trial period because it was perceived to be important for China's economic reform. This trial period was directed by the CPC's policies and the administrative rules of the SCRES, which acted as the central government department in charge of the economic reform. For instance, the SCRES held a Symposium on the Trial of Urban Economic Reform in Changzhou in April 1984. In its minutes, it was clearly stated that, 'the employees of the small-sized state-owned and collective enterprises should be allowed to take shareholding in the enterprise and enjoy the interest'.[25] At that time, securities companies were registered under the rules of local governments.[26]

During that period, senior officials of the central government also pushed for the development of the securities market. As mentioned earlier, Deng Xiaoping sent a share to the President of the New York Stock Exchange in 1986, and then Communist Party Chief of Shanghai, Jiang Zemin, visited Shanghai's first securities trading firm: Jing'An Securities Trading Department.[27]

During the 1990s, the Stock Exchanges had been issuing regulatory documents, such as listing rules and business rules. The operational body of the State Securities Commission (SCSC) at that time, the CSRC, started issuing regulatory documents after its establishment in 1992. These documents were not administrative rules because the CSRC had not been given administrative powers. In practice, these CSRC rules could not be properly enforced because of the CSRC's lack of authority and local protectionism.

Before a national regulatory body was set up, the securities markets were governed by a number of departments at the national level within their respective categories of powers. For instance, the SCRES made a number of rules on the trial of the shareholding system; the former State Planning Commission[28] decided which SOEs could adopt the shareholding system; the PBOC decided which companies could issue shares to the general public; and the State Council's Production Office *(Sheng Chan Ban)* decided which enterprises could adopt the shareholding system and/or issue shares to the public. These five departments jointly issued the

---

25. Li, Zhangzhe, *Finally Successful: Report of the Development of China's Securities Market*, 68.
26. *Ibid.*
27. *Ibid.*, 86.
28. In March 2003, the SCRES, the State Planning Commission, and the State Commission for Economics and Trade were merged into the State Development and Reform Commission.

Measures for the Trial of the Shareholding System on 15 May 1992. In addition to this joint Regulation, the SCRES released two administrative rules on the same day: the Standard Opinions on Limited Liability Companies and the Standard Opinions on Joint Stock Limited Liability Companies. These became the first three important documents guiding the adoption of the shareholding system.

Up until the early 1990s, most enterprises in the PRC were SOEs. For several decades, they had been acting as organs of the government. The change of the business form of these SOEs became the first priority of the central and local governments at that time. The basic principles of Western securities markets had not been studied and therefore were not adopted in the PRC. Openness, fairness, and justice, as the fundamental principles of securities markets, were not adopted in the first relevant national regulations, which instead were focused on what kind of enterprises were allowed to experiment with the shareholding system; how to structure shareholding companies; the functions of the departments of these companies; takeovers and mergers of the companies; and the liquidations and dissolutions of the companies. No provisions for disclosure were made in these rules. This outcome was a result of the fact that the development of the Chinese securities market was initially driven by the transformation of SOEs into companies. The securities markets had just re-emerged, share issuing had not become a major means of capital raising, and regulation of share issuing had not been put on the agenda of the government.

Before the establishment of the SCSC and the CSRC, no single department was clearly given the power to regulate the securities market. Although the PBOC played an important role, given that the regulation of financial institutions was within its portfolio, its role was limited to the approval or denial of the establishment of securities companies.

The establishment of the CSRC started a new stage in the PRC's securities regulatory history. The first Chairman of the CSRC, Liu Hongru, had been the Executive Deputy Governor of the PBOC and had a lot of experience in finance. He recruited Gao Xiqing, one of the first Chinese people who had obtained a juris doctorate (JD) from one of the top American law schools and had several years of work experience on Wall Street, as the CSRC's Chief Counsel. Gao Xiqing later became the Executive Deputy Chairman of the CSRC, and currently is the General Manager and an executive director of the PRC's sovereign wealth fund: the China Investment Corporation. Many other American-trained Chinese people were also employed by the CSRC. They had brought back the American ideas of securities regulation and drafted the first administrative regulation on securities regulation: the Interim Administrative Regulation Concerning Share Issue and Trading Regulations for the State Council of April 1993 (hereinafter the 1993 Interim Regulation).

In this Regulation, openness, fairness, and honesty are accepted as three basic principles.[29] Promoters, directors, and underwriters are subject to an obligation to guarantee that there is no false or seriously misleading information, or any major

---

29. Article 3.

omission in prospectuses.[30] The Regulation pays particular attention to the issue of disclosure by devoting a chapter to it. Chapter 6 is entitled 'Information Disclosure of Listed Companies.' Listed companies are required to submit a half-yearly financial report within sixty days after the first six months of the financial year.[31] They are also required to submit a yearly financial report, audited by a registered accountant, within 120 days after the end of the financial year.[32] Chapter 6 not only lists the contents of the half-yearly and annual financial reports,[33] but also sets the requirement for disclosure of major events that may have a material effect on the share price.[34] Article 60 lists about thirteen items that are deemed to be major events. For the first time, the shareholdings of directors, supervisors, and senior management staff were required to be disclosed.[35] Listed companies are also required to correct any inaccurate information that may affect share prices.[36] This Regulation unified the means by which disclosure is to be made by requiring listed companies to publish news in the national newspapers and local newspapers designated by the CSRC,[37] which also imposed on listed companies the duty to disclose documents to the public.[38] This Regulation also has exceptions to disclosure. Commercial secrets and the information acquired by the CSRC during the process of investigation and other non-public information need not be disclosed.[39]

The State Council's 1993 Interim Regulation is the first piece of national regulation relating to securities disclosure. On the one hand, it has an important function in standardizing the PRC's securities market. For the first time, it clearly stated the principles of disclosure that are the fundamental rules of securities markets. On the other hand, there is no general disclosure requirement, and the matters on the list to be disclosed are very limited. Many important matters do not have to be disclosed simply because they do not fall into the categories listed. Article 74 imposes penalties on those who are involved in giving false and misleading disclosure information. However, it only contains administrative liabilities, such as warnings, confiscation of illegal profits, and fines. These penalties clearly are not severe enough to prevent people from contravening the law.

Because of the loopholes of the 1993 Interim Regulation, many companies continued to give false information in disclosure after they had been fined, given a warning, or even had their illegal profits confiscated. Another shortcoming of this Interim Regulation is that although it states that giving false and misleading information may result in criminal and civil liabilities, the Criminal Law did not have

---

30. Article 17.
31. Article 57.
32. *Ibid.*
33. Articles 58 and 59.
34. Article 60.
35. Article 62.
36. Article 61.
37. Article 63.
38. Article 64.
39. *Ibid.*

relevant implementing sections for a long time.[40] To date, there is no clear civil liability section in the General Principles of the Civil Law of 1986 or the Securities Law of 1998. This shortcoming led to the occurrence of a large of number of cases in breach of the disclosure rules. These cases will be analysed and discussed in later chapters.

The 1993 Interim Regulation provided experience for the drafting of the PRC's first Company Law, which was enacted by the Standing Committee of the NPC on 29 December 1993. The three principles of openness, fairness, and honesty were reworded as 'openness, fairness, and justice' in the Company Law.[41]

Because the PRC's main purpose in enacting a company law was to establish a modern enterprise system, issues such as how a company should be formed, how the departments of a company should be formed, and what the functions of the departments should be were put at the centre of this Law.[42] This Law does have articles on share issuing and trading, although these are simply copied from the 1993 Interim Regulation.

The 1993 Interim Regulation requires companies applying to issue shares to provide a financial report without false statements[43] and to publish a prospectus.[44] It even has articles on liabilities for giving false information.[45] However, there are several problems with these provisions. Firstly, the standards of disclosure are not clearly stated in the Company Law. In a civil law country such as the PRC, this problem indirectly encourages some companies and directors to give false disclosure, as they only need to follow clearly written rules. Secondly, the penalties are limited to warnings and small fines, which also indirectly encourages companies and directors to violate the basic principles of the Company Law. Thirdly, although the Company Law provides that giving false information might make a person subject to criminal liability,[46] detailed criminal liability legislation was not enacted until 28 February 1995, when the Standing Committee passed the Decision Concerning Punishment of Crimes against the Company Law. These criminal liability provisions were later incorporated into amendments to the Criminal Law on 14 March 1997. Under these criminal liability articles, a company, a director, a supervisor, or any other persons who are involved in false disclosure may be subject to imprisonment for three to five years and/or a criminal fine of up to 10% of the company's registered capital or the illegal profits. However, as a result of the poor enforcement of law in the PRC,[47] companies, directors, and other company officers who violated the criminal liability provisions were rarely prosecuted.

---

40. The Criminal Law of 1979 was first amended in 1997.
41. The PRC Company Law of 1993, Art. 130.
42. *Ibid.*, Art. 1.
43. Article 137.
44. Article 139.
45. Articles 206, 207, and 208.
46. *Ibid.*
47. See the discussion in Ch 2.

At the same time, when the first Company Law was being drafted by the LAC, the Finance and Economics Committee of the NPC formed a working group headed by Professor Li Yining to draft the PRC Securities Law. However, because of the slow process of lawmaking in the NPC and the lack of experience in regulating securities markets, this Law was not enacted until 29 December 1998.

The drafting by Professor Li's group had been greatly influenced by US securities regulation. Members of Professor Li's group comprised a number of lawyers and economists educated in Western countries (mainly the USA) who were brave to draw foreign experience into PRC securities market regulation. However, the draft of Professor Li's group had to be passed on to the LAC for revising before it could be submitted to the Standing Committee. The staff members of the LAC are mainly local lawyers who are very experienced in China's domestic practices but unfamiliar with foreign experiences. They made significant changes to the draft of the securities law that was submitted by the Finance and Economics Committee. Although the Securities Law was finally enacted at the end of 1998, the members of the Finance and Economics Committee's drafting group and the CSRC were very disappointed with this piece of legislation because it was very conservative and lagged behind current practical needs.[48]

During the drafting process of the first Company Law and the Securities Law, the PRC's securities market continued to develop. In need of market regulation, the CSRC released a set of rules on disclosure to prevent and punish misconduct involving false and misleading disclosure, as disclosure is a fundamental issue in the development of a securities market.

Before the State Council passed the 1993 Interim Regulation in April, the CSRC released the Circular Concerning Issues Relevant to Share Issue and Disclosure of Listed Companies on March 18. This was the first administrative rule that was enacted specifically to regulate disclosure. It provides the content and standards of disclosure. It also designates *Financial Times, China Securities Daily, China Daily,* and *Securities Weekly* as the national newspapers in which disclosure is officially made (the CSRC soon added *Shanghai Securities Daily, Securities Times,* and *Economics Daily* to the list for publishing disclosure documents).[49] Unfortunately, this Circular was very general. It did not cover all the major issues that should be disclosed. On June 3, the CSRC had to issue Rule No. 1 on Content and Format of Disclosure by Listed Companies – Prospectus. To supplement this Circular, the CSRC issued the Implementing Rules for Disclosure by Listed Companies (for Trial) on June 12. This Circular was also issued under the guidelines of the 1993 Interim Regulation.

Because of a lack of details in the national laws and regulations, the CSRC has to issue many administrative rules to set out in detail the standards, contents, and

---

48. Author's interviews with then Deputy Chairman of the CSRC, Gao Xiqing, and Wang Lianzhou, the Head of the Drafting Group of the Securities Law of the Fiscal and Economics Committee, in September 2000.
49. Li, Zhangzhe, *Finally Successful: The Report of the Development of China's Securities Market,* 262.

formats of disclosure documents. By the end of April 2003, it had released No. 1–19 Rules on Contents and Formats of Disclosure by Listed Companies. Because these Administrative Rules were made in response to the changing needs of practice, the CSRC has to keep amending them. This means that many of the CSRC's rules are short-lived. Sometimes, listed companies find it a burden to follow the changes of disclosure requirements because they are too complicated and change so frequently.[50] All in all, in the past decade, the PRC securities market has been very vulnerable, and the frequent changes of policies and rules on securities regulation is one cause of this vulnerability.

During the drafting process of the Company Law and the Securities Law, and the issuing of administrative rules by the CSRC, the State Council from time to time releases circulars and policies on share issuing and trading. These documents are treated as administrative regulations. Some of them contain provisions on disclosure. For example, the State Council issued the Circular on Further Strengthening Macro-Management of the Securities Markets, which had provisions on disclosure, on 17 December 1992. The State Council's ministries and commission also issued a number of administrative rules involving disclosure within their jurisdiction. For instance, the Ministry of Finance issued Accounting Standards – Disclosure in 1998.

Before the CSRC was given sole regulatory power in late 1997,[51] the provincial governments had securities regulatory offices. These offices assisted their local governments in releasing regulatory documents in the form of local administrative rules. Some of these documents dealt with disclosure. The local governments and the CSRC also jointly regulated the securities market until late 1997. This produced many conflicts between local administrative rules and the administrative rules of the CSRC. Thus, these offices were merged into the CSRC in late 1997, and the provincial governments no longer have regulatory power with regard to the securities market.

The CSRC was made the national regulator of the securities market in August 1997 by a Circular of the State Council.[52] Under this Circular, the general managers and deputy general managers of the two stock exchanges were to be appointed by the CSRC, and the Chairpersons and deputy chairpersons of the two stock exchanges were to be elected from a list of candidates nominated by the CSRC. The Securities Law of 2005 has changed this practice and gives the CSRC the power to appoint the general managers of the stock exchanges.[53] The CSRC has issued many administrative rules and documents on disclosure, which make up the guidelines for joint stock companies. In later chapters of this book, these regulatory rules will be discussed.

---

50. Author's interview with a deputy general manager of Shanghai Shenxin Textiles Ltd in August 1999.
51. Zheng, Zhenlong (ed.), *A Concise History of Chinese Securities Development* (Beijing: Economic Science Press, 2000), 327.
52. *Ibid.*
53. The PRC Securities Law of 2005, Art. 107.

4.1.2.   Corporate Disclosure Rules

As discussed in Chapter 2, the laws in the PRC include the following forms: the Constitution and laws, administrative regulations and local regulations, departmental administrative rules, and local administrative rules. The corporate disclosure regime in the PRC can be summarized as having three levels: the Securities Law and the Company Law provide guidelines and principles that are of the highest effectiveness; the State Council's 1993 Interim Regulation and then other administrative regulations are the next levels of regulatory documents. These administrative regulations contain the guidelines, principles, and standards of disclosure, as well as some implementing provisions; the CSRC's rules on disclosure are the core provisions dealing with this issue. These departmental administrative rules contain detailed provisions for the implementation of the guidelines and principles, but they have less authority than administrative regulations. The ministries and commissions of the State Council, within their respective jurisdictions, issue their own administrative rules on particular issue regarding disclosure.

These administrative rules of other ministries or commissions are supplementary to the CSRC's rules. Before the CSRC was made the sole regulatory body of the securities market, other ministries and commissions, such as the SCRES and the PBOC, had made a number of administrative rules to regulate the securities market. Currently, most of the administrative rules on securities regulation are issued by the CSRC. Sometimes, the CSRC still jointly releases rules with other ministries and/or commissions of the State Council. For instance, the CSRC and the State Commission of Economics and Trade jointly released the Code of Corporate Governance for Listed Companies in January 2002. This is an administrative rule. It requires listed companies to disclose all the information that may have a substantial effect on the decision-making of shareholders and other investors. The disclosure regime in the PRC is improving. With knowledge of the regulatory regime of corporate disclosure in mind, we can now move on to a consideration of the functions of the gatekeepers in the securities market.

4.2.   THE REGULATOR OF THE CHINESE SECURITIES
            MARKET: THE CSRC

4.2.1.   Regulation by Other Bodies of the Central Government
            before 1998

In August 1997, the State Council transferred the two stock exchanges of the PRC to the control of the CSRC. That was the first step for the CSRC to become a national securities regulatory body. The Securities Law of 1998 formally clarified the status of the CSRC as the national regulatory body.[54] Before 1998, apart from

---

54. Article 7.

the regulation of the local governments and the PBOC, other departments of the State Council were also involved in securities regulation within their respective areas. For instance, the SCRES issued administrative rules on implementing the shareholding system, the State Tax Bureau issued rules on stamp duties and other taxes on share issue and trading, the Ministry of Finance and the former State Planning and Development Commission decided on the T-bonds' issue scale, and the Ministry of Finance was in charge of the setting of Accounting Standards. This multi-department regulation caused a number of problems, including share trading in the black market, market manipulation, and insider trading.[55]

4.2.2. TRYING TO CENTRALIZE SECURITIES REGULATION

To solve the problems of inconsistency among all kinds of administrative rules, the State Council formed the Share Markets Working Meeting, which consisted of the PBOC, the State Planning Commission, the Ministry of Finance, the State Foreign Exchange Authority, and the State Tax Bureau.[56] This Meeting undertook the day-to-day regulation of the securities market on behalf of the State Council.[57] In June 1992, this Meeting was dissolved and the State Council's Securities Regulatory Working Meeting was set up. Its working body was the securities regulatory office within the PBOC.[58] However, the Securities Regulatory Working Meeting did not become a real national securities regulatory body.

While the two stock exchanges, in Shanghai and Shenzhen, were becoming national share trading sites, the differences between the administrative rules released by different local governments caused inconsistencies in practice between the different markets. These inconsistencies led to unfair competition between the markets. It became necessary to set up a national regulatory body and release a set of national securities regulations.

To improve the regulation of the securities market and ensure its stability, the State Council decided to set up a national body to regulate the securities market. This national body, the SCSC, was established in October 1992. It was the national authority responsible for exercising centralized market regulation.[59] Its working body, the CSRC, was also established at the same time with the responsibility of conducting market supervision in accordance with the law. Under the State Council's Circular Concerning Further Strengthening Macro-Management of Securities Markets, released on 17 December 1992, the PRC's securities regulatory structure consisted of the SCSC and the CSRC, other government bodies, and the Securities Industry Association.

---

55. Ye, Lin, *China's Securities Law* (in Chinese) (Beijing: China Audit Press, 1999), 110.
56. Li, Zhangzhe, *Finally Successful: Report of the Development of China's Securities Market*, 93.
57. Zheng, Zhenlong (ed.), *A Concise History of Chinese Securities Development*, 325.
58. Ye, Lin, *China's Securities Law*, 110.
59. Zheng, Zhenlong (ed.), *A Concise History of Chinese Securities Development*, 325.

4.2.3.   THE FUNCTIONS OF THE SCSC AND THE CSRC

It is worth pointing out that both the SCSC and the CSRC were not established by the NPC in a usual way by which a governmental ministry or commission in the PRC is established. A ministry or a commission is usually set up by a proposal of the State Council and then approval by the NPC. However, the SCSC and the CSRC were both established by an administrative regulation issued by the General Office of the State Council on 12 October 1992. This was because the SCSC was set up as a macro-management and coordination body, while the CSRC was established as a working body for the SCSC.[60] However, neither of them had been given enough authority and resources to fulfil their functions properly. The establishment of two commissions demonstrated that the central government either had not realized the importance of the regulation of the securities market or had not decided how to regulate the securities market rationally.

The SCSC was a quasi-ministry of the State Council. It was chaired by the former Deputy Premier and later by a former Premier Minister, Zhu Rongji. It made policies guiding the development of the securities market and consisted of representatives from relevant government departments, including the People's Bank of China, the State Planning Commission,[61] the State Commission for Restructuring the Economic System,[62] the State Council Economic and Trade Commission, the Ministry of Finance and the Ministry of Foreign Trade and Economic Co-operation, the Ministry of Supervision, the State Administration of Industry and Commerce, the State Administration for Tax, the State Bureau for State-Owned Assets, the State Administration for Foreign Exchange, the Supreme People's Court, and the Supreme People's Procuratorate.[63]

The functions and powers of the SCSC and the CSRC were formally announced by the State Council in its Circular on Further Strengthening the Macro-Management of the Securities Market on 17 December 1992. Under this Administrative Regulation, the SCSC was the department in charge of national macro-management. It had the following functions and powers:

(i)   to organize the drafting of the securities law and regulations;
(ii) to investigate and make policies and administrative directives on the securities market;
(iii) to plan the development of the securities market and make relevant suggestions;

---

60. *Ibid.*
61. In the restructure of the State Council in March 1999, it was renamed as the State Development Planning Commission. In March 2003, it was merged with the Ministry of State Economics and Trade Commission and the successor of the SCRES – the Office for Restructuring Economic System as the State Development and Reform Commission.
62. In the restructure of the State Council in March 1999, it was changed into the Office for Restructuring the Economic System. In March 2003, it was merged into the newly established State Development and Reform Commission.
63. Li, Zhangzhe, *Finally Successful: Report of the Development of China's Securities Market*, 93.

(iv) to guide, coordinate, supervise, and inspect the work relevant to the securities market in all provinces and all departments; and

(v) to administer the CSRC.

The CSRC was defined in this Circular as the working body for the SCSC. It consisted of experts with theoretical and practical knowledge about securities. It was an 'institutional legal entity' (*shi ye dan wei*). Thus, the CSRC was not established as an administrative department under the State Council.

The 1993 Interim Regulation further clarified the status and functions of the SCSC and the CSRC. Under Article 5, the SCSC was the department in charge of securities markets, and it conducted national regulation of the markets; the CSRC was the working body of the SCSC, and it conducted supervision and regulation of the activities in securities issuing and trading in accordance with laws and administrative regulations.

This regulatory framework had its defects from its inception. First of all, as most of the members of the SCSC were deputy ministers from the relevant ministries and commissions under the State Council who had other, more important duties, they often could not attend the meetings of the SCSC. Second, some of these deputy ministers had little knowledge of securities, let alone regulation of the market. To a great degree, during policy making, the SCSC depended on the advice of the CSRC. The SCSC in fact was an 'empty body' (*kong jia zi*). As discussed above, the CSRC is comprised of people who are well qualified. Therefore, in fact, the CSRC was in charge of the day-to-day supervision and regulation of the securities market. However, because at that time the CSRC was not an administrative subordinate of the State Council, but rather an institutional legal entity, its documents were not treated as administrative rules. Thus, these documents might not be recognized by other ministries or commissions of the State Council. In particular, its documents were not recognized by the local governments. (The local governments even had doubts about the authority of ministerial administrative rules; sometimes the local governments would not implement such rules issued by the CSRC because it had no directive power over local governments.) In short, under this system, there was some degree of ambiguity between the functions of the SCSC and the CSRC. The CSRC lacked supremacy over other ministries and commissions, and local governments in securities regulation. In practice, there had been conflicts between the CSRC's rules and the local administrative rules, and the CSRC's rules were often ignored. These problems led to the acceptance of the argument that a sole and powerful regulatory body should be established.[64]

The SCSC began to issue regulatory documents, including those regulating disclosure. It publicized the Interim Measures Concerning Administration of Stock Exchanges on 1 July 1993. This Administrative Rule had eight chapters

---

64. Liu, Shuqiang, *Annotation of the Securities Law* (in Chinese) (Beijing: People's Court Press, 1999), 36.

and fifty-nine articles on the establishment and dissolution of stock exchanges, their functions, departments, and regulation. It was the first administrative rule regulating securities trade in the securities market. On 15 August, the SCSC issued the Interim Measures Prohibiting Securities Fraud. It had provisions on insider trading, market manipulation, fraud, and false statements. This was the first administrative rule that had clear provisions prohibiting false disclosure.[65]

During the process of coordinating securities market regulation, the SCSC often delegated some powers to the CSRC. On August 17, it issued the Circular to Delegate Powers to the CSRC to Investigate and Punish Conduct Violating Securities Laws and Rules. With this delegation, the documents released by the CSRC started becoming more authoritative than before, but at the same time, there was a question about whether the SCSC, as an administrative organ of the State Council, had the power to delegate the power that was given to it by the State Council.

This problem was later resolved by the State Council. In March 1995, the State Council formally approved the Organisational Plan of the China Securities Regulatory Commission, thereby confirming the CSRC as a deputy-ministry rank unit directly under the State Council and the executive body of the SCSC. The CSRC was authorized to conduct supervision and regulation of the securities and futures markets in accordance with the law.[66]

In August 1997, the State Council decided to put the Shanghai and Shenzhen Stock Exchanges under the direct supervision of the CSRC.[67] In November 1998, the State Council held the annual National Finance Conference and decided to reform and re-organize the national securities regulatory mechanism.[68] It decided that the securities regulatory departments of the provincial governments would be supervised directly by the central government through the CSRC. It also decided that organizations that were engaged in securities trading and formerly supervised by the People's Bank of China were to be put under the centralised supervision of the CSRC.[69]

In April 1998, pursuant to the State Council's Plan for Institutional Reform, the SCSC and the CSRC were merged into one ministerial ranking commission: the CSRC, which is directly under the control of the State Council.[70] After the merger, both the powers and the functions of the CSRC were significantly strengthened. A centralized securities supervisory system was thus established. In September 1998, the State Council approved the Provisions Regarding the CSRC's Functions,

---

65. Articles 11, 12, 13, and 22.
66. Zheng, Zhenlong (ed.), *A Concise History of Chinese Securities Development,* 326.
67. Gong, Haocheng & Dehuan Jin (eds), *The First Ten Years of the Shanghai Securities Market* (in Chinese) (Shanghai: Shanghai University of Finance and Economics Press, 2001), 192.
68. Li, Zhangzhe, *Finally Successful: Report of the Development of China's Securities Market,* 549.
69. *Ibid.*
70. Zheng, Zhenlong (ed.), *A Concise Hisotry of Chinese Securities Development,* 328.

Internal Structure and Personnel (hereinafter Provisions of 1998),[71] further confirming the CSRC as one of the institutional legal entities *(shi ye dan wei)* directly under the State Council and the authorized department governing the securities and futures markets of China. This Administrative Regulation further strengthened and clarified the CSRC's functions and powers.

Under this Regulation, the CSRC has the following basic functions:

(1) To establish a centralized supervisory system for securities and futures markets and to assume direct leadership over securities and futures market supervisory bodies.

(2) To strengthen the supervision over securities and futures business, stock and futures exchange markets, the listed companies, fund management companies investing in the securities, securities and futures investment consulting firms, and other intermediaries involved in the securities and futures business. To raise the standards of information disclosure.

(3) To increase the abilities to prevent and handle financial crisis.

(4) To organize the drafting of laws and regulations for securities markets; to study and formulate the principles, policies and rules related to securities markets; to formulate the development plans and annual plans for securities markets; to direct, coordinate, supervise and examine matters related to securities in various regions and relevant departments; to direct, plan and coordinate test operations of futures market.

(5) To exercise centralized supervision of securities business.[72]

In addition, the CSRC is given the following major responsibilities:

(1) To study and formulate policies and the development plans regarding securities and futures markets; to draft relevant laws and regulations on securities and futures markets; and to make relevant rules on securities and futures markets.

(2) To supervise securities and futures markets and exercise vertical power of authority over regional and provincial supervisory institutions of the market.

(3) To oversee the issue, trading, custody and settlement of equity shares, convertible bonds, and securities investment funds; to approve the listing of corporate bonds; and to supervise the trading activities of listed government bonds and corporate bonds.

(4) To supervise the listing, trading and settlement of domestic futures contracts; and to monitor domestic institutions engaged in overseas futures businesses in accordance with relevant regulations.

---

71. The General Office of the State Council, *Circular [1998]131 Concerning the CSRC's Functions, Internal Structure and Personnel.*

72. *Ibid.*

(5) To supervise the conduct of listed companies and their shareholders who are responsible for information disclosure in securities markets.

(6) To supervise securities and futures exchanges and their senior management in accordance with relevant regulations, and securities associations in the capacity of the competent authorities.

(7) To supervise securities and futures companies, securities investment fund managers, securities registration and settlement companies, futures settlement institutions, and securities and futures investment consulting institutions; to approve in conjunction with the People's Bank of China, the qualification of fund custody institutions and supervising their fund custody business; to formulate and implement rules on the qualification of senior management for the above-mentioned institutions; and to grant licenses to the people engaged in securities and futures-related business.

(8) To supervise direct or indirect overseas issue and listing of shares by domestic enterprises; to supervise the establishment of securities institutions overseas by domestic institutions; and to supervise the establishment of domestic securities institutions by overseas organizations.

(9) To supervise information disclosure related to securities and futures and is responsible for the statistics and information resources management for securities and futures markets.

(10) To grant, in conjunction with other relevant authorities, the qualifications to law firms, accounting firms, asset appraisal firms, and professionals in these firms, engaged in securities and futures intermediary businesses; and to supervise their relevant business activities.

(11) To investigate and penalize conduct violating securities and futures laws and regulations.

(12) To manage the foreign relationships and international cooperation affairs in the capacity of the competent authorities.

(13) Any other duties as commissioned by the State Council.[73]

The functions and responsibilities of the CSRC were again confirmed in the Securities Law of 1998.[74] Under the State Council's Provisions of 1998, the CSRC had one chairperson, four vice-chairpersons, one secretary general, and two deputy secretary-generals. It had thirteen functional departments or offices, three subordinate centres, and one special committee. It also had regional offices set up in key provinces and cities across the country.

To ensure the fairness and quality of the examination and verification of securities issuance, a Public Offering and Listing Review Committee was set up

---

73. *Ibid.*
74. Chapter 10.

by the CSRC in 1993. The function of this Committee was clarified in the Securities Law of 1998:

> the securities supervisory agency under the State Council shall set up a Public Offering and Listing Review Committee, examining and verifying issuance applications in accordance with law. Comprising professionals in the agency and relevant experts specially engaged from outside, the Committee shall cast votes over a stock issuance application and reach a resolution on it.[75]

In April 1998, the SCSC was dismantled, and its working staff members were transferred to the CSRC as a result of the reduction of the size of the State Council. The SCRES had no longer had the power to make policies on the securities market since March 1998, when it became the State Council's Restructuring Economic Reform Office, with its main function being to conduct policy research on economic reform. In March 2003, the Restructuring Economic Reform Office became a department of the State Development and Reform Commission. The CSRC not only acquired the powers of the SCSC and the SCERS to make rules and policies on the development of the securities market, but it also became a ministerial-level commission of the State Council.[76] With the enactment of the Securities Law at the end of 1998, the CSRC became the sole securities regulatory body, established by national legislation.[77]

Meanwhile, the CSRC started setting up regional offices based on the American model. The Securities Law of 1998 was enacted after the State Council's 1998 Circular Concerning the Functions of the CSRC. It gave the CSRC the power to establish branch offices according to the needs of regulation.[78] By July 1999, the CSRC basically formed a centralized national regulatory regime. It established nine regional securities regulatory offices in medium-sized and large cities: Tianjian, Shenyang, Shanghai, Jinan, Wuhan, Guanzhou, Shenzhen, Chengdu, and Xi'an.[79] These offices implement laws, administrative regulations, and administrative rules on behalf of the CSRC. They also undertake initial investigations. The CSRC has become a sophisticated regulatory body.

To date, the CSRC has expanded its size. Its current senior officials include one Chairman, three deputy Chairmen, three assistants to the Chairman, and one Chief of the Disciplinary Committee.[80] The current organizational structure of the CSRC is illustrated in Figure 4.1.[81]

---

75. Article 14.
76. Zheng, Zhenlong (ed.), *A Concise History of Chinese Securities Development* 328.
77. The PRC Securities Law of 1998, Art. 7.
78. Article 7.
79. <www.csrc.gov.cn/CSRCSite/exorg/pcjg.htm>, Jul. 2003.
80. <www.csrc.gov.cn/n5754458/index.html>, 11 Feb. 2008.
81. <http://csrc.gov.cn/en/department/dep_index_en.jsp?path=(200T>EN>Departments>, 31 Jul. 2005.

Figure 4.1   Organisational Structure of the China Securities Regulatory Commission

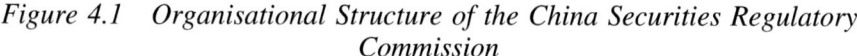

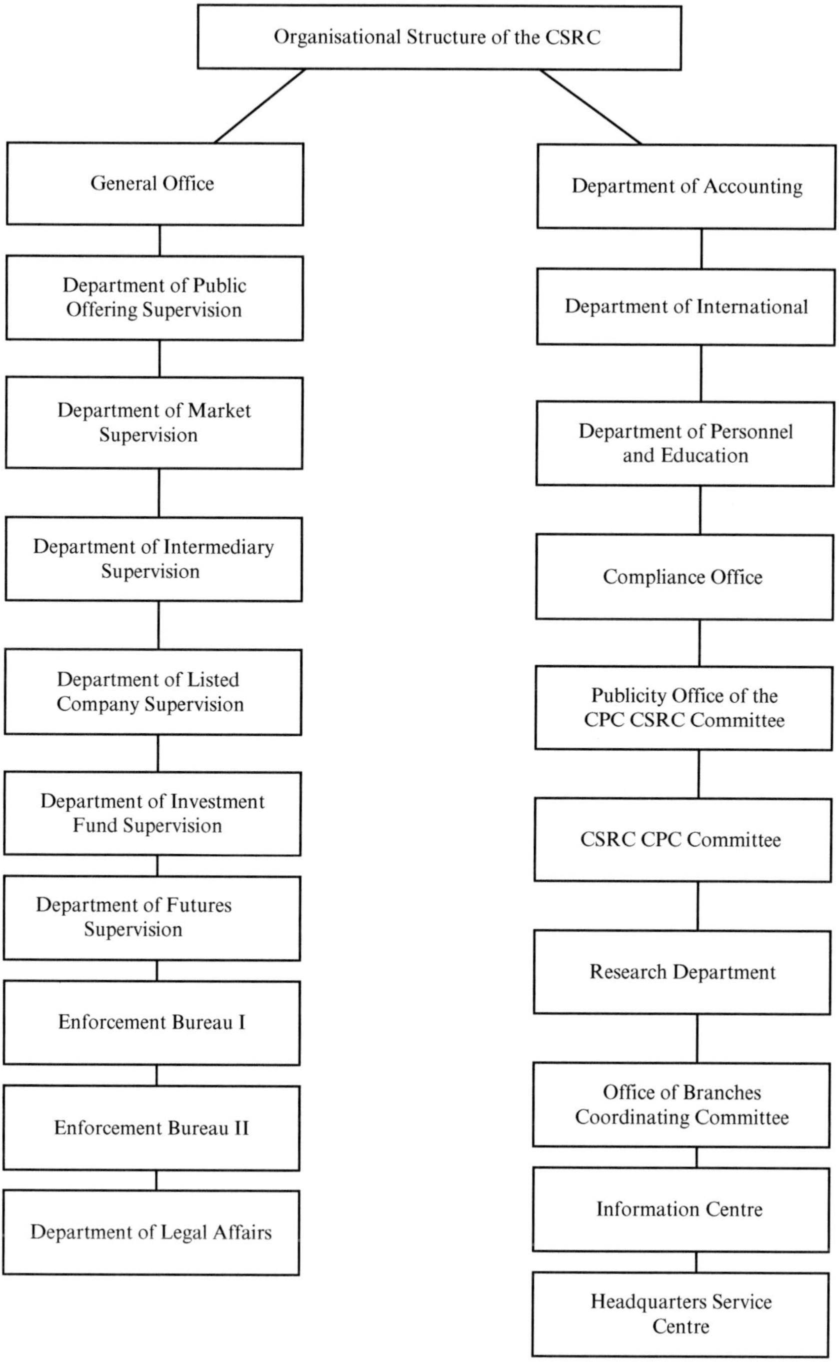

Organisational Structure of the CSRC

General Office	Department of Accounting
Department of Public Offering Supervision	Department of International
Department of Market Supervision	Department of Personnel and Education
Department of Intermediary Supervision	Compliance Office
Department of Listed Company Supervision	Publicity Office of the CPC CSRC Committee
Department of Investment Fund Supervision	CSRC CPC Committee
Department of Futures Supervision	Research Department
Enforcement Bureau I	Office of Branches Coordinating Committee
Enforcement Bureau II	Information Centre
Department of Legal Affairs	Headquarters Service Centre

Even though the SCSC was dissolved in 1998, the administrative rules issued on its behalf continue to be effective unless they are clearly invalidated by the CSRC, which may amend the old rules. Sometimes the CSRC only makes minor changes. For instance, in December 2001, it issued an administrative rule entitled Measures on the Administration of Stock Exchanges, which is just a copy of the administrative rule of the SCSC that was released on 21 August 1996 with the same title.

4.2.4.   THE CSRC'S RULES ON DISCLOSURE

One of the major functions of the CSRC is to make a range of rules regulating the securities markets. These rules can be classified as rules governing the conduct of listed companies, such as the rules on initial public offerings (IPOs) and securities trading, as well as disclosure rules. Some disclosure rules are about the financial reporting standards for listed companies. Disclosure of listed companies is regulated through rules at four levels.

First, the Rules on the Content and Format of Disclosure by Listed Companies set the basic standards and content. To date, there are 23 rules that have been released in this regard. Many of these rules have been updated almost every year.

Second, some of the Disclosure Reporting Rules by Listed Companies are about how the Rules on the Content and Format of Disclosure should be applied in particular industries, such as disclosure of financial companies; some are about how the Content and Format Rules should be applied in particular activities of listed companies, such as mergers and acquisitions; and some are about how to implement the Content and Format Rules, such as how to disclose profit forecasts.

Third, apart from the Content and Format Rules as well as the Disclosure Reporting Rules, the CSRC also releases Questions and Answers. These are about the questions and problems that have occurred in practice. The CSRC has a duty to answer inquiries and questions. However, for a long time, the CSRC did not publicize these questions and answers. This caused differences between the regulators and those who were subject to regulation. The decision to publicize the Questions and Answers is a reflection of openness and fairness.

Fourth, since 2001, the CSRC has been publicizing Opinions on Individual Cases and Case Analysis on Disclosure by Listed Companies.

The CSRC also issues administrative rules on the administration of the participants in the securities market. On 28 December 2001, it released Measures Concerning Administration of Securities Companies, which became effective on 1 March 2002. In this Rule, it is clearly stated that the CSRC is in charge of regulation of securities companies, including the establishment, change, and dissolution of securities companies.[82]

The CSRC has another important function, that is, to investigate any breach of securities laws and regulations.[83] The CSRC has investigated a large number of

---

82. Article 3.
83. The PRC Securities Law of 1998, Art. 168.

cases violating the securities laws, regulation, and rules since its establishment. Many of these cases involve disclosure, such as the *Shenzhen Yuanye Co.* case in 1991, the *Hainan Qiongminyuan Co.* case in 1997, the *Sichuan Hongguang Co.* case in 1998, the *Yinchuan Guangxia Co.* case in 20001, the *Shenzhen Maikete Co.* case in 2001,[84] *Kelong Electric Appliances in 2005,* and *Hangxiao-ganggou in 2006.* The CSRC punished the companies, company directors and managers, relevant accounting firms and accountants, and relevant law firms and lawyers by giving them warnings, imposing fines, and disqualifying them from conducting securities businesses.

4.2.5.   OVERVIEW OF THE FUNCTIONS OF THE CSRC

Although the PRC has made great progress in developing its securities market, this market still has apparent transitional problems. The problems associated with the current securities regulatory framework can be summarized as follows.

First, departmental administrative rules are not enforceable by the courts under the current Chinese legal system, and therefore the rules of the CSRC may not be complied with by other state organizations.[85]

Second, the CSRC has not been given enough power to enforce its rules or decisions. For instance, it does not have the power to initiate civil or criminal litigation, while many securities regulatory bodies in other countries, such as the Australian Securities and Investments Commission, are clearly given such power by law. The poor cooperation between legal institutions in the PRC often causes a failure to prosecute listed companies and their directors who breach securities laws and rules. This situation also leaves the interests of the investors in the securities market unprotected.

Third, the poor enforcement of law in the PRC also affects the integrity of the CSRC. For instance, the CSRC has the power to disqualify a director or manager of a listed company from conducting business for that company in the securities market, but it does not have the power to ban such a person from being appointed as a director or manager at another company. For example, a deputy chairman of the board of directors of the Shanghai Shenyin-Wanguo Securities Company was banned by the CSRC from any involvement in securities business for misleading and fraudulent conduct. Soon after he was fired from this company, he was appointed as a deputy chairman of a high-tech company in Shanghai by the Shanghai municipal government. The CSRC knew of this appointment but could not do anything to stop the Shanghai municipal government from making such an appointment.[86] In other cases, there are no detailed provisions on when and how the directors should bear personal liability if they breach disclosure provisions.

---

84.   Xu, Zhaohong & Hui Zheng (eds), *Concise Analysis of Securities Law Cases* (Beijing: Oriental Press Centre, 2001).
85.   See the discussion in Ch. 2, para. 2.3.2.
86.   Author's interview with a senior officer of the Shanghai Stock Exchange in November 2001.

Therefore, most of the directors of listed companies or securities companies who breach the disclosure provisions are only banned from holding director positions but do not bear any civil compensation liability. Later on, they can use the money they made from their former company to invest in the securities market as individual investors. These situations obviously discourage the participants in the securities market to comply with the rules. They are among the most important reasons why, in the PRC's securities market, false disclosure cases occur again and again.

Fourth, although the CSRC should be given more power to fulfil its role as a national regulatory body, it is unnecessary to regulate all the activities of the participants in the market. For instance, the Securities Law of 1998 gives the CSRC the power to supervise listed companies,[87] stock exchanges,[88] securities companies,[89] securities registration and clearing companies,[90] securities trading services companies,[91] and even the securities industry association.[92] This power was affirmed in the Securities Law of 2005.[93] The problem is not whether the CSRC should be given the power to supervise these securities institutions, but rather what kind of power it should be given. Under the relevant articles, the supervision of the CSRC is still marked by a planned economy. The two national stock exchanges may make listing rules and trading rules, but these rules must be approved by the CSRC.[94] In December 1997, the CSRC approved the listing rules of the Shanghai and Shezhen Stock Exchanges, but these two sets of listing rules were virtually the same, except for two articles. The two stock exchanges amended their listing rules in 2001 and 2006, but these two sets of rules remain the same. There is no difference except for the names of the stock exchanges. The newly adopted listing rules of the Shanghai and the Shezhen Stock Exchanges came into effect on 1 December 2001. The general managers of the two stock exchanges are appointed by the CSRC under the Securities Law of 2005.[95] Securities consulting firms must have their business rules approved by the CSRC.[96] From the provisions of the Securities Law and the CSRC's administrative rules, it is not difficult to draw the conclusion that a real market economy has not formed in the PRC. This obviously limits the ability of the stock exchanges in the PRC to act as self-regulatory bodies. It also causes extra work for the CSRC, which is already too busy with its own policy making. The Securities Industrial Association is a self-regulatory community entity[97] but has to do what it is told by the CSRC under Article 164.

---

87. Chapters 2, 3, and 4.
88. Articles 96, 100, 108, 110, and 113.
89. Articles 117, 119, 126, and 136.
90. Articles 146, 149, and 154.
91. Articles 157 and 158.
92. Article 164.
93. Chapters 5–9.
94. Article 96.
95. Article 107.
96. Article 157.
97. Article 162.

This provision puts the Securities Industrial Association in a position as a subordinate of the CSRC.

Finally, securities companies are under the tight control of the CSRC. Under the law, not only the establishment of securities companies must be approved by the CSRC, but also, the scope of some businesses must be decided by the CSRC.[98] This framework does not necessarily benefit the interests of the clients of the securities companies and is also not consistent with the principles of a market economy. Under the Securities Law of 1998, there were two types of securities companies: comprehensive securities companies and brokerage securities companies.[99] The minimum registered capital for a comprehensive securities company was CNY 500 million.[100] The minimum registered capital for a brokerage securities company was CNY 50 million. Such high requirements for registered capital lead to two results: first, most of the securities companies could only act as brokers; second, most of the securities companies were state-owned or state-controlled companies. The state-owned and state-controlled companies became places where the officials of the CSRC could find well-paying jobs. According to one statistic, more than ten chief executive officers (CEOs), deputy CEOs, general managers, or deputy general mangers of big securities companies were former officials of the CSRC at the end of 2001.[101] The securities-regulators-turned-securities-company-mangers no doubt use their connections and knowledge obtained before in conducting securities trading business. There have been doubts about fairness in the securities market. The confusion of the roles of regulators and regulatory subjects might easily jeopardize the principle of fairness in the securities market. In this sense, the CSRC has not become an independent and objective body. These facts also demonstrate that the PRC's securities regulation is still at a developing stage. The Securities Law of 2005 no longer separates the securities companies' brokerage business from their comprehensive business; the minimum paid-up registered capital remains at CNY 50 million.[102] This shows that the Chinese government still has very strict control over the setting up of securities companies.

To improve regulation, the CSRC has been trying to increase the skills of its staff by recruiting a number of professionals. These people include junior staff members and senior staff members. For instance, in its Listing Department and Legal Affairs Department, some people were educated in Western countries. The CSRC's previous Chairman and the current Governor of the PBOC, Zhou Xiaochuan, was a banker with a doctoral degree.[103] Laura Cha, an experienced securities lawyer educated in the USA, was a deputy chairperson of the CSRC from

---

98. Articles 124 and 128.
99. Article 119.
100. Article 121.
101. 'The Securities Companies under the Control of the "Gang" of the CSRC', *The Economic Observer* (in Chinese), 19 Nov. 2001, 1.
102. Article 127.
103. Walter, Carl E. & Fraser J.T Howie, *Privatizing China: The Stock Markets and Their Role in Corporate Reform* (Singapore: John Wiley & Sons (Asia) Pte Ltd), 65.

February 2001 to August 2003. Prior to her appointment at the CSRC, she was a deputy chairperson of the Hong Kong Securities and Futures Commission for some years. Since her appointment at the CSRC in February 2001, she constantly worked to bring the corporate governance ideas and experiences of Hong Kong into mainland China.[104] The adoption of independent directors in Chinese listed companies is one of her endeavours. A former deputy executive chairman, Gao Xiqing was educated at a top American law school and has been a law professor for a long time. He brought in many American lawyers, legal academics, and securities practitioners to introduce American securities regulatory theory and practices. The CSRC also provides all kinds of training courses for its staff and participants in the securities market. The CSRC has staff members with relatively good professional skills. This has laid a significant foundation for the improvement of securities market regulation.

Although there are several major defects in the regulatory regime of the PRC, its securities market regulation has achieved great success. Through more than fifteen years of practice, the CSRC has accumulated substantial experience in securities regulation and rule making and has become a nationally recognized regulatory body. With the work of the CSRC, the PRC securities market has been moving towards maturity, although it still has a long way to go.

4.3.	THE REGULATORS OF THE CHINESE SECURITIES MARKET: OTHER DEPARTMENTS UNDER THE STATE COUNCIL

The growth of securities regulatory bodies came after the re-emergence of share issuing. The national securities regulatory body was established long after the re-emergence of the securities market and the establishment of the two stock exchanges. One might say that it was the re-emergence of the securities market that pushed the emergence of the securities regulatory regime; but it is the continuous development of the securities market that improves this regime.

Before the CSRC was given the status as the sole regulator of the Chinese securities market, there had been a long period of debate over which department was the most appropriate one to be responsible for securities regulation. During that period of time, many other departments of the central government played very important roles in securities regulations within their respective areas. The most powerful body among them was the PBOC.

4.3.1.   REGULATION BY THE PBOC

Securities trading markets were first established as regional markets. The Shanghai and the Shenzhen Stock Exchanges were first established as local securities markets. The Shanghai and Shenzhen municipal governments were heavily

---

104. *Ibid.*, 66.

involved in securities policy making. In the meantime, securities markets were seen as a part of the financial market, which is regulated by the PBOC. Thus, the branches of the PBOC in both Shanghai and Shenzhen first exercised regulatory powers together with local governments in these two securities markets. This is because under the Interim Regulation Concerning Administration of Banks of 1986, the PBOC was clearly given the power to approve the establishment of banks and other financial institutions and to regulate enterprise shares and bonds.[105] For a long time, the PBOC was in charge of the licensing of securities companies and investment funds, as well as the establishment of stock exchanges and securities trading centres. It also issued a number of administrative rules, such as the Circular on Enterprise Shares, Bonds and Other Financial Services Administration, and the Circular on Strict Control of Share Issue and Transfer. The PBOC was gradually moved out of securities regulation following the State Council's decision to make the CSRC the sole regulatory body in August 1997.

In the 1980s, the PBOC was given many powers to regulate securities issuing as a result of the problems with the traditional division of functions among the ministries and commissions under the State Council. The PBOC had been in charge of the administration of all the banks and other financial institutions in China. The Ministry of Finance was and still is in charge of financial and fiscal matters. Nevertheless, securities regulation is different from either banking regulation or financial regulation. When the securities market started re-emerging in the early 1980s, no department had clear power to regulate this area.

On 12 January 1991, the PBOC issued the Circular on Strict Administration of Foreign Securities Investment. Under this Circular, if any foreign investment fund wants to enter into China's domestic securities market, it must obtain approval from the head office of the PBOC; provincial governments or their departments themselves cannot approve such investments.

Because of the problems that resulted from the lack of regulation of the securities market, the PBOC first started regulating share issuing in the 1980s. This regulation was tacitly approved and confirmed by the State Council in its Administrative Regulations passed from 1987 to 1989. Under some provisions of the Interim Regulations on Banks Administration, the Interim Regulations on Administration of Enterprise Bonds, and the Circular on Strengthening Administration of Shares and Bonds, the PBOC was made the major regulatory body of securities matters.

However, this arrangement was not welcomed by many other ministries and commissions of the State Council at that time, such as the State Planning Commission, the Ministry of Finance, the State Commission of Restructuring Economic Reform, etc. Within the PBOC, its departments were also fighting for regulatory power. In early 1992, the PBOC set up its Department of Shares to regulate the shares market, but the 'August 10 Incident'[106] led to a change in the

---

105. Article 5.
106. On 10 Aug. 1992, many people went to the Shenzhen Stock Exchange to buy newly listed shares. Because of over-speculation of the market, there were riots happening during the

securities market regulator. The change of the regulatory role of the PBOC will be discussed later.

During the process of the re-emergence and development of the Chinese securities market, different administrative bodies made inputs. In the mid-1980s, the PBOC was the first national body in charge of the issue of shares, as it treated issuing share as a financial matter.[107] The branches of the PBOC were asked to take strict control of the continuing share issuing by SOEs. Without the approval of the PBOC, the shares of newly established shareholding enterprises could not be listed.[108] At the same time, local governments also played a very active role in share issuing by local enterprises.[109]

The two stock exchanges were originally established by the Shanghai municipal government and the Shenzhen municipal government, respectively. Both governments set up securities market supervision commissions to oversee securities issuing and trading in these two markets. After the CSRC was established, the regulatory powers of the securities market were gradually transferred to it. However, the head of a stock exchange council was elected from the candidates recommended by the CSRC. The recommendation of the CSRC had to be approved by the local government.[110] The general manager of a stock exchange was appointed from a list of candidates that was recommended by the CSRC and also approved by the local government.[111] In the central government, many other departments were involved in securities market regulation. Because the shareholding system was mainly implemented in SOEs, the former State Planning Commission and the State Economy and Trade Commission were in charge of the share issuing by SOEs. Because the implementation of the shareholding system was one aspect of the reform of the economic system, the SCRES was also involved in the regulation of share issuing. These ministries and commissions, together with the State Council, passed many regulations either jointly or separately with respect to particular areas of share issuing.[112]

---

process of the selling of permits to buy shares. This is called the 'August 10 Incident' in Chinese securities history.

107. The Shanghai Branch of the People's Bank of China promulgated Provisional Regulations on Share Issue in 1984. Article 5 of the Interim Regulations on Banking Administration provided that the People's Bank of China was in charge of enterprise shares and bonds as well as the financial market.

108. The State Council, Circular on Strengthening the Administration of Shares and Bonds 1987 (in Chinese).

109. The Shenzhen Municipal Government promulgated Provisional Regulations on the Trial of Shareholding System in State-owned Enterprises in Shenzhen Special Economic Zone in October 1986. The Shanghai municipal government promulgated Provisional Measures for the Administration of Shares in Shanghai in 1987.

110. The Measures for Administration of Stock Exchanges 1993, Art. 22.

111. *Ibid.*

112. The State Commission for Restructuring the Economic System (SCERS), the State Planning Commission, the Ministry of Finance, the People's Bank of China, and the State Economic and Trade Commission jointly promulgated Measures for the Trial of Shareholding System in May 1992. The State Council promulgated Standard Opinions on the Limited Liability

There were many conflicts between the regulations issued by different departments at the beginning of the development of the securities market. This was because of power conflicts, different opinions, and a lack of coordination among these regulatory bodies. Many compromises were therefore made at both the central and local government levels.[113] These central government departments and the two local governments in Shanghai and Shenzhen made separate regulations with respect to the problems regarding their powers. Before the State Council empowered the CSRC to regulate the national securities market in 1992, few of these regulations dealt with information disclosure.

With the rapid development of the securities market in China, there was an urgent need for a national regulatory body and a set of national securities regulations. Thus, the SCSC and the CSRC were established. Because the members of the SCSC came from relevant ministries and commissions of the State Council, as well as from the courts and procuratorates, there was close cooperation among the branches of the central government department.

While it is arguable whether a body with delegated powers, such as the SCSC, can re-delegate those powers to another body – the CSRC[114] – the experience in the first five years after the SCSC and the CSRC were established had shown that the CSRC should be established as an administrative body so as to standardize the securities rules and regulate the securities market more effectively.

In August 1997, the State Council released a Circular to put the two stock exchanges under the direct control and administration of the CSRC.[115] The State Council also put investment funds under the control of the CSRC. In the restructuring of the departments of the State Council in early 1998, the SCSC was dismissed and its functions were transferred to the CSRC. From 1992 to 1997, the CSRC gradually became the sole regulator of China's securities market, but still under the guidance of the SCSC. Its status was finally clarified by the Securities Law at the end of 1998. Article 7 of the Securities Law of 1998 authorizes the CSRC to supervise and administrate the national securities market. Article 167 gives the CSRC a number of powers, including the power to make securities decrees and rules, and the power to examine and approve or verify share issuing

---

Companies and Standard Opinions on the Joint Stock Limited Liability Companies, which were drafted by the SCERS at the same time. The State Planning Commission and the SCERS promulgated Provisional Regulations on the Macro-management of the Trial Shareholding Enterprises in Jun. 1992.

113. Gao, Xiqing, 'Developments in Securities and Investment Law of China', *Australian Journal of Corporate Law* 6 (1996): at 239.

114. Fang, Liufang, 'China's Corporatization Experiment', *Duke Journal of Comparative & International Law* 5 (1995): at 177. Gao Xiqing, the first Chief Council of the CSRC, held that the critics on the SCSC's authority to re-delegate the power to the CSRC 'has no logical foundation and no basis in reality', and that the CSRC was established as the administrative, supervisory, and enforcement arm of the SCSC in his article 'Developments in Securities and Investment Law of China'.

115. *Securities Times (Zheng Quan Shi Bao)*, 13 Aug. 1997.

applications. The status and the functions of the CSRC are reaffirmed in the Securities Law of 2005.[116]

Before the State Council's 1997 Circular was released, a variety of different administrative bodies dealt with the stock exchanges; these included the PBOC, ministries and commissions of the State Council, local governments, and the CSRC.

To prevent the establishment of securities companies without approval of the central government, the PBOC released a circular requiring (a) that the securities companies and other similar financial institutions be established after the prior examination of the local branch of the PBOC and later the approval of the head office of the PBOC, which would issue the license once it was approved; (b) that these companies must be separate from the industrial patrons and be transferred to the administration of the PBOC and its branches at the same level; (c) that the PBOC was a state department in charge of the administration of the financial industry and thus administered the financial institutions and markets; and (d) that local governments and other departments of the central government had no power to approve the establishment of securities companies or similar financial institutions. The securities companies established with the approval of local governments were illegal.[117]

The problem with this document is that, as a department of the State Council, the PBOC has the same ranking as a provincial government or a ministry. The fact that the PBOC gave regulatory powers to itself could not gain support from other ministries or other provincial governments. Obviously, the circulars of the PBOC could not be enforced properly, but this is not to say that its circulars were useless. Under the assignment of the functions of each ministry by the State Council, the PBOC was given the power to regulate the establishment of financial institutions and financial markets. In a broad sense, financial institutions included securities companies. However, the enactment of the Securities Law of 1998 changed this practice. Securities companies were no longer under the control of the PBOC. The regulation of these companies was transferred to the CSRC. However, this does not mean that the PBOC had no role to play in securities regulation. It still decided on the issuing of financial debentures together with the CSRC.[118] Some of the functions of the PBOC were transferred to the CSRC after 1998, demonstrating that the PRC government aimed to improve the efficiency of its securities regulation.

4.3.2.   OTHER DEPARTMENTS OF THE STATE COUNCIL

The SCRES was another department of the central government that played an important role in the process of adopting the shareholding system of SOEs

---

116. Articles 7 and 179.
117. The State Council, *Interim Regulation Concerning Administration of Banks 1986*, Art. 5.
118. The Law Committee, *Report on Review of the PRC Securities Bill of 20 December 1993*, cited by Shuqiang Liu in his *Annotation of the PRC Securities Law* (in Chinese) (Beijing: the People's Court Press, 1999), 477.

before 1998. In 1993, the SCRES clarified the principles for the adoption of a shareholding system: (a) to protect the ownership of state assets, the shareholding system should not be used to convert state-owned assets into private assets; (b) to protect the freedom of investing in shares, the same shareholding enjoys the same rights, enjoys the same interests, and shares the same risks; and (c) shareholding must follow the same national rules and measures.[119]

Other ministries and commissions of the State Council were to be involved in the administration with the release of Trial Measures for the Adoption of the Shareholding System in SOEs by the SCRES in 1987. Under this departmental Administrative Rule, the following ministries were given a role to play in the regulation of the securities market:

(a) The Legal Affairs Bureau (renamed the Legal Affairs Office in April 1998) of the State Council was to be in charge of drafting the regulations on limited liability companies and on joint stock limited liability companies. It also initiated the research on the drafting of regulations on how to convert SOEs into shareholding enterprises;

(b) The State Assets Administration Bureau (renamed the State Assets Supervision and Administration Commission in early 2003) was established and was in charge of making rules concerning the evaluation of the state-owned assets of SOEs and in charge of drafting the regulations on management of state-owned assets;

(c) The POBC was in charge of drafting the regulations on share issuing and regulation of securities markets;

(d) The Ministry of Finance was in charge of making measures for the administration of finance and accounting of shareholding enterprises;

(e) The State Administration of Industry and Commerce (hereinafter SAIC) was in charge of registration measures for shareholding enterprises;

(f) The Ministry of Personnel and Labour (later split into two ministries) was in charge of making measures for personnel administration and labour administration.

Since the Securities Law of 1998 made the CSRC the sole securities regulatory body, the functions of other departments of the central government were diminished. Nevertheless, other departments still have some regulatory functions with respect to their areas. For example, although the CSRC approves the applications for the formation of securities companies, these companies have to be registered by the SAIC. The courts and procuratorates are no longer involved in the policy making of securities market regulation. The State Development and Reform Commission no longer has a major role to play because the quota system was abolished. However, it still plays a part in deciding which SOEs are allowed to raise capital by share issuing. The PBOC only maintains the powers to register and deregister banks and other financial institutions. Other departments of the State Council, such as the Ministry of Labour and Social Security, may still be involved

---

119. *Ibid.*

in the securities issues within their jurisdiction. One of the functions of the State Assets Management Commission was to make policies dealing with the transfer of state shares in state-owned companies.

With the development of the securities market, one ministry of the State Council is becoming more and more heavily involved in securities regulation: the Ministry of Finance. At the beginning of the re-emergence of the securities market, disclosure was not treated as a major issue. After the first big cases of false statements that occurred in the 1990s, disclosure was put at the top of the agenda of the development of the securities market. Because most of the false statements were about financial disclosure, the Ministry of Finance had to establish rules on corporate financial reporting.

To solve the problem of false disclosure, the CSRC began closely cooperating with the Ministry of Finance. Traditionally, the Ministry of Finance (hereinafter the MOF) has been in charge of setting accounting standards in relation to disclosure regulation. It issued enterprise accounting standards in 1992. With the influence of globalization, the MOF established the International Accounting Standards Department. The MOF is also in charge of applying the accounting standards of the International Accounting Standards Commission, which was established in 1973. The international accounting standards were first adopted in listed companies in the PRC in the mid-1990s. In 1997, the MOF released a detailed accounting rule: Enterprise Accounting Rule – Disclosure of Related Parties and Their Transactions. Because disclosure mainly involves accounting and financial reporting, the Ministry of Finance sets the standards and the CSRC ensures the implementation of these standards and punishes conduct in breach of these standards.

The establishment of the Chief Accountant Office of the CSRC was based on the American model. The Chief Accountant of the CSRC summarized the functions of his office as stimulus, critique, and enforcement.[120] He said that the MOF sets the accounting standards and rules; his office draws on practical experiences that may stimulate the improvement of these standards and rules. His office also criticizes the defects in the accounting standards. Finally, his office enforces the accounting standards. In addition to setting up the accounting and financial reporting standards, the MOF also continues to be in charge of the issue of state debentures.[121]

The State Economics and Trade Commission (Its function of regulating SOEs was merged into the State Development and Reform Commission, which was established in March 2003.) was the managerial authority of SOEs. It had an important role to play in securities regulation because most of the listed companies are state-owned companies. It used to decide which SOEs could go public under the share issuing examination system. After the examination system was abolished, the State Economics and Trade Commission no longer had direct influence on the

---

120. Interview with the Chief Accountant of the CSRC in September 2002.
121. The Law Committee, *Report on Review of the PRC Securities Bill,* The Fifth Plenary Meeting of the Standing Committee of the NPC, cited by Shuqiang Liu in *Annotation of the Securities Law* (in Chinese), 475.

securities market. However, as corporate governance became a hot issue that affected the quality of securities regulation in the late 1990s, this Commission played a very important role in maintaining the level of corporate governance in SOEs. The frequent occurrence of breaches of securities law cases is a sign of poor corporate governance in the PRC.

In 2001, improving corporate governance became a focus of the CSRC. After several symposia held by the stock exchanges in association with the CSRC and based on the Shanghai Stock Exchange's Corporate Governance Standards of Listed Companies, the CSRC and the State Economics and Trade Commission jointly released the Code of Corporate Governance of Listed Companies on 7 January 2002. This Administrative Rule contains provisions on shareholders' rights, shareholders' general meetings, related-party transactions, controlling shareholders, directors and boards of directors, the independent director system, supervisory boards, and supervisors. More importantly, it has a chapter on disclosure and transparency.[122]

The State Assets Management Commission was established in early April 2003. Because the state shares are treated as state assets, this Commission is in charge of drafting rules on handling shares in state-owned companies. It is predicted that these rules might include provisions requiring shares trading by state-owned companies to be open and competitive.[123] Many people expect that these rules may bring some clarity to the current share issuing and sale process, which has often been chaotic, secretive, and subject to the changing whims of officials.

Sometimes ministries and commissions have regulatory powers over the same matters. Even the CPC sometimes issues policies that have an impact on the securities market. For instance, on 22 September 1999, the Fourth Plenary Meeting of the Fifteenth Conference of the CPC passed the CPC's *Resolution on Major Issues Concerning SOEs' Reform and Development.* It was decided in the Resolution that state-owned listed companies with good reputations and great development potential should be allowed to reduce part of the state's shareholding. In December 1991, a senior official of MOF pointed out that the first step of state shareholding reduction was to decrease the state's shareholdings in listed companies to 51% and the second step was to reduce state shares according to the actual need. In June 2001, the State Commission of Economics and Trade issued the Measures for State Shares Reduction. However, the shareholders did not accept the fact that state shares would be sold at the market price, although they were issued at face value. The issuance of the Measures caused the securities market to slump sharply. The CSRC had to suspend the reduction in August 2001 to save the securities market. As there were no acceptable measures for such a reduction, the State Council had to formally stop the state shares reduction in June 2002.[124] The frequent change of government policies on securities regulation again shows

---

122. Chapter 7.
123. A. Batsob, 'China Rides Another Privatisation Wave', in *The Australian Financial Review,* 13 May 2003, 13.
124. See *China Securities Daily* from June–October 2001.

that the PRC's securities market is still in a transitional period and is underdeveloped.

In conclusion, at the beginning of the re-emergence of the securities market, many departments were involved in its regulation. This caused conflicts between different departments. With the enactment of the Securities Law of 1998, a centralized regulatory system has been formed with the CSRC as the national regulator. The cooperation between the CSRC and other relevant departments makes the regulatory framework more functional.

4.4.   THE REGULATORS: LOCAL GOVERNMENTS

4.4.1.   REGULATION BY LOCAL GOVERNMENTS BEFORE THE CSRC WAS ESTABLISHED

At the beginning of the re-emergence of the securities markets in the PRC, local governments were the regulators of local securities markets, dealing with the problems incurred during the process of share issuing in local securities markets. As a result, both the Shanghai and Shenzhen Stock Exchanges were established with the approval and support of their local municipal governments. Local governments drew upon experiences of local practices and issued several local administrative rules to guide and control the development of the local markets. These rules played an active role in regulating the re-emergence of the markets. Sometimes local governments issued rules jointly with the departments of the central government. For example, on 10 August 1984, the Shanghai municipal government approved the Shanghai branch of the PBOC's Interim Regulation Concerning Share Issue. This was the first local administrative rule on securities regulation, but this Interim Regulation aimed at the development of local securities markets. In May 1987, the Shanghai municipal government promulgated the Shanghai Interim Measures on Shares Administration. The Shenzhen municipal government also passed several local administrative rules on securities regulation. For example, it released the Circular on Strengthening Securities Regulation and Prohibiting Illegal Off-Market Trading. However, the regulations by the local governments were terminated on 13 August 1997 when the State Council decided to transfer the administration of the two stock exchanges and the appointment of the general managers of the two stock exchanges to the CSRC.

At the beginning of the re-emergence of the securities market, local governments played an active role in cracking down on illegal securities trading and preventing over-speculation. However, this was not consistent with the needs of a market economy. Local protectionism exercised by the local governments gradually became an obstacle in the development of the securities market. This forced the central government to abolish the local governments' involvement in securities market regulation.[125]

---

125. Zheng, Zhenlong (ed.), *A Concise History of Chinese Securities Development*, 328.

In the PRC, state-owned companies or enterprises are classified into two categories: national companies, which are under the control of the central government, and local companies, which are under the control of the provincial governments. Although China claims that it is a socialist market economy, to a great degree, its economy is still subject to government plans.

Before the enactment of the Securities Law, not only the central government, but also local governments were actively involved in the development and administration of the securities markets. As the shareholding system was first adopted for trial in SOEs at both the central and local levels, local governments, of course, had a role to play in adopting such a system in SOEs. Following the CPC's Thirteenth Report on the Shareholding System in 1987, local governments passed their own local administrative regulations. For instance, Fujian Province passed the Interim Regulations of Fujian Province on Shareholding Enterprises and the Interim Measures of Fujian Province on Administration of Shares in 1987.

The Shanghai municipal government drafted the Interim Measures for the Trial of Shareholding in Shanghai on 10 January 1989. The Shenzhen municipal government issued the Shenzhen Interim Measures for Administration of Printing of Shares and the Business Rules for Securities Brokers, and passed the Principles on Examination and Approval of Share Issue by Enterprises in 1988. Unfortunately, these documents were released with red-letter letterhead *(hong tong wen jian)* and were not made public.[126] Under the Chinese legal system, these are not laws but administrative directives that may or may not be enforced by the courts. However, the release of these documents was a sign of the local governments' involvement in the regulation of the securities market.

The department within a local government that is most involved in the regulation of the securities market perhaps is the Securities Supervision Commission. The Shanghai Securities Supervision Commission was established in May 1992. It had full control of the establishment of joint stock limited companies and share issuing by these companies. The local Securities Supervision Commissions complied with the administrative rules of the ministries of the State Council to pass its detailed implementing rules. For instance, the SCRES and State Planning Commission jointly released the Trial Measures for the Trial of the Shareholding System in May 1992. The Shanghai municipal government issued the Shanghai Interim Regulation on Joint Stock Companies three days later.

Local governments played a very active role in share issuing by local enterprises.[127] Even the two stock exchanges were originally established by the Shanghai municipal government and the Shenzhen municipal government. The first listing rules of the two stock exchanges were made by the two local

---

126. These are the government's internal documents, which are usually released on government paper with red letterhead.
127. The Shenzhen municipal government promulgated Provisional Regulations on the Trial of Shareholding System in State-owned Enterprises in Shenzhen Special Economic Zone in October 1986. The Shanghai municipal government promulgated Provisional Measures for the Administration of Shares in Shanghai in 1987.

governments and the two stock exchanges. After the CSRC was established, the regulatory powers over the securities market were gradually transferred to it. Since 1993, the Shanghai and Shenzhen governments no longer participated in the making of the listing rules, but they maintained the power to appoint the heads of stock exchange councils and the general managers of the two stock exchanges from the candidates recommended by the CSRC[128] until the end of 1997.

Before August 1997, almost every provincial government or the same level of local government had a securities regulatory commission. The function of such commissions was to propose a share issuing and listing plan for the local governments. They also conducted preliminary reviews of the enterprises applying for share issuing or listing with the local governments' economic commissions. With the centralization of securities markets, local securities regulatory offices were transferred to the CSRC.

Before 1998, the general manager of a stock exchange was appointed by the stock exchange council from a list of candidates recommended by the CSRC and in consultation with the local government.[129] All these practices indicate the important role that local governments had at the beginning of the re-emergence of the securities market.

4.4.2.   THE ROLE OF LOCAL GOVERNMENTS AFTER 1998

The administrative role of the local governments in securities regulation ended with the centralization of the functions and personnel of the securities regulatory offices of the local governments in 1998. At this time, the local governments' role in securities regulation is limited to approving the share issuing applications of local government-owned companies. Local governments may still have control of the SOEs that are listed companies. However, this control is limited to supervising the corporate governance structure of listed companies rather than direct interference in the market.

4.5.   OTHER REGULATORY BODIES:
         THE STOCK EXCHANGES

4.5.1.   WHY THE SHANGHAI AND SHENZHEN STOCK EXCHANGES
           WERE ESTABLISHED

The establishment of stock exchanges came later than the adoption of the share-holding system in SOEs, and also later than the establishment of securities companies. The main reason why stock exchanges were established was to solve the problems caused by the black-market trading of shares and trading without rules.

---

128. Listing Rules 1997, Art. 22.
129. *Ibid.*, Art. 24.

The proposal to establish stock exchanges in Shanghai and Shenzhen was initiated by the SCRES in January 1989.[130] The reason why these two cities were selected is that Shanghai is a typical big commercial city and Shenzhen is a Special Economic Zone. Initially, the local governments were very reluctant to be the trial cities because there were big risks. However, both governments agreed to try out the idea with the encouragement of the SCRES,[131] which demonstrates the extent of the government's strong involvement in the development of China's securities markets.

When the Shanghai and Shenzhen Stock Exchanges were established, there was no national regulatory body for the securities market. As has been discussed, these two stock exchanges were under the control of the local governments. Within the Shanghai and Shenzhen municipal governments, there were securities offices governing securities. Each government adopted its own rules governing its securities market. The localism of securities regulation caused strong local protectionism and therefore prevented harmonization in the development of the securities markets. The need to solve this problem led to the CSRC finally becoming the sole national regulatory body of the securities market in China.

The two mainland stock exchanges now assist the CSRC in guiding and supervising listed companies seeking to issue and trade their securities on a stock exchange. The stock exchanges must not only disclose trading information,[132] but also must supervise information disclosure in the securities market. This role is not only stipulated in the State Council's regulation entitled Measures for the Administration of Stock Exchanges,[133] but is also confirmed in the listing rules of the two stock exchanges.[134] Under the Securities Law, the supervisory function of the stock exchanges was once again clearly established.[135]

4.5.2.   THE SHANGHAI STOCK EXCHANGE (SSE)

The Shanghai Stock Exchange was established on 26 November 1990, following the construction of the Pudong New Area.[136] It was officially opened to replace the over-the-counter-trading market on 19 December 1990.[137] To date, the Shanghai Stock Exchange is still the largest stock exchange in Asia. It has 1,608 trading seats and is connected electronically with more than twenty securities trading centres

---

130. Li, Zhangzhe, *Finally Successful: Development Report of Chinese Shares Market,* 101.
131. *Ibid.*
132. *Ibid.,* Art. 106.
133. *Ibid.,* Art. 11.
134. Shanghai Stock Exchange Listing Rules, Art. 2.1.1 and Shenzhen Stock Exchange Listing Rules, Art. 2.1.1.
135. Article 111of the Securities Law of 1998 and Arts 103, 107, and 108 of the Securities Law of 2005.
136. The Shanghai Stock Exchange, *Guidelines for Listed Companies,* 1997, 12.
137. *Ibid.*

within the mainland. It has more than 6,000 computerized trading terminals.[138] The Shanghai Stock Exchange solely owns the Shanghai Securities Central Registration and Clearing Corporation, which is a centralized registration, depository, and clearing body.

The SSE is one of the mainland's two securities exchanges that provide places for centralized securities trading. It is a non-profit, membership, institutional legal entity.[139] It has been working to supply a fair, transparent, and highly efficient trading environment for market participants and to ensure normal operation of the securities market under the supervision of the CSRC.

During the first decade after its establishment, the SSE became a safe, efficient, and sizable securities market with a rich variety of choices and wide coverage. By the end of 1998, the SSE's trading floor was handling the following:

(i) 438 listed companies with market capitalization of CNY 1,062.6 billion, equivalent to 13.3% of China's gross domestic product (GDP);

(ii) 528 listed securities of various types, including equity shares, securities investment funds, government bonds, corporate bonds, and corporate convertible bonds;

(iii) 333 members; and

(iv) 19.99 million investment trading accounts.[140]

By the end of 1998, the SSE had raised a total of CNY 140.814 billion for listed companies, of which 2.477 billion US Dollars (USD) had been from foreign investors.[141]

To minimize the paper-based operations, the SSE uses a computerized trading system that is based on the principle of price priority and time priority. The system automatically matches the closest offer and has the capacity to handle 5,000 deals per second. Supplied with the largest satellite-based telecommunications network for securities trading in China, the SSE utilizes electronic trading technology, and trading information can be instantly delivered to all parties across the country.[142]

The Shanghai Securities Central Registration and Clearing Co., a wholly owned subsidiary of the SSE, is responsible for the central registration, deposit, management, and settlement of securities. This company is capable of simultaneously completing stock transfers for A shares and stock pre-transfers for B shares based upon a deal constructed within the computerized system. Before 2001, the A-share market had adopted the T+1 settlement system and the B-share market had used T+3. Since 1 December 2001, B-share trading also started using the T+1 settlement system under the new business rules of the SSE.

---

138. *Ibid.*, 13.
139. The Securities Law of 1998, Art. 95.
140. The SSE Year Book 1998, 4.
141. *Ibid.*
142. *Ibid.*

As both the Shanghai and Shenzhen Stock Exchanges were established by their respective local governments, they had also been supervised and administered by the local governments until 1997, when the CSRC took over responsibility for the supervision of stock exchanges.[143] These two stock exchanges had their own listing rules for some years until 1997. After the CSRC was established, it issued guidelines for the listing rules. Under these guidelines, the two stock exchanges passed very similar listing rules with only small differences. Although there was strong pressure from other provincial governments to establish more securities exchanges, the central government insisted on keeping only two stock exchanges for the sake of good governance. Also, the Shanghai and Shenzhen Stock Exchanges were intentionally opened to compete with each other.

When the two stock exchanges were set up, they were non-profit institutional legal entities *(shi ye fa ren)*[144] and operated on a membership system. Under the articles of association *(zhang cheng)* of the stock exchanges, the Members' General Meeting is the highest body of the stock exchange. The Council (*Li Shi Hui)* is the body that makes general policies. It consists of several executive council members and several non-executive members. The general manager is the legal representative of the stock exchange and is in charge of day-to-day business.

The status of a stock exchange as a *shi ye* legal entity[145] was confirmed by the SCSC, which issued the Measures for Administration of Stock Exchanges on 21 August 1996. This Administrative Rule confirmed that a stock exchange is a non-profit *shi ye* legal entity that operates on a membership system.[146] It listed the contents of the memorandum of association of a stock exchange. Among the eight main functions of a stock exchange, two are related to the supervision of listed companies and information disclosure on the stock markets. Based on this document, a stock exchange has a members' general meeting, a council, and several special commissions.[147] On 29 December 1998, the Sixth Meeting of the Standing Committee of the Ninth National People's Congress enacted the first Securities Law. This law recognizes the functions of the councils of stock exchanges.

The status of a stock exchange was changed as a result of the enactment of the Securities Law. According to this Law, a stock exchange is a non-profit legal entity.[148] For some reason, the Law does not say whether a stock exchange is a *shi ye* legal entity. Under the Securities Law, it is not clear whether a stock exchange adopts a membership system. Under a membership system, a stock exchange is managed in a more democratic way. The members' general meeting has the power

---

143. In a decision by the State Council in August 1997, the stock exchanges were put under the direct supervision and administration of the CSRC.
144. The General Principles of the Civil Law of 1986, Art. 50 allows some institutions associated with the government to be established as legal entities without going through formal registration procedures. *Shi ye* means a legal entity that is neither a company nor a governmental department with administrative authority.
145. *Ibid.*
146. Article 3.
147. Article 16.
148. The PRC Securities Law of 1998, Art. 95.

to formulate and amend the articles of association of the stock exchange, to elect and remove the members of the council, to examine and approve the working reports of the council and of the general manager, to examine and pass the budget, etc.[149] However, the Securities Law is strongly characterized by state control: a stock exchange can only be established or dissolved upon a decision by the State Council;[150] the formulation and amendment of the articles of association of a stock exchange must be approved by the CSRC;[151] a stock exchange may formulate its trading rules, the administrative rules for the management of its members, and the code of conduct for the securities business professionals with the approval of the CSRC.[152] The stock exchanges to some degree have become subordinates of the CSRC. The independence of stock exchanges will affect their ability to provide a fair and competitive trading market.

However, the SSE has tried very hard to improve its work. It has paid great attention to international exchanges and cooperation. During its early days of operation, it established cooperation with foreign counterparts. It signed a memorandum of understanding with the London Stock Exchange in March 1995. Many European securities dealers, including SBC Warburg and Barclays, have been engaged in B-share transactions on the SSE. Southeast Electric Power Ltd has listed both B shares in Shanghai and global depository receipts (GDRs) on the London Stock Exchange. In October 1998, the memorandum of understanding with the London Stock Exchange was renewed in the presence of Tony Blair, then Prime Minister of the UK. Mr Blair even wrote an inscription for the SSE during the event.[153]

The SSE has been playing a major role in improving corporate governance in the PRC. It held the first International Symposium on Corporate Governance in the PRC in late 2000. It issued the first Guidelines on Corporate Governance of Listed Companies for the companies listed with it. Because of the SSE's experience in this area, the CSRC delegated power to the SSE to draft the national Code of Corporate Governance of Listed Companies,[154] which was released jointly by the CSRC and the State Commission of Economics and Trade on 7 January 2002.

This Administrative Rule contains eight chapters and ninety-five articles, including provisions on disclosure. It emphasizes that listed companies must strengthen disclosure of corporate governance by disclosing all the information that may have a substantial effect on shareholders and other investors' decision-making.[155] It also ensures that all the shareholders have an equal opportunity to acquire information.[156] The issuance of the corporate governance standards shows that the PRC's central government has paid great attention to this matter, but also

---

149. Article 17 of the Measures of the Administration of Stock Exchanges of the SCSC.
150. The PRC Securities Law of 2005, Art. 102.
151. *Ibid.*, Art. 103.
152. *Ibid.*, Art. 118.
153. Li, Zhangzhe, *Finally Successful: Development Report of Chinese Shares Market*, 569.
154. Author's interview with a senior research officer at the SSE in September 2001.
155. Article 88.
156. *Ibid.*

demonstrates that poor corporate governance widely exists in many listed companies. It is impossible to rely solely upon these companies to improve corporate governance. Thus, outsiders' help is needed.

4.5.3.   The Shenzhen Stock Exchange (SZSE)

Set up on 1 December 1990 as a non-profit, self-disciplined institutional legal entity with a membership system,[157] the SZSE has been providing a market operation environment with appropriate facilities for concentrated and organized securities trading. It has been fulfilling responsibilities as stipulated in relevant state laws, regulations, rules, and policies under the supervision of the CSRC.

The SZSE, guided by the principles of standards, fairness, efficiency, and safe operations, has been rapidly expanding in size, increasing its products, and aggressively seeking growth opportunities. It has successfully moved from the manual matching of offers and bids into the stage characterized by automated trading, and it has been upgraded from a local market to a nationwide one. By the end of 1998, the SZSE's trading floor was handling the following:

(i)   413 listed companies with market capitalization of CNY 888 billion, equivalent to 11.13% of China's GDP;
(ii) 483 listed securities, of which 454 were equity shares, 10 were funds, and 19 were bonds;
(iii) 19,117,300 investor accounts;
(iv) 329 members; and
(v)   over 2,400 interconnected retail branches.[158]

The SZSE had raised capital worth CNY 128 billion for listed companies by the end of 1998 and played an important role in promoting the restructuring of SOEs and bringing forth a socialist market economic system.

The SZSE adopted a market trading system based on modern computerized and telecommunications technology and fully electronically automated trading. Based on the principles of price priority and time priority, the system offers concentrated bidding and matches offers and bids deal-by-deal, with a daily capacity of commissions of CNY 10 million. It has exercised a 10% price cap for both rise and fall margins within the day for shares and funds trading to maintain market stability and stay out of daunting fluctuations in share prices. To strengthen the front-line monitoring functions, it has developed and gradually improved an automatic real-time market monitoring system. Its information system delivers market updates in a timely manner to all domestic business points, as well as to

---

157. The Shenzhen municipal government's Shenzhen Interim Measures for Share Issue and Trading of 1991, Art. 54.
158. The *SZSE Annual Report 1998* (Beijing: China Finance Press), 3.

more than 150 countries and regions in the world via its trading network and the Internet.[159]

Within the operating system of the SZSE, there are four sub-systems: a trading system, a clearing and settlement system, a disclosure system, and a surveillance system. The Shenzhen Securities Clearing Company, a subsidiary wholly owned by the SZSE, is responsible for the registration, custody, and settlement of shares listed on the SZSE. An omni-directional, tri-dimensional operation system has been set up with four sub-systems: a trading system, a settlement system, an information-management system, and a market-monitoring system.

For years, the SZSE, having taken an open-minded stance, has been working to tighten links and cooperation with the global securities industry and has actively tapped the B-share market. By the end of 1998, it had listed fifty-four B shares with a market capitalization of CNY 10.6 billion, with more than 100,000 B-share investors from 108 countries and regions. The Shenzhen Special Economic Zone Real Estate and Properties Group issued American depository receipts (ADRs) in the USA in 1994. The listing of the Shenzhen Merchants Shekou Port Service Co. Ltd. in Singapore in 1995 symbolized the SZSE's growing openness.[160]

With China's rapid economic growth, the SZSE has been playing an important part in attracting capital from wealthy southern China and neighbouring Macau and Hong Kong. With the changing role of stock exchanges, their nature has been designated as 'self-regulatory legal entities which provide the venue and facilities for centralized trading of securities and responsibility for organizing and supervising securities trading'.[161]

4.5.4.   OVERVIEW OF THE ROLE OF STOCK EXCHANGES IN THE PRC

Although the mainland stock exchanges are defined as self-regulatory legal entities under the law, some scholars believe that they are still government agencies.[162] They were set up by the government, their listing rules and their amendments to such rules are approved by the CSRC, and they have delegated administrative powers from the government.[163] Some people have doubts about the independence and transparency of the stock exchanges. However, lawmakers have decided that the stock exchanges should be given some administrative powers in view of following the precedents of the stock exchanges in other countries, such as the UK.[164] The PRC stock exchanges view their supervision of the securities market as

---

159. *Ibid.*
160. *Ibid.*
161. The Securities Law of 2005, Art. 102.
162. Interview with a professor of company law at China University of Politics and Law in February 1998 in Beijing.
163. The 1993 Interim Regulations, Art. 11.
164. Interview with two drafting members of the draft of the PRC Securities Law in February 1998 in Beijing.

day-to-day supervision, mainly in regard to technical and procedural matters.[165] They do not administer the securities market in the same way as a government department.

It can be seen from the short history of the securities market in China that the regulatory structures for information disclosure were formed as the securities market developed. Arguably, disclosure guarantees the healthy growth and development of the securities market by facilitating greater transparency within the market.

4.6.   SELF-REGULATORY ORGANIZATIONS

4.6.1.   SECURITIES INDUSTRY ASSOCIATION

The China Securities Industry Association (CSIA) was established on 28 August 1991 with the approval of the State Council.[166] It was registered with the Ministry of Civil Affairs as an independent non-profit entity[167] and is under the leadership of the CSRC.[168] It is a self-regulatory body composed of securities brokerage institutions as its members. Under the Securities Law, there may be national securities associations and local securities associations. The national body, the China Securities Industry Association, is a national self-regulatory body. On 15 December 1991, the CSIA had a members' meeting that passed new articles of association to meet the requirements under the Securities Law. It also adopted a number of internal rules, including the Code of Conduct for the Securities Industry, the Interim Measures for CSIA Membership Administration, and the Ethical Rules for Chinese Securities Analysts.

The Securities Law of 2005 confirms the status of this Association. The nature and function of the Securities Association is clearly stipulated in Articles 174–176. Under these Articles, the CSIA is a self-regulatory organization with a separate legal status. Securities companies are required to join the Association.

Apart from the Securities Law, the CSIA must comply with the requirements of the Regulation Concerning Registration of Social Institutions of 1998. Under the requirements of this Regulation, the SCIA must have thirty or more institutional members or fifty or more individual members; it must have professional personnel to conduct relevant work; the registered capital must be CNY 100,000 or more if it is registered as a national body; and the Association must have a charter. Although the Securities Law does not prevent individuals from becoming members of the SCIA, most of the members are institutions, and, although non-securities

---

165. Interview with a deputy general manager of the Shenzhen Stock Exchange in February 1998.
166. Zheng, Zhenlong (ed.), *A Concise History of Chinese Securities Development*, 334.
167. *Ibid.*
168. *Ibid.*

brokerage institutions are allowed to become members, most of the members are securities companies.[169]

The CSIA consists of the following main departments: the Council, the Supervisory Board, and the special committees. There is a standing committee that works for the Council. It is managed by a Secretariat. There are six major departments of the Secretariat: the Administrative Section, the Membership Department, the Investigation Department, the Research Department, the Training Department, and the Foreign Affairs Department. The CSIA has the following functions: to educate and organize the members to comply with the provisions of laws and administrative regulations; to safeguard the lawful rights and interests of members according to law and to report members' suggestions and requests to the securities regulatory authority; to collect and process information on securities and provide service to its members; to formulate rules to be observed by its members; to arrange for vocational training for the employees of its members and to promote professional exchanges among members; to mediate the disputes between members and between members and their clients; to make arrangements for members to research the development, operation, and other matters related to the securities industry; to supervise and inspect member's conduct; and to impose disciplinary sanctions on any member who violates laws, administrative regulations, or the charter of the Association.[170]

However, in Chinese culture, there is a tradition to respect authority. Self-regulation in China has not played an important role, and this is why there are so many securities companies involved in giving false information. The weak role of SROs is one of the signs that the PRC's securities market is under strong government control.

A unique characteristic of the CSIA is that it is under the strict control of the CSRC. Its charter must be formulated by the members' general meeting and submitted to the CSRC for the record.[171] It has to fulfil the responsibilities given to it by the CSRC.[172] These provisions limit the Association's ability to function as a real self-regulatory body. To some degree, the CSIA is still seen as a body attached to the government. The development of the securities markets and the traditional function of the government has made the Securities Industry Association dependent on the government since its inception.[173] Unlike self-regulatory bodies in countries with developed and complicated securities markets, the CSIA cannot really exercise self-regulatory functions. Its main functions are focused on assistance, training, research, and mediation.[174] However, the establishment of the CSIA has laid a foundation for securities self-regulation.[175]

---

169. Ye, Lin, *China's Securities Law,* 370.
170. The PRC Securities Law of 2005, Art. 176.
171. *Ibid.*, Art. 175.
172. *Ibid.*, Art. 176.
173. Ye, Lin, *China's Securities Law,* 374.
174. The PRC Securities Law of 2005, Art. 176.
175. Yang, Zhihua, *Study of Securities Systems* (Beijing: China University of Politics and Law Press, 1995), 201.

4.6.2.   OTHER SROS

The CSIA is a statutory SRO. Apart from the CSIA, there are other SROs in the securities market, such as the China Securities Analysts Association, established in 2000. As the PRC securities market is under the strong control of the government, SROs do not have a significant role to play.

4.7.   CONCLUSION

The process of establishing an effective regulatory body has gone through non-regulation, to local government regulation, to combined regulation between the local governments and the departments of the central government, to the primary regulation by the CSRC. This process is a result of the development of the PRC's domestic securities market and the influence of foreign experiences. There have been a number of regulators in the PRC securities market, although the CSRC is now the most important one. Many government departments were, and even still are, involved in the regulation of the securities market. This is natural in a country that is strictly controlled by a centralized government. However, this structure is very different from that of most Western securities markets, where there is a statutory regulatory body that is not subject to the control of the executive government.

The formation of securities regulators in the PRC is a result of its political structure. It is also a reflection of the divergence hypothesis. The multiple-level regulation of course diminishes the efficiency of the securities market. Nevertheless, the weakening of the government departments' role in securities regulation is a sign of further development of a market economy. The regulation of the PRC's securities market is developing to achieve higher transparency and efficiency. This is consistent with the trend of convergence, which results from globalization of securities regulation. Each gatekeeper in the securities market has been issuing regulatory documents according to their respective powers. These documents have formed the securities regulatory framework of the PRC. Identifying the gate-keepers of the PRC securities market can provide a basis for further review of the securities regulatory framework, which will be discussed in the next chapter.

Chapter 5

Regulatory Rules Dealing with Disclosure in the PRC's Securities Market

5.1.   INTRODUCTION

Securities legislation is essentially concerned with information regulation and market conduct. Investors are deemed to be adequately protected if all the aspects of the securities market are fully and fairly disclosed.[1] In a securities market, investors make the decisions of buying and selling securities based on the information that is available to them. Transparency is one of the key features of a well-functioning securities market. One of the key functions of securities regulators is to supervise companies' compliance with securities rules in the market to ensure that they disclose accurate and relevant information. In this way, investors can make informed investment decisions. Many of the legal requirements found in the securities market are related to information disclosure issues.

As discussed in Chapter 4, issuing securities in the PRC was first used by collective enterprises to meet their capital needs. This situation is dramatically different from the experiences of Western countries. As China's economic reform continued, issuing shares was mainly used by the Chinese government at both the local and central levels as a means to help SOEs in financial trouble to raise capital so as to meet the deficiency of funds that could no longer be provided by the government through state-owned banks. Such a purpose for securities issuing and the strong government involvement in the development of the securities market have created unique features in the PRC's securities market and its regulation.

The PRC securities market re-emerged long before the government's regulation of the market started. The development of the PRC's securities market

---

1. T.L. Hazen, *The Law of Securities Regulation* (St. Paul: West Publishing Co., 1985), 7.

has shown the unique environment surrounding this market and the strong involvement of the government. These unique features of the PRC's securities market caused the PRC to establish a securities regulatory regime with some unique characteristics. This chapter will give an overview of the PRC's securities regulatory scheme by examining its disclosure rules. It will also demonstrate that the development and improvement of the disclosure rules in the PRC have also reflected the influence of both the corporate law theory of path dependency and the theory of convergence.

The regulation of the securities market in the PRC went through the process of 'bottom to up'[2] and then the process of 'top to down'.[3] This regulation began with the local governments. The administrative documents of local governments were the first rules regulating the re-emerging securities market. Later, the ministries and commissions of the State Council came to join the regulatory team. To avoid abuses of the share issuing scheme and prevent fraudulent misconduct, local governments first started releasing regulatory documents on share issuing. As the national securities markets were only operated in Shanghai and Shenzhen, SOEs in each province and region had to compete to be listed on either of these two markets.[4] Sometimes, SOEs had to use all the means they could to be listed on a stock exchange. The ministries and commissions of the central government had to separately or jointly release regulatory rules to punish and prevent misleading, deceptive, and fraudulent conduct in the process of listing. Because of a lack of coordination and cooperation, the rules of all gatekeepers in the securities market had conflicts among themselves. This practice resulted in an inefficient and fraudulent market. It caused the frequent occurrence of fraudulent and deceptive listings in the mid-1990s. Only after a number of serious fraudulent cases occurred did the PRC's central government begin to draw on lessons and experiences from foreign countries, to centralise regulatory power, and to make uniform regulatory rules.

Based on the model of the Securities and Exchange Commission (SEC) of the USA, the CSRC was given more authority to become the sole regulator of securities trading in late 1997.[5] In the primary market, even though the Ministry of Finance, the PBOC, and the State Development and Reform Commission still maintain the power to approve the issuing of state bonds, financial bonds, and enterprise bonds, respectively, the listing of these securities has to be approved by

---

2. Share issuing was first used by collective enterprises in the countryside to raise capital, then by enterprises in the cities, then by the SOEs of the local governments, and then by the SOEs of the central government. The regulatory rules were first made by the local governing bodies, then by the local governments, then by the central government, and then by the Standing Committee of the NPC.
3. After the central government decided to adopt the shareholding system in SOEs in the early 1990s, it took control of securities issuing by centralizing the power to decide which enterprises could issue securities and to make rules at different levels.
4. Walter, Carol E. & Fraser J.T. Howie, *Privatizing China: the Stock Markets and Their Role in Corporate Reform* (Singapore: John Wiley & Sons (Asia) Pte Ltd, 2003), 90.
5. Zheng, Zhenlong (ed.), *A Concise History of the Chinese Securities Market* (Beijing: Economic Science Press, 2006), 328.

the CSRC. The rules released by the ministries and commissions of the State Council or local governments are focused on the requirements for securities issuing and the liabilities for contravention of these rules. Few of them are concerned about information disclosure. Although the State Council's 1993 Interim Regulations contain principles of securities disclosure, these provisions are too general to be implemented properly. The CSRC started issuing regulatory rules on disclosure soon after its establishment. However, these rules of the CSRC were not treated as administrative rules[6] until the end of 1998. The rules of the CSRC released before then were often ignored by companies and even by other government departments. Even after the CSRC rules were made administrative rules, they still may not be complied with because administrative rules are not enforceable by the courts in the Chinese legal system, as discussed in Chapter 2. The practices in the PRC demonstrated that multi-level rules without coordination did not function well.

To tackle the problems with the multi-party regulatory structure, the PRC government decided to enact a national law regulating the securities market. Consequently, the Securities Law of 1998 came into effect, and via legislation, it made the CSRC the sole regulator of the securities market. However, administrative regulations made by the State Council and administrative rules made by the relevant ministries or commissions of the State Council continue to play a role in securities regulation. The day-to-day supervision and regulation of the securities market has been delegated to the CSRC. Thus, the administrative rules on securities disclosure released by the CSRC constitute the core body of the securities disclosure regime.

During the process of drafting laws, administrative regulations, and administrative rules, the PRC sets the rules, which have 'Chinese characteristics' to deal with the problems in practice. It also draws on lessons from Western countries. When the Chinese securities market re-emerged in the mid-1980s after forty years of non-existence, it was in great need of the experiences of other jurisdictions. Many legal concepts and principles were then borrowed from Western countries. The officials of the CSRC who were educated in the USA naturally intended to adopt the US model in securities regulation, especially because the US securities market was seen as the most developed market in the world. As Hong Kong was seen as the biggest financial centre in Asia and it is culturally, geographically, and economically closer to the PRC than any other jurisdiction, the experience of securities regulation in Hong Kong also became a model that the PRC central government thought would be more appropriate and easier to adopt. The PRC has learned a great deal about Hong Kong securities regulation since 1993, when several SOEs sought listing on the Hong Kong Stock Exchange. Of course, the rule makers also looked at the development of its domestic securities markets. To deal with the problems that occurred in practice, they set some rules with 'Chinese characteristics'. In learning from foreign experiences, China's lawmakers

---

6. As discussed in Ch. 2, administrative rules are the rules made by an administrative commission or ministry of the State Council. The CSRC was not given administrative status until the passage of the PRC Securities Law of 1998.

traditionally preferred to adopt civil law models. This can be seen from the law reform in the late Qing Dynasty, which was modelled on Japanese law and German law.[7] However, the drafting of the securities laws and regulations was one of the few exceptions. Apart from the fact that some of the senior officials were educated in the USA, the Tokyo securities market was considered insignificant and the drafters of the laws lacked knowledge about the European markets.

It is worth noting that Articles 59–63 of the PRC Company Law of 1993 impose a duty on directors not to use their positions to make personal gains, and a duty not to conduct the same business as the company's business for their personal interests or for other people's personal interests. Article 20 of the PRC Company Law of 2005 repeats these duties and imposes the duty of loyalty and the duty of care on directors, supervisors, and other senior executive officers. Under the requirements found in these provisions, directors of listed joint stock companies (similar to public companies in Western countries) have the duty of information disclosure. This is in accordance with one basic policy of securities regulation, that is, to ensure that informed decisions are made by investors. However, in contrast to provisions on the duty of information disclosure imposed upon companies in the PRC Company Law and the Securities Law, the provisions on the duty of information disclosure imposed upon directors and other senior officers of companies were only clarified in the 2005 amendments of these two Laws. In contrast with Australian corporations laws, these provisions are still very general and vague. One reason might be that disclosure duties have already been imposed on company directors in the State Council's administrative regulations and the CSRC's Administrative Rules. The legislators did not want to have too much repetition of regulation and rules.

The first part of this chapter analyses what securities markets are, the relationship between the duty of information disclosure by listed companies, and the duty of information disclosure by directors of such listed companies. It then examines the contents of information disclosure in the PRC and gives an overview of the liabilities for violations of duty of information disclosure. After that, it makes comments on the current statutory duty of information disclosure by the directors of listed companies.

Later, this chapter undertakes a review of all kinds of rules dealing with corporate disclosure. It looks into disclosure regulation in both the primary market and the secondary market. Furthermore, this chapter discusses the process of formation of disclosure rules and their functions. In this process, it traces how laws and rules were made. In particular, it elaborates on how foreign experiences were drawn upon in the process of Chinese lawmaking. Based on this analysis, this chapter concludes that the current PRC corporate disclosure regulatory regime is not very effective, as many rules were directly borrowed from other countries without empirical study and they do not suit the Chinese environment. The development of the securities market in the PRC demonstrates the application

---

7. J.M. Otto et al., *Lawmaking in the People's Republic of China* (The Hague: Kluwer Law International, 2000), 23.

of the differentiation hypothesis with a stronger influence of divergence. However, the corporate disclosure regime in the PRC has been more strongly influenced by the convergence of the securities market development. In the end, this chapter makes a suggestion in relation to legal transplanting: the way in which the PRC government adopts Western experiences, including Western corporate disclosure rules, needs to be improved so that these rules can function effectively and efficiently.

5.1.1.   WHAT IS THE CONCEPT OF SECURITIES USED IN THIS BOOK?

To understand how the PRC securities market is regulated, it is essential to know what kind of market it is. This requires a definition of the term 'securities' first. The term 'securities' has been used in two ways in the PRC: in the narrow sense, under the Securities Law of 1998, 'securities' only refers to shares, corporate bonds, and other securities recognized by the State Council.[8] In the broad sense, 'securities' not only refers to shares and corporate bonds, but also to state treasury bonds, enterprise bonds, financial bonds, convertible enterprise bonds, and derivatives. The choice of adopting a narrow definition of 'securities' in the Securities Law of 1998 was made by the Chinese legislators considering the early stage of the market's development and the constant changes in the Chinese securities market. This approach also determines how the Chinese securities market functions. As the Chinese securities market was in an early stage of its development, shares, state treasury bonds, and company bonds were the major types of securities. Professor Wu Zhipan classified the securities regulatory models of the world into two types: the government-directed model, such as that of the PRC, and the market-oriented model, such as that of the USA.[9] However, this narrow concept of securities was broadened to include government bonds, investment funds, and some derivatives in the Securities Law of 2005 after the PRC securities market had moved to a new stage.[10] The current concept of 'securities' is the broad one.

Although the definition of 'securities' in the Securities Law of 1998 was very narrow, this did not mean that only shares and company bonds existed in the Chinese securities market. Securities such as local government bonds, financial bonds, and derivatives had been issued under a plan of the state and administered by some ministries of the State Council, and very often they were issued in a procedure that was different from the issuing of shares and company bonds to the public. These securities were issued in a similar way to shares and company bonds issuance.

---

8. The PRC Securities Law of 1998, Art. 2.
9. Wu, Zhipan, 'Review of the Design of the Securities Regulatory System: From the Perspective of the Securities Definition', in *Law and Practice of Securities Transactions,* ed. Wu Zhipan & Bai Jianjun (eds) (Beijing: CUPL Press, 2000), 9–10.
10. The PRC Securities Law of 2005, Art. 2.

5.1.2. COMPANIES' DUTY OF DISCLOSURE VERSUS
        DIRECTORS' DUTY OF DISCLOSURE

Who has a duty to provide corporate disclosure? Is the duty of information disclosure a company's duty or its directors' duty? In Australia, the answer to this question has been made clear. It is a company's duty as well as the directors' duty.[11] Chapter 6 further discusses this matter.

Before the Amendments to the PRC Criminal Law were enacted in March 1997, the answer to this question in China was not clear. Looking at the provisions in the PRC Company Law and the State Council's 1993 Interim Regulations, all the provisions dealing with information disclosure were related to companies rather than company directors.[12] The concept of 'information disclosure' in the State Council's 1993 Interim Regulations only deal with information disclosure by listed companies. There is a chapter in the Regulations specifically dealing with 'information disclosure by listed companies'. For some time, some people thought that under Chinese law, company directors had no duty of information disclosure because it was the duty of listed companies. As there was no official explanation as to why the duty of information disclosure was confined to companies, people could only guess the reasons for this. One reason might be that when the PRC Company Law was drafted, the problems caused by non-disclosure or misleading disclosure by directors were not very apparent and serious. Another reason might be that, as the disclosure was given on behalf of the company, the company should bear the liability for breaching disclosure rules, even if the breach was committed by company directors or other officers.

Uncertainties in the meaning of the liability provisions of the PRC Company Law of 1993 caused trouble in interpreting the law. The enactment of the 1999 Amendments to the PRC Criminal Law cleared up some of the ambiguities that exist in the Company Law of 1993. Under Article 160 of the amended PRC Criminal Law, companies that make omissions or that make false statements in the prospectus, the subscription of shares, or the measures for bonds issuing will be fined 1% to 5% of the illegally raised funds; and individuals who engaged in the same conduct will be given a penalty of imprisonment of no more than five years or detention. Under Article 180 of the amended PRC Criminal Law, those with inside information (including companies and their directors) who leak information that will fundamentally affect the prices of securities and cause serious effects, will be sentenced to detention or imprisonment of no more than five years. They will also be fined between one to five times the amount of the illegal gains made through this conduct. If the situation is especially serious, they will be sentenced to

---

11. Section 729 of the Australian Corporations Act of 2001 says who is liable for misstatements in, and omissions from, a disclosure document. These include not only the companies, but also the company directors. Chapter 6CA imposes the duty of continuous disclosure on public companies.
12. The PRC Company Law, Arts 140, 153, and 156. The State Council's Interim Regulations on Administration of Share Issuing and Trading of 1993, Arts 13, 49, 57, and 60.

imprisonment of between five to ten years and will be required to pay a fine between one to five times the amount of the illegal gains from their conduct. The 1999 Amendment particularly provides that the penalty of imprisonment or detention applies to the individuals who are responsible for the company's affairs. These people include company directors.

The notion that directors have the duty to disclose information can be illustrated by reference to a set of rules released by the CSRC. In April 1993, before the PRC Company Law was enacted, the State Council passed the 1993 Interim Regulations to meet the needs of the emerging securities market. This legal document contains several provisions about the directors' duty of information disclosure. In June 1993, the CSRC released the Provisional Enforcement Rules of Information Disclosure by Listed Companies in accordance with the State Council's 1993 Interim Regulations.

Although this document mainly contains provisions regarding the content and format of information disclosure by a company, it also provides that the issuer or the directors of the company must ensure that there is no false or seriously misleading information or gross omission in disclosure documents and that the company and its directors have joint liability for this.[13] In June 1993, before the 1993 Interim Regulations were released, the CSRC issued the Provisional Rule No. 1 on the Content and Form of Information Disclosure – Content and Form of Prospectus. This was the first detailed rule on disclosure in prospectuses.

After the enactment of the PRC Company Law of 1993, the CSRC revised the Provisional Rule No. 1 on the Content and Form of Information Disclosure by Listed Companies and continued to release other Rules on the Content and Form of Information Disclosure. It can be seen that, as the securities regulator, the CSRC has always paid great attention to information disclosure issues. It continuously adjusts its regulatory rules to administer and standardize securities transactions. Because the securities market in China re-emerged a short time ago, the regulatory regime is still developing and therefore is continuously updated. The standardization of information disclosure of the Chinese securities market is going through, and will continue to go through, a long period of change. Outsiders of this regime may think that Chinese securities regulation is not stable. Although there is in fact some instability, this instability is the first step towards achieving stability. By mid-2009, the CSRC had released twenty-nine rules especially dealing with the content and form of information disclosure. The basic structure of the information disclosure system has now been formed.

It can be seen that in the PRC Company Law of 1993, there is not a clear provision dealing with directors' duty of information disclosure, although this duty can be deduced from other provisions in the legislation. To avoid ambiguity, a clear statement of this duty should be inserted when the PRC Company Law is to be amended in the future. The Company Law of 2005 has made some changes in this regard by imposing compensatory liabilities on company directors and other senior

---

13. The CSRC's Provisional Enforcement Rules on Information Disclosure by Listed Companies of 1993, Art. 5.

managers for breaches of laws and rules when acting on behalf of the company.[14] It is assumed that this includes breaches of the duty of disclosure.

5.1.3. WHERE ARE THE DISCLOSURE RULES?

5.1.3.1. The Structure of Disclosure Rules

As discussed in Chapter 2, there are four kinds of legal sources on disclosure, from the upper level to the lower level, under PRC law: the Constitution and laws; administrative regulations and local regulations; and departmental administrative rules and local administrative rules. In addition to these disclosure rules of state bodies, the listing rules of the Shanghai and the Shenzhen Stock Exchanges have also set forth disclosure rules in their listing rules.

Since the CSRC became the sole securities regulatory body, the PRC's corporate disclosure rules consist of laws, administrative regulations, and departmental administrative rules of the CSRC, as well as those of other ministries and commissions of the State Council. The relevant laws include the Securities Law of 2005,[15] the Company Law of 2005,[16] the 2006 Amendments to the Criminal Law of 1979[17] and the 2009 Amendments to the Criminal Law of 1979;[18] the relevant administrative regulations, including the Interim Regulations Concerning Administration of Share Issue and Trading of 1993, the Regulations Concerning Domestic Listing of Foreign Investment Shares by Shareholding Companies of 1995; the relevant Departmental Administrative Rules and other directives, including the CSRC's Implementing Rules on Disclosure by Public Shareholding Companies (for Trial) of 1993, Rules No. 1–24 on the Content and Format of Disclosure by Public Shareholding Companies, Rules No. 1–13 on Preparation of Disclosure by Public Shareholding Companies, and the Code of Corporate Governance for Listed Companies issued by the CSRC and the State Economics and Trade Commission. In addition, the CSRC releases Interpretations of Disclosure Rules as well as Opinions on Relevant Cases and Case Citations from time to time. The CSRC Interpretations and Opinions do not bind listed companies, but they provide directive functions in practice. The Listing Rules and Business Rules of the Shanghai and the Shenzhen Stock Exchanges also contain provisions regarding disclosure. The following parts of this chapter will analyse the major information disclosure rules that are found in these sources.

---

14. Article 150.
15. Articles 20, 21, 52, 53, and 63–72.
16. Article 86
17. Articles 160, 161, and 181.
18. Article 180(1).

5.1.3.2. The Disclosure Rules under the National Laws

In three pieces of legislation of the NPC and its Standing Committee are the provisions governing disclosure: the Company Law of 2005, the Securities Law of 2005, and the 2006 and the 2009 Amendments to the Criminal Law. However, all these laws are very general in regard to disclosure.

5.1.3.2.1.   *The Company Law of 2005*

The Company Law of 1993 was the first national law to regulate companies, including shareholding companies. Unfortunately, it only touched on the issue of corporate disclosure, with very few articles requiring listed companies to provide a prospectus. As it focused on setting up a modern enterprise system among SOEs, most articles of this Law were about company registration and organization. Although Article 140 required a company issuing shares to the public to publish its prospectus, there were no criteria for disclosure. As at that time, the PRC government had not put the protection of shareholders into its lawmaking agenda. It also had not realized the emergency and the importance of enacting the Securities Law.

As mentioned earlier, there was no clear statement of directors' duties of information disclosure in the Company Law of 1993. However, the Company Law imposes many duties on directors. According to this Law, directors must comply with the articles of association of the company, faithfully perform their duties, and maintain the interests of the company.[19] Directors must not take advantage of their positions, functions, and powers in the company to seek personal gains. Directors must not accept bribes or other unlawful profits, nor misappropriate the property of the company by taking advantage of their functions and powers.[20] Directors must not misappropriate company funds or lend company funds to others. Directors must not use company assets as security for personal debts of shareholders of the company or other individuals.[21] Directors must not personally or on behalf of others engage in the same category of business as their company, nor engage in activities that may cause damage to the interests of the company. Directors must not enter into contracts or conduct transactions with the company, except as provided for in the articles of association or as approved by shareholders' meeting.[22] It may be deduced that directors must disclose any relevant information about any personal interests as required under the relevant administrative regulations and departmental administrative rules. These duties of directors have now been incorporated into Chapter 6 of the Company Law of 2005.

---

19. The PRC Company Law of 1993, Art. 59.
20. *Ibid.*
21. *Ibid.*, Art. 60.
22. *Ibid.*, Art. 61.

5.1.3.2.2.   The Securities Law of 2005

The first Law to contain clear disclosure rules was the Securities Law of 1998. It was passed after the more than ten-year development of the securities market and seven years of drafting and revising. It drew upon lots of experiences of Western countries, with a foundation from its own practices. It is more focused on disclosure than the Company Law of 1993, not only with the principles of disclosure, but also with the contents of disclosure documents and liabilities for breaches of disclosure rules. However, what are missing in the Securities Law of 1998 are civil liabilities. This problem leaves a loophole for the protection of minority shareholders. This is the biggest defect of the Securities Law of 1995. With strong criticism, civil liabilities were inserted in the Securities Law of 2005.

In both the first Company Law and the Securities Law, openness, fairness, and justice are stipulated as three fundamental rules governing share issuing and trading.[23] In the Securities Law of 1998, Article 5 prohibits fraud, insider trading, and securities manipulation. Article 17 requires the issuer to publish its share issuing documents by public notice and display these documents at public places. Article 13 requires the issuer to provide share issuing documents that are true, precise, and complete. Article 24 provides that underwriters must examine whether the disclosure documents are true, precise, and complete. These articles come from the State Council's 1993 Interim Regulations. The upgrade of disclosure rules from administrative regulations to laws indicates that legislators have gradually realized the importance of compulsory disclosure. The provisions of the Securities Law of 1998 regarding disclosure were also incorporated in the Securities Law of 2005.[24]

A big breakthrough in disclosure regulation in the Securities Law of 1998 is the requirement for continuous disclosure,[25] as the previous regulations, such as the 1993 Interim Regulations, only adopted periodic disclosure. In most Western countries, laws not only require companies to give disclosure at their first securities issuance, but also require companies to continuously provide information that may have a material effect on the share price after the initial public offer.[26] The Securities Law of 1998 not only contains provisions on continuous disclosure, but also provides for three major documents of so-called continuous disclosure: an annual report,[27] a half-yearly report,[28] and an interim report.[29] Interim reporting is required when a listed company is to disclose any major event that may materially affect the share price of that company to the CSRC, the relevant stock exchange, and the public.[30] This structure was adopted because Chinese legislators were

---

23. The PRC Company Law of 1993, Art. 130; the PRC Securities Law of 1998, Art. 3.
24. The PRC Securities Law of 2005, Arts 5, 15, 31, 63–72, and 193.
25. The PRC Securities Law of 1998, s. 3 of Ch. 3.
26. Chapter 6CA of the Australian Corporations Act of 2001 (Cth); the SEC rules on quarterly reports in the USA.
27. Article 61.
28. Article 60.
29. Article 62.
30. *Ibid.*

confused with the concept of continuous disclosure and the concept of periodic disclosure.[31]

The provisions concerning these reports came from Articles 57–60 of the 1993 Interim Regulations. The major difference is that the Securities Law uses the term 'interim report' to refer to the major events that may have a major impact on the trading price of the shares, while the 1993 Interim Regulations directly uses the term 'major events'. However, the requirement for interim reports does not really work, as neither the Securities Law nor the 1993 Interim Regulations clearly states when the 'major event' should be disclosed, providing only that this kind of information be disclosed 'immediately'.[32] That no clear time limit for timely disclosure proved to be one of the problems in the collapse of Enron in the USA. The fact that there is no time limit for disclosure means that there is no continuous disclosure.

In contrast, the Australian legislation requires that information that has a material effect on the price or value of securities be disclosed with Australian Securities and Investments Commission (ASIC) as soon as is practical.[33]

5.1.3.2.3.   The Criminal Law of 1979

Amendments to the Criminal Law of 1979 were made in March 1999, following the urgency of criminal punishment of securities offences that were not provided for in the previous Criminal Law. Later, more amendments to the Criminal Law of 1979 were made in June 2006 and February 2009 in compliance with the changes brought by the 2005 Company Law and Securities Law. The 1999 Amendments contain some articles that impose criminal liabilities on companies and their employees who are directly in charge of company business for false disclosure and misstatements.[34] These amendments constitute the criminal liabilities for breaches of disclosure rules. Before these amendments were made, there were only civil liabilities and administrative liabilities imposed on companies and employees directly in charge of company business.

Under Article 160 of the 1999 Amendments to the PRC Criminal Law, companies that have omitted material information or made false statements in the prospectus or the subscription of shares will be heavily fined; individuals who have engaged in the same type of conduct and are directly in charge of company business will be given detention or imprisonment of up to five years. Under Article 180, those with inside information (including companies and their directors) who leak information that will materially affect the prices of securities and cause serious effects will be sentenced to detention or an imprisonment of up to five years. They will also be fined between one to five times the amount of the

---

31. In both the PRC Securities Law and the 1993 Interim Regulations, annual reporting and half-yearly reporting are listed as continuous disclosure.
32. The PRC Securities Law of 1998, Art. 62; the 1993 Interim Regulations, Art. 60.
33. The Australian Corporations Act 2001 (Cth), s. 675(2).
34. The 1999 Amendments to the PRC Criminal Law, Arts 160 and 161.

illegal gains made by this conduct. If the situation is especially serious, they will be sentenced to imprisonment between five to ten years, as well as being required to pay one to five times the amount of the illegal gains made by this conduct. The 1999 Amendments particularly provide that the penalty of imprisonment or detention applies to the individuals who are responsible for a company's affairs, including company directors. For the conduct of forging and passing false information affecting securities transactions, if it is engaged in by an enterprise, this enterprise will be given a fine between CNY 10,000 to 100,000, and the individuals who are responsible for this conduct will be given criminal detention or imprisonment of up to five years, and/or a fine between CNY 10,000 to 100,000; in very serious circumstances, the imprisonment can be between five to ten years, and a fine between CNY 20,000 to 200,000 can be imposed.[35] These kinds of punishment have been retained in the 2006 Amendments to the Criminal Law.

There is a problem with the imposition of fines on companies and their employees directly in charge of company business. Under the Securities Law of 2005, a company employee who gives false statements or misstatements in the company financial report will be subject to a fine between CNY 10,000 to 100,000.[36] This fine is classified as an administrative fine under Chinese law. Under the Criminal Law, for the same kind of conduct, the employee directly in charge of company business is subject to a fine between CNY 20,000 to 200,000.[37] This fine is classified as criminal fine. Neither the Securities Law nor the Criminal Law clarifies whether a person may be subject to both kinds of fines or whether one fine may replace the other fine. As the courts in the PRC do not have the power to interpret law, there will be some difficulty for the courts in dealing with the application of criminal fines. According to the literal interpretation rule that is used in the PRC, most people likely think that, for the same conduct, an employee directly in charge of company business may be fined twice.

5.1.3.3. Disclosure Provisions under Administrative Regulations

5.1.3.3.1.   *The State Council's Interim Regulations on Administration of Share Issuing and Trading of 1993 (The 1993 Interim Regulations)*

Before the PRC Company Law was enacted at the end of 1993, the State Council had issued two provisional regulations: the Standard Opinions on Limited Liability Companies and the Standard Opinions on Joint Stock Limited Liability Companies in 1992 to standardize the conduct of these types of companies. In accordance with these two regulations, the State Council issued the 1993 Interim Regulations.

---

35. The PRC Criminal Law of 1979, Art. 181.
36. Article 193.
37. Article 161.

The 1993 Interim Regulations for the first time set out basic principles for share issuing and trading: openness, fairness, honesty, and accountability.[38] They further provide that all promoters and directors of a company must sign off on the prospectus.[39] They must ensure that there are no false or seriously misleading statements, nor any gross omissions in the prospectus. Joint and several liability is imposed for breaches of these provisions.[40] The adoption of these provisions makes it clear that the duty of information disclosure is not only imposed on the company, but also imposed on its directors. The 1993 Interim Regulations also require any major lawsuits or arbitration cases against the company or company directors, as well as details concerning the backgrounds of directors, to be disclosed.[41]

Under these Administrative Regulations, a listed company must also provide a listing announcement containing the shareholding structure and the ten biggest shareholders of the company, as well as the shareholdings of the directors.[42] In Chapter 6 of the Interim Regulations, a listed company is required to provide continuous disclosure documents (in actuality, periodic disclosure documents), including its annual report, its half-yearly report, and its interim report. The directors of the company have the duty to disclose information, although the listed company also has the same duty.

The 1993 Interim Regulations have laid the foundation for establishing the disclosure regime in the PRC. Some of its principles and provisions on disclosure were later incorporated into the Securities Law. Even after the enactment of the Securities Law, the 1993 Interim Regulations continue to be used as a supplementation to laws, although some of their provisions that are inconsistent with the Company Law and the Securities Law are automatically invalid under the general rules of Chinese law.

5.1.3.3.2.   *The Regulations on the Issue of Foreign Shares by Listed Companies inside China of 1995*

In December 1995, the State Council released the Regulations on the Issue of Foreign Shares by Listed Companies inside China so as to standardize the issue of B shares. Article 16 provides that listed companies seeking B-share issuance must disclose information to the public in accordance with the law. Although these regulations do not contain provisions that clearly impose a duty of disclosure on directors, Article 6 clearly provides that directors, supervisors, managers, and other senior managerial staff owe fiduciary duties to the company. As one of the aspects of fiduciary duty is the duty of disclosure, it can be argued that Article 6 implies that directors have the duty of information disclosure.

---

38. Article 3.
39. The 1993 Interim Regulations, Art. 17.
40. *Ibid.*
41. *Ibid.*, Art. 15.
42. *Ibid.*, Art. 34.

5.1.3.3.   *The Special Provisions on Share Issuing and Listing outside China by Listed Companies of 1994*

In August 1994, the State Council released the Special Provisions on Share Issue and Listing outside China by Listed Companies so as to standardize the issuing of H shares and N shares. According to Article 23 of this Administrative Regulation, the directors' duty of information disclosure is one aspect of directors' fiduciary duties to the company. According to Article 13, the SCSC has the power to make prerequisite articles in the company's articles of association. With the authorization of this Article, the SCSC and the SCRES jointly issued the Compulsory Provisions in the Articles of Association of Companies Seeking Listing outside China in August 1994. These prerequisite provisions contain more details about companies and directors' duty of information disclosure. Although the relevant regulatory power of the SCRES was transferred to the CSRC in 1998, when the SCRES was re-organized as an Office under the State Council, most of these provisions are still in use. This document mirrors the basic duties of directors provided in Articles 59–61 of the PRC Company Law. However, these duties are expressed in a more detailed form here.

5.1.3.4.   Disclosure Rules under Departmental Administrative Rules

5.1.3.4.1.   *Disclosure Rules in the Accounting Standards Set by the Ministry of Finance*

In the PRC, the Ministry of Finance is responsible for setting accounting standards. In 1992, for the first time, it released the Accounting Standards of Joint Stock Companies. Since then, the Ministry of Finance has been updating the accounting standards from time to time. For example, in 1997, it adopted Accounting Standards – Disclosure. On 15 February 2006, the MOF announced the establishment of the System of Enterprise Accounting Rules and the System of Enterprise Auditing Rules in compliance with the international accounting standards. These two systems were invalidated on 1 January 2007 and applied to listed companies. Other enterprises will gradually adopt these two systems.

5.1.3.4.2.   *Disclosure under the Administrative Rules and Other Regulatory Rules of the CSRC*

(i)   Rules Concerning Disclosure by Listed Companies

As mentioned above, the CSRC exercises the day-to-day administration of and supervision over the securities market. After examining common disclosure problems in the securities market in the early 1990s, the CSRC released several rules governing information disclosure before the PRC Company Law was enacted. In June 1993, the CSRC released the Implementation Rules on Information

Disclosure by Listed Companies (for Trial). Article 4 lists the minimum disclosure documents, including the prospectus, the listing announcement, the annual and half-yearly reports, and the interim report. Under Article 5, directors must ensure that there are no false or seriously misleading statements or gross omissions in the disclosed documents; when such misconduct occurs, the directors and the promoters must bear joint liability. Under Item 2 of Article 22, the personal details and shareholding of directors must be disclosed in the takeover announcement. Most provisions in this Administrative Rule were revised and adopted later in the detailed disclosure rules of the CSRC and the national laws. However, this Rule is still valid.

(ii)   Rules on Content and Format of Information Disclosure by Listed Companies (hereinafter Content and Format Rules)

From March 1993 until the end of 1997, the CSRC issued a vigorous set of rules on the content and format of information disclosure by listed companies. Since 1997, these rules have been amended from time to time to meet the changing needs of the PRC's securities market. Apart from amending these seven rules, the CSRC continues to issue other rules on the content and format of information disclosure. By mid 2009, the CSRC had released Rules No. 1–24 on Content and Format of Information Disclosure by Listed Companies. These Rules cover the main issues of information disclosure, including initial public offering prospectuses, annual reports, half-yearly reports, reports of changes in shareholding, share listing announcements, and prospectuses for issuing new shares. These Rules constitute the core of the corporate disclosure regime. The model of using these Rules comes from the Rules of the SEC in the USA.[43]

(iii)   Making and Reporting Rules Concerning Disclosure by Listed Companies

Since November 2000, the CSRC has been releasing Making and Reporting Rules Concerning Disclosure by Listed Companies to standardize disclosure in the implementation of the Content and Format Rules in specific industries such as finance, energy, and real estate property.[44] These rules are very detailed. Some cover how the Content and Format Rules should be applied in specific industries; some cover how the Content and Format Rules should be applied in takeovers and acquisitions; and some cover the further implementation of the Content and Format Rules. The CSRC realizes that the Making and Reporting Rules are urgently needed to be developed.[45]

---

43.   The CSRC (ed.), *Disclosure Requirements of China Securities Market 2001* (Beijing: Finance and Economics Publishing House, 2001), 1.
44.   *Ibid.*, 3.
45.   *Ibid.*

(iv)   Other Rules Regarding Disclosure

From time to time, the CSRC issues Circulars or Measures that contain disclosure provisions. For example, it released the Circular Concerning Engagement of Accounting Institutions by Companies to Issue Shares. This document requires companies that are to issue shares to provide profit-making forecasting materials. These regulatory rules of the CSRC are an important part of the disclosure regulatory regime.

(v)   Other Documents with Regulatory Purposes

In addition to formal rules, the CSRC also started releasing Questions and Answers Concerning Disclosure Standards by Listed Companies beginning in April 2001. These are the directives of the CSRC on particular questions raised by listed companies. These documents are not legally binding and thus they are only used for guidance to direct the conduct of listed companies. In practice, however, as the CSRC is the sole regulatory body of the securities market, most listed companies follow these Questions and Answers documents. On 31 October 2008, the CSRC decided to change it Questions and Answers documents into 'Interpreting Notices'.[46]

(vi)   Opinions on Individual Cases and Case Analysis

In 2001, the CSRC decided to publish its administrative decisions on the cases in breach of disclosure rules. The purpose was to increase the transparency of the CSRC and send a warning to other listed companies.

5.1.3.5.   Disclosure Provisions Concerning Disclosure in the Listing Rules and Business Rules of the Stock Exchanges

Both listing rules and business rules of the Shanghai and the Shenzhen Stock Exchanges have disclosure provisions. These provisions repeat the disclosure standards and contents adopted in laws, administrative regulations, departmental administrative rules, and further implement these rules regarding the content and standards of disclosure.

The two exchanges in mainland China were first established by the local governments with the approval of the central government. Their first listing rules were made by their local governments and were approved by the PBOC. However, Article 113 of the Securities Law of 1998 changed this practice. It clearly stated that the listing rules and business rules of the stock exchanges must be approved by the CSRC. In fact, when the two exchanges were transferred to the leadership of the CSRC in 1997, their listing rules (LRs) were unified by the CSRC as well.[47]

---

46.   CSRC Bulletin, 2008, No. 4.
47.   There are two articles that are different in the Listing Rules of the two stock exchanges.

The Shanghai and the Shenzhen Stock Exchanges started to use the same LRs in 2001 and these LRs were revised in 2004.[48] The Securities Law of 2005 maintains the CSRC's supervision over the stock exchanges.[49] In 2006, both the Shanghai and Shenzhen Stock Exchanges updated their listing rules and business rules in accordance with the Securities Law of 2005. The listing rules continue to mirror the criteria for disclosure, which have already been written into the Securities Law and summarize the information that should be disclosed.[50]

5.1.4.　　　BRIEF COMMENTS ON THE DISCLOSURE REGIME

As China' securities market is still in a transitional period, the CSRC has to update its regulatory rules from time to time to meet the needs of the market. This kind of updating is beneficial for directing the development of China's securities market, as the changes of the market often occur before the relevant laws are amended. In the Chinese legal system, as discussed in Chapter 2, laws have higher authority than the CSRC's rules. When the CSRC has updated its rules but the laws have not been amended, the authority of the CSRC rules will be undermined by other departments of the government, and even by the courts.

Laws often fall out of date soon after they are enacted. This frequently causes inconsistency between laws and other forms of regulatory rules in the PRC, as the amendment of laws usually take a very long time to happen. For example, the amendments of the Civil Procedure Law of 1992 took almost nine years to finish. The amendments of the Copyright Law took ten years to finish. The rapid changes of the CSRC's rules cannot wait for the changes of laws. Listed companies and investors often face the dilemma of deciding whether they should follow old laws or the CSRC's news rules whenever there is any inconsistency.

Apart from the inconsistencies between laws and rules, there are other problems with laws. Firstly, the Securities Law of 1998 did not have provisions on civil liabilities for breaches of market regulations, including breaches of disclosure rules. The innocent individual investors were left without effective legal protection until the civil liabilities were added in the Securities Law of 2005. Secondly, the Securities Law did not have provisions on litigation to protect minority shareholders' interests. For example, neither class actions nor derivative actions existed. Some had argued that the joint action under the Civil Procedure Law of 1992 could be used,[51] but these people ignored the fact that the purpose of a class action is different from a joint action. Even though the derivative action (called a shareholder representative action in the PRC) has been written into Article 152 of the

---

48. 'Major Events in China's Securities Market in 2004', *China Securities Daily,* 1 Jan. 2005, A07.
49. Article 118.
50. Listing Rules of the Shanghai and the Shenzhen Stock Exchanges 2006, Chs 4–7,
51. Xi, Xiaoming & Wen Jia, 'The Civil Compensation System on False Disclosure in the Securities Market: An Analysis of *Several Provisions on the Civil Compensation Cases of False Disclosure in the Securities Market* Release by the Supreme People's Court on 1 January 2003', *Securities Law Review* 3 (2003): 33–75 at 49.

Securities Law of 2005, this scheme is very confused one. Another problem is the poor enforcement of law in China.[52] These defects affect investors' confidence in the Chinese securities market.

5.2. MAJOR RULES DEALING WITH DISCLOSURE IN FUNDRAISING

5.2.1. DISCLOSURE IN INITIAL PUBLIC OFFERINGS (IPOs)

5.2.1.1. Sources of Rules on IPOs

The establishment of national securities markets in the PRC is modelled on the securities markets of Hong Kong, the USA, and other Western countries. In drafting its first Company Law and Securities Law, the PRC also drew upon lessons and experiences mainly from Hong Kong and the USA, although it also looked briefly at experiences of other Western countries, including Australia. Many legal ideas and concepts were borrowed from Western law.[53] However, the fundamental purposes of company and securities legislation in the PRC are different from those of Western countries. The Company Law of 1993 was enacted when China was at the beginning of establishing its modern enterprise system. It only generally adopts the principles of information disclosure and contains few detailed provisions on disclosure.[54] For a long time, the principles of information disclosure were only contained in the 1993 Interim Regulations. These Regulations not only contain the principles for information disclosure, but also contain many detailed provisions on the publication of the most important document of IPOs – the prospectus. To implement the 1993 Interim Regulations, the CSRC issued the Implementing Rules on Information Disclosure by Public Share Offering Companies in 1993. It lists the contents of information disclosure in more detail. As a day-to-day regulator, the CSRC accumulated more experience from China's securities market and has issued a set of standard rules on content and format for information disclosure since 1997. It also constantly updates these standard rules.

The rules governing IPOs in the PRC can be found in the following sources: the Company Law, the Securities Law; the 1993 Interim Regulations Concerning Administration of Share Issue and Trading; the Implementing Rules Concerning Disclosure, Rule No. 1 on Content and Format of Disclosure – Prospectus, Rule No. 7 of Content and Format of Disclosure – Notice of Share Listing, and Rule No. 9 on Content and Format of Disclosure – Documents for IPO Application.

---

52. This problem was analysed in Ch. 2.
53. See the CSRC (ed.), *Collection of Essays and Articles from the International Symposium on Securities Law Bill* (Beijing: Law Press, 1997).
54. The PRC Company Law of 1993, Arts 130 and 140.

5.2.1.2. IPOs and Offerings of Other Shares

In mainland China, there are two ways to set up a joint stock company: either by means of sponsorship or by means of a share offer.[55] The former means to incorporate a company by subscription from the sponsors of all the shares to be issued by the company. The latter means to incorporate a company through the sponsors' subscription of a portion of the shares while the rest of the shares are to be offered to the public by a public offer.[56] A joint stock company has been a new form of enterprise after the economic reform began. As most of the enterprises in the PRC are state-owned, the establishment of the modern enterprises system in China involves a large number of SOEs. Under the Company Law of 1993, the transformation from a state-owned enterprise to a joint stock company must be conducted by means of a public offering.[57] Up until now, most of the joint stock companies listed on the Shanghai or the Shenzhen Stock Exchange were still SOEs. Thus, in the PRC, most listed companies were incorporated in the latter way described above.

In the PRC, SOEs had been the subordinates of the government for a long time under the planned economic system. The adoption of the shareholding system in SOEs started later than its adoption in non-state-owned enterprises. The procedures for issuing shares reflect the strong control of the state. With the development of the economic reform, SOEs gradually moved towards a modern enterprise system. As a result, the shareholding system was adopted in SOEs, and it is being improved with the deepening of the PRC's economic reform. The shareholding system was first experimented in collective enterprises and then in SOEs.[58] In 1997, the State Council announced the ban on SOEs from issuing shares by public offering.[59] The experiment of share issuing by public offering in SOEs did not resume until 1989.[60]

At the beginning of the adoption of the shareholding system, there were three forms for share issuing: a public offer, pre-decided share issuing (*ding xiang fa xing*), and an internal offer (*nei bu fa xing*). With public offers, the ordinary public had equal rights to decide whether to accept the offer. The shares bought by the public were called public shares, which could be freely transferred. A pre-decided offer meant that the offer was made to particular entities or government departments. The pre-decided shares included legal entities' shares, which were bought by the legal entities, and state-owned shares, which were bought by the government departments before they were offered to the public.

---

55. *Ibid.*, Art. 74.
56. *Ibid.*
57. *Ibid.*, Art. 75.
58. The State Council, *Circular on Strengthening the Administration of Shares and Bonds 1987.*
59. *Ibid.*
60. The State Council, *Circular of the Key Points of the Economic System Reform by the State Commission for Economic Restructuring 1989* stated that only a few large and medium-sized enterprises would experiment with share issues by public offer.

Both state-owned shares and legal entity shares were not freely transferable until late 1999. State-owned shares and legal entity shares existed in state-owned companies, which were in a transitional period. At the beginning of the adoption of the shareholding system, there was debate on the great proportion of state-owned shares in the total numbers of the shares issued by SOEs. In 1999, the State Council selected two state-owned companies to conduct a trial of transferring the state-owned shares to the public shares. In June 2001, the State Commission of Economics and Trade issued the Interim Measures for Reduction of State-Owned Shares.[61] As there were hot debates over how state-owned shares should be converted into public shares, the CSRC had to release an urgent circular to stop the reduction of state-owned shares in August and call upon public submissions on how to reduce state-owned shares.[62] State-owned shares and legal shares are historical products and will disappear with the development of China's securities market. The problem of non-transferability of state-owned shares and legal shares was only solved in September 2005 by the State Council's regulation Measures for Reform of the Division of Shareholding in Listed Companies.

An internal offer is an offer made to a company's employees at a discounted price. Shares issued in this way are called internal employee shares (*nei bu zhi gong gu*). The purpose of issuing employee shares was to raise capital quickly and to stimulate the employees' concern for their company. The issuing of internal employee shares before the IPO ceased in 1999 because of the concerns about fairness to external public investors.

As the PRC government makes specific procedures for the issuing of state-owned shares, legal entity shares, and employee shares, this chapter will only discuss the issuing of shares offered to the public.

There are two major kinds of shares issued by the joint stock companies in the PRC securities market: A shares and B shares. As there were differences between these two types of shares in issuing purposes, issuing objectives, and trading currencies, there were common and separate rules for their IPOs. Because most shares listed on the Shanghai and the Shenzhen Stock Exchanges are A shares, the following part of this chapter mainly analyses disclosure requirements in the IPO of A shares and briefly discusses the disclosure requirements in the IPO of B shares. Another reason for this is that, since February 2001, the ban on Chinese citizens from trading in B shares has been lifted. The substantial differences between A shares and B shares have disappeared.

5.2.1.3. The Verification System Versus the Examination and Approval System in Public Offers of Company Shares

The issuance of shares is subject to different systems under the Securities Law and the Company Law. From the provisions in both Laws, it can be seen that although

---

61. Li, Zhangzhe, *Finally Successful: Development Report of Chinese Shares Market* (in Chinese) (Beijing: World Knowledge Press, 2000), 606.
62. <www.cs.com.cn>, August–October 2002.

the government's involvement in share issuing is being diminished, this involvement will continue to exist for some time. This constitutes one of the unique features of the PRC's securities regulation.

Under the Company Law of 1993, the establishment of a joint stock company must be approved by a body authorized by the State Council or by the local provincial government.[63] This system is called the examination and approval system. Under this system, to incorporate a joint stock company, the examinations and approvals from particular departments of the State Council are compulsory. These departments not only examine the form of the joint stock company's application documents for public offer, but they also examine the substantial contents, including the truthfulness, accuracy, and completeness of the application documents, credibility, business operation, the future of the company, and the amount and price of the shares. Articles 163–166 of the Company Law of 1993 provide that issuing company bonds is subject to the examination and approval system. Articles 139, 131, and 12 of the 1993 Interim Regulations, which was enacted before the Securities Law, also clearly state that share issuing before 1999 was still subject to the examination and approval system.

Under the examination and approval system, the state controlled the quota for the issuance of shares. The quota system was one of the reflections of the Chinese government's cautious attitude toward the development of the securities market. The State Development Planning Commission[64] used to make an annual national shares issuing scheme, which set out the total amount of shares to be issued, the types of the shares, the category of the issuers, and the way to issue shares.[65] The quota was then allocated among the central government and the provincial governments. At the central government level, the quota was allocated among the ministries. The relevant ministries selected some SOEs and recommended them to the central government to issue shares. The recommendations needed to be approved by the State Development Planning Commission. Some of the quotas were allocated among provincial governments. Provincial governments, along with their relevant departments, selected the provincial enterprises to be recommended for share issuing. The CSRC conducted the final review of these recommendations and decided what shares could be issued. This review was a substantial one. It not only examined the forms of the share issuance, but also the contents of the share issuance. Under this system, the government was heavily involved in the administration and supervision of securities issues.[66] The securities market was a market strongly controlled and directed by the government. This was a key feature of a transitional economy.

There were many reasons why the examination and approval system was adopted. Firstly, China's securities market had a very short history, and the relevant regulatory system was underdeveloped. Secondly, the reforms in state-owned

---

63. *Ibid.*, Art. 77.
64. In March 2003, it was renamed as the State Development and Reform Commission.
65. Ye, Lin, *Chinese Securities Law* (Beijing: China Auditing Press, 1999), 38.
66. Ye, Lin, *Chinese Securities Law*, 140.

enterprises, finance, and investment were still evolving, and many issuers were not clear about how to behave professionally. Lastly, the investors in the securities market did not have enough knowledge about the risks in the securities market. At the beginning of the emergence of the PRC securities market, such a system was necessary. However, as there were so many government departments involved in the decision-making of share issuing by joint stock companies, there had been many problems under this system. For instance, all the share issues were capped at the quota decided upon and allocated by the central government. As discussed in the previous chapter, the quota system had caused an inequity between central government-owned enterprises and local government-owned enterprises. This practice caused some damage to the interests of shareholders. After ten years of the practice of capital raising by issuing shares, the issuing of shares has been moving towards the direction that is used in Western countries. Therefore, it is time to move to a more flexible regulatory regime.

The examination system is similar to the old pre-vetting procedure in Australia. The PRC Securities Law of 1998 abolished this examination and approval system by requiring that a share issue by means of a public offer must be certified by the CSRC as well as fulfil other requirements of the Company Law of 1993.[67] The new system is called the verification system. Under this system, the sponsors of the company must submit application documents for public offer to the CSRC. The CSRC has a Share Issue Examination and Approval Committee (*fa shen wei*) to assess the application and make recommendation to the CSRC.[68] The Securities Law of 2005 confirmed this practice.[69]

Although one of the purposes of the Securities Law of 1998 was to diminish the government's direct involvement in the securities market by the abolition of the quota for share issuing, the final context did not set out what the legislators had expected because of the objection from the central government. Under Article 11 of the Securities Law, the quota system had continued to exist for some time. The procedures for the share issuing applications have not been simplified. Instead, the procedures are becoming more and more complicated as a result of the enhancement of the involvement of the CSRC.

However, there is one revision for the certification of the CSRC. The CSRC no longer substantially examines the contents of the applications as the applicants have the duty to ensure truthfulness, accuracy, and completeness of the application documents.[70] The CSRC will only look at the forms of the application documents and then make a decision on an application. It will not make a judgment on the value of the shares to be issued. The sponsors for share issuing must provide the application documents, including the business operation of the company, the financial report and accounting report, the members of the board of directors, the

---

67. The PRC Securities Law, Art. 11.
68. *Ibid.*, Art. 14; Wang, Lianzhou & Cheng Li, *Uneasy Securities Law* (Shanghai: Shanghai Sanlian Bookshop Press, 2000) 297.
69. Article 22
70. *Ibid.*, Art. 13.

credibility of its main managerial staff, the means of public offer, the price for shares, and the usage of fundraising. The sponsors are also required to guarantee the truthfulness, accuracy, and completeness of the documents. The examination and approval system for share issuing was used at the beginning of the re-emergence of the share market for the purpose of ensuring the healthy and stable development of the newly emerging securities market. The certification system is in need of a developed and more mature market. The Securities Law was intended to adopt the verification system for shares in need of the development of the market. In practice, this system, however, is very difficult to implement. Firstly, the state still controls the major decision-making of state-owned companies and would be reluctant to allow all the SEOs that wish to become listed to do what they want. Secondly, the quota system has not been completely abolished, even though it lost its legitimate foundation of existence under the Securities Law of 1998. The Law only does not allow new quotas to be issued.

Currently, to issue shares by public offer, a company must meet the requirements of the Company Law of 1993 and the 1993 Interim Regulations.[71] These requirements include the following:

(i) Production and management of the company must conform to the industrial policies of the State;

(ii) Only one kind of ordinary shares may be issued with equal shares for equal shares;

(iii) The promoters' shares capital must not constitute less than 35% of the total shares capital;

(iv) Of the total shares to be issued by a company, the promoters' shares must not be less than CNY 30 million, except otherwise provided for by the State;

(v) The shares offered to the public must not be less than 25% of the total share capital to be issued. Of these shares company employee-owned shares must not exceed 10% of the amount to be issued to the public; if the total amount of the shares to be issued is in excess of CNY 400 million, the CSRC may reduce the portion to be issued to the public; however, the minimum portion must be more than 10% of the total shares;

(vi) The promoters have no major violations of the PRC law in the past three consecutive years; and

(vii) Other requirements set by the CSRC.[72]

These requirements are for the incorporation of new joint stock companies. If an existing state-owned enterprise is going to be transferred into a joint stock company, it must meet the following requirements, as well as the above:

(i) The net assets account for more than 30% of the total assets and the intangible assets account for no more than 20% of the net assets at the

---

71. The PRC Securities Law, Art. 11; the PRC Company Law, Art. 131.
72. The Interim Regulations on Administration of Share Issue and Trading of 1993, Art. 8.

end of the year prior to the year when the issue takes place, except otherwise provided for by the CSRC;

(ii) The company has been making profits for three consecutive years; and

(iii) Other requirements provided for by the CSRC.[73]

5.2.1.4.   Procedures for IPOs

The procedures for IPOs reflect the requirements for disclosure. Before the enactment of the Securities Law, these procedures were very complicated. The old procedures were mainly provided for in the 1993 Interim Regulations:[74]

(i) The applicant for an IPO must hire an accounting firm, an assets appraisal organization, a law firm and other professional institutions to examine and appraise their credit status, assets and financial situation and prepare legal statements. Then the applicant must lodge application documents with the government of the relevant province, autonomous region or municipality directly under the control of the central government (if the applicant is an enterprise under the control of a local government) or the department in charge of enterprises of the central government (if the applicant is an enterprise under the control of the central government);

(ii) According to the size of issuing set by the state, the relevant local government must examine and approve the share issue applications by local government-owned enterprises; the department in charge of enterprises at the central government must examine and approve the share issue applications by the central government-owned enterprises. The responsible local government or the department of the central government must make a decision of approval or disapproval within thirty working days after the application is received. The decisions of both governments must also be submitted to the CSRC;

(iii) The decision of approval by the local government or the central government department must be sent to the CSRC for review. The CSRC must give its findings within twenty working days after the review application is received. After receiving the consent of the CSRC, the share issue applicant must apply to the listing committee under the stock exchange for share issue and listing. With the approval from the stock exchange the issuer may start to issue shares.

It is not hard to draw the conclusion that the procedures for share issuing applications in China are very bureaucratic and time-consuming, and the application for share issuing is a very slow process. These cannot meet the urgent needs of capital by enterprises. The provisions in the Securities Law aim to change the old system and establish a more efficient share issuing system for Chinese enterprises.

---

73. *Ibid.*, Art. 9.
74. *Ibid.*, Art. 12.

Unfortunately, the old procedures continued to be used for some time even after the enactment of the Securities Law of 1998 because of the lack of implementing rules.

The CRSC's Procedures for Verification of Share Issue was not released until 16 March 2000. Under this Administrative Rule, there are five procedures that a company applying for share issue must follow:

(i) The company, after the approval of the relevant provincial government or the relevant ministry of the State Council, must prepare and submit application documents to the CSRC. The CSRC will make a decision on whether to accept or reject the application within five working days after the application is lodged;

(ii) Once the application is accepted, the CSRC will have a preliminary review of the application documents. The CSRC will notify the applicant and its main underwriter of its preliminary review opinion within thirty days of the acceptance of the application. The applicant may have to lodge supplementary application materials. The CSRC must also ask for the opinions of the State Development Planning Commission and the State Commission of Economics and Trade;[75]

(iii) The CSRC shall transfer the application documents and its preliminary review results to the Share Issuing Verification Commission[76] within sixty days after the acceptance of the application documents;

(iv) The Share Issuing Verification Commission makes the decision on whether or not the share issue application is verified with reasons within three months after the application documents are received;

(v) The applicant whose application has been rejected may apply for an administrative review of the decision by the Share Issuing Verification Commission within sixty days after receiving the written decision. The CSRC should make a decision on whether an administrative review is to be conducted within sixty days after receiving the review application.

These procedures are much simpler than the old ones, but there are still some problems. First, from the time when the application for share issuing is lodged until the time when the decision of administrative review is made, it may take as long as 155 days. This long process still affects the efficiency of the securities market. Second, there are doubts about the necessity of the approval of the provincial governments and the ministries of the State Council on the applications by private enterprises.

While these procedures are still in use, the Securities Law of 2005 also requires the applicant enterprise to have sponsors. The IPO sponsorship system was first introduced by the CSRC in its Provisional Measures on Securities Issuing

---

75. The opinions of the State Development and Reform Commission are needed now. The State Commission of Economics and Trade was later merged into the Ministry of Commerce.
76. This is a commission under the CSRC and consists of external experts and internal officials of the CSRC.

and Listing Sponsorship System. This system was based on the UK model.[77] Article 12 of the Securities Law of 2005 has a list of the documents to be submitted to the CSRC for the IPO application. A prospectus as a major disclosure document must be included with other IPO application documents.

5.2.1.5. Application Documents for IPOs

As mentioned above, neither the Company Law of 1993 nor the 1993 Interim Regulations had been amended after the Securities Law of 1998 was enacted until 2005. Thus, share issuing and trading had to follow the old rules, which were made before the Securities Law was enacted in 1998. To meet the requirements for public share offers, the issuer must submit application documents and other supporting documents to the CSRC. Under the requirements set out in the Company Law, the Securities Law, and the 1993 Interim Regulations, the issuer must submit the following documents to the CSRC:

 (i) application for share issue;
 (ii) the resolution of the promoters' meeting, or the shareholders' meeting on share issue by public offer;
 (iii) the approval documents of establishment of the joint stock company;
 (iv) the business license or the establishment registration of the issuer granted by the Administration for Industry and Commerce;
 (v) the articles of association or the draft articles of association of the joint stock company;
 (vi) the prospectus;
 (vii) a feasibility study report on utilization of the funds and documents of approval issued by the relevant government departments concerning investment projects on fixed assets;
 (viii) the company's financial report for the last three years or since its establishment, which has been audited by an accounting firm, and the auditing report which has been signed by two registered accountants and sealed with the seal of the accounting firm;
 (ix) legal statement signed by at least two lawyers and sealed by their law firm;
 (x) an assets appraisal report signed by at least two professional appraisal personnel and sealed by their offices, a capital rating report signed by at least two registered accountants and sealed by their offices, and the confirmation document by the state assets management department if state assets are involved;
 (xi) the underwriting plan and the underwriting agreement; and
 (xii) other documents required by the CSRC.

---

77. Li, Fei (ed.), *Annotation to the Securities Law 2005* (Beijing: Law Press, 2005), 18.

5.2.1.6. Prospectus

The most important document containing information about IPO is the prospectus. Under the Securities Law of 2005, the issuer must submit the application documents for share issuing to the CSRC according to the requirements in the Company Law.[78] The Company Law of 2005 requires the company to publicize the prospectus when issuing new shares.[79] The 1993 Interim Regulations requires the issuer to publicize the prospectus from the second to the fifth working day before the public offer.[80] Under the Implementing Rules on Enforcement of Information Disclosure by Public Share Offer Companies (for Trial) issued by the CSRC in 1993, companies limited by shares must prepare a prospectus to disclose relevant information to the public.[81] This implementing document includes standard rules on the content and format of prospectuses.

As the shareholding system was new to state-owned companies, the CSRC issued Rule No.1 on Content and Format of Prospectus to guide the shareholding companies in 1997. Since then, the CSRC has revised this document constantly to meet the needs and changes of practices. This Administrative Rule has four chapters and about two hundred articles. One of the principles in this Rule is that the provisions in this Rule are the minimum requirements for disclosure and any information that may have material impact on an investment decision must be disclosed.[82] This Rule also clearly states that the board of directors as a whole and directors individually must ensure truthfulness, accuracy, and completeness of disclosure, and have joint and several liability for any false or misleading statements or major omissions.[83] Rule No. 1 has a standard format for a prospectus:

   (i) format requirements: the cover page of a prospectus; the catalogue of a prospectus; the appendix; a reminder of reading the auditing report; interpretations of key concepts

  (ii) the content of the prospectus contains: names of the issuer, shareholders, and purpose of share issue;

 (iii) the summary of the issuing;

 (iv) general information about this issuing, such as the classification of shares, the issuing price, and the face value per share; the shareholding structure of the company; the usage of the capital to be raised; distribution of profits

  (v) investment risks;

 (vi) detailed information about the issuer;

(vii) scope of business and technical support;

(viii) competition and related party transactions;

---

78. The PRC Securities Law of 2005, Art. 12.
79. Article 135.
80. The 1993 Interim Regulations on Administration of Share Issuing and Trading, Art. 19.
81. Article 6.
82. Article 3.
83. Article 18.

(ix) details of directors, supervisors, senior managerial staff, and major technical staff;

(x) corporate governance scheme;

(xi) accounting and finance information

(xii) targets of the company;

(xiii) proposed use of the raised capital;

(xiv) share issuing price setting and profits sharing policy;

(xv) other major items;

(xvi) statement of directors, accounting firm, law firm, and assets appraisal firm.[84]

When the issuer releases a prospectus, it must also publicize the share listing notice.

In addition to compliance with Rule No. 1 and Rule No. 7, the issuer must prepare IPO documents according to the requirements in Rule No. 9 on Content and Format for Disclosure – Application Documents for IPOs. Rule No. 9 requires all directors of the issuer and the issuer's consulting bodies to ensure truthfulness, accuracy, and completeness of the application documents.[85]

5.2.1.7. Procedures for B-Share Issuing

As mentioned above, A shares and B shares have different objects and are traded in different currencies. Therefore, B-share issuing follows different procedures. From these procedures, we can see that there are some different disclosure requirements in these two kinds of share issuing.

The Securities Law of 1998 authorizes the State Council to make rules concerning the issuing and trading of B shares.[86] This authority maintains provisions of the Securities Law of 2005.[87] Until now, the State Council has not released new rules regarding B-share issuing to implement the Securities Law provisions. Under these circumstance, B-share issuing follows the old rules contained in the State Council's Provisions Concerning Listing of Foreign-Invested Shares by Joint Stock Companies inside China of 1995 and the SCSC's Implementing Rules Concerning Listing of Foreign-Invested Shares by Joint Stock Companies of 1996. B shares were originally issued inside the PRC to investors residing outside the PRC. The procedures for issuing B shares have the following characteristics:

(i) The issuing of B shares must be approved by the CSRC (formerly by the SCSC) if the face value of the proposed shares is less than USD 30 million; or if the face value of the proposed shares is more than USD 30 million; the

---

84. Chapter 2.
85. Article 7.
86. Article 213.
87. Article 239.

issue application must be lodged with the CSRC and then passed to the State Council by the CSRC and get approval by the State Council.[88]

(ii) The total amount of B shares to be issued must be within the total share issue quota.

(iii) B-share investors include foreign natural persons, legal persons and other organizations; natural persons, legal persons and other organizations of Hong Kong, Macau and Taiwan; Chinese citizens residing overseas; other investors prescribed by the SCSC (later CSRC).

(iv) To incorporate a company by public offer of B shares, the following requirements must be met.

    (a) The capital to be raised by B-share offers must be used in line with state industrial policies.

    (b) B-share issues must comply with the state regulation on fixed assets investment.

    (c) The promoter must subscribe no less than 35% of the shares to be issued, the total capital invested by the issuer must not be less than CNY 150 million.

    (d) The shares to be issued to the public must account for 25% or more of the total capital. If the proposed share capital is more than CNY 400 million, the shares to be offered to the public must be 15% or more of the total number of shares.

    (e) The company has not had any major illegal acts in the past three consecutive years.

    (f) The company has made profits in the past three consecutive years.

    (g) Other requirements prescribed by the SCSC (or CSRC).[89]

(v) compared with the requirements for A-share issues, the requirements for B-share issues have similar features as A-share issues:The issuer has to lodge an application to the local government or the central government. It also needs the recommendation to the SCSC (or the CSRC) from either the local government or the relevant department of the central government.

(vi) The SCSC (later, the CSRC), together with the relevant department of the State Council, selects the companies that are approved to issue B shares.

(vii) The company approved to issue B shares must submit the prescribed documents to the CSRC for verification.

(viii) Once the application is verified by the CSRC, it will be submitted to the SCSC for issue approval (after the SCSC was dismantled in early 1998, this procedure is no longer required).[90]

It can be seen from the above that B-share issues was also subject to the national share issue quota. However, which applications should be lodged with the local

---

88. The State Council, *Provisions Concerning Listing of Foreign-invested Shares by Joint Stock Companies inside China 1995*, Art. 2.
89. *Ibid.*, Art. 8.
90. *Ibid.*

government and which applications should be lodged with the central government are not clear and will cause confusion in practice. The companies to issue B shares were selected by the SCSC (or the CSRC), but are required to be approved again by the SCSC (or CSRC) after verification by the CSRC. This repeated approval has no substantial function except that it causes a delay of B-share issuing. It does no good for providing an efficient securities market. The allocation of B-share quotas is also not transparent.

To issue B shares, an applicant must submit the following documents to the CSRC:

    (i) the application report;
   (ii) the name of the issuer, the amount of shares subscribed by the issuer, the types of investment and the capital verification report;
  (iii) the resolution of the promoters in favour of B-share issue;
  (iv) the approval document of the State Council authorized department or the local government;
   (v) recommendation by local government or the department in charge of enterprises under the State Council (namely the State Commission for Economy and Trade);
  (vi) the approval notice of the enterprise named by the State Administration for Commerce and Industry;
 (vii) the draft articles of company association;
(viii) the prospectus;
  (ix) the report of feasibility of capital usage;
   (x) the financial reports of the enterprise in the past three years which are audited by a registered account and his/her accounting firm, and the auditing report by the registered account and his/her accounting firm;
  (xi) an assets appraisal report signed by two professional appraisers and their institutions; if state-owned assets are involved, confirmation and approval documents on state-owned equity issued by the State Assets Administration must also be provided;
 (xii) a legal advice report on relevant share issues signed by two or more lawyers and sealed by their law firms;
(xiii) an underwriting proposal and underwriting agreement on B-share issue; and
(xiv) other documents required by the CSRC.[91]

B-share issuing must also meet the information disclosure requirements. A company that intends to issue B shares is required to have detailed provisions on information disclosure in its articles of association, including the place of disclosure and the means of disclosure.[92] The prospectus of B-share issuing must

---

91. *Ibid.*, Art. 11.
92. *Ibid.*, Art. 16.

be made according to the requirements of Chinese laws and regulations. It must also meet the criteria of truthfulness, accuracy, and completeness.[93]

The documents on B-share issuing must be prepared in Chinese. A commonly used foreign language should also be prepared if necessary. If there is any ambiguity between the Chinese version and the version in a foreign language, the Chinese version prevails.[94]

As from February 2001, Chinese citizens living inside China are allowed to invest in the B-shares market. There are not many differences between A-share issuing and B- share issuing.

5.2.1.8.   Overview of Disclosure Rules Regarding IPOs

The above section has analysed the various sources of disclosure rules regarding IPOs. It has examined not only the requirements, the procedures, and the application documents for A-share issuing, but also the contents for B-share issuing. From the provisions of Chinese laws, regulations, and rules, the conclusion can be drawn that the co-existence of A shares and B shares was for the purpose of absorbing foreign capital. It is also a result of the existence of non-convertible CNY. This co-existence will continue for some time even though the PRC government tried to solve the problem of price differences of shares of the same company caused by the two kinds of shares in its domestic market by allowing Chinese citizens living inside China to trade B shares from 19 February 2001. It also can be seen that the IPO market in China is still in an infancy stage. The procedures for share issuing are very complex and time consuming.

At this time, the governments both at central and local levels still enjoy too many powers of controlling the securities market. This may be necessary, given China's current stage of development. However, it does affect the efficiency of the market and increases the cost for share issuance. Unfairness can easily happen. Lack of competition is another factor that prevents the securities market from moving towards efficiency. In the long run, the role of the government should be reduced so as to meet the needs of a market economy. To improve the efficiency of China's securities market, China should reduce its strong government involvement in the IPO process.

5.3.   CONTINUOUS DISCLOSURE

Articles 63–72 of the Securities Law of 2005 especially deal with continuous disclosure. However, under those articles, the concept of continuous disclosure

---

93. The SCSC, *Implementing Rules on ForeignInvested Share Issue by Joint Stock Companies inside China1996*, Article 12.
94. The Listing Rules of the SSE and the SZSE, Art. 17.

has been confused with periodic disclosure; while in Western countries, continuous disclosure and periodic disclosure are two different concepts.

The term 'continuous disclosure' is not used in the State Council's 1993 Regulation. However, the content of continuous disclosure was already set in that Regulation.

Since 7 January 2002, listed companies have been required to implement the Code of Corporate Governance in Listed Companies jointly released by the CSRC and the State Economics and Trade Commission. Chapter 7 of this Administrative Rule is entitled Information Disclosure and Transparency. The standards for disclosure are again written into this Code.[95] Listed companies are called to timely disclosure for all information that may have a material impact on the decision-making of shareholders and other stock holders in listed companies.[96] This Regulation also clarifies the responsibilities of secretaries of the boards of directors of listed companies. Moreover, this Regulation for the first time required listed companies to disclose information about corporate governance of the companies.[97] This information must include (i) the directors and supervisors of the company and their backgrounds; (ii) the work of the board of directors and the supervisory board and the evaluation on their work; (iii) the work of independent directors and their evaluation; (iv) the structure of the committees of the company and their work; and (v) the plan and measures for improving corporate governance.[98]

Disclosure of corporate governance is a result of international corporate governance practices. This code shows that the PRC securities market continues its rapid development.

5.4. SPECIAL DISCLOSURE RULES OF THE CSRC

Apart from the Rules on Content and Format of Information Disclosure, which are about general disclosure, and the Rules on Making Disclosure, which are specific rules on particular types of companies, the CSRC has also released special rules on particular kinds of disclosure. For example, the CSRC released Rules on Disclosure by Securities Investment Funds in July 2004. Since June 2004, the CSRC started releasing Rules on Content and Format of Disclosure by Securities Investment Funds.

---

95. Article 87.
96. Article 88.
97. Article 91.
98. *Ibid.*

5.5.   MAJOR ISSUES ON DISCLOSURE

5.5.1.   THE THEORIES OF GOVERNMENT REGULATION
OF THE SECURITIES MARKET

The economists in the PRC have observed seven basic functions of the securities market.[99] Firstly, the process of selling and buying of shares is in essence a process of allocation and re-allocation of capital resources. Secondly, the securities market provides investors with another way of investment and therefore enhances the efficiency of investments. Thirdly, investment in the securities market is a way in which investors evaluate the operation of companies and encourages the companies to improve their operation. Fourthly, what investors buy and sell are not the value of the securities themselves but rather the prospective profits that may come with holding the securities at some with risk. Fifthly, securities capital is movable, and this provides the incentive for companies to improve their operations. Sixthly, the securities market speeds up the interchange of information and reduces transaction costs. Finally, for the government, the securities market is an effective means to maintain macro-economic control.[100]

PRC economists have also noted that a fully functioning market depends on an effective securities market.[101] However, in reality, such a securities market does not exist. The reality is that market failure causes the low efficiency of resource allocation. This reality provides the basis for the government to regulate the securities market. PRC economists believe that in Western countries, the market failure theory became the basis for government regulation. The original purpose for securities regulation was to overcome failures and improve the securities market.[102]

Information is the most important factor that affects the function of the securities market. Information failure is the major reflection of market failure. The regulation of disclosure naturally becomes the most important part of securities regulation and the focus of the regulatory body.[103] According to the First Chief Counsel of the CSRC, Gao Xiqing, the most common and serious breach of law in the securities market is directly related to the width, depth, and timeliness of disclosure.[104] His ideas have had a strong influence in forming China's disclosure rules. To ensure fair access to information is the key to enhancing the investors' confidence and protecting the investors' interests. Only securities regulation can ensure the completeness and symmetry of information so as to reduce information failures.

---

99. Hong, Weili, *Securities Regulation: Theory and Practice* (Shanghai: Shanghai Finance and Economic Press, 2000), 19–26.
100. *Ibid.*
101. *Ibid.*, 34.
102. *Ibid.*
103. *Ibid.*, 84.
104. Gao XiQing, 'Compulsory Disclosure System and the Effectiveness of the Securities Market', *Shanghai Securities,* 25 Feb. 1997, 1.

In the USA, there were two major approaches on disclosure regulation. The approach of mandatory disclosure aims at avoiding market failure caused by fraud and insider trading. Justice Louis Brandeis was the most well-known person to advocate mandatory disclosure.[105] The other theory was against mandatory disclosure. There was a situation that, in the first two years after the SEC was established, the share prices did not change as a result of mandatory disclosure. George Stigler used this case to argue that compulsory disclosure did not increase the profits of investors and therefore it was ineffective.[106] It was the Great Depression of 1929–1932, which was caused by fraud, false disclosure, and manipulation, that made the US securities market break down. This breakdown of the securities market led the US government to adopt mandatory regulation, including mandatory disclosure.

In the PRC, there was little theoretical research on disclosure systems during the drafting of the first Company Law and the Securities Law.[107] The CSRC's issuance of a number of disclosure rules was mainly driven by the occurrence of numerous cases of serious breaches of openness, fairness, and justice principles in corporate disclosure.

5.5.2.   WHY SHOULD THE PRC ADOPT COMPULSORY DISCLOSURE?

In the USA, apart from Stigler's theory, which opposed compulsory disclosure, the US Congress held an anti-regulatory ideology in the 1990s. Then Chairman of the House of Representative's Commission on Telecommunications and Finance, Jack Fields, made a proposal to delete the provisions on protection of investors and reduce investors' access to information. His arguments were the following: this might reduce costs in the securities market; mandatory disclosure might legalize misleading conduct; the SEC's full disclosure requirement might weaken the agents' power; and finally, these would reduce the costs of the SEC.[108]

What kind of disclosure regulation a country should adopt depends on the development of its economy. Taking the PRC as an example, the government has always been actively involved in almost every aspect of the country. Without a sound financial system and a developed market, regulation by the government will not ensure the establishment and improvement of the domestic capital market and financial system because past regulation has made the market solution impossible.[109] Another major reason for compulsory disclosure in a new market

---

105. L. Brandeis, *Other People's Money and How the Bankers Use It* (Chevy Chase: National Home Library Foundation, 1933), 62.
106. G. Stigler, 'Public Regulation of the Securities Market', *Journal of Business of the University of Chicago* 37, no. 2 (1964).
107. Gao, Xiqing's article mentioned in n. 104 is one of the few influential ones on theoretical debates.
108. R. Simon, 'How Washington Could Tip the Scales against Investors', *Money* (1995): 122–128.
109. The World Bank, *World Development Report 1989* (Beijing: China Finance and Economics Press, 1989), 3.

economy such as that of China is that a country with a new securities market faces the serious problem of information failure. Slow economic development, less development of the information industry, and a lack of sound information law make the new securities market a weak one with asymmetry, manipulation, and fraud. These require the government to adopt rigid and direct regulation of the market.

Shareholders make investment decisions based on the information disclosed to them. The nature of the securities market is to provide shareholders with an open and fair trading site. This requires the securities market to adopt three principles, namely openness, fairness, and justice.[110] Information disclosure is an effective way to implement these three rules. What kind of information must be disclosed? To what extent should it be disclosed? How should it be disclosed? These questions suggest that the Securities Law should set out the criteria for disclosure.

5.5.3.   CRITERIA FOR DISCLOSURE

As discussed in previous chapters, openness, fairness, and justice are three principles that are believed to be fundamental to the disclosure system.[111] Openness means that all the significant events on investments must be disclosed, all the securities regulations are to be published, and all information and state policies must be published. Fairness means that all the market participants, such as listed companies, investors, and securities firms, are equal under the law. Justice means that disclosure should be given to all investors, not just selected investors.

The principles of truthfulness, accuracy, and completeness were first established in the 1993 Interim Regulations.[112] They were reiterated in the Implementing Rules on Information Disclosure of the CSRC (for Trial) of 1993[113] and the Securities Law.[114] Some people held the view that, in addition to these three principles, another principle – that of timeliness – was necessary.[115] However, it is very hard to define what timely disclosure means.[116]

Truthfulness means that issuers of shares must disclose true information. The issuers must not disclosure false information. Accuracy means that the information disclosed must be clear, accurate, and not misleading. Completeness means that the information disclosed must be complete and without major omissions.

---

110. The PRC Securities Law 2005, Art. 3.
111. Lu, Fengqiang, *Legal Analysis of Information Disclosure* (Beijing: People's Courts Press, 2000), 23.
112. The PRC Securities Law of 1998, Arts 17, 18, and, 21.
113. Article 5.
114. Article 3 of the Securities Laws of 1998 and 2005.
115. Ye, Lin, *Chinese Securities Law* (in Chinese) (Beijing: China Auditing Press, 1999), 149; Qi, Bin, *Legal Supervision of Information Disclosure in the Securities Market* (in Chinese) (Beijing: Law Press, 2000), 118.
116. Hu, YZ, *Legal Supervision of the Securities Market* (in Chinese) (Beijing: China Legal System Press, 1999), 41.

5.5.4.   WHAT SHOULD BE DISCLOSED?

To disclose complete information does not mean that an issuer of shares must disclose everything about the issuance. It only requires that an issuer disclose major facts that may have a material effect on the share price.[117]
  Such major facts include the following:

  (i) major contracts entered into by the company which may have substantial effect on the company assets, debts, interests and/or operation;
  (ii) major changes in company operation policy or operation projects;
  (iii) the company's major investment or purchase of expensive long term assets;
  (iv) the company's major debts;
  (v) the company's breach of contract by not paying debts due;
  (vi) the company's major losses;
  (vii) major damage to the company assets;
  (viii) major change in the company's operational environment;
  (ix) newly released laws, regulations and rules which may have a material effect on company business;
  (x) the change of the chairman of the board of directors, or a change of 30% or more of company directors, or a change of the general manager;
  (xi) the increase or decrease of one type of shares held by a shareholder who holds more than 5% of the company's shares;
  (xii) major lawsuits involving the company; and
  (xiii) liquidation or insolvency of the company.[118]

The above is a very detailed list of the major facts that should be disclosed by a company, However, this does not mean those facts must be disclosed at every disclosure. Under certain circumstances, the duty of disclosure may be waived by the CSRC. If the issuer has strong reasons to believe that disclosure of some material facts to the public may bring damage to the interests of the company, and non-disclosure will not cause a material change of the share price, it may not disclose this information with the agreement of the stock exchange.[119] It is widely accepted that commercial secrets do not need to be disclosed.
  Currently, in the PRC, there is only one kind of disclosure document for the initial share issuance – the prospectus. However, in Western countries, other alternative disclosure documents have been accepted.[120] Thus, the PRC's disclosure rules were made for the punishment of securities fraud, and market efficiency is not one of the considerations. Since the first release of Rule No. 1 on Content and Format of Disclosure – Prospectus in 1993, the CSRC has revised this document

---

117. The 1993 Interim Regulations, Art. 60.
118. *Ibid.*
119. *Ibid.*
120. For example, under Ch. 6D of the Australian Corporations Act of 2001 (Cth), disclosure documents include prospectuses, profile statements, and offer information statements.

several times. The last substantial changes were passed in 2001. These changes contain very detailed provisions on the prospectus. There are about 180 articles in this document. Rule No. 1 not only repeats the criteria of disclosure provided in laws and administrative regulations, but it also lists the information to be included in the prospectus. It requires listed companies to disclose risks, related party transactions, and the corporate governance structures of the companies.

The Securities Law of 1998 authorizes the State Council to make rules concerning the issue and trading of B shares.[121] To date, the State Council has not released new rules to update the regulation concerning B-share issuing. Under this circumstance, B-share issuing still follows the old rules reflected in the State Council's Provisions Concerning Listing of Foreign-Invested Shares by Joint Stock Companies inside China of 1995 and the SCSC's Implementing Rules Concerning Listing of Foreign-Invested Shares by Joint Stock Companies of 1996. With the opening of B shares market to Chinese citizens living inside China since February 2001, there are no longer substantial differences between A shares and B shares, except that these two kinds of shares are traded in different currencies. Consequently, the disclosure rules released after 2001 apply to both A and B shares.

One important aspect of enhanced information disclosure in Western countries is continuous disclosure. Listed companies not only have a duty of information disclosure when they initially issue their shares, but they also have a duty to continuously disclose any material information that may have a material effect on the trading of the companies' shares. The Australian Corporations Act of 2001 has a chapter on the scheme of continuous disclosure.[122] Unlike Australia, US legislation does not use the concept of 'continuous disclosure,' but it has requirements for annual reports, half-yearly reports, and quarterly reports, as well as current reports.[123]

The concept of 'continuous disclosure' had not been formally used in PRC legislation until the Securities Law of 1998 was enacted, even if Article 60 of the 1993 Interim Regulations contain what should be disclosed after the IPO. There are two main reasons for this. One is that at the time of enactment of the Company Law of 1993, information disclosure was not considered by the legislators as one of the key issues; the other is the lack of in-depth theoretical research and understanding of lessons from Western countries in respect to this area. Nevertheless, as the regulator of the Chinese securities market, the CSRC always pays great attention to the continuous disclosure issues. One of its officers pointed out that besides the prospectus and listing announcement, listed companies also bear liability to continuously disclose information affecting the operation of the companies, the rights and interests of the shareholders, and the price of shares.[124]

---

121. Article 213.
122. Chapter 6CA.
123. See Listing Rules of the NYSE.
124. Nie, Qingping, 'Chinese Securities Market and Its Supervision System', in *Business Law of the People's Republic of China* (Hong Kong: Butterworths, 1997), 90.

Before the Securities Law of 1998 was enacted, although there were some provisions in the CSRC's regulations concerning continuous disclosure of information, and the CSRC officials[125] had addressed the importance of continuous disclosure of information, the requirement of continuous disclosure had not been clearly established in the State Council securities regulations. This demonstrated that the senior officials of the central government had not paid enough attention to the protection of shareholders for some time. This loophole in China's securities regulation left some listed companies with the chance to avoid disclosure of material information after their IPOs were conducted. This kind of omissions in regulation may not be a problem in a common law system, under which companies and their directors have fiduciary duties under case law. However, in a civil law country that does not have a clear fiduciary duty imposed upon company directors, such as the PRC, this kind of omissions does cause difficulties. Many listed company officials thought that they only had the duty to disclose information at the time when they were issuing shares. They saw the duty of information disclosure as a one-time action. The non-requirement for continuous disclosure in the national law before the enactment of the Securities Law of 1998[126] probably is one of the contributors to the constant occurrence of false disclosure in the securities market.

Under the CSRC's Rules on information disclosure, company directors, as well as their listed companies, bear a duty of continuous disclosure. The concept of continuous disclosure is used in the same manner as that of continuous disclosure.[127] The documents that must be provided by listed companies are the following:

- The annual report.
- The half-yearly report.
- The quarterly report.
- The interim report.

As American companies have to release quarterly reports to keep information disclosed in a timely manner, the PRC adopted quarterly reports as of 2001 in ST[128] and PT[129] companies.[130]

---

125. Nie, Qingping said in his 'Legal Structure of the Securities Market in China', *Commercial Laws in the PRC* (Hong Kong: Butterworths, 1995), 90, that apart from the prospectus and announcement of listing, a company has an obligation to continuously disclose information that influences its business, its shareholders' rights and interests, and the prices of its shares.
126. See the 1993 Interim Regulations.
127. The Securities Law of 1998, Arts 58–66.
128. ST stands for 'special treatment'.
129. PT stands for 'particular treatment'.
130. 'Stock Exchanges Emphasis Quarterly Report Rules', *China Securities Daily*, 28 Mar. 2002, 1.

5.5.4.1. The Annual Report

The State Council's 1993 Interim Regulations require listed companies to provide an annual report each year and list main items that must be included in it.[131] To standardize information disclosure,[132] the CSRC released Rule No. 2 on Content and Format of Information Disclosure by Listed Companies (provisional) in January 1994. In December 1995, the CSRC revised this provisional Rule and formally issued Rule No. 2. In 1999, this Rule was revised again.

In Article 1(3) of Rule No. 2, it is provided that the board of directors of a company must ensure that the information in the annual report is true, accurate, and complete, and that the directors bear joint liability for ensuring this. This requirement was not made into law in the USA until the passage of the Sarbanes-Oxley Act in 2002. This is a very rare case in which the Chinese securities regulatory rules are more advanced than American law. The requirement for the board of directors' guarantee of the contents of the annual report has put more pressure on the directors to fulfil their duties. Meanwhile, Rule No. 2 also provides guidance to directors in fulfilling their duty of information disclosure. It was in 2005 when directors' guarantee duty was written into the Securities Law and this duty was also extended to company supervisors and senior managerial personnel.[133]

The annual report must include the report of the chairman of the board of directors or the general manager.[134] In his or her report, the chairperson of the board of directors must review the operation of the company's business in the past year, mainly regarding matters such as the achievements of the company, the financial statements of the company, the investment activities of the company, the business achievements of any wholly-owned subsidiary companies and shareholding companies, a statement regarding the company's employees, a statement regarding the problems in the operation of the company and the resolutions to these problems, and other related issues.

The report of the board of directors must also be included in the annual report.[135] It must contain the work that the board of directors has done, the information regarding company shares and shareholders, and any changes to them. The report of the board of directors must also include information about the directors, supervisors, and senior managerial staff, major lawsuits, and arbitration cases involving the company or company directors. In the statement about directors, the particulars and biographical details about the directors must be set forth. The shareholding of each director and the changes of directors' shareholdings at the beginning and the end of the year must be included in the same statement. The remuneration of directors must also be included.

---

131. The State Council's 1993 Interim Regulation, Art. 59.
132. See the Interpretations of Rule No. 2 on the Content and Form of Information Disclosure by Listed Companies.
133. Article 68.
134. *Ibid.*, Item 3.
135. *Ibid.*, Item 4.

The general requirement for the annual report of listed companies is also provided in the Securities Law of 2005.[136]

5.5.4.2.   The Half-Yearly Report

The PRC Company Law of 1993 required a listed company to release a half-yearly accounting report,[137] but this article has been moved to the Securities Law of 2005.[138] The State Council's 1993 Interim Regulations specifically require listed companies to provide the half-yearly report[139] and list the main items to be included in this report.[140] The CSRC issued Rule No. 3 on Content and Format of Information Disclosure by Listed Companies (provisional) in June 1994. In June 1996 and June 2000, the CSRC revised this rule and reissued it. The revised Rule No. 3 contains more details to be included in the half-yearly report.

5.5.4.3.   The Quarterly Report

This report was not required until 2002.[141] The purpose for this requirement is to ensure timely disclosure.[142] However, this is a requirement only reflected in the CSRC's Administrative Rules. The Securities Law of 2005 has not set such a requirement.

5.5.4.4.   The Interim Report

In addition to annual reports and half-yearly reports, which are to be disclosed periodically, listed companies are required to disclose any event that may affect the trading price of shares. The 1993 Interim Regulations contain the requirement to disclose any major event that may have a material impact on shares price immediately after the event happens.[143] In addition, the Securities Law of 2005 provides that a listed company shall immediately disclose any major event that may have a material impact on the share price immediately after it happens.[144] But what does 'immediately' mean? Is there a deadline? No definition or explanation of 'immediately' can be found in the laws or the regulations. As the PRC courts do not have the power to interpret legislation, there is no doctrine of precedent. This general approach to legislation interpretation causes confusion in practice.

---

136. Article 66.
137. The PRC Company Law of 2005, Art. 156.
138. Above n. 128.
139. Article 57.
140. *Ibid.*, Art. 58.
141. Research Centre of the Shanghai Stock Exchange, *Report on China's Corporate Governance 2003* (in Chinese) (Shanghai: Fudan University Press, 2003), 231.
142. *Ibid.*
143. Article 60.
144. Article 67.

No clear statutory deadline leaves a loophole for companies to avoid their continuous disclosure duty.

To implement the requirements in law and administrative regulations, the CSRC issued a number of administrative rules and directives concerning interim reports. One event that listed companies often have to disclose is their takeover activities. Chapter 4 of the 1993 Interim Regulations have very detailed provisions on the procedures and disclosure requirements for takeovers, while the Securities Law of 2005 has a general requirement.[145]

5.5.4.5. Related Party Transactions

A related party is usually referred to as a related legal person or a natural person. Related party transactions, in some jurisdictions called affiliated transactions or connected transactions,[146] refer to the transactions between a company and its related companies and related persons. To reflect the enterprise value of such a company, it is considered to be essential in the PRC that public shareholders have confidence that the companies will be run in the interests of the shareholders as a whole, and that profits of other forms will not be improperly diverted to the companies' affiliates.[147] This is a reflection of the extremely high percentage of state ownership that has characterized China's enterprises. Most common law countries and areas have detailed regulations concerning control and prohibition of improperly related party transactions. For instance, in American law, there are substantive limitations on transactions between a company and its affiliates, as well as requirements of disclosure by public companies of all significant transactions between public companies and their affiliates.[148] In Hong Kong, Chapter 14 of the Listing Rules of the Hong Kong Stock Exchange set out special approval procedures for five types of important transactions; one of which is connected transactions.[149] However, the CSRC did not have detailed provisions on related party transactions until 2001. Related party transactions are also required to be disclosed in interim reports.

On 7 January 2002, the CSRC and the former State Economics and Trade Commission jointly issued the Code of Corporate Governance in Listed Companies. This Administrative Rule drew upon many experiences from overseas.[150] Articles 87–89 contain a clear duty of continuous disclosure. However, this Code does not provide a definition of continuous disclosure.

---

145. *Ibid.*
146. Such as Hong Kong and the USA
147. S. Curley, 'Presentation on the United States Securities Laws Governing Affiliated Transactions', in *Collection of Essays and Articles from the International Symposium on Securities Law*, ed. CSRC (Beijing: Publishing House of Law, 1997), 205.
148. *Ibid.*, 206.
149. Ho, Betty M.F., 'Regulating Affiliated Transactions in Hong Kong', in *Collection of Essays and Articles from the International Symposium on Securities Law*, ed. CSRC (Beijing: Publishing House of Law, 1997), 183.
150. See the Preface.

From the above analysis, it is clear that although the concept of 'continuous disclosure' has been used in the PRC,[151] it is different from the concept of 'continuous disclosure' that is used in Australia, where disclosure in the annual reports and the half-yearly reports is called 'periodic disclosure' and is different from continuous disclosure. The confusion between continuous disclosure and periodic disclosure requirements in the PRC cannot ensure timely disclosure in its securities market.

5.6.　　　　　THE FORMATION OF DISCLOSURE RULES AND
　　　　　　　THEIR FUNCTIONS

It can be concluded from the previous analysis that disclosure rules of the PRC are mainly reflected in the administratirules of the CSRC. Laws and administrative regulations only contain the principles and criteria for disclosure. This is one of the characteristics of the PRC's securities regulation that are consistent with the Chinese legal system. The CSRC's disclosure rules show a strong influence of overseas experiences as a result of convergence of the economy. However, these rules do not appropriately reflect the stronger persistence of divergence in the development of the PRC's securities market. Therefore, CSRC corporate disclosure rules are well written, but are not very functional in practice.

Another problem with disclosure was caused by a defect in the PRC's legislation. One of the legislative guidelines in the PRC is that laws should be general and not too detailed. The purpose is to leave some degree of flexibility with the implementing bodies to make detailed implementing rules in compliance with practices. The Chinese legislators have always been reluctant to enact long and detailed legislation. There are very few national laws that have more than 200 articles.[152] It is not uncommon that a piece of legislation has less than thirty articles. To some degree, the generality of legislation affects the adoption of the rule of law.

It is very useful to examine how the disclosure rules were adopted so as to understand their functions. Unfortunately, the legislature of the PRC rarely publishes materials or documents used in the legislative debates by either the deputies of the NPC or the members of the Standing Committee of the NPC. It was only from the early 1990s that the staff of the committees or commissions that were involved in the legislation started publishing some of the documental materials used in the drafting process. From these dispatched sources, we can track the legislative process.

---

151. The PRC Securities Law of 1998, Arts 58–66; the PRC Securities Law of 2005, Arts 63–72.
152. Among the longest legislation, the PRC Criminal Procedure Law of 1991 has 270 articles, The PRC Maritime Law of 1993 has 278 articles, the PRC Company Law of 1993 has 230 articles, the PRC Criminal Law of 1979 has 452 articles, the PRC Securities Law of 1998 has 214 articles, and the PRC Contract Law of 1999 has 428 articles.

Taking the Securities Law as an example, the drafting of this Law was greatly influenced by foreign laws, even if it was aimed at domestic situations. In terms of disclosure provisions, the people who drafted the Law had drawn upon experiences from countries and regions such as the USA, Japan, Australia, the UK, Hong Kong, and Taiwan.[153] Because of the use of the same language, the Hong Kong and Taiwan experiences have been easier for the PRC legislators to research, most of whom do not speak English. The importance of the experiences of the USA and the UK was the main reason why they were adopted by the PRC. Japan, as a traditional civil law country and a close neighbour, has always been a resort for Chinese legislators. The dominant foreign influence came from the US Securities Act of 1933 and the US Securities Exchange Commission Act of 934, as well as other American acts. During the drafting of the Securities Law, there was extensive cooperation between the SEC and the CSRC. For instance, on 28 April 1994, then Chairman of the SEC, Arthur Levitt, signed a Memorandum of Understanding (MOU) with the CSRC, advising the PRC securities regulators on developing Chinese financial markets.[154] However, as a result of the generality of national legislation, the PRC Securities Law only picked up the principles of disclosure, which were widely accepted in Western countries, and several provisions of 'continuous disclosure' (in fact, these are similar to Western countries' periodic disclosure). The Securities Law of 1998 lacked detailed provisions for implementing the principles. There has been some improvement in the Securities Law of 2005 regarding the disclosure issue. However, substantial details have yet to be added into the national laws.

Under the Chinese legal system, the next level of law below national laws is called administrative regulations. The most important Administrative Regulation on Disclosure is the 1993 Interim Regulations. The problem with these Regulations is that they were adopted in 1993 at the beginning of the development of the securities market. At that time, the problem with information disclosure had not become a serious problem and the rule makers had not realized the importance of regulating disclosure. The Regulations only contain periodic disclosure and interim disclosure[155] and administrative liability for false and misleading disclosure.[156] These provisions had been reworded into the Securities Law.

The real functioning disclosure rules are those released by the CSRC. They are very up-to-date. They are focused on the problems that occur in practice. However, as the CSRC has acknowledged, its disclosure rules were mainly modelled on the Hong Kong and US markets.[157] These two markets are free and relatively

---

153.   Wang, Lianzhou & Cheng Li (eds), 'Preface', *The Drafting of the Securities Law* (Shanghai: Shanghai Sanlian bookshop Press, 2000), 310 and 311; the CSRC, *Collection of Essays and Articles from the International Symposium on Securities Law* (Beijing: Law Publishing House, 1997), 1.
154.   Cited in Yu, Gunaghua and Minkang Gu *Laws Affecting Business Transactions in the PRC* (The Hague: Kluwer Law International, 2001), 89.
155.   Chapter 6.
156.   Chapter 7.
157.   The CSRC, *Disclosure Requirements of China Securities Market 2001*, 1.

developed markets. Even in a free market with a sound legal system, there are serious problems in the compliance with disclosure requirements, such as those exposed in the cases of Enron and WorldCom, let alone an emerging market that is closely controlled by the government and lacks the rule of law, such as that of the PRC. This is why in theory the CSRC has adopted relatively comprehensive disclosure rules, while in practice these rules do not have much impact on the quality of disclosure.[158]

5.7. OVERVIEW OF THE CORPORATE DISCLOSURE REGIME IN THE PRC

5.7.1. THE ENFORCEMENT OF LAWS AND REGULATIONS

The Securities Law was enacted and substantially amended by the Standing Committee of the NPC. It is a national law. The 1993 Interim Regulations are administrative regulations passed by the State Council. Both were passed by following prescribed procedures. Thus, they can be enforced by the courts.

The rules released by the CSRC and other ministries of the State Council are administrative rules. The procedure for passing these rules are, however, much simpler and informal than those for the passing of laws and administrative regulations. Therefore, administrative rules may not be enforced by the courts under the Administrative Litigation Law of 1989.[159] Generally speaking, these rules still apply to the companies listed either on the Shanghai or Shenzhen Stock Exchanges. However, if there is a lawsuit, the party that follows the CSRC's rule that is inconsistent with the laws may not be protected. As laws and administrative regulations are very general, the CSRC's administrative rules often play a more important role in the regulation of securities market than any law or administrative regulation in practice. However, a lack of enforceability to some degree diminishes the function of the CSRC's rules.

5.7.2. THE DEFECTS IN THE NATIONAL LAWS

Provisions for civil liabilities and derivative actions did not exist in laws until the passage of the Securities Law of 2005. Without such provisions, the securities investors and shareholders of listed companies could not be effectively protected. These provisions, together with other suggestions, such as the establishment of a shareholders' foundation system[160] for the protection of shareholders and the

---

158. According to *China Securities Daily*, there was at least one false disclosure case every month in 2001, which was named 'the year of supervision' by the CSRC. It is not difficult to imagine that there were many such cases in other years.
159. Article 5.
160. Anthony Nheo, Special Council of the CSRC, 'Several Issues in the Chinese Capital Market Development of Regulation', *Securities Law Review* (in Chinese) 1 (2001): 15.

fundamental amendments to the Company Law of 1993 and the Securities Law of 1998 were not established until 2005. However, how effective these provisions are is yet to be tested.

5.7.3.   How Should Foreign Experiences Be Adopted?

As mentioned above, the PRC has learnt many lessons from foreign experiences in its lawmaking. However, from books and other published materials, it can be seen that before adopting foreign laws, legislators and rule makers have rarely conducted empirical studies of foreign laws. Their knowledge of foreign laws mainly comes from the introduction of foreign experts, as well as short meetings with foreign legislators and legal experts during their about ten-to-fifteen-day trips to each target country. This approach to the transplantation of foreign laws has raised doubts about the accuracy and completeness of PRC legislators' and lawmakers' understanding of foreign law. This might be one of the major reasons why the PRC has formed a disclosure regulatory regime, but this regime does not work very well. For this reason, the Australian approach towards the transplantation of foreign laws is worth studying by PRC legislators and rule makers. The Australian approach will be examined in Chapter 6.

5.8.   CONCLUSION: WHAT CAN THE PRC LEARN FROM THE US MODEL IN TERMS OF DISCLOSURE?

It was pointed out at the beginning of this chapter that the securities regulatory regime in the PRC was mainly based on the US model and the Hong Kong model. The CSRC's rules on disclosure were also mainly based on the rules of the SEC. This was not only because the dominant rule makers in the PRC thought that the US market was a complicated market with a well-functioning regulatory regime, but also because there was a trend towards adoption of the US model in Germany and the UK in the 1990s.[161] For a long time, the US model was seen as a perfect regulatory model in the PRC.

Unfortunately, with the collapse of Enron Corp., which was the seventh-largest company in the USA, a fairy tale was destroyed. Not only the SEC, but also the regulators in other countries had to rethink the American approach. At the core of the Enron collapse is the issue of inadequate disclosure. In the Enron case, three of the six audit committee members owned shares of Enron Corp. worth more than USD 7.5 million.[162] The requirement for independence of the audit committee and the disclosure rules should deal with these problems. To deal with such problems, the SEC had to examine its rules and propose new ones to improve the quality, amount, and timeliness of public disclosure of extraordinary corporate

---

161. *Ibid.* 34, 123–124.
162. L. Lavelle, 'Enron: How Governance Rules Failed', *Businessweek*, 21 Jan. 2002, 38–39.

events. Under the SEC's proposal that was released on 12 June 2002, new items and events must be reported on Form 8-K, which is also known as the current report.[163] In addition, the SEC proposed that Form 8-K reports be filed within two days of such items and events instead of five to fifteen days.[164]

The PRC has to draw upon lessons from the USA. Fortunately, senior officials have realized that China should correct its own methods as it adopts Western models. As a past Chairman of the CSRC pointed out, simply borrowing rules of mature markets and inserting them into a transitional market is unrealistic and may cause problems.[165]

With respect to disclosure, the PRC has to realize that the disclosure rules of the USA were aimed at its domestic market. When transplanting these rules into China, the CSRC should make adjustments in response to its own domestic markets. For example, the problem of timeliness is a key issue to be clarified in the CSRC's disclosure rules. Currently, there are no detailed rules on timely disclosure in the PRC.

The independence of the auditors and audit committees has been a major issue in improving the quality of disclosure in complicated markets such as that of the USA[166] and Australia.[167] With the exposure of many listed companies' poor auditing quality, such as the *Ninguangxia* case in 2000, it is urgent that the PRC put the independence of auditors and accountants into its rule-making agenda. Otherwise, there is no way for the PRC to improve its corporate governance. After the collapses of Enron and WorldCom, the US Congress passed the Sarbanes–Oxley Act in July 2002, a benchmark law to strengthen information disclosure and corporate governance in listed companies. The Sarbanes-Oxley Act contains strict provisions requiring CFOs and CEOs to certify the genuineness of their companies' financial statements.[168]

The CSRC drafted rules that mirrored this US Act soon after its passage. In January 2003, Zhang Weiguo, a former Chief Accountant of the CSRC and now the PRC's Representative on the International Accounting Standards Commission, said that the CSRC would release new rules including those on strengthening the accounting responsibilities of chief executives and chief accounting officers of listed companies in the coming one to two years in order to boost information disclosure requirements relating to economic activities among managing teams and major shareholders.[169] Zhou Daojiong, a former Chairman of the CSRC, said that other plans to be launched in the next twenty-four months would include a number of regulations to streamline the sound performance of

---

163. <www.sec.gov/press/2002-88.htm>, 8 Aug. 2002.
164. *Ibid.*
165. Zhou, Xiaochuan, then Chairman of the CSRC, A Speech at the International Symposium of 2002 on Development of China Securities Investment Funds, <www.peopledaily.com.cn>, 19 Jun. 2002.
166. The US Sarbanes–Oxley Act of 2002 has sections dealing with this issue.
167. The Australian CLERP 9 Act of 2004 (Cth) has sections dealing with this issue.
168. Section 302.
169. <www.chinadaily.com.cn/news/2003-01-13/101034.html>, 13 Jan. 2003.

accounting firms, such as an effective auditing system, restrictions on accounting firms providing non-accounting services, the keeping of backup accounts, and the prohibition of accountants' holding positions in the listed companies for which they provide services.[170] Zhang Weiguo also indicated that a national, independent, accounting supervision committee would be established.[171] This committee would be the decision-maker for a number of important issues, including the development of accounting rules, supervision of the accounting sector, and punishment for illegal practices. On 15 February 2006, the MOF announced the establishment of the System of Enterprise Accounting Rules and the System of Enterprise Auditing Rules. These two systems became effectiveon 1 January 2007 and had been applied in listed companies by that date. Other enterprises will gradually adopt these two systems. It would therefore seem that the CSRC moves very quickly in updating its rules. However, it has again chosen the American model as its major model. Whether this practice will work is still in question.

---

170. *Ibid.*
171. *Ibid.*

Chapter 6

The State of the Securities Market and Disclosure in the PRC

6.1.   THE DEVELOPMENT OF THE SECURITIES MARKET

6.1.1.   RE-EMERGENCE OF THE SECURITIES MARKET IN THE PRC

Chapter 5 discussed and assessed the PRC's securities regulatory framework by analysing laws, administrative regulations, administrative rules, and stock exchange listing rules governing corporate disclosure. This chapter first draws a rough picture of the Chinese securities market: it briefly reviews the history of the formation and development of the Chinese securities market; it lists different types of securities in this market; and it describes the current state of the PRC securities market. Then the chapter reviews how the PRC disclosure regulatory regime works in practice. It focuses on the problems under the current disclosure framework and analyses the reasons why these problems occur.

By analysing the classic cases that occurred in the PRC securities market since its re-emergence, this chapter argues that the current disclosure regulatory regime cannot function properly, although the regulation has been much improved since 1998. There are three major reasons for this. Firstly, disclosure has not been seen as the highest priority of regulation by the policy makers. Secondly, the Chinese regulatory authorities have insufficient regulatory powers, and their rules are not always enforced. Thirdly, some important provisions, such as those on directors and other company officers' civil liabilities and criminal liabilities, did not exist for a long time, and some provisions, such as those on disqualification, are too vague to be implemented. Finally and most importantly, many regulatory rules were directly borrowed from other securities markets, especially those in the USA and Hong Kong, without empirical study. These rules do not necessarily suit the needs of the PRC securities market and are often lost in the process of transplantation.

The reasons for this reflect the historical, political, economic, and cultural factors influencing the PRC securities market. With the influence of these factors, the process of establishing an appropriate corporate disclosure regulatory regime will follow the particular pathway that is relevant to the system of government and the operation of the markets in the PRC. Corporate disclosure practices have demonstrated that the PRC has to examine the way it makes use of foreign experiences and practices if it intends to build an effective securities market.

As pointed out in the previous chapter, the term 'securities' is used in two ways in the PRC. The concept of 'securities' in the narrow sense was adopted in the Securities Law of 1998. It only refers to the domestic market, where shares, corporate bonds, and other securities recognized by the State Council are issued and traded.[1] After a long period of criticism and the market's development,[2] the Securities Law of 2005 expanded this concept to include shares, corporate bonds, treasury bonds, securities investment funds, and derivatives.[3] As, in this market, the majority of investors are trading in shares, company bonds, and funds, most of the disclosure rules discussed in this book are concerned with these types of securities.

The securities market of the PRC re-emerged in the mid-1980s after its disappearance in the early 1950s. However, this market developed very quickly. At the end of 1991, which was the first year of the establishment of the Shenzhen Stock Exchange, there were twenty listed companies; the value of their shares was CNY 3.5 billion.[4] By the end of 1991, there were only eight types of shares listed on the Shanghai Stock Exchange. The other thirty-seven types of securities were state treasury bonds (seven), financial bonds (twelve) and company bonds (eighteen).[5] Up until April 2002, there were 1,175 companies listed on the two stock exchanges, which raised capital of CNY 810.1 billion, and the market value of these securities reached CNY 454 trillion. There were 67 million investors and 118 securities companies.[6] By the end of September 2002, there were 1,212 listed companies, and the market value of these shares reached CNY 45,000 trillion, which was equal to 50% of the GDP. There were nineteen investment funds and 68 million investors.[7] On 15 February 2008, the SSE had 861 listed companies and 1,130 listed securities, and their market vale reached CNY 233.4 trillion;[8] the SZSE had 680 listed companies and 878 listed securities, and their market value

---

1. The PRC Securities Law of 1998, Art. 2.
2. Fu, Jian and Yuan Jie, *PRC Company & Securities Laws: A Practical Guide* (Singapore: CCH Asia, 2006), 117.
3. Article 2.
4. Li Zhangzhe, *Finally Successful: The Report of the Development of Chinese Share Market* (in Chinese) (Beijing: World Knowledge Press, 2000), 188.
5. *Ibid.*
6. The speech of Zhou Xiaochuan, then Chairman of the CSRC, at the Second International Symposium on China Securities Market, Beijing, 7 Jun. 2002, <www.csrc.gov.cn>, 19 Jun. 2002.
7. <www.peopledaily.com.cn>, 27 Oct. 2002.
8. <www.sse.com.cn/sseportal/ps/zhs/home.html>, 17 Feb. 2008.

reached CNY 55 trillion.[9] Even the outbreak of the global financial crisis did not have much of a negative impact on the Chinese securities market in comparison with the impact on most Western securities markets. On 9 September 2009, the SSE had 866 listed companies and 1,298 listed securities, and their market value was CNY 16.180118 trillion;[10] the SZSE had 756 listed companies and 798 listed securities, and their market value was CNY 78.117 billion.[11] The PRC securities market will continue its rapid development, even though there have been and will continue to be ups and downs in this market. Why did the PRC market re-emerge? How did it develop so quickly? Does this market function properly? These issues have been touched on in the previous chapter. This chapter will provide a more detailed discussion. It will demonstrate how the Chinese securities market has been shaped under historical, cultural, economic, and political influences.

6.1.2.   THE HISTORY OF SECURITIES MARKETS IN CHINA BEFORE 1949

Although the PRC securities market only re-emerged in the mid-1980s, securities were not new to the Chinese. If state treasury bonds[12] are treated as one type of security, the history of the Chinese securities market can be traced back to the late Qing Dynasty.[13] As early as 1869, the Changli Company already was trading in shares of foreign companies.[14] In 1872, then Prime Minister of the Qing Dynasty,

---

9. <www.szse.com>, 17 Feb. 2008.
10. <www.sse.com.cn/sseportal/ps/zhs/home.html>, 10 Sep. 2009.
11. <www.sse.com.cn/sseportal/webapp/datapresent/SZEverydayMarketAct?reportName=Biz CompSZEverydayMarketRpt&TRADING_DATE=&CURSOR=1>, 10 Sep. 2009.
12. State treasury bonds refer to securities issued by the central government. Since 1981 they have been issued by the State Council through its Ministry of Finance.
13. Zhang, ZJ, 'Securities Market and Securities Regulation in China', *North Carolina Journal of International Law and Commercial Regulation* 22, no. 2 (1997): 558–629 at 575. According to him, the Qing government started to issue bonds in 1867. There are different opinions on when securities formally came into use in China. For example, Li, Zhangzhe, in his book *Finally Successful: The Report of the Development of Chinese Share Market* stated that Chinese businessmen first invested capital that accounted for one-tenth of the total capital raised by an American company, Qiongjiang Merchants, in Shanghai in 1856, 23. He also stated that the first state bonds of the Qing Dynasty were issued in 1898 even though they were called '*zhaoxin shares*'. These bonds were issued to repay the debts to the Japanese government as a result of the Sino-Japanese War in 1895. Zheng, Zhenlong (ed.), in *A Concise History of Chinese Securities Development* (in Chinese) (Beijing: Economic Science Press, 2000), held the view that China first borrowed foreign debts in 1865 when the Qing Dynasty borrowed twenty-year-long debts worth GBP 1,431,664 and 2 shillings from the UK to pay debts owed to the Russians resulting from the Yili Convention. Zheng also held that the first domestic debts were '*xi jie shang kuan*' in 1894, which were stopped in the second year because of the strong protest from the ordinary people. Zheng held that '*zhao xin shares*' were the second bonds issue in Chinese history.
14. Zhang, Hong, 'The Chinese Securities Regulation and Its Theoretical Development', *Civil and Commercial Law Review* 2 (2000): 154–221 at 160–165.

Li Hongzhang, established the first Chinese joint stock company – the China Merchant Company.[15]

The first securities market in China came into being at the beginning of the twentieth century. Foreign businesspeople set up the first stock exchange of China – the *Shanghai Gufen Gongsuo* (the Shanghai Shareholding Public Site) in 1891 to trade in foreign shares.[16] In 1905, the government of the Qing Dynasty converted it into the *Shanghai Zhongye Gongsuo*, or the Shanghai Stock Exchange. The first Chinese organization of securities dealers was the Shanghai Shares Business Association, which was established by the Shanghaiese businesspeople with the approval of the North Ocean Government in 1914.[17] In the same year, the North Ocean Government enacted the Stock Exchange Law, which was the first national securities law in Chinese history, although there were no stock exchanges.[18] In June 1920, the North Ocean Government established the Shanghai Securities and Commodity Stock Exchange, which started business on 1 July 1920.[19] Other securities markets were also established in Beijing, Hankou, and Tianjin.[20] Later on, other stock exchanges were set up. The Nationalist Government (which took power in 1927) enacted a new Stock Exchange Law in 1929.[21] This Law was more comprehensive than the one enacted by the North Ocean Government, and it was later inherited by Taiwan and constituted the foundation of current Taiwanese securities legislation.[22] Unfortunately, the securities markets under the control of the Nationalist government did not operate on the basis of normal market rules, as they were controlled by the government, which focused on trading in government bonds in the stock exchange.[23] However, because of the frequent changes of the government and the Second World War, the securities market became extremely volatile and almost out of control.[24] The securities regulatory rules developed in the USA in the 1930s did not have much influence on the lawmaking of the Nationalist government because the regulation of the Chinese securities market was under the strict control of the government and the capital needed by industries was mainly raised by taxation and business profits.[25] In summary, prior to the founding of the PRC, China's securities market had the following characteristics:

---

15. Dong, SP, *The Policies on the Chinese Securities Market and the Share Trading* (Beijing: Economy and Management Press, 1997), 1.
16. Zheng, Zhenlong (ed), *A Concisef History of Chinese Securities Development* (in Chinese) (Beijing: Economics Science Press, 2000), 127.
17. *Ibid.*
18. Jin, Dehong, *Contemporary Securities Market of China* (in Chinese) (Shanghai: Shanghai Finance and Economics University Press, 1999), 16.
19. Zheng, Zhenlong(ed), *A Concise History of Chinese Securities*, 128.
20. Zhang, Hong, 'The Chinese Securities Regulation and Its Theoretical Development', 160–165.
21. Jing, Dehong, *Contemporary Securities Market of China*, 17.
22. Zhang, Hong, 'The Chinese Securities Regulation and Its Theoretical Development', 154–221 at 157.
23. Jin, Dehong, *Contemporary Securities Market of China*, 17.
24. *Ibid.*, 17 and 18.
25. *Ibid.*, 19.

slow development, imbalanced development, colonized development, and development separate from industries.

6.1.3.   THE SECURITIES MARKET AFTER THE FOUNDING OF THE PRC

The Nationalist *(Kuomintang)* legal system was completely abolished by the CPC after the founding of the PRC in 1949.[26] The institutions established by the Nationalist government were also abolished.[27] The CPC established its first stock exchange in Tianjin based on the old Tianjin Stock Exchange on 1 June 1949.[28] The Beijing Stock Exchange started business on 1 February 1950.[29] However, these two stock exchanges did not last long because they were set up to absorb moving capital *(you zi)*, and from June 1950, the PRC central government moved this capital from the securities market to other industries as a result of adjustments of its industrial and commercial policies. Soon after, the PRC government adopted the Soviet Union type of socialist planned economy and stopped the issuing and trading of shares and other securities. The Tianjin Stock Exchange was converted into the state-owned Tianjin Investment Company in February 1952.[30] The Beijing Stock Exchange was dissolved in October 1952. From then on until the late 1970s, a securities market did not exist in the PRC. Even after the open-door policy was adopted in late 1978, no securities were issued until the early 1980s, and there were no relevant securities regulations in China because of the dominance of the planned economy. This reflects the fact that historically, issuing securities was not used as a major means for capital raising in China.

6.1.4.   THE SECURITIES MARKET SINCE THE 1980s

From 1952 until the late 1970s, the PRC had a highly centralized planned economy. Business was done according to the state development plan. There were no securities at all. Although the PRC adopted an open-door policy in 1978, it continued with the planned economy for several years afterwards.[31] To encourage foreign investment so as to solve the funding problems partly arising from the

---

26. Zheng, Zhenlong(ed), *A Concise History of Chinese Securities Development*, 154.
27. *Ibid.*
28. Zheng, Zhenlong(ed), *A Concise History of Chinese Securities Development*, 154.
29. *Ibid.*
30. *Ibid.*, 156.
31. The planned economy was not replaced by the planned commodity economy until 1984 in the Resolution on Economic System Reform by the Third Meeting of the Twelfth Plenary Session of the CPC. The planned commodity economy was not replaced by the market economy until 1992 by the Fourteenth Session of the CPC. See Wu, Jinglian, *Reform: Now at a Critical Point* (in Chinese) (Beijinjg: Sanlian Bookshop Press, 2002), 325, 326, and 337.

heavily subsidized loss-making SOEs, Western business ideas and legal forms had to be introduced.[32]

Firstly, the notion of a company as a separate legal entity (but not merely as a subordinate of the government) was gradually accepted into the PRC during the 1980s.[33] Although the concept of a 'company' was still articulated differently in China in the 1980s when contrasted with the practices in Western countries, the incorporated entity gradually became a major vehicle for business in China. Afterwards, the concept of capital raising by issuing of securities was also introduced.

As a result of the enterprise reforms of the 1980s, SOEs were no longer under the direct control of government, and thousands of companies were set up. The operation of companies was no longer directly subject to state planning. The state could not derive its revenue from the profits made by SOEs, instead having to resort to taxation of such entities.[34] The central question then became how enterprises could find new ways of capital raising, as they could no longer rely solely upon the governmental budget. Up until the early 1980s, many people still held negative views regarding share issuing because of past negative experiences, such as China's securities market in the late 1940s.[35] Consequently, the leaders of the PRC cautiously started to reform the capital-raising system by issuing state treasury bonds to the general public.

State treasury bonds (as the first type of securities) were first issued in the PRC to government institutions in early 1981. The issue of state treasury bonds was the beginning of the re-emergence of the securities market in the PRC. Since then, several other types of securities have developed in China's capital market. Among them were financial bonds, enterprises bonds, and shares. These securities were widely welcomed, while derivative securities were only reluctantly accepted. In 1984, permission was given to a certain number of SOEs to issue enterprise bonds through approved financial institutions.[36] Individuals were first allowed to purchase treasury bonds through the enterprises that they were working for. In 1986, the Shanghai Branch of the PBOC first allowed the Industrial and Commercial Bank of China to establish an over-the-counter (OTC) market for bonds and shares.[37] In 1988, shares of the Shenzhen Development Bank were first traded on the Shenzhen OTC market.[38]

---

32. R. Nottle, 'The Development of Securities Markets in China in the 1990s', *C&SLJ* 11, no. 8 (1993): 503–523 at 503.
33. The Resolution of the Third Meeting of the Eleventh Plenary Session of the CCP Congress for the first time officially used the concept of 'company'; see Li, Zhangzhe, *Finally Successful: The Report of the Development of Chinese Share Market*, 59.
34. The State Council started the 'taxation replaces profit' reform by approving the Ministry of Finance's Measures Concerning Application of Taxation Replacing Profit in SOEs in April 1983. See Wang, Yuming & An Jiang, *The Economic Law Perspective of State-owned Enterprises Reform* (Beijing: China People's Public Security University Press 2001), 10.
35. Li, Zhangzhe, *Finally Successful: The Report of the Development of Chinese Share Market*, 32.
36. *Ibid.*, 85.
37. *Ibid.*, 80.
38. *Ibid.*

Issuing and administration of treasury bonds is a responsibility of the Ministry of Finance. At the beginning of the 1980s, as interest rates of treasury bonds were relatively high, treasury bonds were very attractive to investors. With the continuous cuts in interest rates paid on treasury bonds, share issues became a more attractive means of capital raising. Companies that raised capital by issuing shares were widely expected to pay dividends to the shareholders. While the interest rate paid on bonds tended to be fixed, the rates of the dividends paid by companies obviously varied, depending upon the success of the company. Shareholders were generally more active than bondholders, as the former could be involved in the decision-making processes of a company, such as attending and voting at shareholders' general meetings. In contrast, bondholders did not participate in the management of a company. Their interest in a company was fixed but stable. However, shareholders had the freedom to transfer their shares by selling them, while the trading of treasury bonds was prohibited until May 1988. In 1991, the primary market for state bonds trading was established.[39] To regulate the primary market of state bonds and develop the secondary market of state bonds, the CSRC joined the Ministry of Finance as regulators to release the 1993 Interim Regulations. The poor reputation of the share market that existed prior to 1949 was gradually forgotten as investors were driven by the lure of high profits that might be made within a short period of time. Consequently, in the mid-1980s, the share market started to grow rapidly.

Since the mid-1980s, with the need for capital raising by small business organizations and small companies that could not get loans from the banks, which were state-owned, share issuing has become a major means of capital raising.[40] To regulate securities issuing and trading and to prevent fraudulent capital raising, the Shanghai and the Shenzhen municipal governments opened the Shanghai and the Shenzhen Stock Exchanges, respectively, as lawful share-trading sites. These two stock exchanges became national securities markets in mainland China on 19 December 1990 and 3 July 1991 with the approval of the State Council.[41] To date, these two stock exchanges apply the same LRs and in fact function as a single market.

By the end of 1992, these two stock exchanges were still under the supervision of their local municipal governments, and the share issuing and trading rules were also established by the local governments with the approval of the PBOC.[42] Apart from the local governments, the People's Bank of China and other ministries of the State Council also released numerous rules on the issuing and trading of company shares and debentures. With the occurrence of the August 10 Incident,[43] the central

---

39. Walter, Carol E. & Fraser J.T. Howie, *Privatizing China: the Stock Markets and Their Role in Corporate Reform* (Singapore: Hoh Wiley & Sons (Asia) Pte Ltd), 37.
40. Li, Zhangzhe, *Finally Successful: The Report of the Development of Chinese Share Market*, 60.
41. The State Council is the executive body of the PRC.
42. Shenzhen Interim Measures for Share Issue and Trading of 1991 by the Shenzhen municipal government.
43. The investors in the Shenzhen Stock Exchange had fought for buying the subscription certificates to shares and had bloody clashes with the police.

government decided to interfere with the regulation of the securities markets by establishing a national securities regulatory body. The SCSC and its working body, the CSRC, were thus established in October 1992.[44]

The State Council provided that the Shanghai and the Shenzhen Stock Exchanges were under the administration of their local governments while being supervised by the CSRC.[45] This structure was confirmed in the Interim Measures of Administration of Stock Exchanges in July 1993. However, as discussed in Chapter 3, there were other ministries and commissions of the State Council that had regulatory powers within their functional categories.[46] Each department made its own regulatory rules when necessary. Some departments released joint regulatory rules whenever necessary. The transformation from SOEs to shareholding companies was approved either by the provincial or the central government, according to the rankings of these SOEs.[47] Multiple regulators and multiple rules led to high costs and inefficiency of the securities markets. This was most evident in the case of the CSRC and the local governments. They had different focuses on securities regulation, and thus the dual regulation of the stock exchanges prevented the markets from functioning properly.

To further improve the efficiency of the securities markets, a nationwide treasury bonds trading system, the Securities Trading Automated Quotations System (STAQ), was established on 5 December 1990 and was modelled on the US National Association of Securities Dealer Automated Quotation system (NASDAQ).[48] The National Electronic Trading System (NET), which was sponsored by the PBOC, was established in January 1991.[49] However, in 1997, both the STAQ system and NET system ceased to function because of policy changes of the CSRC.

The term 'company' was given statutory recognition in the PRC Company Law of 1993, although this form of business had already been recognized as a separate entity in the mid-1990s. This Law provides for two types of companies: limited liability companies and joint stock limited liability companies.[50] Companies were treated as a legal entity,[51] but China's Company Law adopted a corporate governance structure that reflected the attitude of the decision-makers. As China had not done enough research on company laws in common law countries, especially

---

44. Jin, Dehong, *Contemporary Securities Market of China* (in Chinese), 328; Zheng, Zhenlong (ed), *A Concise History of the Development of the Chinese Securities* (in Chinese) (Beijing: Economic Science Press, 2000), 325.
45. The State Council, *Circular on Further Strengthening Macro-Administration of Securities Markets*, December 1992.
46. There was a time when the securities markets were regulated by twelve ministries and commissions of the State Council in addition to the Supreme People's Court and the Supreme People's Procuratorate.
47. Zheng, Zhenlong (ed), *A Brief History of Chinese Securities Devlopment*, 26.
48. Walter, Carl E. & Fraser J.T. Howie, *Privatizing China: The Stock Markets and Their Role in Corporate Reform*, 37.
49. *Ibid.*, 39.
50. The PRC Company Law of 1993, Art. 2.
51. *Ibid.*, Art. 3.

in the area of their development, its first Company Law was very different from the company legislation of most common law countries. For example, in China, the general meeting of shareholders was seen as the supreme body in a company;[52] among other things, it decided upon the principles that governed the operation of the company and its investment plans.[53] Another example is that the board of directors in a Chinese company was a body under the control of the shareholders' general meeting; the board formulated the companies' operation plans and adopted investment proposals on the basis of the operational principles and investment plans set by the shareholders' general meeting.[54] These provisions were not changed in the Securities Law of 2005. In contrast, in Western countries, the board of directors and the shareholders at the general meeting are two divisions of a company that are vested with different powers.[55]

Following the German model,[56] the PRC Company Law of 1993 provided that larger limited liability companies could have a supervisor or a supervisory board,[57] whilse joint stock limited liability[58] companies must have a supervisory board.[59] The supervisor or the supervisory board inspected the financial records of the company and supervised the directors and managers of the company to monitor violations of laws, regulations, or the company's articles of association.[60] This system was retained in the Securities Law of 2005[61] and differs from the unitary corporate governance models found in common law countries. Instead, China has a two-tier governance structure with a supervisory board and a board of directors; the shareholders' general meeting exercises supervision over these two boards. In common law countries, the unitary board – the board of directors – is only subject to very general supervision of the general meeting of shareholders. The governance structure of Chinese companies as provided for under the PRC Company Law has the potential to cause confusion and conflict among the shareholders' meeting, the supervisory board, and the board of directors when each exercises its respective powers.

The rapid development of the securities market not only attracted the Chinese people, but it also attracted foreign investors. With the issue of B-shares[62] on the domestic stock exchanges and the listing of Chinese companies on foreign stock

---

52. *Ibid.*, Arts 37 and 102.
53. *Ibid.*, Arts 38 and 103.
54. *Ibid.*, Arts 46 and 112.
55. Austin, Robert & Ian Ramsay, *Ford's Principles of Corporations Law*, 12th edn (Sydney: LexisNexis Butterworths, 2005), 212.
56. Chen, Xi, 'A Consideration of the Establishment of Our Company Supervisory Board', in *Comparative Studies on Company Law* (in Chinese), ed. You QR (Beijing: People's Court Press, 2005), 29.
57. Article 52.
58. Joint stock limited liability companies in China refer to companies issuing shares to the public.
59. Article 24.
60. Articles 54 and 126.
61. Articles 52 and 54.
62. The Chinese shares are classified as A-shares, B-shares, N-shares, and S-shares according to the place of issue and the people who are allowed to trade these shares.

exchanges, more and more investors in Hong Kong, Macao, Taiwan, and even Western countries began to invest in the Chinese share market. On 5 November 2002, the CSRC and the PBOC jointly issued an Administrative Rule entitled Interim Measures Concerning Administration of Investment inside China by Qualified Foreign Institutional Investors (hereinafter QFII Measures).

6.2. LISTED SECURITIES

Currently, there are limited types of securities that may be listed and traded on either the Shanghai Stock Exchange or the Shenzhen Stock Exchange. Dual listing is not allowed within the PRC. Shares, state treasury bonds, enterprise bonds, funds, and some derivatives are allowed to be listed on the domestic stock exchanges.

6.2.1. A-SHARES AND B-SHARES IN THE DOMESTIC MARKETS

The classification of shares in the PRC is very different from that in most Western countries. According to the trading currency and the investors, shares can be classified as A-shares and B-shares in the PRC. The differences between them were discussed in the previous chapter. On 5 November 2002, the QFII Measures were released. On 1 December 2002, China formally introduced QFII Measures.[63] Under the QFII Measures, foreign investors that satisfy prescribed qualifications will be able to invest in A shares, state bonds, corporate bonds, and other financial instruments approved by the Chinese authorities.[64] Although the PRC is opening up its securities market, under the QFII Measures, foreign investors have to open a special CNY account with a Chinese bank and Chinese securities companies for trading.

B-shares are also called 'special CNY shares' or 'domestically listed shares with foreign investment'. According to Article 4 of the State Council's Regulations Concerning Domestically Listed Shares with Foreign Investment by Joint Stock Limited Companies of 1995, investors of B-shares were limited to (a) foreign citizens, foreign legal entities, and other organizations; (b) natural persons, legal entities, and other organizations resident in Hong Kong, Macau, and Taiwan; (c) PRC citizens who reside in other countries; and (d) other investors designated by the SCSC. The purpose of differentiating B-shares from A-shares was mainly to encourage investment from outside mainland China while the CNY was not freely convertible.

---

63. <www.1.chinadaily.com.cn/news/cb/2002-11-8/93019.html>, 8 Nov. 2002; also see the CSRC's *Interim Measures for Administration of Domestic Investment by QFII*, which were released on 5 Nov. 2002.
64. Article 18.

Although the State Council first regulated B-share trading in 1995, the trading of B-shares on the two stock exchanges started long before that time. Shenzhen was the first city where B-shares were issued and traded in Hong Kong Dollars (HKD) in 1988 by the Shenzhen Development Bank. One of the characteristics of the Chinese securities market is that regulation is always behind practice. The Shenzhen municipal government and the PBOC jointly issued the first legal document regulating B-shares, the Shenzhen Interim Measures Concerning Administration of RMB [CNY] Special Shares on 5 December 1989. The first formal issuing of B-shares started in Shenzhen in December 1991, when China South Glass Joint Stock Company issued its B-shares successfully.[65] The Shanghai Stock Exchange finished its first B-share issue in February 1992, when Shanghai Electronic Vacuum Parts Company became the first company to issue B-shares in Shanghai.[66] It is worth noting that although a joint stock company may issue either A-shares or B-shares or even both, it is not allowed dual listing on both stock exchanges. This reflects the fact that the PRC government is very prudent in approving share issues.

As the Chinese securities market is still underdeveloped and quite volatile, the Chinese government has to interfere with this market from time to time. For example, as there were black currency markets because of the control of foreign exchange by the central government, Chinese citizens were attracted to invest illegally in B-share trading before the opening of the B-share market to domestic investors on 19 February 2001.[67] For some time, there had been many illegally opened B-share trading accounts. The CSRC had to issue the Circular on Strict Control of Opening of B-Share Trading Accounts in June 1996 to crack down on B-share trading by domestic Chinese nationals. Although having different shares was intended to attract different investors,[68] this difference, together with the handling of B-share trading by the Chinese government, demonstrates the non-market economy feature of the PRC securities market.

After the B-share market was established, it was never as active as the A-share market because of limited investment from abroad. In addition, with its accession to the WTO at the end of 2001, China had been considering gradual termination of foreign currency control and free conversion of CNY.[69] Also worried about the rule of national treatment under the WTO agreements and the weak market of B-share trading, the CSRC opened the B-share market to domestic investors with certain limitations on 19 February 2001. Based on the CSRC's decision, only domestic investors with foreign currency deposited at a bank that was located within mainland China were allowed to open B-share trading accounts and trade

---

65. Zhou, Yousu (ed), *General Theories on Securitiesy Law* (in Chinese), 34.
66. Li, Zhangzhe, *Finally Successful: The Report of the Development of Chinese Share Market*, 218.
67. CSRC, *The Decision on Domestic Residents' Investment in B-share Market*, 19 Feb. 2001.
68. Li, Zhangzhe, *Finally Successful: The Report of the Development of Chinese Share Market*, 173–174.
69. The PRC adopted managed floating of CNY on 22 Jul. 2005. See <www.peopledaily.com.cn>, 22 Jul. 2005.

B-shares. This policy temporarily stimulated the B-share market. However, on 1 June 2001, the CSRC completely opened its B-share market to domestic investors to crack down on the black foreign currency market, and all Chinese people could trade in the B-shares market. On December 2001, both the Shanghai and the Shenzhen Stock Exchanges adopted new business rules, of which most provisions apply to both A-share and B-share trading.[70]

In conclusion, at this time, there are only three differences between A-share and B-share trading. Firstly, B-shares are still calculated in USD or HKD, while A shares are calculated in CNY. Secondly, B-share trading must be done through designated brokers, while investors may directly trade in A shares. Lastly, A-shares are still not open to foreign investors. The central government has been considering the merger of A-shares and B-shares for some time. The inconvertibility of CNY, however, remains the major hurdle. The changing of the business rules of the two stock exchanges is another step towards the merger between A-shares and B-shares. This merger will happen once CNY becomes completely floating.

6.2.2.   FOUR TYPES OF SHARES IN SHAREHOLDING COMPANIES CONVERTED FROM SOEs

Shares in the PRC can be classified as state shares, legal entity shares, employee shares, and public individual shares, according to the ownership of shares. These are the four types of shares in state-owned companies. In companies that are established by share issue, there are state shares, legal entity shares, and public individual shares. However, in companies converted from SOEs, there are state shares, legal entity shares, and employee shares, as well as public individual shares.

State-owned shares include state shares and legal entity shares.[71] The concept of state-owned shares came from the adoption of the shareholding system by the government in SOEs starting in 1992. The percentage of state-owned shares in the total number of shares of a state-owned company is completely decided upon by the government. To date, this percentage is still very high. Generally, it is above 40%; in some companies, it may be as high as 80%.[72] As most listed companies in the PRC are converted from SOEs and state-owned shares were not freely transferable, most shares of most listed companies were not transferable until May 2005, when the State Council released the Regulation on Division of State-owned Shareholding. This situation demonstrates that the shareholding structure in PRC listed companies is inappropriate and irrational. The shareholding structure forced the government to be heavily involved in the management of listed companies. With this structure, it was unlikely that a real market economy could be formed in

---

70. See the CSRC, *Disclosure Requirements of China Securities Market*, 311–352.
71. Li, Zhangzhe, *Finally Successful: The Report of the Development of Chinese Share Market*, 606.
72. Hu, Ruyin and Di Liu, 'Conclusions and Policy Suggestions', in *Corporate Governance: International Experience and China Practice* (in Chinese), ed. Tu, Guangshao & Congjiu Zhu (Beijing: People's Press, 2001), 173.

the PRC. This structure also put the minority shareholders in the PRC in a disadvantageous situation and led to the constant occurrence of infringement upon public shareholders by the controlling shareholders in state-owned companies. As the majority of listed companies are SOEs, the government had to focus on SOEs' ability to raise capital by issuing shares rather than consider the issue that disclosure and transparency were important regulatory tools in ensuring the confidence of investors.

In 1992, SOEs started transforming into shareholding companies.[73] As the senior managerial staff of SOEs were appointed by the government, these people were first responsible to the state. Because modern corporate management was not included in the companies transformed from SOEs until 1992, the senior managerial staff of these companies had not established a sense of loyalty to their companies. They could not be easily removed from their positions once they had been appointed, and consequently, some of them abused their powers for personal interests. For instance, during the process of transformation from SOEs into shareholding companies – except for state-owned shares – company directors and senior managerial staff had the power to divide employee shares and public individual shares. In China, there is a big difference between the internal issuing price and the public issuing price; the issuing price for employee shares is much lower than the price for publicly issued shares. The holders of more employee shares could benefit greatly from selling these shares at the market-trading price. In most cases, directors and senior managerial staff of the state-owned companies received more employee shares than did ordinary employees, which reflects the fact that at the beginning of the establishment of the shareholding system in SOEs, the principle of fairness was not adopted.

A big problem with state-owned shares is that they are not freely transferable. With the distribution of dividends and the allotment of new shares in most companies, the state became the largest shareholder and formed 'a dominant single shareholding' (*yi gu du da*).[74] This means that the state has the dominant holding of shares with voting rights. Currently, state shareholding on the average accounts for at least 65% of the total value of shares.[75] Non-transferability of state-owned shares is a sign that this securities market is not sophisticated.

---

73. The General Office of the State Council, the State Commission for Restructuring Economic Reform, the State Planning Commission, the Ministry of Finance, and the People's Bank of China jointly released the *Measures Concerning the Experiment of Shareholding System in SOEs* in 1992. See Wang, Yuming & An Jiang, *The Economic Law Perspective of State-owned Enterprises Reform*, 17.
74. *Yi gu du da* has become a special term in China to refer to the state-dominated shareholding structure in most listed Chinese companies. See Xu, Hongtang, 'Corporate Self-Regulation and the Reform of Company Law: Focused on Corporate Governance' in unpublished essays of the 2002 Annual International Symposium on Corporate Law Reform under the Global Economic Competition at the School of Law, Tsinghua University, Beijing, September 2002, vol. 2; Wu, Jinglian, *Reform: Now at a Critical Point* (Beijing: Sanlian Bookshop Press, 2002), 161.
75. Li, Zhangzhe, *Finally Successful: The Report of the Development of Chinese Share Market*, 606.

In practice, some SOEs tried to sell their state-owned shares, but this has been strictly controlled by the government. For instance, in August 1994, the SSE allowed Sichuan Changhong Company to trade the allotment of its state-owned shares.[76] Soon after that, the CSRC announced that this trading was prohibited. It publicly criticized the SSE and confiscated the profits made by the brokerage companies. Another example is Yuehuadian Company. On 9 May 1995, the SZSE allowed Yuehuadian Company's allotment of legal entity shares to be traded. Two days later, the CSRC held a press conference to clarify that state-owned shares were not allowed to be traded after their allotment.[77] These cases illustrate that listed companies wanted to reduce their shares that were either directly or indirectly controlled by the government, but the central government was not comfortable about allowing them to do so.

There are two technical questions that may explain why, for a long time, state-owned shares were not transferable. The first is, Who can represent the state as the owners of state-owned shares?[78] The second is, At what price should state-owned shares be sold?[79] Related to the first question, another question is whether the State Council should establish a separate department to supervise the floating of state-owned shares or whether the boards of directors may decide how to float state-owned shares. Related to the second question, another question is whether state-owned shares should be sold at the same market price as the individuals shares even though they had an issuing price different from that of public individual shares. Up to this time, there have been no clear answers to these questions.

After about ten years of debate, the central government decided to reduce the state's shareholding in companies. The decision to reduce part of the state's shareholding was made in September 1999 by the Fourth Meeting of the Fifteenth Congress of the CCP. It is worth noting here that it is the CCP – not the NPC – that makes the most important policies in China. Strong influence from the CCP is one of the unique features of the PRC securities market. The CCP set two steps for the state's shareholding reduction: the first was to reduce the state's shareholding to 51% of the total shares; the second was to further reduce the state's shareholding by need.[80] To implement this policy, the CSRC selected two companies to conduct an experiment of such a reduction through share allotment in October 1999. The state-owned shares were first sold to the holders of the transferable shares in the same company at a price higher than the value of company assets but ten times less than the issuing price.[81] It can be seen that the focus of the PRC government's regulation was how to control the market rather than how to serve the

---

76. Li, Zhangzhe, *Finally Successful: The Report of the Development of Chinese Share Market*, 410.
77. *Ibid.*
78. Wang, Yuming & An Jiang, *The Economic Law Perspective of State-owned Enterprises Reform*, 17.
79. *Ibid.*
80. Li, Zhangzhe, *Finally Successful: The Report of the Development of Chinese Share Market*, 606.
81. *Ibid.*

interests of shareholders. This reflects one of the key features of the PRC securities market, called a 'policy market'.[82]

In June 2001, with the approval of the State Council, the Ministry of Finance released the Measures on Reduction of State Shareholding. However, this document caused a plunge of the securities markets in Shanghai and Shenzhen. The CSRC had to stop the implementation of that Administrative Directive with the State Council's approval on October 23. After that, the CSRC sought public opinions and suggestions on the means of the reduction of state shareholding. However, in June 2002, with the approval of the State Council, the CSRC formally stopped the reduction of state shareholding in domestic markets,[83] although based on the decision of the CSRC, the companies listed overseas could only continue their state shareholding reduction with an understanding in certain circumstances, demonstrating that state shares are treated differently. This practice breaches the principle of 'equal share equal treatment'.[84] The CSRC also made the statement that even if state shares could not be traded on the stock exchange, they could continue to be traded by transfer agreements.[85] Government interference in the securities market is another sign of a non-market economy. China has to abolish such interference on its way towards a market economy. However, as the market is underdeveloped and has inexperienced investors, Chinese investors have to rely upon the government from time to time to save the market from collapsing. The CSRC, as the regulator, is often in a dilemma. The controlling position of the state in state-owned companies was only changed after the beginning of the shareholding division system experiment on 29 April 2005.[86] At the same time, the experimental companies and their directors must ensure that there are no false or misleading statements or gross omissions.[87]

Legal entity shares are the shares purchased by companies and other legal entities. In state-owned companies, legal entity shares and state shares are usually referred to as state-owned shares together. In the transformation from SOEs into state-owned companies, a big problem was that many senior officers of SOEs did not represent the interests of their companies. They abused their managing power to sell themselves more employee shares or even convert legal entity shares into their own. The above-mentioned Administrative Rules have provisions regarding legal entity shares. With the implementation of these rules and the gradual standardization of the corporatization of SOEs, the problems associated with legal entity shares were gradually solved. In companies that are not SOEs, legal entity shares refer to shares issued to legal entities other than the issuing company itself. Legal entity shares are also not freely transferable at this time.

---

82. This means this market is controlled by government policies rather than regulatory rules.
83. <www.cs.com.cn>, 24 Jun. 2002,
84. Article 130 of the PRC Company Law of 1993 contains such a principle.
85. Li, Zhangzhe, *Finally Successful: The Report of the Development of Chinese Share Market*, 606.
86. The CSRC, *Circular on Experiment in Shareholding Division in Listed Companies*.
87. Article 8.

Employee shares are the shares that a company issues internally to its employees. Like state-owned shares, employee shares are not issued at the same price as that of public individual shares. On the contrary, employee shares are usually sold to employees at a minimal price. Therefore, employee shares are a form of benefit to company employees. The creation of employee shares was to provide incentives to employees. Employee shareholding started in the early 1980s, when some enterprises needed capital to expand their operations but the government did not allow enterprises to issue shares to the public. When SOEs were converted into shareholding companies in the early 1990s, the senior staff of the companies kept some of the company shares for its employees after the proportion of state shareholding was decided upon by the government. Once employee shares were sold on the market, employee shareholders would make a lot of money because the market price was usually much higher than the par value of the employee shares. Even if the holders of employee shares did not sell their shares, they could receive dividends and were entitled to the new share allotment, which, again, was cheaper than the market price.[88]

In most companies, managers and other senior employees of the company were given the opportunity to buy more employee shares than were ordinary employees. In a country that does not have a sound legal system, this unequal share-allotment was not treated as illegal. However, by its nature, the means of the issuing of employee shares in the PRC is not consistent with the principle of fairness.

As employee shares were not issued to the public, the government did not allow the transfer of such shares for some time, even if the holders of these shares were entitled to dividends and new share allotments. However, by the end of 1992, many problems arose regarding employee shares: (a) employee shares were traded openly in the way same as were the shares issued to the general public, which was apparently unfair to the investors who traded in the securities market; (b) China had had the quota system for share issuing for some time and the government also set the ratio of employee-share issuing to prevent the loss of state assets, but, in practice, many state-owned companies breached this ratio without punishment; and (c) some senior officers of the companies abused their power by buying legal entity shares with company money that were registered under the names of public individuals.[89] As there was a big gap between the price of legal entity shares and employee shares, and the price of the shares issued to the public, a black market of securities trading came into being. This situation caused great capital losses in state-owned companies.

Because of the problems of employee shares, the State Council distributed an administrative directive of SCRES: the Urgent Circular Concerning Immediate Prohibition on Non-standard Issue of Employee Internal Shares, on 3 April 1993. Under this Circular, new companies would not be approved to issue employee shares

---

88. Li, Zhanhzhe, *Finally Successful: The Report of the Development of Chinese Share Market*, 260.
89. Li, Zhangzhe, *Finally Successful: The Report of the Development of Chinese Share Market*, 260–261.

for the time being; employee shares could not be transferred within three years after their issue; these shares could only be transferred between company employees three years after the issue; these shares could only be traded in the market three years after its listing; and the black market of share trading must be closed. As the SCRES was then the body in charge of the economic reform policy, it released a number of administrative rules to limit and prohibit the over-speculation on employee shares. In its Regulation Concerning Employee Shareholding in Companies Issuing Shares to Designated People released on 5 July 1993, there were limitations on the issuing and trading of employee shares. The Circular Concerning Correction of Irregular Practices of Employee Shareholding by Joint Stock Companies Issuing Shares to Designated Companies was released on July 5. It required the companies that issued employee shares after April 3 to cancel such share issues and refund the capital and interest to their employees. From then on, the problems of the unlawful issuing and transfer of employee shares gradually stopped. The black market of share trading, such as the famous Chendu Red Temple market, soon disappeared.[90]

In 1994, the PRC government stopped the practice of establishing companies by share issues to designated people. Employees were no longer able to buy shares before the IPOs, but employee shares continued to exist in the form of 10% of the quota of an IPO to be offered to the employees of the company.[91] As there was a big gap between the IPO price and the price in the secondary market, these shares were usually sold after the six-month non-transferable period. Thus, company employee shareholding was criticized as being 'short-term security' to employees. The purpose of this employee shareholding system is far from the incentive purpose of the employee shareholding system in Western countries. The CSRC prohibited the adoption of the employee shareholding system in new share issuing in December 1998 in its Circular Concerning Stopping the Issue of Company Employee Shares. This was one step to move the PRC securities market into a free market without government interference, but it does not mean that employee shareholding was abolished. In 2001, the Shanghai and the Shenzhen Stock Exchanges adopted the same listing rules, which were amended in 2004 and 2006. These two sets of new listing rules both have provisions on the listing of company employee shares in Section 4 of Chapter 3. When discussing the types of shares of the PRC, it is important to distinguish those shares that are issued outside mainland China by Chinese companies or companies associated with Chinese companies.

H-shares are issued by the Chinese companies listed on the Hong Kong Stock Exchange. They can only be subscribed and traded by Hong Kong residents and foreign investors. The main reasons why H-shares are issued include the following: (a) the trading of B-shares was not convenient for foreign investors, as CNY are not freely convertible and cannot attract much foreign investment; (b) these companies have adopted the financial and accounting systems that are consistent with those

---

90. *Ibid.*
91. The Shanghai Stock Exchange, 'SOEs: Their Real Value and Practice', in 2001 (7) *Listed Companies* (in Chinese), 26.

used in foreign companies while most domestic companies adopted very different accounting and financial systems; and (c) the Chinese legal system could not meet the requirements for international investments. These reasons forced the Chinese government to provide other means for capital raising from overseas. The name of H-shares came from the first initial of 'Hong Kong'. Precisely, H-shares should be defined as a type of CNY special shares that are listed and traded on the Hong Kong Stock Exchange. The face value of H-shares is marked in CNY but subscribed and traded in HKD.

The listing of H-shares is required to be approved by the State Council as well as to meet the listing requirements of the Hong Kong Stock Exchange. The first nine listings of H-shares were approved by the State Council in September 1992. On 19 June 1993, the Hong Kong Stock Exchange and Hong Kong Securities and Futures Commission entered into a Memorandum of Regulatory Cooperation with the CSRC as well as the SSE and the SZSE in Beijing. Tsingtao Brewery Company was the first Chinese company listed on the Hong Kong Stock Exchange (HKSE). The H-shares of this company began listing on the HKSE on 15 July 1993.[92] Some companies registered in Hong Kong are funded by the Chinese government. These are often called 'window companies' of the Chinese government at all levels. The shares of these companies are often called 'red chips'. The share issuing of these companies in Hong Kong has to comply with the relevant rules in Hong Kong, but it is not subject to the laws and regulations of mainland China.

N-shares are the shares that are issued on the New York Stock Exchange (NYSE) to foreign investors by Chinese companies.[93] Like H-shares, N-shares are also marked in CNY but subscribed and traded in USD. The first N-shares were not directly listed on the NYSE, but rather through American Depository Receipts, which were negotiable instruments issued by the Depository. The first official N-shares were issued in 1994. On 28 April 1994, the CSRC and the SEC of the US signed a Memorandum of Regulatory Cooperation.[94] In fact, the first Chinese company listed on the NYSE was Shenyang Jinbei Automobile Company, which did so through another company it controlled.[95] As this type of indirect listing was not approved by the CSRC, it was soon ordered to stop by the central government. One of the reasons why Shenyang Jinbei did not apply to the CSRC for approval was that the CSRC was not a regulatory body then and its authority was not recognized at the local government level. The *Shenyang Jinbei* case also showed that there were no uniform rules regulating securities issuing in the PRC at the beginning of the formation of the securities market.

---

92. Li, Zhanhzhe, *Finally Successful: The Report of the Development of Chinese Share Market*, 270–271.
93. Zhou, Yousu (ed), General Theories on Securities Law (in Chinese). (Chengdu: Sichuan People's Press, 1999), 94.
94. Li, Zhangzhe, *Finally Successful: The Report of the Development of Chinese Share Market*, 329.
95. Author's interview with an official of the SSE in September 1999.

In addition to the above discussed four major types of shares, there are other types of shares in the PRC. *L-shares* are the shares issued by Chinese companies on the London Stock Exchange.[96] *S-shares* are the shares issued by Chinese companies on the Singapore Stock Exchange.[97]

There are two major problems with the issuing of different kinds of shares. First, in the same issuance, the price of state shares is decided by face value, but legal entity shares and individual shares are sold at higher prices than face value. The result is that in the same share issuance, there are different share prices for different kinds of shares. This is in breach of the principles of 'equal shares equal rights' and 'equal shares equal interests'. In fact, the interests of legal entities and individual investors are often infringed upon by state shareholders. Secondly, some companies issue A-shares, B-shares, and H-shares at different prices. The issuing prices for B-shares and H-shares are often lower than A-share prices so as to attract investors outside China. However, the holders of different shares are paid similar dividends. As a result, the holders of B-shares and H-shares to some extent infringe upon the interests of A-shareholders. These two problems cannot be solved under the Securities Law or the 1993 Interim Regulations.

6.2.3.   BONDS

Apart from shares, bonds are another major type of security traded on the two domestic stock exchanges. Bonds include state treasury bonds (or T-bonds), corporate bonds, and financial bonds.[98] In 1981, the PRC started issuing state treasury bonds.[99] In 1993, the SSE launched the T-bond repo, an investment alternative that helped to stimulate the market and bring forth the mortgage function of T-bonds.[100] So far there are four types of bonds: treasury bonds, construction bonds, corporate bonds, and financial bonds.

The government started to issue state treasury bonds to raise capital from the public in 1981. Treasury bonds are securities with fixed interest rates. They are issued by the Ministry of Finance and are floated to cover budget deficits and to raise funds for large domestic construction projects. They were the first type of security issued after the PRC's economic reform started.[101] Construction bonds are issued by the Ministry of Finance to finance major construction projects or infrastructure projects. Financial bonds are issued by banks and other non-banking financial institutions as an additional resource of funding and are usually used for specific financial projects.[102] Corporate bonds are issued by trading enterprises to

---

96.   Zhou, Yousu (ed), *General Theories on Securities Law*, 94.
97.   *Ibid.*
98.   Jin, Dehong, *Contemporary Securities Market of China* (in Chinese), 109.
99.   Zhou, Yousu (ed), *General Theories on Securities Law*, 109.
100. The SSE, *Stock Exchange Fact Book 2000*, 1.
101. Zhou, Yousu (ed), *General Theories on Securities Law*, 109.
102. *Ibid.*, 115.

supplement their general capital raising by share issuing.[103] The trading of investment funds started in 1998. By the end of 2000, sixteen securities investment funds had been traded on the SSE.[104] For a few decades after the PRC was founded, the Chinese government relied upon collecting funds and taxes mainly from SOEs as a means of capital raising.[105] The reform of the economic system starting in the late 1970s brought about changes in national revenue collection. Taxes collected by the state dropped dramatically. Enterprises and individuals therefore could retain more profits after the payment of taxes than before.

The issuing of state treasury bonds is done through a quota system. Each year, the Ministry of Finance announces the quota on the issue of state treasury bonds, the term, and the interest rate of state treasury bonds that are to be issued after approval is given by the State Council.[106] Initially, only ten-year long-term bonds were issued. Because the interest rate of such bonds was much lower than the interest rate of bank savings, and especially because state treasury bonds were not transferable, the Chinese were not very interested in buying them. The issuing of such bonds was very difficult in the 1980s. The government had to force the Chinese people to buy state treasury bonds in the name of a political task. The government departments at all levels were given a quota to buy such bonds. The government departments then distributed the quota among its employees.

With the issuing of shares starting in 1983, the issuing of state treasury bonds was subject to competitive pressure from the issuing of shares.[107] Gradually, the Chinese government started to reduce the term of state treasury bonds from ten-year terms only to a variety of terms, including eight years, five years, three years, one year, and even six months, given that investors were more interested in short-term investments.[108] In 2001, China for the first time issued twenty-year long-term state treasury bonds to encourage long-term investments.

Capital raising by issuing state treasury bonds had some disadvantages. Before the mid-1980s, China was in the process of building a planned commodity economy and the government still planned many aspects of the state economy. For instance, the government decided the total amount, the term, and the interest rate of state treasury bonds. The interest rate of long-term state treasury bonds was slightly higher than that of the same term for deposits in banks. The purchase of state treasury bonds was compulsory before 1988; each state-owned enterprise and government department had to fulfil the quota decided upon by the Ministry of Finance by purchasing treasury bonds.[109] Thus, the employees of state-owned

---

103. *Ibid.*, 101.
104. *Ibid.*
105. I. Tokley & T. Ravn, *Company and Securities Law in China* (Hong Kong: Sweet & Maxwell, 1998), 62.
106. The Regulations on State Treasury Bonds of the State Council 1992, Art. 4.
107. In July 1983, Shenzhen Bao'an County Joint Investment Limited Corporation became the first corporation incorporated by issuing shares to the public.
108. Zheng, Zhenlong (ed), *A Concise History of Chinese Securities Development* (in Chinese) (Beijing: Economics Science Press, 2000), 127; Zhou, Yousu (ed), *General Theories on Securities Law*, 111.
109. Zhou, Yousu (ed), *General Theorieson Securities Law*, 113.

enterprises and government departments were directly compelled to purchase state treasury bonds. During the first few years, state treasury bonds were not allowed to be traded. Ordinary Chinese people knew little about state treasury bonds, as the government did not seek to benefit the people in the value of these bonds.

Gradually, enterprises and individuals became reluctant to buy state treasury bonds because of the low interest rate of state treasury bonds. In 1984, the State Council granted permission to some enterprises to issue enterprise bonds to meet the capital needs of these enterprises.[110] These enterprise bonds were for shorter terms. However, because the government controlled the amount and interest rates of enterprise bonds to be issued, they could not meet the needs of people looking for investment opportunities. This situation fundamentally led to the emergence of share issuing in the Chinese securities market. Another problem with state treasury bonds and enterprise bonds was that they were only issued to Chinese citizens who resided inside China. Even the Chinese who lived overseas or in Hong Kong, Macao, or Taiwan were not eligible to invest in such bonds, let alone foreigners. This approach limited the development of the bonds market in the PRC.

In September 1984, the first standard joint stock company, Beijing Tianqiao Department Store, was established.[111] Shanghai and Shenzhen followed this step by establishing their joint stock companies. In 1988, China opened its state treasury bonds market. These bonds could be underwritten by non-financial institutions.[112] At the same time, state treasury bonds started to be traded over-the-counter. Government administration in the state treasury issuance was gradually minimized. The openness and the over-counter-trading of state treasury bonds, the issuing of enterprise bonds, and the establishment of the joint stock enterprises were the experiments for the establishment of the securities market.

6.2.4.   FUNDS

The emergence of funds occurred before the issue of B-shares. In 1987, the Bank of China and the China International Trust and Investment Corporation started to set up mutual funds.[113] However, these funds were on a small scale, with the focus on attracting foreign investors.[114] The first fund targeting domestic investors, the Zhuxin Fund, was set up in July 1991 with the approval of the Shenzhen Branch of the PBOC.[115] In 1992, over twenty funds, both open-ended and close-ended, were launched for the wide institutional and retail investor interests in the Chinese securities market.[116] All the funds management companies were established by the

---

110. *Ibid.*, 129.
111. R. Nottle, 'The Development of Securities Market in China in the 1990s', *Company and Securities Law Journal* 11, no. 8 (1993): 504.
112. *Ibid.*
113. Zhang, Zhenlong (ed), *A Concise History of Chinese Securities Development*, 285.
114. *Ibid.*
115. *Ibid.*, 286.
116. Jin, Dehong, *Contemporary Securities Market of China* (in Chinese), 175.

government. This again shows the strong feature of government control of the securities market. However, up to now, the trading of funds only accounts for a very small proportion of the entire trading volume.

6.3. OPENING OF THE PRC SECURITIES MARKET AFTER ITS WTO ACCESSION

China formally became the 143rd member of the WTO on 11 December 2001. In its WTO Accession Agreement, China made the following concessions on securities market access: (a) foreign securities institutions might directly trade in B-share trading; (b) China offices of foreign securities institutions might become members of the Shanghai and the Shenzhen Stock Exchanges; (c) foreign securities institutions might set up joint venture companies to trade in investment funds with foreign investment of less than 33%; in three years, foreign investments might reach up to 49%; and (d) three years after China joined the WTO, foreign securities companies might establish joint venture companies to underwrite A-share issues and trade in B-shares, H-shares, government bonds, and corporate bonds, and also might establish funds with foreign investments of less than one-third of the total investment.[117] Although foreign companies may trade Chinese shares, they cannot issue shares in the PRC securities market. This is an indication that China has not completely opened its securities market, nor has it adopted a real market economy.

The CSRC also pointed out that the opening of the securities industry was different from the opening of the securities market. The latter was about whether foreign investors are allowed to freely trade in Chinese securities. The CSRC claimed that the issue of opening the securities market was not within the WTO's financial services category.[118] This claim suggested that foreign investors might not be able to enter into the PRC securities market for some time after China's WTO accession was fulfilled. As for foreign investors, it is not very safe to enter into this market before it has become a transparent market.

6.3.1. MEANS FOR SHARE ISSUING

The CSRC treated share issuing on the Internet as one of the main methods of securities issuance in its Interim Circular on Share Issue and Subscription of 1996. In the CSRC's Interim Regulation Concerning Means of Share Issue and Subscription released on 26 December 1996, Internet issues, paid-up subscriptions, and savings subscriptions were clarified as three means of share issuing. In July 1999, it released another Circular on Further Improvement of Share Issue Methods. Under this Circular, listed companies are allowed to issue shares to individual investors

---

117. 'CSRC Publishes the Main Concessions on the Securities Market Access in China's WTO Accession' (in Chinese), *The Chinese Weekly*, Melbourne, 14 Dec. 2001, 21.
118. *Ibid.*

on the Internet while issuing shares to legal entities by allotment *(pei shou)*. Internet issuing has become a major means of share issuing. It is a sign of further development of the Chinese securities market.

Before 1 July 1999, when the Securities Law of 1998 came into effect, both the central government and local governments controlled share issuing under the quota system. The Securities Law abolished the quota system and adopted the 'hashing system' (verification system). The Securities Issue Verification Commission *(Fa Shen Wei)* was established to review the applications for share issuing. On 19 August 1999, the State Council approved and published the Regulation Concerning Securities Issue Verification Commission. According to this Regulation, the Securities Issue Verification Commission is composed of eighty members. Among them, the CSRC's Chief Investigator, the Chief Council, and the Chief Accountant, as well as the General Managers of the Shanghai and the Shenzhen Stock Exchanges, are automatic members.[119] There are eight members from the State Planning Commission, eight members from the Economic Management Department or ministries. There are other fifteen professionals from the CSRC and six experts from the two stock exchanges. There are five experts from state-owned banks, and one expert from the All-China Association of Industry and Commerce. There are five experts from the China Academy of Science or the China Academy of Social Science. Another eight experts should come from the China Securities Industry Association, the China Registered Accountants Association, the All China Lawyers Association, or other professional bodies. Another eight securities experts, three university professors, and five famous people sit on the Commission.[120] The adoption of the verification system is a further step moving towards a market economy.

The Securities Law clarifies the difference between share issuing and share listing.[121] In practice, the shares issued to the public could be listed in two weeks' or one months' time.[122] This has caused a number of problems: first, the direct listing after the share issuing made trading outside the stock exchanges impossible; second, it limited the number of companies to be listed; and finally, it caused the high capital gains in the trading after listing and therefore created the bubble phenomenon in the securities market.

6.3.2.   FORMATION AND ABOLITION OF THE QUOTA SYSTEM FOR
          SHARE ISSUING

China's transition from a planned commodity economy to a socialist market economy has been a long process. The re-emergence of the securities market was under the strict control and supervision of the government, either at the local or the

---

119. Article 4.
120. Above n. 116.
121. The Securities Law of 2005, Art. 50.
122. Zheng, Zhenlong (ed), *A Concise History of the Chinese Securities Development*, 200.

central government level. As most enterprises are SOEs, their transformation into shareholding companies was designed and controlled by the government. The two stock exchanges were first established by the local governments and later on were transferred to the direct control of the central government through the CSRC. The senior officers of the stock exchanges are appointed by the central government. Before the stock exchanges were transferred to the administration of the central government, neither the Shanghai nor the Shenzhen municipal government used quotas to control share issuing. Although with the deepening of economic reform, the government's direct involvement in securities issuing and trading was diminishing, its involvement in securities market regulation still existed. The use of the quota system for share issuing is such an example.

Adopting a quota system for share issuing was a specific feature of the PRC securities market. Under this system, the former State Planning Development Commission and the CSRC set an annual quota as to the size of share issuing.[123] This plan needed to be approved by the State Council before it came into effect. The quota for share issuing by the companies under the control of the local governments was distributed to the relevant local government. The local government examined and approved the share issue applications by local companies.[124] The quota for share issuing of the companies under the control of the central government was distributed to the relevant patron ministry or commission. The relevant ministry or commission, after consultation with the local government where such a company was located, examined and approved the share issuing by the companies under the leadership of the central government.[125] Thus, any company that wanted to issue shares had to apply to its local government and relevant patron ministry or commission of the State Council for approval. If the quota for a particular year had been used up, other companies could not apply for issuing shares, even if they met all the other requirements for share issuing. If the quota for a particular year had not been used up, it might be used in the following year.

Although the quota system was convenient for the government to control the development of the securities market, it caused unfairness. First, in the developed provinces, the quota for share issuing might not have met the needs of the companies seeking to raise capital by share issuing, while in less-developed provinces, the quota might have been greater than what was needed.[126] In these provinces, the local government sometimes forced its local companies to apply for share issuing, even if these companies did not meet other share issuing requirements. This was referred to as packaging listing *(bao zhuang shag shi).*[127] Packaging listing was one of the major reasons for giving false information in the securities market.

---

123. Zhou, Yousu (ed), *General Theorieson Securities Law*, 179.
124. The *State Council's 1993 Interim Regulation*, Art. 12.
125. *Ibid.*
126. Zhou, Yousu (ed), *General Theoriess on Securities Law*, 180.
127. Hua, Sheng, *The Economic Analysis of China's Securities Market* (Beijing: Economic Science Press, 2004), 40.

Second, the quota system disadvantaged private companies. As the quota was distributed to the companies according to their affiliation with the local or the central government, private companies were outside these two categories because they had no affiliation with the government. Thus, they had to apply for special consideration for share issuing applications. Because there was no rule on share issuing by private companies, the CSRC had the final say in approving such share issuing applications.

Third, the quota system was not fair to joint ventures that were outside the categories of companies under the leadership of the local government or the category of companies under the leadership of the central government. The share issuing applications by those companies were also subject to special consideration.

Lastly, as the quota was decided and controlled by the central and local governments, there was no transparency at all in the process of allocating the quota. The problems of lack of transparency and fairness caused great debate and criticism and finally forced the PRC government to abolish the quota system for share issuing.[128]

The quota system for share issuing was formally abolished by the Securities Law at the end of 1998.[129] Any company that wants to issue shares and be listed on the stock exchange only needs to apply to the CSRC and submit the supporting documents. However, the quota system was not completely abolished at the end of 1998, because the CSRC issued a circular in June 2000 recognizing the validity of the 1997 year's quota and allowing the use of the quota until it was used up.[130] This may be seen as an indication that the PRC government had not treated transparency and disclosure as high priorities in the development of its securities market.

6.3.3.   FROM AN EXAMINATION AND APPROVAL SYSTEM
          TO A VERIFICATION SYSTEM

Countries such as the USA and Australia have registration systems that do not require government approval of company listings. So long as the stock exchange has reviewed all the securities issue application documents submitted by a company and is satisfied with their accuracy and completeness, the securities issuance may go ahead. In contrast, countries such as Germany, France, and Belgium have an examination and approval system.[131] Under this type of system, the securities regulator not only reviews the true situation of the company applying for securities issuance, but also examines whether the company has met all the requirements for securities issuance set out by the securities regulator.

---

128. Zhou, Yousu (ed.), *General Theoriess on Securities Law*, 181.
129. The PRC Securities Law of 1998, Art. 43.
130. The CSRC, *Circular on Relevant Issues on Year 1997 Share Issue Quota*, 7 Jun. 2000.
131. Wang, Lian Zhou & Cheng Li (eds), *The Making of the Securities Law* (in Chinese) (Shanghai: Sanlian Bookshop, 2000), 295.

Given the poor quality of listed companies, the frequent misconduct of officers of listed companies, and the primitive stage of the PRC securities market, PRC legislators decided to adopt a system that was somewhere between the above-mentioned two systems – the verification system.[132] Since the early 1990s, the issuing of securities had to be examined and approved by the SCSC or the CSRC because the quota was not great enough for the companies that wanted to raise capital in the securities market. The problems caused by the quota system finally led to the abolition of this system. It is to be hoped that, under the new system, the issue of transparency may attract more attention from the PRC government.

6.3.4.   THE MAIN BOARD AND THE HIGH-TECH BOARD

The development of the PRC securities market has been designed and directed by the CCP and the executive government. Although the issuance of A and B shares belongs to the main boards at the SSE and the SZSE, other trading boards also exist. On 20 August 1999, the CCP and the State Council released the Resolution on Strengthening Technical Invention and Developing High Technology and Industrialization. This policy proposed to give preferential support to competent high-tech companies to enter into domestic and international capital markets. It also directed the SSE and the SZSE to establish high-tech securities markets.

Following this policy, the Standing Committee of the NPC made an amendment to the Company Law of 1993 by adding an article to allow the high-tech joint stock limited liability companies to apply for listing on either the SSE or the SZSE.[133] In January 2000, the CSRC decided to establish high-tech markets on the SSE and the SZSE so as to create separate indexes of the shares of high-tech companies. With the support of the CCP's policy, the national law, and the CSRC's administrative rule, high-tech shares suddenly boomed. In April, the CSRC drafted Measures for Share Issue by High-Tech Companies. This document mainly drew on experiences from the growth enterprise market of the HKSE.

At the same time, the CSRC created a 'secondary board' to take the place of the 'high-tech board' to broaden the category of the new companies.[134] In June, it was initially decided that the SSE would become the main board market while the SZSE would become the secondary board market. Because the CSRC was worried that the difference between these two boards might affect the stability of the securities market, in September it adopted the term 'growth enterprise market' to take the place of the 'secondary market'.[135] Because many high-tech companies used this opportunity to issue shares without approval and because of the lack of confidence in the new market, the growth enterprise market did not open. Instead,

---

132. *Ibid.*
133. The PRC Company Law of 1993, Art. 229.
134. Li, Zhangzhe, *Finally Successful: The Report of the Development of Chinese Share Market,* 731.
135. *Ibid.*, 732.

in 2004, the medium and small business board was opened in the SZSE. This board was replaced by the growth board in June 2009.[136]

6.4.   INVESTORS IN THE SECURITIES MARKET

In the development of the securities market, legislators had not paid much attention to the disclosure regime because the main purpose of the lawmaking was to establish a so-called modern enterprise system – a shareholding system in SOEs.[137] The regulator, CSRC, had only become more active on cracking down on misleading and deceptive disclosure after it was given the authority as the sole regulator in 1997. The investors in the PRC securities market had not realized that they were entitled to full and accurate disclosure by listed companies. However, with the deepening of the economic reform, the ordinary people in the PRC had accumulated fairly large sums of savings. They had to invest in the securities market as there were not many choices for investments.

However, individual investors in the securities market generally are not sophisticated. The SZSE conducted a survey entitled 'China Individual Investors on the Chinese Market' in early 2002.[138] According to this survey, most of the individual investors had gained their securities knowledge from non-educational channels. Of those surveyed, 70.4% had gained their knowledge from friends and relatives, securities analysts, and newspapers, while 51.5% made their investment decisions based on securities analysts' recommendations, friends and relatives' recommendations, or even hearsay. About 20% made investments without any investment analysis.[139]

6.5.   SECURITIES COMPANIES

Under the Securities Law of 1998, only securities companies can act as brokers. Securities companies could be classified as comprehensive securities companies or brokerage securities companies.[140] Securities companies must apply for a business license. Comprehensive securities companies might engage in the following businesses: (a) brokerage; (b) the securities business as a principal; (c) securities underwriting; and (d) other businesses verified by the CSRC.[141] Brokerage securities companies were not allowed to conduct other types of business except brokerage

---

136. The SZSE released its Listing Rules for Growth Enterprises on 6 June 2009 and they became effective from 1 July 2009.
137. Wang, Lianzhou & Cheng Li (eds), *Uneasy Securities Law* (in Chinese). (Shanghai: Shanghai Sanlian Bookshop Press, 2000), 295.
138. Chen, B, Li XM & YZ Du, 'Survey of Individual Investors on Chinese Securities Market', *China Securities Daily*, 15 Apr. 2002, 13.
139. *Ibid.*
140. The PRC Securities Law of 1998, Art. 119.
141. *Ibid.*, Art. 129.

business.[142] This classification was a feature of the developing securities market in China. It showed the government's strong control of this young market. The Securities Law of 2005 no longer uses this classification of securities companies. The scope of business of securities companies has been broadened to include not only acting as brokers and principals, but also as financial and investment consultants, and securities assets mangers, as well as listing sponsors.[143]

6.6. CLASSIC CASES INVOLVING DISCLOSURE ON THE PRC SECURITIES MARKET

Before the amendments to the Securities Law were made in October 2005, the PRC government had been focused on encouraging the development of its securities market. From the provisions of the Company Law of 1993 and the Securities Law of 1998, it was clear that the ruling party and the legislature did not put corporate disclosure as its highest priority in lawmaking. Instead, using the securities market as a tool to transfer SOEs into the business form of companies became the highest priority of the CCP and the lawmakers. The CSRC, as the sole regulator of the securities market, still lacks authority to enforce its regulatory rules. The majority investors in the PRC securities market – individual investors – have not realized their rights to proper disclosure. These problems, together with the defects in the Chinese legal system, in particular, the lack of cooperation between government departments and the poor enforcement of law (discussed in Chapter 2) caused the frequent occurrence of fraudulent and misleading cases in the securities market. During this establishing process, there have been many cases regarding violations of laws, regulations, administrative directives, and listing rules. Even after the enactment of the Company Law of 2005 and the Securities Law of 2005, there were still breaches of disclosure law. The *Hangxiaoganggou* case of 2007 is such an example. The following section examines some classic cases of disclosure and highlights the key problems in the Chinese securities disclosure regime.

6.6.1. THE *BAOYAN* INCIDENT

By 30 September 1993, a subsidiary company of Shenzhen Bao'an Company Group had already taken over 16% of the shares of Shanghai Yanzhong Company, according to a notice of this subsidiary company. On October 5, Shenzhen Bao'an Company Group denied this takeover, but several days later, Bao'an announced that it had taken over 18% of Yanzhong shares and called for a shareholders' meeting of Yanzhong Company. This demand was refused by Yanzhong Company. The CSRC decided that Bao'an had violated Article 47 of the 1993

---

142. *Ibid.*, Art. 130.
143. Article 125.

Interim Regulations by not disclosing its takeover of Yanzhong shares. The CSRC fined the Bao'an (Shanghai) Company CNY 1 million for false disclosure.[144]

6.6.2.   THE CASE OF BEIHAI ZHENGDA COMPANY'S TAKEOVER
              OF THE SHARES OF SUSANSHAN COMPANY

In November 1993, one of Hainan Province's newspapers, *Special Economic Zone Daily*, released the news about Beihai Zhengda Real Estate Company's takeover of the shares of Zhejiang Province's Susanshan Company. It also published a letter written to the newspaper by Beihai Company. In this letter, it was confirmed that Beihai Zhengda Company had taken over 5.006% of the transferable shares of Susanshan Company. With the news in *Special Economic Zone Daily*, there was a big change in the share price of Susanshan Company. The CSRC immediately investigated with the SZSE and found that the so-called takeover had not happened. The letter to the newspaper editor by Beihai Zhengda Company was forged by an individual investor. The seal of Beihai Zhengda Company on the letter sent to the newspaper was also forged. *Special Economic Zone Daily* did not verify the seal and the letter before it published the letter and released the news about the takeover. The person who forged the news was heavily fined by the CSRC. *Special Economic Zone Daily* was given a warning by the CSRC for disclosing false information.[145]

6.6.3.   THE *QIONGMINYUAN* CASE OF A FALSE FINANCIAL REPORT

Qiongminyuan Modern Agriculture Development Joint Stock Company was listed on the SZSE in April 1993. Its share price had always been low since its listing. At the beginning of 1997, it issued its annual financial report for1996, claiming that it had made a profit of CNY 570 million. According to this figure, this company's profit in 1996 was 1,000 times that of 1995. This reporting raised the suspicion of the CSRC. It conducted an investigation and found that out of the so-called profit of CNY 570 million, CNY 540 million did not exist. The accounting firm engaged by Qiongminyuan had provided a false assets evaluation report. The auditing firms jointly gave a false audit report. The company, the accounting firm, and the two auditing firms had all violated the State Council's 1993 Interim Regulations and the accounting rules of the Ministry of Finance. The *Qiongminyuan* case was the fist serious false disclosure case in the PRC securities market. More than 40 thousand investors suffered losses because of false disclosure. The CSRC gave

---

144. Li, Zhangzhe, *Finally Successful: The Report of the Development of Chinese Share Market*, 304 and 306; Ren, Zili, *The Theories of the Chinese Securities Law and an Analysis of Classic Cases* (in Chinese) (Beijing: China Procuratorate Press, 2000), 357–360.
145. Hu, Jinmiao & Weilin Li, *Analysis of Securities Investment Cases* (Jinan: Shangdong University Press, 2000), 248–250.

a warning to the Qiongminyuan Company. One auditing firm was recommended for de-registration and the person in charge at that firm was disqualified from practice. The other auditing firm was given a warning, with six months of disqualification from practice, and its auditor was disqualified for three years. The accounting firm was fined CNY 300,000 and suspended from evaluating securities companies for six months, and its accountant who was directly in charge was disqualified from practice for three years. The Qiongminyuan Company and its holding company were fined CNY 2 million, respectively, and their illegal profits were also confiscated.[146] However, no criminal prosecution was brought against any individuals who were involved in the false disclosure, nor was any civil compensation liability imposed. This was a result of the limitations of the Securities Law of 1998.

6.6.4. THE *CHENGDU HONGGUANG* CASE OF PROFITS FORGERY AND FRAUDULENT LISTING

This was the second serious false disclosure case. Hongguang Company was converted from an SOE to a shareholding company in 1993. It obtained approval to issue shares to the public in 1997. Later, the CSRC found that it had gotten approval for share issuing by fraud. In its application for listing, the Hongguang Company claimed to have had a profit of CNY 103 million when in fact it had a loss of CNY 5.4 million. After the IPO, it claimed a loss of CNY 19.8 million in 1998 when in fact the real loss was CNY 22.952 million. In addition, the Honggunag Company did not disclose that it used most of the capital raised by issuing shares for a purpose other than that claimed in the capital-raising documents. The CSRC took the following actions: (a) it confiscated the illegal profit of CNY 4.5 million of the Hongguang Company; (b) the Hongguang Company was fined CNY 1 million; and (c) the Chairman, the General Manager, and the Chief Financial Officer were banned from the securities market for life. The individuals involved in this case did not have civil compensation liability imposed on them.

6.6.5. THE *YINGUANGXIA* FRAUD CASE

The *Yinguangxia* case is so far the most serious fraudulent disclosure case in PRC securities history. In August 2001, *Caijing* magazine disclosed the fraudulent conduct of Yinguangxia Company after its 440% share price increase in 2000. The CSRC then formed an investigation group. The group released its preliminary report in September 2001, which disclosed that Guangxia (Yinchuan) Company (known as Yinguangxia) had forged a profit of CNY 750 million during the period from 1999 to 2000.[147] The accounting firm of Yinguangxia, Shenzhen

---

146. *Ibid.*, 254–255.
147. <www.npcnews.cn/gb/paper8/6/class000800002/hwz171644.htm>, 12 Sep. 2001.

Zhongtianqin Accounting Firm, and its accountants who were involved in giving false accounting reports were de-registered by the Ministry of Finance. Under the Securities Law of 1998 and the 1993 Interim Regulations, the company and the individuals who had breached laws would be subject to administrative liability and criminal liability. However, neither the Company Law of 1993 nor the Securities Law of 1998 had detailed civil liability sections. It was extremely difficult for the investors who suffered losses because of the breach of disclosure provisions to sue for compensation.

There were a few specific problems with compensation litigation. First, who could be the plaintiff? The PRC has not adopted the concept of a class action in its legislation, and the courts have been reluctant to accept cases claiming civil compensation. Second, who should be the defendant? The law is not clear as to whether the broker and professional firms should be defendants. Third, how much compensation should the plaintiff be given? There was no clear idea among the courts about whether the innocent investors should be paid the real losses or the losses of predictable gain. Fourth, which court should have jurisdiction? Fifth, who had the onus of proof? It would have been very difficult for the plaintiff to collect evidence. Finally, how should the investors be paid? If they were to be paid out of the company's money, it would be in fact their own money.

6.6.6.   HAINAN KAILI COMPANY V. THE CSRC

In August 2000, Hannan Kaili Company sued the CSRC for its rejection of Kaili Company's listing application. The CSRC for the first time became a defendant and lost this case, showing that the principle of fairness has been adopted in the PRC securities market. The legal environment for securities regulation is being improved.

6.6.7.   REASONS FOR THE FREQUENT OCCURRING OF FALSE DISCLOSURE CASES

Through the analysis of a number of classic cases of securities disclosure, it is clear that false and misleading disclosure has been and continues to be a very serious problem in the PRC's securities regulation. In Western securities markets, false disclosure, such as in the Enron case in the USA and the One. Tel case in Australia, occurs from time to time. However, it occurs much less frequently than it does in the PRC.

There are unique reasons for the occurrences of false disclosure in the PRC. First, under the quota system, preferential treatment was given to many SOEs that did not meet the listing requirements. False packaging *(xu jia bao zhuang)* for public listing, which was encouraged by either the central government or local governments, affected the quality of listed companies.[148] Second, the purpose of

---

148.   Wang, Lianzhou & Cheng Li (eds), *Uneasy Securities Law*, 295.

solving the SOEs' problem of capital shortage by issuing securities became one of the motives for the legislature to pass the Securities Law.[149] This might be interpreted as a means for the government to thrust its financial burden upon ordinary people. A prominent economist, Professor Jinglian Wu, called this phenomenon 'robbing money by public listing' *(shang shi quan qian).*[150]

6.7.	EXCHANGE AND COOPERATION WITH SECURITIES REGULATORY BODIES IN OTHER COUNTRIES

6.7.1.   THE INTERNATIONAL ORGANIZATION OF SECURITIES COMMISSIONS

The International Organization of Securities Commissions (hereinafter IOSCO) is the largest international securities regulatory cooperative institution. It was formed in 1983 from the transformation of its predecessor, the Inter-American Regional Association, which was created in 1974.[151] It is not a real international economic organization but rather a non-profit-making industrial liaison body. The mission of IOSCO is cooperation and transfer of expertise, in particular, between the developed and emerging markets.[152] The PRC is one of the emerging markets on IOSCO's list.[153] The rules of IOSCO do not bind its members. IOSCO makes uniform regulatory rules, which may or may not be adopted by its member states. It passes resolutions, which may be adopted by its members. There had been more than 180 members by 2005.[154]

The PRC became a member of IOSCO in 1995.[155] Through its membership in IOSCO, it has established broad contacts with other securities market regulators. Since 1992, the CSRC has also signed more than twenty-six memoranda of understanding (MOUs) with foreign securities regulatory bodies under Article 4 of the Special Regulations Concerning Overseas Listing of 1994. These MOUs will undoubtedly lead to further standardization of Chinese securities regulation, especially in the area of information disclosure. Chinese joint stock companies seeking share issuing and listing overseas must therefore abide by the requirements for information disclosure under Chinese rules as well as the rules of the country where the shares are going to be issued and listed. This means that Chinese joint stock companies seeking overseas listing will bear a heavier burden of information disclosure than do companies listed solely on either the Shanghai Stock Exchange or the Shenzhen Stock Exchange.

---

149. *Ibid.*
150. Wu, Jinglian, *On Ten Year History of the Securities Market* (in Chinese) (Shanghai: Shanghai Far East Press, 2001), 162.
151. <www.iosco.org/about/index.ctm?section=history>, 30 Jul. 2005.
152. *Ibid.*
153. <www.iosco.org/lists/display_committees.cfm?emtid=8>, 30 Jul. 2005.
154. <www.iosco.org/about/index.ctm?section=history>, 30 Jul. 2005.
155. Li, Zhangzhe, *Finally Successful: The Report of the Development of Chinese Share Market*, 416.

On 11 July 1995, the CSRC became a member of IOSCO at the IOSCO Twentieth Annual Meeting in Paris.[156] On 20 September 1996, the Shanghai and the Shenzhen Stock Exchanges became subsidiary members of IOSCO at the IOSCO Twenty-First Annual Meeting.[157] On 27 June 2005, China signed an MOU with Vietnamese Securities Commission on cooperation in securities regulation.[158] By then, the CSRC had signed MOUs with their counterparts in twenty-six countries and regions, including the USA, Hong Kong, Singapore, the UK, Australia, Japan, Luxembourg, Germany, and Malaysia.[159] Through listings on foreign stock exchanges and communications with its foreign counterparts, the CSRC has accumulated much knowledge about securities regulation.

6.7.2.   THE INTERNATIONAL ACCOUNTING STANDARDS COMMITTEE

The International Accounting Standards Committee (IASC) plays an important role in the uniformity of financial disclosure, especially in cross-border securities issuing and listing. IASC was established in 1973 as a private organization. However, since 1983, all the members of the international accounting bodies have become members of IASC. The target of IASC is to unify the accounting standards throughout the world. As a member of IASC, the PRC's Ministry of Finance established the International Accounting Standards Commission to review and adopt the international accounting standards. The MOF released the new Enterprise Accounting Standards and Auditing Standards that are in compliance with IASC Accounting Rules in February 2006.[160] Both Standards became applicable to listed companies on 1 July 2007.

6.7.3.   RAISING CAPITAL FROM ABROAD

The PRC central government released the State Economic Construction Bonds Regulation on 9 December 1953.[161] Since the promulgation of this Regulation, the PRC started issuing state bonds. However, on 2 April 1958, the CCP released the Resolution on the Issue of Local Bonds. This Regulation terminated the issuing of central government bonds, although local governments were allowed to issue economic construction bonds. In 1965, the PRC entered into a no-foreign-debts period. In 1982, the China International Trust and Investment Company, an SOE,

---

156. See *China Securities Daily*, 6 Jan. 2003.
157. *Ibid.*
158. <www.csrc.gov.cn/cn/Jsp/detail.jsp?infoid=1120447808100&type=CMS.STD&path=ROOT% 3ECN%3E%D%C2%CE%C5%B%BC%B6%C1>, 30 Jun. 2005.
159. *Ibid.*
160. Jin, Renqing (Minister for Finance), Speech at the News Conference on the New Enterprise Accounting Standards and Auditing Standards, < http://www.mof.gov.cn/news/20060220_ 2246_12569.htm>, 26 Apr. 2007.
161. Zheng, Zhenlong (ed), *A Concise History of the Chinese Securities Development*, 415.

issued company bonds worth Japanese Yen (JPY) 10 billion. This was the first time that China raised capital from an international market.[162]

China did not raise capital from an international market through mutual funds until December 1985, when China Oriental Company established the China Oriental Fund in Hong Kong and London.[163] In 1993, large Chinese companies started going public in Hong Kong. To do so, the PRC strengthened connections with the Hong Kong Stock Exchange. On 17 January 1994, China issued universal bonds worth USD 10 billion in the USA. This was the first time that China entered into the American capital market.[164]

6.8. CONCLUSION

Compared to the securities markets of Western countries, the PRC securities market has a very short history, but it has developed very quickly. The re-emergence of the securities market is a result of the development of China's economic reform. The Chinese securities market now has most of the common features of other securities markets. This process of development demonstrates the influence of economic convergence. The asymmetry of information among listed companies and investors also exists in China. As China is in the process of an economic transition, its securities market also reflects some unique features of such a transition. The problems caused by the asymmetry of information are more obvious and serious in China than in other countries.[165] This perhaps is a result of the influence of economic divergence. Thus, the current state of the PRC securities market demonstrates the applicability of the differentiation hypothesis.

Currently, the major problems of disclosure in the PRC securities market are as follows. First, most of the listed companies are state-owned, and therefore the companies usually get information about changes in state securities policies before ordinary investors do. Consequently, the institutional shareholders often acquire information earlier than do individual investors. Because China lacks detailed insider trading rules and statutory duties on company directors and other officers, these officers, their friends, and relatives who have gained inside information before the investors did have often been involved in insider trading. The possibility of huge profits from securities trading has induced senior officers of listed companies to violate securities regulations, especially as the liability provisions are not effectively enforced.

Second, the PRC has not adopted a real market economy, and the government tightly controls the development of the securities market. This can be seen in the

---

162. Jin, Dehong, *Contemporary Securities Market of China*, 120.
163. *Ibid.*, 175.
164. Li, Zhangzhe, *Finally Successful: The Report of the Development of Chinese Share Market*, 516.
165. Gao, Xianmin (ed), *The Secrets of Listed Companies* (in Chinese) (Beijing: WorldPublishing Company, 2001), 158.

adoption of the shareholding system, in the establishment of the SSE and the SZSE, in the quota system for securities issuing, in the changes of market regulators, and in the types of securities allowed to be issued. High requirements for IPOs have forced some companies to forge profit statements and disclose false information to obtain approval for IPOs. Packaging listing *(bao zhuang shang shi)* is not rare in listed companies.

Third, as issuing securities in the PRC was mainly used by SOEs to meet their capital needs, which were no longer met by the government, at the beginning of the re-emergence of this market, the principle of fairness was not adopted. There are two problems that resulted from this approach. One is that it was very difficult for private companies to raise capital by share issuing. The other is that many state-owned companies that did not meet the requirements for share issuing and listing were allowed to issue shares to the public after the packaging that was forced by the government at different levels. In many cases of false disclosure, the local governments indirectly encouraged this misconduct so as to transfer the financial burden of SOEs to individual investors. To use a Chinese expression, local governments encouraged some state-owned companies to 'rob the money' *(quan qian)* out of the pockets of ordinary Chinese individual investors. This is one of the reasons why so many state-owned companies are involved in false disclosure.

Fourth, as China has not become a country with the rule of law, the situation of poor enforcement of law has indirectly encouraged some directors and other senior officers of state-owned companies to give false information so as to increase the share price of their companies and then abuse their powers to make profits for themselves. For example, although there were many cases of giving false information, few directors or other senior officers of the companies have been prosecuted. Civil actions against individual directors are hardly ever brought. This situation has encouraged company directors and managers to make profits for themselves by using their positions in the companies. Most Chinese investors are still not sophisticated and do not know how to protect their interests with the limited legal remedies available to them.

Finally, as China's securities regulatory laws and rules are not sophisticated, there are some loopholes. Thus, the people who are involved in fraud on the securities market will not be punished and innocent investors have no proper remedies to seek compensation. For example, China securities regulations lack detailed disqualification provisions. Most of the company officers or underwriters who have been involved in false disclosure can continue their business by transferring to another position. The lack of civil liability provisions in the Securities Law of 1998 also had left innocent investors without proper compensation. The civil liability provisions in the Securities Law of 2005 are rarely tested. Although the corporate disclosure rules are well written, they do not suit the Chinese situation because the PRC securities market has clearly unique features that demonstrate the application of the hypothesis of differentiation advocated by Professors Pistor and Wellons. The current disclosure rules have focused too much on the convergence of economic development. Overall, the Chinese securities market is not a sophisticated market, having unsophisticated regulators, unsophisticated investors, and an unsophisticated regulatory system. It has not acquired enough experience to become a modern market in which a market economy is fully established. This will require PRC corporate disclosure rules to show more divergence in economic development.

6.9.   INFORMATION AVAILABILITY, MECHANISM FOR
         ENFORCING SECURITIES REGULATIONS, AND
         REMEDIES FOR INVESTORS WHO HAVE
         SUFFERED LOSSES

6.9.1.   INFORMATION AVAILABILITY

Currently, the Chinese securities market has some unique features. First, listed companies have not realized that it is their duty to actively comply with disclosure rules. They treat compliance with disclosure requirements as a burden.[166] In practice, many companies disclose minimal information. When there is an opportunity for non-disclosure, they will often take this opportunity. The fundamental reason for this conduct is that those companies usually have problems that will affect their share prices if information is disclosed. Therefore, some companies try to avoid disclosure, which may have a negative impact on their share price.[167]

For example, Daheng New Century Technology Company (hereinafter Daheng New Century) became the first company that did not disclose its forecast of profit making. Daheng New Century was listed on 3 November 2000. Under the CSRC's Circular Concerning Share Issue of 1996, the responsible person involved in giving a false forecast of profit-making will be punished. In the CSRC's Circular Concerning Issues of Engagement of Auditing Institutions by Companies to Issue Shares to the Public of 2000, these companies must disclose and provide materials for the forecast of profit-making. This Circular also states that company directors should be responsible for the prediction of profit-making and that they will be punished according to the relevant provisions if the forecast is not met. As Daheng New Century Technology Company directors were not clear about its predictable profits and did not want to take responsibility, they chose to avoid the duty to disclose the forecast of profit-making.

Second, there is uncertainty in the disclosure rules. Although there are plenty of disclosure rules, the content and timing of disclosure gives listed companies the opportunity to make selective disclosure or non-disclosure, even if this information may have a material impact on share prices. For example, under the CSRC's Circular Concerning Engagement of Auditing Institutions of 2000, the companies that have issued shares but are not listed on a stock exchange may choose not to

---

166. Interview with a senior manager of Shanghai Shenxin Textile Company in August 1999. He bitterly complained that the CSRC disclosure rules were too complex to follow.
167. Gao, Xianmin, (ed)., *The Secrets of Listed Companies* (in Chinese) (Beijing: World Publishing Corp., 2001), 167.

disclose the forecast of profit-making. This creates much insider information and hearsay. The main cause of this is the incompetence of some senior officers of listed companies.[168]

Third, some disclosure by listed companies has violated continuous and timely disclosures requirements. The securities market is not static. This requires disclosure to be continuous. However, many listed companies cannot or do not want to meet this requirement. Their disclosure is neither timely nor continuous. For example, Jilin Tansu Company released a notice on 17 November 2000 stating that the company's performance would be affected as a result of the price increase of raw materials. Such disclosure was normal, but the lateness of such disclosure is abnormal, given that the price increase occurred in the first half-year. There are two reasons for late disclosure: first, deliberate actions of listed companies, and second, disclosure is required to be published in the newspapers, and this can take a long time.[169]

Fourth, much disclosure is of poor quality. Misleading and deceptive disclosure and major omissions are three common problems in the quality of disclosure by listed companies in the PRC. Investors are often confused by the meaning of the disclosure documents of listed companies. They call such disclosure documents 'riddles'.[170] For example, Jingying Company's public notices in 2000 confused many investors. The Jingying Company was listed in April 2000. In its prospectus and its first half-yearly report, Jingying claimed that it made profits. Investors thought that this company was doing well. In mid-2001, Jingying issued a notice stating that, because of the increase in raw materials prices, several subsidiary companies had lost money in the first half-year. This notice indicated that the performance of the company in the second half-year would be affected. Many investors thought that Jingying was not doing well and lost interest in it. They quickly sold their shares in the company. In fact, the share price of Jingying went up instead of going down. The investors reached the conclusion that no matter what they read in annual reports or half-yearly reports, they may be trapped.[171] The reasons for the problems of giving false disclosure, misleading information, and misstatements are the speed of and large amount of capital raising to be obtained from the securities market and the low risks of being punished for misconduct.

The following part this chapter analyses information availability on the Chinese securities market by looking at the legal framework and practices of the securities market. Although the Securities Law, the Company Law, the administrative regulations and rules of the State Council, and especially the rules of CSRC have many provisions on disclosure, the practice of disclosure is very disappointing. Since the establishment of the two stock exchanges, a frequent problem on the securities market has been to give false, untimely, or incomplete disclosure.

---

168. *Ibid.*
169. *Ibid.*
170. *Ibid.*, 170.
171. *Ibid.*, 172.

6.9.2.   Information Availability under the Law and in Practice

Under Chinese law, true, accurate, complete, and timely information must be available for investors. Both the Company Law[172] and the Securities Law[173] require the issuer to prepare and publish a prospectus. However, often, the disclosure provisions are not complete. For example, although Article 17 of the Securities Law requires a company to prepare free copies of disclosure documents at a designated place for the investors to read, there are no liabilities provisions dealing with the companies that fail to do so. Article 64 requires disclosure to be made in designated newspapers and other publications.

In addition to these places, disclosure must be made at a company's business address and on the stock exchange where it is listed. In fact, most shareholders do not live in the same city where listed companies are located and do not live in the same city where the stock exchanges are located. As there is no requirement for listed companies to send copies of documents to the investors and no requirement for Internet disclosure, the function of disclosure in the PRC has been greatly diminished. Although Article 19 of the Interim Regulations of 1993 requires an issuer to provide copies of documents to investors and underwriters, and to display a prospectus at its business site, in fact, information is only available in form – not in substance. In addition, the laws and regulations do not contain liabilities provisions on non-compliance with the above-mentioned Articles.

The CSRC's Rule No. 1 on Content and Format of Disclosure by Listed Companies: Prospectus has very detailed provisions on the preparation and availability of prospectuses to investors. For example, it makes clear that all the information that may have a material impact on investors' decision-making must be disclosed.[174] It repeats three principles of disclosure and limits the effective period of prospectuses. However, it does not have an article that relates at all to punishment for violations of this Rule.

As for periodic disclosure, from the national laws to the CSRC's administrative rules, there are requirements for annual reporting, half-yearly reporting, and interim reporting. China did not formally adopt quarterly reporting until 2002. Again, this was borrowed from the US experience. The information disclosed by listed companies is often not precise and out of date. Another problem is that investors do not really get information from these reports. There are two main reasons for this: first, the poor quality and false information in these reports have made most investors lose confidence in them; and second, as most computers are not widely used in China, many investors cannot get information from the Internet but instead find information on the companies they are interested in from the newspapers designated for disclosure. The public library system is also very poor.

---

172. Article 88.
173. Article 17.
174. Article 3.

Information disclosed by listed companies in designated publications or places is not effective for other reasons as well. First, most Chinese investors are inexperienced. They are prone to the influence of their friends and hearsay but not to the information disclosed on formal documents. Of course, this phenomenon is related to the nature of the Chinese securities market – 'the policy market' – which means that the PRC securities market is dominated by the government's policies.

Second, the liability system dealing with false disclosure is incomplete. There are articles relating to punishment only for false disclosure but not for the non-displaying of securities issuing documents or for not sending prospectuses to investors. The Securities Law and the Company Law of 2005 have provisions for civil liability, criminal liability, and administrative liability imposed for conduct involving false disclosure, fraud, and major misstatements. However, the civil liability provision lacks details and is very hard for implementation in practice. In addition, there is no liability for late disclosure, even though listed companies are required to give timely disclosure. The problems with civil, criminal, and administrative liabilities will be discussed later.

6.9.3.   BODIES INVOLVING ENFORCEMENT OF SECURITIES REGULATIONS

As discussed in previous chapters, the national regulator in charge of the PRC securities market is the CSRC. Several other bodies still have regulatory roles to play in their respective areas. For instance, the Ministry of Finance is in charge of setting accounting standards, issuing accounting licenses, and punishing accounting firms and individual accountants who are involved in misconduct of disclosure. The State Bureau of Industry and Commerce is in charge of registration and de-registration of companies.

The CSRC is the most active body in charge of securities regulation and enforcement by administrative means. On particular issues, it has to cooperate with other bodies. For instance, it has to jointly issue business licenses to securities companies, securities law firms, accounting firms specializing in securities, and their professional staff with the State Bureau of Industry and Commerce.

In addition to the administrative bodies, the courts also play an important role in enforcement of securities regulations by dealing with securities cases. The courts not only handle disputes between issuers and securities investors, disputes between issuers and underwriters, and disputes between underwriters and investors, but also, disputes between issuers and the CSRC. A lawsuit between an issuer and the CSRC is called administrative litigation. The PRC Administrative Litigation Law of 1989 broke the Chinese tradition that 'ordinary people do not sue the officials' *(min bu gao guan)* and represented a step forward in the development of democracy in China. In 2000, the CSRC was sued by Hainan Kaili Company for not approving its listing application. The CSRC became a defendant for the first time and lost the case in 2001. This shows that although the CSRC has been given a broad range of powers, it still has to act within its authority.

6.9.4.　　THE POWERS OF THE CSRC DEALING WITH CASES INVOLVING CONTRAVENTION OF DISCLOSURE PROVISIONS

The CSRC is the main body that enforces securities regulations. It is given the following powers under the laws:

(i) Stop Order: No company is allowed to issue shares to the public without the approval of the CSRC. If a company receives approval to issue shares to the public by giving false information to the CSRC, the CSRC has the power to order the company to stop issuing shares and refund the money paid by the shareholders.[175] The CSRC may stop underwriters without licenses from trading in securities as brokers.[176] In the Chinese tradition, the executive government has great authority. The CSRC's authority has rarely been challenged. Thus, a stop order is rarely used by the CSRC.

(ii) Confiscation: The CSRC has the power to confiscate the profits of underwriters without approval of brokers.[177] Together with administrative fines, confiscation is an important and commonly used tool to implement securities regulations.

(iii) Order to Correct False, Misleading Information and Misstatements.[178] When the CSRC finds out that there is any of the above-mentioned conduct, it has the power to order the company to correct it. This means that correction order is often used together with an administrative fine and a warning.

(iv) Warning: The CSRC has the power to issue a warning to company officers who are involved in obtaining share issue approval by giving false information. It also has the power to issue a warning to company officers who are directly involved in giving false, misleading information or misstatements.[179] A warning is not used as a remedy in other countries' securities regulation. The function of a warning is only to remind the persons or institutions of violations of securities regulations. It has little punitive function. If a person or a body ignores the CSRC's warning, the CSRC has to use other means of punishment. As the CSRC is reluctant to punish the individual officers of state-owned companies involved in false disclosure, a warning is often used by the CSRC. For example, in the case of the Shijiazhong Electronic Window Company's violation of disclosure rules, the Company did not disclose an operation problem that occurred in early 1997 until 30 April 1998. The CSRC only gave a warning to the company and a warning to the fourteen directors of the company. The ineffectiveness of punishment provisions indirectly encouraged the misconduct in information disclosure.

---

175. The PRC Securities Law of 2005, Art. 179.
176. *Ibid.*
177. *Ibid.*
178. *Ibid.*
179. *Ibid.*

(v) Administrative Fine: The CSRC has the power to impose a fine between CNY 30,000 and 300,000 on company officers who are directly involved in obtaining share issue approval by giving false information.[180] Persons who forge and pass on false securities information will be fined between CNY 30,000 and 300,000.[181] Accountants, assets evaluators, or lawyers who give false reports or false legal statements will be fined between CNY 30,000 and 100,000.[182] As discussed above, administrative fines are usually used together with confiscation.

(vi) Disqualification: The CSRC has the power to disqualify the professional staff of stock exchanges, securities companies, securities registration and settlement companies, and other securities professionals if they are involved in false disclosure.[183] The CSRC also has the power to jointly disqualify accountants, assets evaluators, and securities lawyers from securities market with the Ministry of Finance, the State Assets Bureau, and the Ministry of Justice. The CSRC has the power to disqualify securities companies from securities business if they are involved in giving false documents or fraud.[184] However, it is disappointing that the CSRC has rarely used this power. This has also indirectly encouraged violations of securities regulatory rules.

Compared to the Australian securities market regulator – ASIC – the CSRC has not been given enough regulatory powers. For example, ASIC has the power to investigate a case and collect evidence, and to initiate civil or criminal litigation.[185] However, under the PRC Civil Procedure Law of 1991, only people who suffer loss or damage by illegal actions may bring a civil action against the wrongdoers. Under the PRC Criminal Procedure Law, only the Public Security Department has the power to investigate and collect evidence and only the People's Procuratorate has the power to initiate criminal proceedings. The CSRC, as a department of the executive government, only has the power to make administrative decisions, as discussed above. The status of the CSRC determines that it cannot act as a regulatory body as powerful as the SEC in the USA or ASIC in Australia. From this point of view, it is not very appropriate for the PRC to simply copy the disclosure regime of the USA.

Even with the powers given to it by the law, the CSRC has not exercised them effectively. For some time, giving a warning was the most common form of punishment by the CSRC. In the *Northwest Medicine Company* case of 1998,[186] the Northwest Medicine Company violated the Enterprise Accounting Standards and

---

180. *Ibid.*, Art. 189.
181. *Ibid.*, Art. 191.
182. *Ibid.*, Art. 200.
183. *Ibid.*, Art. 233.
184. *Ibid.*, Art. 222.
185. Australian Securities and Investments Commission Act of 2001(Cth), ss 49, 50, and 51.
186. The *CSRC Official Bulletin 1998/3*, 53–54.

Accounting System of Shareholding Trial Companies. It put the money to be used to pay taxes into its costs and therefore forged profits of CNY 19, 950. The CSRC later found that it had given false and seriously misleading disclosure as a result of a violation of Article 11 of Interim Measures Preventing Securities Fraud and Article 74(2) of the Securities Law. In the case of *Shenyang Accounting Firm*, the firm knew that a company had prepared a false financial report but it helped the company hide the truth by giving a supportive auditing report. Shenyang Accounting Firm violated Articles 73 and 35 of the Interim Regulations of 1993. The CSRC took the following actions:

(i) It issued a warning to Northwest Medicine Company;
(ii) It issued a warning to the Chairman of the Board of Directors and the General Manager, Wu Tingbao;
(iii) It issued a warning to Shenyang Accounting Firm and a fine of CNY 300,000;
(iv) It issued a warning to three accountants who were involved in giving a false auditing report.

In the *China Guotai Securities Company* case,[187] the CSRC found that China Guotai Securities Company's Beijing Branch (hereinafter Guotai Beijing) bought a large number of shares of Beijing Tianqiao Company from April 1997 to January 1998. Guotai Beijing had a 5.28% shareholding in the Beijing Tianqiao Company. Under Article 47 of the Interim Regulations of 1993, when a company holds more than 5% of the ordinary shares in another company, it must disclose this shareholding to the CSRC, the Stock Exchange, and the target company within three days. The CSRC took the following actions:

(i) it imposed a fine of CNY 1 million on Guotai Beijing;
(ii) it issued a warning to the person in charge, the Manger of the Business Department of Guotai Beijing;
(iii) it confiscated the illegal profits, worth CNY 390, 000.[188]

In the *Chengdu Hongguang Company* case,[189] the CSRC found that the Hongguang Company had committed the serious misconduct of false disclosure and misstatements in its listing application documents and prospectus. In its share issue application in 1996, it claimed profits of CNY 5.4 million made in 1996, while in fact it had lost CNY 10.3 million. In its prospectus, Chengdu Hongguang Company claimed that it would use the capital raised by share issuing on the production of new products. In fact, it only used 16.5% of the capital raised by listing for this purpose. Most of the capital was used to repay the company's bank loan. The company did not disclose this. In its listing application, Hongguang Company also did not disclose that its main machinery had serious problems that had already affected the company's operation.

---

187. The *CSRC Bulletin 1998/10*, 29.
188. *Ibid.*
189. *Ibid.*, 1998/11, 51–58.

The CSRC also found that the main underwriter of Hongguang Company, Zhongxing Trust and Investment Company, also violated disclosure rules. Zhongxing Company signed off on the prospectus of Hongguang Company in 1996, knowing that Honggunag Company had forged profits. Zhongxing Company also carelessly ignored the change of the use of capital and the facility problem of Hongguang Company. It was found that Zhongxing Company, as the main underwriter, had violated Article 17 of the Interim Regulations of 1993, which require the main underwriters to guarantee that there is no false, misleading information or misstatements. It was also found that Zhongxing Company had violated Article 11 of the Interim Measures to Prevent Securities Fraud, which prohibits any institution or individual from involvement in false or misleading disclosure or avoidance of disclosure.

Under the LRs of the SSE and the SZSE, any company seeking listing must have two listing referees.[190] The CSRC found that Guotai Securities Company and Chengdu Securities Company, as referees of Hongguang Company, did not investigate and substantially check the company's situation but still signed off on the referee's report. These two companies were found in breach of Article 74 of the Interim Regulations of 1993 and Article 11 of the Interim Measures Preventing Securities Fraud.

The CSRC also found that the law firms for Hongguang's listing – Sichuan Economic Law Firm and Beijing Guofang Law Firm – also violated disclosure regulations. Sichuan Economic Law Firm, as the consulting firm for Hongguang, and Beijing Guofang Law Firm, as the consulting firm for Zhongxing Trust and Investment Company, did not check the documents for the Hongguang listing but signed off on these documents and provided the law firm's report. They violated Article 11 of the Interim Measures and Article 74 of the Interim Regulations of 1993.

The CSRC found that Chengdu Shudu Accounting Firm violated Article 18 of the Interim Regulation of 1993, which imposes the duty to ensure true disclosure on accounting firms and law firms and their professionals. The CSRC found that Chengdu Assets Evaluating Firm violated Articles 11 and 12 of the Interim Measures. Chengdu Assets Evaluating Firm was engaged by Hongguang Company to evaluate its assets in March 1997. It changed an evaluation report made previously according to the direction of Hongguang Company so as to increase the value of Hongguang assets.

The CSRC made separate punishment decisions on violations of disclosure by the above institutions and relevant individuals. The main actions regarding violations of disclosure rules were the following:

(i) the illegal income of Hongguang Company worth CNY 4.5 million was confiscated. It was also fined CNY 1million;

(ii) the Chairman, the General Manager, and the Finance Director of Hongguang Company were disqualified from being reappointed as senior officers of listed companies or securities institutions for life;

---

190. Listing Rule 2.3.1.

   (iii) Twelve directors of the Hongguang Company were given a warning;
   (iv) Zhongxing Trust and Investment Company's illegal income of 8 million CNY was confiscated. It was also fined 2 million CNY;
    (v) Zhongxing Company was disqualified from securities brokering and self-dealing;
   (vi) The General Manager of Zhongxing Company as well as other three company officers who were involved in violations of disclosure rules were disqualified from the securities market for life;
  (vii) Guotai Securities Company was fined CNY 1.32 million and Chengdu Securities Company was fined CNY 500,000;
 (viii) Sichuan Economic Law Firm was fined CNY 460,000. Its illegal income of CNY 230,000 was confiscated. It was disqualified from the securities business for three years;
   (ix) Two lawyers of Sichuan Economic Law Firm who signed the Lawyers' Report for Hongguang's listing were banned from the securities business and from appointment as senior officers of listed companies for three years;
    (x) Beijing Beifang Law Firm was fined CNY 400,000. Its illegal income of CNY 200,000 was confiscated. It was banned from the securities business for one year;
   (xi) Two partners of Guofang Law Firm who signed the Lawyers' Report were banned from the securities business for one year;
  (xii) Chengdu Shudu Accounting Firm was fined CNY 600,000. Its illegal income of CNY 300,000 was confiscated. It was disqualified from the accounting business for thee years;
 (xiii) Two accountants who signed off on the auditing report of Hongguang Company Assets were disqualified from the securities business for life;
  (xiv) Chengdu Assets Evaluation Firm was fined CNY 200,000. Its illegal income of CNY 100,000 was confiscated. The firm was banned from the securities business for three years.[191]

From the above cases, it is clear that before the CSRC was made the national securities regulatory body, it mainly used warnings as punishment for violations of disclosure rules. A warning is a special kind of liability in the PRC. It is effective only for the companies and individuals who care about their reputations and treat warnings seriously. However, as the PRC is a country that does not have a tradition of business ethics, a warning has little punitive function.

With the clarification of its regulatory status, the CSRC started using disqualification as an important tool to punish the companies, firms, and individuals who violated disclosure regulations. However, the periods of these disqualifications were not very long. This diminished the educational function of disclosure rules. Unlike the Australian Corporations Act of 2001 (Cth), which prohibits disqualified persons from being reappointed as directors of either public companies or private

---

191. *Ibid.*

companies,[192] the PRC only prohibits disqualified persons from being reappointed at listed companies. This has also undermined the function of liabilities for breaches of disclosure rules.

6.9.5.   The Remedies Available to Investors Who Have Suffered Losses

Under the PRC securities regulations, the investors who have suffered losses may have civil, criminal, and administrative remedies. As the CSRC is a department under the State Council, the remedies the investors can obtain from the CSRC's decisions are called administrative remedies. The civil remedies can be imposed by courts or arbitration commissions. The criminal remedies can only be imposed by courts. In the PRC, administrative remedies can be imposed, as the CSRC is in charge of the day-to-day regulation of the securities market. Civil and criminal remedies are rarely given as a result of the courts' reluctance to hear such cases caused by the lack of relevant laws and difficulty in evidence collection.

6.9.5.1.   Administrative Remedies

The CSRC has very broad powers to enforce the securities regulations and supervise the securities market. It may use its powers (discussed in the previous sections) and impose administrative liabilities on companies and their officers who are involved in the contravention of disclosure rules. Administrative liabilities are not direct remedies for the investors who suffered losses, as the illegal profits that are confiscated and the fines both go to the state's revenue. Warnings and disqualification only prevent further breaches of disclosure provisions. However, they do not compensate the investors.

6.9.5.2.   Criminal Remedies

The criminal remedies are provided for in the Amended Criminal Law and include criminal fines,[193] detention,[194] and imprisonment.[195] These means can be used separately or jointly. A big problem with criminal remedies is that punishments are not severe. The range of criminal fines is 1%–5% of false registered capital if a company obtains registration by false documents.[196] If a company has falsely registered capital, the criminal fine is 2%–10% of the falsely registered capital.[197] If there is false information in a prospectus or other company document, the

---

192. Article 206.
193. Article 158.
194. Article 159.
195. *Ibid.*
196. Article 158.
197. *Ibid.*, Art. 159.

criminal fine is 1%–5% of the illegally raised capital.[198] The directly responsible officers of the company will be fined CNY 20,000–200,000.[199] From these provisions, it is clear that criminal fines are not severe at all in China. This encourages further violations of disclosure rules. In fact, company officers are rarely fined by the courts, as few provisions on criminal fines apply to individual officers. The company directors who are not directly involved in misconduct of disclosure are not fined at all. The terms of imprisonment for misconduct of disclosure are very short. The maximum term is five years.[200] Up to this time, very few company officers who breached their duties have been imprisoned.

6.9.5.3.   Civil Remedies

Civil remedies are direct remedies that may be granted to investors who suffered have losses. There are serious flaws in the civil remedies regime in the PRC. Under the Chinese legal system, only national laws can contain provisions on civil compensation remedies. Unfortunately, there was no clear provision on investors' right to civil compensation even if it could be deduced from Article 207 of the Securities Law of 1998, which provides that, 'Violation of this Law shall bear civil compensation liability.' Although the legal theorists and the courts agreed with this conclusion, they also recognized that without detailed rules, it was troublesome to determine how to apply and grant such compensation. This Article was not workable. As the courts in the PRC do not have the power to interpret law, Section 207 cannot be used by the courts. The lack of a detailed civil compensation regime is a serious problem that urgently needs to be solved. The General Principles of the Civil Law of 1986 only provides civil compensation principles. The courts in 1998 did not accept the civil compensation claims brought by the shareholders of Honggunag Company because of the lack of relevant articles in the Securities Law of 1998.

In the *Ninggunagxia* case, more individual investors suffered losses from deceptive conduct in the process of share issuing and listing of a large SOE. Individual investors brought civil compensation actions in many provinces. Again, these actions were not accepted for lack of specific articles in the Securities Law of 1998 until 15 January 2002, when the Supreme Peoples' Court released a judicial interpretation entitled Circular Concerning Civil Torts Cases of False Disclosure in the Securities Market. This Circular became effective on the date of release. However, the Circular set a prerequisite for acceptance of such cases that requires the alleged false disclosure conduct to be investigated and dealt with by the CSRC first.[201] This prerequisite raised much criticism from the public. Consequently, the Supreme People's Court amended the Circular by releasing another judicial interpretation entitled Several Provisions on Civil Compensation Cases of False

---

198. *Ibid.*, Art. 160.
199. *Ibid.*, Art. 161.
200. *Ibid.*, Arts 158, 159, 160, and 181.
201. Section 2.

Disclosure in the Securities Market on 9 January 2003. This Interpretation became effective on 1 February 2003. However, the 2003 Interpretation does not invalidate the prerequisite of the 2002 Interpretation. The prerequisite has been changed to require that the alleged false disclosure conduct must have been dealt with by the CSRC or have been tried by a criminal court.[202] Apparently, the courts are still very reluctant to hear cases involving false disclosure.

Based on the criticism of the lack of clear civil compensation in the Securities Law of 1998, Article 232 clearly provides for the priority of civil compensation in the Securities Law of 2005. However, the lawmakers leave the details for implementing this Article to the courts. So far, the Supreme People's Court has not released detailed rules on implementing this Article. This situation again diminishes the function of the Securities Law as a tool for the protection of shareholders.

6.9.6. CONCLUSION

Generally speaking, the information disclosure regime in the PRC was established to meet the needs of the market. It appears to suit the current situation in the PRC, although there are still some distinct shortcomings. Such shortcomings include the following: there are multi-regulatory bodies that have caused multi-level administration; the dispute over sharing the power of regulating the securities market causes conflicts between the different regulations and rules and the inefficiency of their administration; the lack of detailed civil liabilities provisions for violations of the securities regulations and rules increases the frequency of violations in the securities market; the longstanding unclear status of the CSRC and its lack of enforcement powers also causes difficulties in maintaining stability in the securities market. All these problems are fundamentally caused by the strict of the control of the securities market by the PRC government.

With respect to the information disclosure system in the securities market in particular, one big problem is the lack of a statutory statement of the standards to specify the kind of information that should be disclosed. All the regulations and rules about information disclosure try to list the items that should be disclosed. However, this listing cannot be complete. Thus, the making of regulations and rules always lags behind the current market problems. This situation causes trouble in continuously updating the regulations and rules of the PRC's securities market.

Another big problem is the longstanding omission of disqualification and civil compensation provisions for breaches of disclosure rules. Article 232 is an improvement, but without detailed implementing rules, it is useless. Maybe this is one of the features of the transitional market. In the process of development, there are still many issues to be resolved by trial and error as various participants develop more experience.[203]

---

202. Article 6 of s. 2.
203. R. Nottle, 'The Development of Securities Markets in China in the 1990s', *C&SLJ* 11, no. 8 (1993): 503–519 at 519.

The third problem with respect to disclosure is closely related to the second problem. China's provisions on information disclosure, which are found in laws, regulations, and rules, rarely set out the procedures for information disclosure. This causes the regulatory bodies to either abuse their administrative powers or to be confused as to how to supervise joint stock companies so that they properly disclose information. This causes difficulties for joint stock companies and other relevant parties in fulfilling the requirements for information disclosure.

The fourth problem arises with the enforcement of the rules for information disclosure. Although some of these rules are administrative regulations, most of these rules are administrative rules (such as the CSRC's Rules No. 1–19 on the Content and Format Information Disclosed by Listed Companies), the courts will only use administrative rules as references under Article 5 of the PRC Administrative Procedure Law. In other words, the courts are not legally bound by administrative rules. Thus, administrative rules lack enforceability. In addition, it is still arguable whether or not the CSRC can both make securities market rules and enforce these rules. A possible solution to solve this problem is to incorporate some of the CSRC rules into laws of the PRC or at least into administrative regulations of the State Council.

In any event, it can be said that the establishment of a regulatory regime for the securities market in the PRC was the first step in a new 'Long March'. The formation of this regulatory regime was a result of the re-emergence and development of the Chinese securities market. The securities regulations should direct the development of the market. Of course, the improvement of rules has to keep pace with the development of the securities market. The PRC has a long way to go in developing its securities market rules and regulations, although it has made massive progress in a very short period of time.

Chapter 7

Key Elements of the Australian Corporate Disclosure Regulatory Regime

7.1.   INTRODUCTION

In the previous chapters, the development and the characteristics of the PRC securities market and regulation were discussed. How the PRC securities market has become what it is now was also analysed. As this book is a comparative study, it will use the Australian securities market as an example to compare the differences in historical development, the driving forces behind the development and characteristics of these two markets, and the corporate disclosure regimes of these two markets. This book argues that in the process of forming a relatively complicated market, Australia has not simply followed in the footsteps of the USA or the UK, although it did borrow heavily from these two models.[1] The history of the Australian corporate disclosure regime shows that this regime was formed and being constantly reformed after comprehensive study of foreign laws and domestic circumstances had been conducted. From this point of view, the Australian experience is recommended to the PRC for improving its corporate disclosure regime.

The theory of convergence developed by Professors Hansmann and Kraakman opines that at the beginning of the twenty-first century, there was rapid convergence on the standard shareholder-oriented model as a normative view of corporate structure, and this normative convergence produces substantial convergence as

---

1.   B.R. Cheffins, 'Corporate Governance Convergence: Lessons from Australia', *The Transitional Lawyer* 16, no. 1 (2002): 13–44 at 19.

well in the practices of corporate governance and in corporate law.[2] Under this theory, this convergence is driven by three principal factors: the failure of alternative corporate models, the competitive pressures of global commerce, and the shift of interest groups in favour of shareholders.[3] The theory of convergence in corporate law further states that regulation of routine disclosure to shareholders is also converging conspicuously,[4] and that mandatory disclosure for public companies is startlingly similar across the major commercial jurisdictions.[5] This chapter compares the similarities between the Australian securities regulatory regime and other regimes, such as those of the UK and the USA, especially between Australia and the USA. As was observed by the authors of *Ford's Principles of Corporations Law:*

> Starting with the enactment of the first Australian state securities industry laws early in the 1970s, Australia has developed a legislative policy on securities market regulation in which disclosure of material information is a central requirement . . . The development of Australia's disclosure policy has been strongly influenced by the approach to securities market regulation in the United States.[6]

This chapter also demonstrates that the theory of convergence explains why such similarities occur.

On the other hand, the theory of path dependency in corporate law developed by Professors Bebchuk and Roe argues that corporate ownership and governance differ among advanced economies in the world because of path dependence, although economies and business practices have converged in many countries in the world.[7] The theory of path dependence labels two sources of path dependence: structure-driven path dependence and rule-driven path dependence.[8] Structure-driven dependence concerns the direct effect of initial ownership structures on subsequent ownership structures, and rule-driven path dependence arises from the effect that initial ownership structures have on subsequent structures through their effect on the legal rules governing corporations.[9] The theory of path dependence explains the unique features of different regulatory jurisdictions.

---

2. H. Hansmann & R. Kraakman, 'The End of History for Corporate Law', in *Convergence and Persistence in Corporate Governance*, ed. J.D. Gordon & M.J. Roe (Cambridge: Cambridge University Press, 2004), 35–36.
3. *Ibid.*, 36.
4. *Ibid.*, 52.
5. *Ibid.*, 53.
6. Austin, Robert & Ian Ramsay, *Ford's Principles of Corporations Law*, 12th edn (Sydney: LexisNexis Butterworths, 2005), 499.
7. L.A. Bebchuk, & M. Roe, 'A Theory of Path Dependence in Corporate Ownership and Governance', in *Convergence and Persistence in Corporate Governance*, ed. J.D. Gordon & M.J. Roe (Cambridge: Cambridge University Press, 2004), 69.
8. *Ibid.*, 70.
9. *Ibid.*

Like China's, the Australian corporate disclosure regime is a result of the combined interaction of convergence and divergence and thus falls within the differentiation hypothesis; unlike China's, the Australian corporate disclosure regime has a stronger influence of convergence. This is because Australia has a free market economy, like other Western countries. It has built a corporate disclosure regime in which historical background, cultural influence, lawmaking processes, and enforcement of law fit together. Although Australia has learnt much from the UK and US experiences in establishing its corporate disclosure regulatory regime, it developed its own unique features, which can be used by other countries. These unique features of the Australian corporate disclosure regime will be discussed in this chapter as well. This chapter also argues that by looking into the ways in which Australia draws upon foreign corporate disclosure experiences, the PRC, as an emerging[10] and transitional market,[11] should not simply copy foreign models in the process of developing its own securities market and regulatory regime, because simply copying these models is the main reason why the PRC corporate disclosure regulatory regime has failed. This chapter finally suggests that the PRC can learn from the Australia experience in adopting foreign models and establish a corporate disclosure regulatory regime that is based on the empirical study of foreign experiences and suits the PRC's own domestic situation.

To support these arguments and suggestions, this chapter first traces the history of the Australian securities market. It reviews the securities regulatory regime in Australia. Then it focuses on the co-regulation of Australian Securities and Investment Commission (ASIC) and the Australian Securities Exchange (ASX), and on the corporate disclosure rules, which consist of legislation, listing rules, and accounting standards. It analyses the reforms of securities regulation that have taken place in Australia and how these reforms have impacted legal reforms in other common law countries. It also reviews the driving forces behind these reforms. A comparison is made between the development of the securities market and the corporate disclosure regime, and the driving forces of the developments in the PRC and Australia. This chapter concludes with a number of suggestions for the adoption of a suitable disclosure framework for emerging and transitional economies, such as the PRC's.

---

10. The PRC is on the list of emerging markets of IOSCO, <www.iosco.org/lists/display_committees.cfm?emtid=8>, 30 Jul. 2005.
11. Cheng, Siwei (ed.), 'Pandect', *Diagnosis and Treatment: Revealing the Stock Market of China* (Beijing: Economics Science Press, 2002), 33; Shang, Fulin, *To Amend the Securities Law for the Protection of the Securities Market*, <http://business.sohu.com//22/99/article212039922. shtml>, 29 Aug. 2003; Zhu, Congjiu, *To Strengthen the Self-Regulatory Function of the Stock Exchanges*, <http://business.sohu.com/02/19/article212571902.shtml>, 29 Aug. 2003; Shang, Fulin, *The CSRC Party Committee Makes the Implementation of the State Council's 'Opinions' the Work Focus of the CSRC in 2004*, <www.cs.com.cn/01/11/t20040203-17497.htm>, 3 Feb. 2004.

7.2.   THE BRIEF HISTORY OF AUSTRALIAN
          SECURITIES MARKETS

7.2.1.   The Emergence and Development of Securities Markets
          in Australian Colonies before 1900

Before reviewing the Australian experience in adopting foreign securities regulatory models, it is necessary to have a brief look at the history of the Australian
securities markets so as to understand the driving forces behind these markets. This
review will show that Australia has its unique history of securities markets and that
this uniqueness has determined its differences in corporate regulation from other
common law countries. In contrast to the PRC, where the first modern stock
exchange was not formed until 1990, Australia has had a much longer history
of development of stock exchanges, although its first national market was not
formed until 1987.[12] Stock exchanges in Australia at one time were completely
private markets, unregulated by any legislation.[13] They were subject only to the
regulation of their members; they owed no legal duty to the public. Any one was
free to establish new exchanges.

The emergence and development of securities markets in Australian colonies
was greatly influenced by its English heritage and economic development. These
first securities markets in Australia emerged more than 100 years earlier than those
in China. In Australia, stock brokering started as early as 1829, when Matthew
Gregson advertised that he had received permission from the Bank of New South
Wales to trade in its shares.[14] During the period from 1860 to 1890, each colony
established a stock exchange in its capital city. The first market for the exchange of
shares was formed in Sydney in 1837, although the first exchange was not established there until 1871.[15] The Melbourne Stock Exchange, established in 1861, was
the first Australian stock exchange.[16] The Adelaide Stock Exchange was established in 1887; the Perth Stock Exchange was established in 1889; the Hobart Stock
Exchange was established in 1882, and the Brisbane Stock Exchange was established in 1884.[17]

---

12. R. Baxt, H.A.J. Ford & A.J. Black, *Securities Industry Law*. 6th edn (Sydney: Butterworths,
    1996), 133.
13. *Ibid.*, 138.
14. <www.asx.com.au/about/13/HistoryASX-AA3.htm>, October 2002.
15. Quoted by M. Hefferman, 'The Economic Role of the Australian Stock Exchange', in *Securities
    Regulation in Australia and New Zealand*, ed. G Walker (Sydney: LBC, 1996), 132. According
    to Salsbury and Sweeney, the most solid evidence that the Sydney Stock Exchange was founded
    in 1871 is a rule book preserved in the Exchange's records – *The Sydney Stock Exchange,
    Instituted May 1871: Rules and Regulations* (Sydney: Joseph Cook & Co. Printers, George
    Street, no date); see S. Salsbury & K. Sweeney, *The Bull, the Bear & the Kangaroo: The History
    of the Sydney Stock Exchange* (Sydney: Allen & Unwin, 1988).
16. <www.asx.com.au/about/13/HistoryASX-AA3.htm>, 31 Jul. 2002.
17. Hefferman, M, 'The Economic Role of the Australian Stock Exchange', in *Securities
    Regulation in Australia and New Zealand*, ed. G Walker (Sydney: LBC, 1996), 132. According
    to Graeme Adamson, the Perth Stock Exchange opened on 1 Oct. 1888, but it only traded twice a

The impetus for the establishment of the first stock exchange in Melbourne came from the needs of the gold-mining business and the associated rail transport construction.[18] Before the boom of gold-mining, only three or four firms (notably, Edward Khull, William Clarke & Sons, and Baillie and Butters) conducted a share trading business.[19] However, soon after the boom, there was a rapid formation of brokers' offices throughout the towns on goldfields. As a result of the influx of newcomers into the goldfields' economy and the rapid increase in the volume of transactions in Melbourne, it became apparent that there was a need to have more organized methods of conducting operations in the share market. The first step occurred on 2 October 1859, when the brokers assembled at Temple-Court and discussed the need for establishing a daily official list of prices for buying and selling shares.[20] However, the new brokers could not reach an agreement. Meanwhile, the established firms, under the leadership of Baillie and Butters, began to take steps to establish a stock exchange. Their purpose was clearly stated in the Baillie and Butter's *Weekly Share Market Commentary* of 22 October 1859.[21]

The proposed exchange did not take on a definite shape until May 1860. At meetings chaired by Edwin Bryant and attended by about twenty 'gentlemen' at the Criterion Hotel on 9 and 10 May 1860, the report of a provisional committee, which had drawn up a set of rules based on the procedures and practices of the London and Liverpool Exchanges, was discussed and adopted.[22] Thus, the establishment of the first stock exchange in Australia was influenced by the English model. However, this exchange was not in the form of a simple association of share brokers, but was to be a company with 100 shares of GBP 50 each. Applications for shares were to close on June 1.[23] Although there was a Committee of the Stock Exchange and committee meetings were held, the proposed exchange was not established until the beginning of 1861. After a series of meetings through March into April 1861, a majority of the brokers agreed to a set of rules based on those of the London and Liverpool Exchanges but adapted to the local situation.[24]

In February 1851, Edward Hargraves discovered gold near Bathurst. This discovery started a gold rush, first in New South Wales, and then in Victoria.[25] Trading in the shares of mining companies boomed as a result. However,

---

week; the Stock Exchange of Perth was formed on 22 Jul. 1989 by the rebel brokers to move to a daily quotation. As in the eastern states, mining provided the necessary impetus for the Exchange. See Adamson, Graeme, *Miners and Millionaires: The First One Hundred Years of the People, Markets and Companies of the Stock Exchange in Perth 1889–1989* (Perth: Australian Stock Exchange (Perth) Limited, 1989), 1, 3, and 8.

18. A.R. Hall, *The Stock Exchange of Melbourne and the Economy 1852–1900* (Canberra: ANU Press, 1986), 2 and 22.
19. *Ibid.*
20. *Ibid.*, 23.
21. *Ibid.*
22. *Ibid.*
23. *Ibid.*, 24.
24. *Ibid.*, 31.
25. Salsbury, Stephen & Kay Sweeney, *The Bull, the Bear & the Kangaroo: The History of the Sydney Stock Exchange* (Sydney: Allen & UNWIN, 1988), 23.

New South Wales lagged behind Victoria. In Victoria, the gold rush resulted in the formation of stock exchanges in Bendigo, Ballarat, and Melbourne.[26] There were no less than ten specialized brokerage houses in Melbourne, while in Sydney, there were only two specialized brokers in the 1850s.[27] One of the differences in the formation of the Melbourne Stock Exchange and the Sydney Stock Exchange was that the Sydney Stock Exchange arose not only from gold-mining, but also from a boom in the mining of Cornish metals, copper, and tin.[28] It therefore is clear that in Australia, the early stock exchanges emerged with the development of the mining industry.

Queensland was granted a self-governmental status only in late 1859. In 1860, the major industry in the colony was the pastoral industry, of which over 90% of exports were derived.[29] It seemed that the incentive for Brisbane to form a stock exchange was different from those of other colonies. According to *The Brisbane Courier*, 'The large dimensions that the limited liability companies of the colony are now assuming render it desirable that some supervision as to their status should be exercised, and this can only be done by a properly conducted exchange'.[30] However, the significant increase in the trading of mining companies' shares in the period of 1881–1883 was brought about by gold-mining and the availability of funds for speculative dealings. All of these ensured that a stock exchange should be established.

Interestingly, when the stock exchanges were being established, there was no specific securities legislation in any colony: companies were all subject to companies laws enacted in the colonies. In the late nineteenth century, the English Companies Act of 1862 was adopted by most of the Australian colonies.[31] Such adoption was considered important to the maintenance of investments by British companies in the Australian colonies. It was thought that the integration of British and colonial companies legislation would also allow companies to secure listing more easily on both British and Australian share markets, thus facilitating the negotiability of their shares.[32] Colonial company legislation was largely seen in the 1860s as servicing the 'home' country's needs, rather than Australian interests.[33] Although companies acts were passed, the Australian colonies did not establish specific bureaucracies to enforce such legislation. Each colony's companies act was administered by different departments.[34]

---

26. *Ibid.*, 24.
27. *Ibid.*
28. *Ibid.*
29. A.L. Lougheed, *The Brisbane Stock Exchange 1884–1984* (Brisbane: Boolarong Publications, 1984), 1.
30. Cited by Lougheed in *The Brisbane Stock Exchange 1884–1984*, 18.
31. The Lavarch Report 1991, 5.
32. R. McQueen, 'Limited Liability Company Legislation: The Australian Experience', *Australian Journal of Corporate Law* 1, no. 1 (1991): 22–46 at 24.
33. *Ibid.*
34. *Ibid.*

While the colonial company legislation was derived from the equivalent English legislation, there were some Australian innovations. One of these was the introduction of a standard form of financial reporting for limited liability companies. Professor Harold Ford noted that:

> There were some notable innovations in Victoria . . . in 1896 compulsory audit and annual presentation of financial statements were legislated for at the prompting of the Victorian Attorney-General, Issac Issacs.[35]

The laxity of company regulation, the absence of proper financial reporting by companies, and the disdain with which controllers treated shareholders were all implicated in the collapse of large numbers of companies in Victoria during the early 1890s.[36] In response to these problems, the Victorian government had to change its corporate legislation. When a new Limited Liability Act was proposed in 1895, there were more than 173 new provisions. Most of these were aimed at increasing the responsibilities of corporate controllers for financial mismanagement or criminalizing fraudulent practices.[37]

Although there was neither uniform companies legislation nor a uniform regulator in the nineteenth century, the Australian colonies undertook the inclusion of regulatory provisions in their companies acts while the same process was occurring in England.[38] Most of the recommendations of the English 'Davey Committee' were adopted wholesale in the Victorian Companies Act of 1896.[39] The Davey Committee recommendations had primarily concentrated on the improvement of the regulatory provisions of the Limited Liability Act. In England, these recommendations were only accepted piecemeal. In Australian colonies, after the introduction of the 1896 Act, the level of compliance with the Companies Act did not appreciably improve. With respect to the administration of company legislation in the nineteenth century and the early twentieth century, nothing further had been done to create a more uniform system of regulation.[40]

The inconsistencies between the provisions of the colonies' companies acts, the differences in administrative practices between the various colonial departments charged with overseeing the acts, and the different interpretation of the acts by the courts in each colony all led to considerable inconvenience in administration and rules for the business community. This situation led to a strong lobby among the business sector to have a national or a uniform system of company law under the Federation in the early 1900s.[41]

However, the business community always envisaged that a uniform Australian Companies Act would be a replica of the latest English Act rather than a unique Australian product because of the prevailing level of integration between

---

35. H.A.J. Ford, *Principles of Company Law*, 4th edn (Sydney: Butterworths, 1986), 13.
36. Austin, Robert & Ian Ramsay, *Ford's Principles of Corporations Law*, 499.
37. *Ibid.*
38. *Ibid.*
39. *Ibid.*
40. *Ibid.*
41. *Ibid.*, 41.

Australian and English businesses. For instance, the President of the Sydney Chamber of Commerce, writing in 1907 to the Under-Secretary of the Federal Department of the Attorney-General and of Justice, suggested that, 'uniformity of Bankruptcy and Company Law be best obtained by legislation by agreement in identical terms by the Parliament of the individual states' and that 'it was desirable that legislation should follow the lines of the latest English legislation'.[42]

The history of the securities markets in the Australian colonies reveals that the practices of securities regulation in England did not have much influence on the formation of the securities markets in the Australian colonies, although the English companies legislation had some influence on the companies legislation in the Australian colonies. For example, the Melbourne Stock Exchange had looked at the listing rules of the stock exchanges of London and Liverpool in the UK, but it moulded them into its own system of market regulation.[43] It seemed that securities regulation in England had relatively little influence on the establishment and regulation on other securities markets in Australia in the nineteenth century.

The history of the emergence of the Australian securities markets reveals that these markets started early and drew upon English experiences based on their own domestic situations. In contrast, before 1900, securities markets had not been formed in China at all. This was because of the reluctant and slow adoption of capitalism in the feudalist Qing Dynasty of China. Compared to Australia, China's securities markets started late and have a very short history. This is one of the major reasons why they have not become mature and complicated markets thus far. China needs to learn from the Australian experience so as to establish mature and complicated securities markets.

7.2.2.   THE MOVEMENT TOWARDS A UNIFORM COMPANIES ACT AND A UNIFORM SECURITIES MARKET SINCE THE 1930s

The unification of companies legislation in Australia has gone through a long and slow process. Despite the continuing concern of achieving uniform companies legislation, it was not until 1961 that an agreement was reached by the states that a uniform Companies Act should be passed, and it was passed in all Australian states.[44] However, the major problem with the Uniform Companies Act of 1961 was that the states and the Commonwealth had amended their respective legislation separately, as regulation of companies traditionally and constitutionally had been a matter for the states rather than the Commonwealth.[45] In the case of *Huddart, Parker & Co Ltd v. Moorehead* (1909) 8 CLR 330, the High Court of Australia

---

42. McQueen, Robert 'Limited Liability Company Legislation: The Australian Experience', *Australian Journal of Corporate Law* 1, no. 1 (1991): 22–46 at 42.
43. A.R. Hall, *The Stock Exchange of Melbourne and the Economy 1852–1900*, 31.
44. R. Tomasic, S. Bottomley & R. McQueen, *Corporations Law in Australia*, 2nd edn (Sydney: The Federation Press, 2002), 21.
45. R. Baxt, K. Flecher & S. Fridman, *Afterman & Baxt's Cases and Materials on Corporations and Associations*, 8th edn (Sydney: Butterworths, 1999), 164–165.

narrowly interpreted section 51(xx) of the Commonwealth Constitution. Five members of the court unanimously decided that the legislative powers of the Commonwealth Parliament under section 51(xx) is confined to foreign corporations and trading or financial corporations already in existence and does not extend to the creation of corporations.[46]

Section 51(xxxvii) of the Commonwealth Constitution gives states the power to refer their corporation legislative powers to the Commonwealth. Although the deferral of such powers did not happen until mid-2001, such a means of solving the constitutional problems caused by the narrow interpretation of section 51(xx) of the Constitution by the High Court of Australia had been considered as early as 1924. On 28 November 1924, the Parliamentary and Industrial Committee of the Adelaide Chamber of Commerce considered a letter from the Melbourne Chamber of Commerce that suggested a reconsideration of formulating a national system of regulation rather than simply considering tactics in relation to the adoption of uniform legislation:

> It was suggested that the Chambers of Commerce might take steps to ascertain from leaders of all parties in the State Parliaments their ideas on the subject of referring to the Commonwealth Parliament under s 51 of the Constitution, subsection xxxvii – the power to legislate in the direction indicated. It was asked that this Chamber would advise its opinion as to whether the reference of the required powers to the Commonwealth was advisable.
>
> After carefully considering the matter, it was resolved that this Committee is of the opinion that while uniform company law under conditions satisfactory to traders might be desirable, there is no such pressing necessity or urgency as would justify conferring jurisdiction upon the Parliament of the Commonwealth and abandoning the possibility of the State parliaments adopting a uniform Bill.[47]

Although the stock exchanges had been established, the right to trade on a stock exchange was limited to stockbrokers who were members of the exchange. As the London Stock Exchange had a formal constitution and gained formal recognition in London at the beginning of the nineteenth century, stock exchanges in Australia obtained formal recognition much later than that.[48] Initially, a stock exchange was merely an unincorporated association. Until the late 1970s, exchange membership could only be secured by the purchase of the 'seat' of a retiring member. In the case of the Sydney Stock Exchange, this practice lasted until 1983.[49]

The stock exchanges in Australia had a long history of autonomy and self-regulation in the governance of their businesses. However, the Australian Associated Stock Exchanges (AASE) was only formed in 1937 by the separate exchanges,

---

46. *Ibid.*
47. McQueen, 'Limited Liability Company Legislation: The Australian Experience', *Australian Journal of Corporate Law* 1, no. 1 (1991): 22–46 at 43.
48. *Ibid.*
49. *Ibid.*

namely the Stock Exchanges of Sydney, Melbourne, Brisbane, Adelaide, Perth, and Hobart,[50] to deal with the issuing of shares in companies that had national significance.[51] Although the AASE had representatives from all exchanges, it did not have the power to speak for any member, or to change the rules of any member exchange. Each stock exchange was later incorporated as a company limited by guarantee. The requirements for listing and the quotations of securities were harmonized into a uniform body of rules at the 1939 Conference of the AASE.[52] A company listed on one stock exchange was automatically listed on the other AASE exchanges. The 1939 Conference also encouraged companies to issue interim reports and circulate their reports so as to give shareholders an early indication of trends on the securities market. During the 1920s and the 1940s, the securities markets were very quiet, even though there was a bull market that occurred as a result of a gold boom in the 1930s.[53]

During the period from 1961 to 1962, each state passed a Uniform Companies Act. The revised uniform listing requirements also became effective. However, following the passage of the Uniform Companies Act, New South Wales (NSW), Victoria, Queensland, and Western Australia passed a uniform Securities Industries Act, which introduced more elaborate provisions for establishing stock exchanges, regulating securities industry participants, and creating new offences of false trading, market rigging, and the making of false statements about securities.[54] Each state also established its Commission for Corporate Affairs to enforce the Securities Industries Act.[55] Section 5 of the Uniform Companies Act required a company to issue a prospectus if it wanted to issue securities. In addition, it contained sections that imposed civil and criminal liabilities for false or misleading statements in a prospectus.[56] At that time, the prospectus was the only disclosure document. Section 375(2) was amended to catch misleading and false statements in reports, returns, and certificates required by the Uniform Companies Act. Section 73 of the Securities Industries Act of NSW and Victoria created a new offence with respect to false and misleading conduct in securities trading:

> A person shall not with respect to any securities, make any statement or disseminate any information which at the time it is made or disseminated, he knows or has reasonable grounds for knowing is false or misleading in a material particular.

---

50. <www.asx.com.au/about/13/HistoryASX-AA3.htm>, February 2002.
51. Tomasic, Bottomley & McQueen, *Corporations Law in Australia*, 556.
52. Adamson, Graeme, *Miners and Millionaires*, 70.
53. *Ibid.*, 47–78.
54. New South Wales was the first state to enact the Securities Industry Act, in 1970. This was followed by other states.
55. CCH, *A Guide to Australian Securities Industry Law and Stock Exchange Control* (CCH, 1971), 5.
56. Sections 39, 46, and 47.

This provision was not a revolutionary one, as it embodied principles of law that were stated in the nineteenth century.[57] However, this section did not provide any civil or criminal liability. To prove an offence, the statement had to have material defect. The question of materiality was decided by the jury. The scope of section 73 was very broad, including not only the persons who made the statement to induce investors to buy shares, but also those who made the statement to influence the newspapers and other sellers of information about the stock exchanges.[58] Apart from the prospectus provisions, sections 46 and 47 of the Uniform Companies Act applied to misleading and false disclosure in takeover bids.

As the state Corporate Affairs Commissions could not implement the Uniform Companies Act, the Commonwealth and the states reached an agreement in 1978 to form a cooperative regime for companies and securities legislation following the recommendations made in the Report of the Senate Select Committee on Securities and Exchange (also known as the Rae Committee, chaired by Senator Peter Rae) in 1974. The Rae Report was made after a number of corporate collapses resulting from malpractice following the mining boom in the late 1960s and the early 1970s. During that period of time, in Australia, as in America, national regulation posed constitutional issues. The major part of the Senate Committee's public investigations took place from 15 July 1970 to 20 October 1971, but the Committee did not issue its Report until 1974.[59] These investigations proved to be painful for all the stock exchanges: the Committee did an analysis of brokerage house failures in Melbourne and Adelaide, an analysis of conflicts of interest in the Perth and Adelaide Exchanges, and an in-depth analysis of underwriting by the two largest Sydney mining underwriters, Ralph W. King & Yuill and Patrick Partners. In addition, the Committee conducted a thorough analysis of how geologists' reports had influenced the mining boom.[60]

One of the most important recommendations made in the Rae Report was to enact a piece of national securities legislation and establish a national securities regulatory body, similar to the SEC of the USA. This Report espoused the view that a national regulatory body was needed to 'eliminate the variation in administrative practice and standardise the quality of administrative action' in the securities industry.[61] Before a national securities body could be established by the Liberal-Country Party Coalition, state governments in New South Wales, Victoria, and Queensland entered into their own agreement in 1974 to establish the Interstate Corporate Affairs Commission (ICAC); Western Australia joined this agreement in 1975.[62] Each of these states amended its Uniform Companies Act of 1961 and

---

57. Hefferman, M, 'The Economic Role of the Australian Stock Exchange', in *Securities Regulation in Australia and New Zealand*, ed. G Walker (Sydney: LBC, 1996), 132.
58. *Ibid.*
59. Salsbury, Stephen & Kay Sweeney, *The Bull, the Bear & the Kangaroo: The History of the Sydney Stock Exchange*, 371.
60. *Ibid.*
61. The Rae Report of 1974, *Australian Securities Markets and Their Regulation*, (Canberra: AGPS, 1974), para. 16.3.
62. Tomasic, Bottomley & McQueen, *Corporations Law in Australia*, 22.

enacted the uniform Securities Industry Act of 1975, with greater uniformity than the 1970 legislation. Each of these states reached an agreement in 1978 to establish a cooperative scheme.

All six states, the Northern Territory, and the Commonwealth government reached an agreement on 22 December 1978 to create a Commonwealth-State Scheme for Co-operative Companies and Securities Regulation (known as the Formal Agreement). In the Formal Agreement, all these governments acknowledged the importance of having uniform laws relating to companies and the regulation of the securities industry. They also acknowledged the importance of having uniformity in the administration of the states and territories of Australia of the laws relating to companies and the securities industry. They agreed to provide for the introduction of legislation and for the establishment and operation of a Ministerial Council and a National Companies and Securities Commission. The National Companies and Securities Commission Act of 1979 was passed in the following year, and the Formal Agreement became a Schedule of that Act. The Formal Agreement was subsequently amended by the First Amending Agreement on 24 February 1981, the Second Amending Agreement on 30 December 1983, and the Third Amending Agreement on 16 October 1986.

There were a number of pieces of legislation passed as a result of the 1978 Co-operative Scheme, including the Companies Act of 1981(Cth), the Securities Industry Act of 1980 (Cth), and the Futures Industry Code of 1986 (Cth).[63] Each Act was referred to as a Code in the state legislation. As each state continued to have its own Corporate Affairs Commission responsible for the day-to-day operation of the cooperative scheme, federal politicians were dissatisfied with their diminished power under the scheme. The Commonwealth therefore passed the Corporations Act of 1989 (Cth) to cover all the areas of companies and securities previously dealt with by the Companies Code, the Securities Industry Code, and the Futures Industry Code. The Australian Securities Commission Act of 1989 (Cth) was also passed to replace the National Companies and Securities Commission Act. However, these Acts were challenged by the states; the High Court held in *New South Wales v. Commonwealth* (1990) 8 ACLC 120 that the Commonwealth government had no power under section 51(xx) of the Constitution to legislate for the incorporation of trading and financial corporations. This decision rendered the Corporations Act of 1989 (Cth) inoperative. The states and the Northern Territory had to reach an agreement on a new national scheme for uniform companies and securities regulation to be based on the two Acts passed in 1989. This was achieved in Alice Spring in June 1990.[64] This cooperative scheme, which was established under the Alice Spring Agreement, continued until 2001, when the Corporations Act of 2001 (Cth) and the Australian Securities and Investments Commission Act of 2001(Cth) were passed on 15 July 2001, after the states deferred their corporations legislative power to the Commonwealth.[65]

---

63. *Ibid.*
64. *Ibid.*, 27.
65. *Ibid.*

In 1987, all the six capital city stock exchanges agreed to the formation of the ASX as a single national stock exchange.[66] This single national exchange came into being only three years before the establishment of the PRC's first major stock exchange in Shanghai in 1990. The ASX was formed on 1 April 1987, and it amalgamated the six separate stock exchanges that formed the AASE in 1937.[67] The six capital city exchanges became wholly owned subsidiaries of the Australian Stock Exchange Ltd, a company incorporated under an act of the Commonwealth Parliament as if it were a company limited by guarantee in the Australian Capital Territory. Change was also brought about by the Australian Stock Exchange and National Guarantee Fund Act of 1987 (Cth).[68] In the same year, computerized screen trading was also introduced; this provided investors in remote areas with equal access to the national trading floor. More recently, the ASX was converted from a mutual organization to a 'for profit' limited public company in October 1998, following the enactment of the Corporations Amendment (ASX) Act of 1997. The responsibility of the ASX was also expanded. This Act allowed the ASX to be listed as a company traded on its own stock market. Currently, the ASX is the most significant securities market in Australia, in which over 99% of listed disclosing entities are listed.[69] On 7 July 2006, the Australian Stock Exchange and the Sydney Futures Exchange were merged. On 5 December, Australian Stock Exchange Ltd changed its name to Australian Securities Exchange Ltd.[70]

To date, the ASX operates as a co-regulatory organization with ASIC, supervising the trading of securities of the companies listed on its own market. It seeks to maintain an efficient, informed, competitive, and fair securities trading market. It supervises the activities of participants in its market. It has two components:

(i) a primary market to enable listed companies, trusts, and semi-governmental authorities to raise new or start-up capital; and

(ii) a secondary market to provide for the trading of securities already listed on the ASX.

The ASX is also a self-regulatory body, and its regulatory powers are supplemented by the Corporations Act.[71] It makes its own business rules and listing rules. The business rules include the constitution of the ASX and any other rules, regulations, or by-laws made by ASX except listing rules; listing rules are rules that regulate admission to the trading market, admission to the Official List of the ASX,

---

66. Baxt, Ford & Black, *Securities Industry Law* (Sydney: Butterworths, 1996), 133.
67. *Ibid.*
68. *Ibid.*
69. CLERP Proposals for Reform Paper No. 9: *Corporate Disclosure: Strengthening the Financial Reporting Framework*, (Canberra: Canprint Communications, 2002), 132.
70. <www.asx.com.au/about/asx/history/history_ASX.htm>, 31 Aug. 2009.
71. Section 674(1) imposes an obligation on listed disclosing bodies to disclose in accordance with the ASX's Listing Rules. Section 674(2) imposes a continuous disclosure obligation on listed disclosing entities and makes the breach of such obligation an offence; and it is subject to a civil penalty provision under s. 1317E and may be issued an infringement notice.

removal from the official list, and the activities or conduct of listed entities.[72] The ASX updates its listing rules and business rules from time to time.

Currently, the ASX is the only national securities market in Australia recognized by legislation. Before 1996, under the articles of association, membership in the ASX was not transferable[73] and there could be no distribution to members of profits or income of the exchange.[74] The ASX was established as a mutual organization, but on 18 October 1996, its members voted to demutualise it into a public company. The Company Law Review Act of 1998 (Cth) was passed to further simplify drafting prospectuses; it also replaced memoranda and articles of association by a company constitution, and it abolished the concept of par value. Under the Financial Sector Reform (Amendments to Transitional Provisions) Act of 1998 (Cth), Australian Securities Commission (ASC) was replaced by Australian Securities and Investments Commission (ASIC) with added regulatory powers over insurance consumer protection and other financial services. The ASX was demutualized and became a listed company on its own market. The decision to demutualise was justified by the want of identity, the undesirability for long-term control of the entity to reside with one group of stakeholders, and the need for flexibility and swiftness of decision-making for competing with other securities markets resulting from global capital mobility. The demutualization of the ASX broke the requirement for a connection with the ASX for listing.

In addition to the national market run by the ASX, there are regional exchanges in Newcastle (in the State of New South Wales), Bendigo, and Ballarat (both in the State of Victoria). The Newcastle Stock Exchange Limited (NSX) first commenced trading in 1937 but was inactive for many years, until trading re-commenced in December 2000.[75] It is a market for the securities of small to medium and regionally based companies. By the end of September 2002, there were four companies listed with the NSX.[76] The Bendigo Stock Exchange Limited (BSX) is moving in a similar direction; it re-commenced trading on 15 August 2001. It is a fully Internet-based exchange that intends to specialize in emerging companies and rural-based companies. By the end of September 2002, there was only one listing on the BSX.[77] The Ballarat Exchange has not listed any securities and may be seen as a local association of dealers.[78] On 11 August 2004, Australia Pacific Exchange Limited was granted a market license by ASIC. Its operation commenced on 20 January 2005. On 22 December 2008, its name was changed to

---

72. A. Shaw & P.V. Nessen, 'The Legal Role of the Australian Securities Commission and the Australian Stock Exchange', in *Securities Regulation in Australia and New Zealand*, ed. G. Walker, 2nd edn (Sydney: LBC, 1998), 175.
73. The ASX Listing Rules, Art. 35(3).
74. *Ibid.*, Art. 81.
75. <www.newsx.com.au/nsx.html>, 15 Jul. 2002.
76. <www.newsx.com.au/nsx.html> July 2002; CLERP Paper 9: *Corporate Disclosure: Strengthening the Financial Reporting Framework*, 132.
77. <www.bsx.com.au>; CLERP Paper 9: *Corporate Disclosure: Strengthening the Financial Reporting Framework*, 132.
78. <www.asx.com.au>, 15 Jul. 2002.

Asia Pacific Exchange Limited. By April 2009, it had three listed companies and one participating broker.[79] The ASX is Australia's only significant stock exchange and has well over 99% of listed disclosing entities.[80] In this book, therefore, the term 'the Australian securities market' refers to the ASX market.

The Australia securities market is an integral, although small, part of world investment markets. This market is rapidly globalizing. It depends on the investors in those markets to help support its economic growth and demand for funds. Although Australia has strong traditional ties with the United Kingdom, it has also developed close ties with the USA and Europe in recent times. Large Australian companies' shares may be traded quite actively in the capital markets in London, Europe, New York, Tokyo, and Hong Kong. With the globalization of securities markets, Australian securities regulation has been greatly influenced by foreign experiences. In the following parts, this influence will be discussed in the context of further development of the Australian securities market.

It is worth noting that while the development of the Australian securities market is closely associated with its company law reform, the development of the PRC securities market has mainly been directed by the national policy of the controlling Communist Party.[81] In the PRC, the securities market is widely called 'the policy market', as the securities price is greatly affected by the policies of the government.[82] The development of this market had not had the support of national law for a long period of time.[83] Even though the PRC passed its first Company Law in 1993, this Law is mainly focused on issuing shares with few provisions on the securities trading market. The PRC Securities Law of 1998 is still too general, and the CSRC has to frequently make administrative rules under the direction of the CPC's policies to meet the changes of the market. Consequently, the changeable nature of Party policy is one factor that contributes to the vulnerability of the PRC securities market. Lack of the support of national law determines the unique feature of the PRC securities market – strong control of the government.

7.2.3.   CURRENT DEVELOPMENT OF THE SECURITIES MARKETS
          IN AUSTRALIA

Although stock exchanges in Australia were established relatively early, compared to the securities markets in most Western countries, the scale of the Australian

---

79.   ASIC, *Market Assessment Report: Asia Pacific Exchange Limited*, April 2009, 6.
80.   Above n. 78.
81.   According to Li, Zhangzhe, *Report on the Chinese Shares Market Development*, 91, the term 'shareholding system' was first officially used by the State Council in the Circular Concerning Several Issues on Commercial System Reform in 1986. In December 1986, the State Council for the first time allowed the SOEs to adopt the shareholding system.
82.   Wang, Chunfeng, Chapter 2 'Political Influence: Is It a Policy Market?', in *Diagnosis and Treatment: Revealing This Stock Market in China*, ed. Siwei Cheng (Beijing: Economics Science Press, 2002), 118.
83.   The securities market of the PRC re-emerged in the mid-1980s, but the Securities Law was only promulgated on 29 Dec. 1998.

market has never been very big. For example, at the end of June 1992, the domestic market capitalization in the ASX was Australian Dollars (AUD) 198 billion. By the end of June 2002, it had increased to just AUD 700 billion. By the end of November 2002, 1,349 domestic and 67 foreign companies had their equities on the ASX.[84] As of 30 June 2009, the domestic market capitalization was AUD 1.09 trillion, and the number of listed companies was 2,198. However, this small market has been very efficient and successful. By examining some features of the Australian securities market, this book demonstrates that the success of this market is built upon its regulatory regime, which absorbed foreign experiences and also fit its domestic situations.

7.2.3.1.   Stock Exchange Automated Trading System (SEATS)

Since October 1987, the ASX has adopted and has maintained an automated or screen-based system whereby brokers can execute transactions for their clients through a central computer. This Stock Exchange Automated Trading System (SEATS) had been used on a trial basis until October 1990, when it was expanded to the entire market. SEATS has transformed share trading in Australia by removing it from the trading floor to terminals in brokers' offices.[85] This system enables the matching of buying and selling orders automatically, with the best-priced orders taking priority. If there is more than one order at the same price, the order that was placed first takes precedence.

Like NASDAQ, SEATS has also influenced the PRC's adoption of an automatic securities trading system. On 5 December 1990, the Securities Trading Automated Quotations Systems (STAQS), which was modelled on NASDAQ,[86] was formally established to provide a secondary market for government treasury bonds.[87] In January 1991, another trading system, the National Electronic Trading System (NETS) was established[88] to provide a unified national electronic market for all securities, including 'central government bonds, municipal government bonds, state bank bonds, corporate bonds, shares, investment fund bonds and other securities'.[89] However, as computers in the PRC are not as commonly used as they are in Australia, the PRC's automatic trading system has not been broadly and efficiently used by investors. With the strengthening of the Shanghai and the Shenzhen Stock Exchanges, both STQS and NETS ceased to function in 1997.[90] In October, the ASX replaced SEATS with the CLICK XT platform, which offers integrated trading for all cash equity and equity derivative products.[91]

---

84.   <www.asx.com.au>, January 2003.
85.   Hefferman, M, 'The Economic Role of the Australian Stock Exchange', 146.
86.   Walter & Howie, *Privatizing China*, 37.
87.   *Ibid.*, 38.
88.   *Ibid.*, 38.
89.   *Ibid.*, 40.
90.   *Ibid.*, 39, 40.
91.   <www.asx.com.au/about/asx/history/history_ASX.htm>, 8 Sep. 2009.

7.2.3.2.   Clearing House Electronic Sub-register System (CHESS)

The ASX implemented a clearing and settlement initiative, the Clearing House Electronic Sub-register System (known as CHESS), on 19 September 1994. CHESS is operated by the ASX Settlement and Transfer Corporation (ASTC), a wholly owned subsidiary of the ASX.[92] As a clearing house, CHESS enables the transfer of titles or legal ownership of securities between sellers and buyers and facilitates the transfer of money for these securities. As a sub-register, this system registers the ownerships of securities. In the PRC, the SSE and the SZSE have adopted a similar clearing and settlement system.

7.2.3.3.   Influence of Foreign Markets

There are a number of factors that may have an influence on a securities market. These can be historical, cultural, psychological, economic, political, and/or social, as well as being of international, regional, or national significance. The Australian securities market has been closely cooperating with foreign exchanges. Through these ties, it was greatly influenced by other markets, notably, the New York Stock Exchange, the London Stock Exchange, and the Tokyo Stock Exchange, which have exercised a dominant influence on Australian investment behaviour.[93] In 1996, the ASX signed MOUs with the Kuala Lumpur Stock Exchange and the Korea Stock Exchange.[94] In 1997, it signed MOUs with the Jakarta Stock Exchange, the Surabaya Exchange, and the Taiwan Stock Exchange.[95] In 1998, the ASX entered into an MOU with the Philippine Stock Exchange.[96] In 1999, the ASX signed MOUs with the Thailand Stock Exchange and the Singapore Stock Exchange.[97] In 2000, the ASX signed MOUs with the Tokyo Stock Exchange and the Hong Kong Stock Exchange.[98] In September 2002, it signed an MOU with the Shanghai Stock Exchange.[99]

The signing of MOUs between stock exchanges is a result of globalization. Through these MOUs, Australia has learnt a lot from its foreign counterparts, and in return, has influenced other countries. As a member of IOSCO, Australia also follows IOSCO's corporate governance rules. On 3 July 2002, the Financial Reporting Council announced its formal support for the adoption of IASB Standards by 2005.[100] The IASB Standards were formally adopted in January 2005 in Australia. From the development of the Australian securities market, it can be seen

---

92. P. Lipton & A. Herzberg, *Understanding Company Law*, 12th edn (Sydney: Thomson Law Book, 2004), 210.
93. *Ibid.*
94. <www.asx.com.au>, 15 Aug. 2004.
95. *Ibid.*
96. *Ibid.*
97. *Ibid.*
98. *Ibid.*
99. *Ibid.*
100. *Ibid.*

that this market has become very complicated. The Corporate Law Economic Reform Program (CLERP). Policy Framework echoes what the Financial System Inquiry Final Report[101] pointed out that 'the productivity, dynamism, and global integration of Australia's business and financial markets have greatly increased in recent years'.[102]

Since the 1990s, the CSRC has also strengthened its cooperation with other countries by signing MOUs. In this way, the Chinese securities market to some degree has been influenced by foreign experiences, as it is still in a stage of transition. This nature of development has been a determinant that the PRC has not been able to form a securities regulatory regime with very strong Chinese characteristics.

7.2.4.   FINANCIAL DISCLOSURE AND COMMITTEES OF ENQUIRY IN
         THE PROCESS OF CORPORATE LAW REFORM

The changes of corporate disclosure rules in Australia have been the consequences of reports of committees of enquiry appointed by the Commonwealth Parliament following a financial crisis or large corporate collapses. Corporate disclosure debates have been mainly focused on financial disclosure. The analysis of the reports of these committees helps explain the purposes and rationales underlying the existing laws. In this section, an analysis of some key reports in relation to corporate disclosure is conducted.

As Australia inherited English law, it is useful to start with an examination of some key committee reports of the UK from the nineteenth century. The discussions and recommendations on corporate disclosure in these reports influenced the development of the corporate disclosure regime in Australia. In more recent times, Australia has formed a number of inquiry committees to review its corporate disclosure regime from time to time. Some of the reports by these committees will be briefly reviewed. From the review of these reports, it is possible to trace back how foreign experiences have influenced the formation and development of the Australian corporate disclosure regime and how Australia has adjusted foreign experiences to its own domestic circumstances. The aim of this review is to provide an example from which the PRC can learn.

7.2.4.1.   The Select Committee on Joint Stock Companies and the Joint Stock Companies Acts of 1844 and 1856

In 1844, the first English Companies Act was passed. It followed a report by a Select Committee on Joint Stock Companies chaired by William Gladstone and

---

101.   This is also called the Final Wallis Report (Canberra, AGPS, 1997). The then Treasurer, Peter Costello MP, established the Financial System Inquiry in June 1996, which was chaired by Stan Wallis, who was the President of the Business Council of Australia at the time.

102.   The CLERP 9 Discussion Paper, 103.

commissioned by the House of Commons in England to combat regular abuses such as fraudulent accounting. The Committee recommended a statutory regime that required honest financial disclosure by companies.[103] Under the Companies Act of 1844, for the first time, companies could be incorporated through registration, in addition to the granting of a royal charter or the passing of a special act by Parliament. Under this Act, the promoters of companies seeking public subscriptions were obliged to disclose all relevant facts by registering the company's prospectus. Disclosure through a prospectus was inherited by the Australian colonies.

7.2.4.2. The 1895 Davey Report of the UK, the Companies Act of 1896 (Victoria), and the 1906 Loreburn Report of the UK

In 1895, the Davey Committee[104] of the UK adopted three basic principles:

- (a) legislation cannot protect people from the consequences of their own imprudence, recklessness, or want of experience;
- (b) because a person who is invited to subscribe for shares on the basis of a prospectus has no opportunity of making any independent inquiries, therefore that person deserves the greatest protection;
- (c) it is more difficult to regulate the administration of companies for the benefit of members and creditors. *Inter alia*, then, more stringent provisions respecting accounts, balance sheets, and audits and better provisions for better securing the responsibility of directors, may be made with advantage and safety.[105]

It took almost thirty years for the recommendations of the Davey Committee to be adopted in the UK. However, the colony of Victoria enacted requirements corresponding to the recommendations by the Davey Report in its Companies Act of 1896, including the following:

- (a) the keeping of proper books of accounts on the affairs and transactions of the company;
- (b) preparation of an annual shareholders' balance sheet at the company's general meeting;
- (c) a requirement that the balance sheet and accounts be audited to certify whether they were correct or not.[106]

---

103. Cited by PeterLittle in 'Financial Disclosure by Corporations', *Australian Journal of Corporate Law* 1, no. 2 (1991): 87–116 at 88.
104. Report of the Departmental Committee appointed by the Board of Trade, to inquire what amendments are necessary in the Acts relating to Joint Stock Companies with limited liability under the Companies Act.
105. Cited by Peter Little, 'Financial Disclosure by Corporations' (1991) 1(2) *Australian Journal of Corporate Law* 87–116 at 89.
106. *Ibid.*, 90.

In the UK, the Loreburn Report of 1906 contained recommendations that led to the legislative adoption in 1907 of a requirement for public companies to file an annual audited balance sheet.[107]

7.2.4.3. The Greene Report of 1925–1926 and the Companies Act of 1929 of the UK

The English Companies Act of 1929 followed widespread abuse through non-disclosure of information, related party transactions, takeover and merger malpractice, and breaches of directors' duties. The Greene Report required all companies to keep proper accounts, including profit and loss accounts, and to file them with the Registrar.[108] Although the professions acknowledged at the time that the public had a legitimate right to certain information, they supported the imposition of broadly defined minimum statutory standards. This resulted in minimum standards being imposed based on the government's trust of industry leaders and the accounting profession.[109]

The UK Companies Act of 1929 was later adopted not only by Australia, but also by Hong Kong. In 1993, when the PRC was enacting its first Company Law, it borrowed some contents of the Hong Kong Companies Act. Perhaps to some extent the PRC Company Law has similarities to the Australian Companies legislation. However, the PRC Company Law was passed to 'meet the needs of establishing a modern enterprise system'.[110] It did not aim to regulate the securities markets because the PRC securities market had just begun to emerge. Thus, the Law had few detailed articles on corporate disclosure, although it did contain the principles of openness, justice, and fairness.[111]

7.2.4.4. The Cohen Report of 1945 of the UK

In 1945, the Board of Trade of the UK produced a Report of the Committee on Company Law Amendment, which considered that abuse would be lessened by 'the fullest practicable disclosure of information concerning the activities of companies'.[112] The Report recommended the insertion of a definition of a profit and loss account and a requirement that it be audited together with the balance sheet so as to determine the prosperity of a company and the value of its assets.[113]

---

107. *Ibid.*, 92.
108. *Ibid.*
109. *Ibid.*, 93.
110. Article 1.
111. Article 130.
112. The Cohen Report, para. 5.
113. *Ibid.*, para. 97.

7.2.4.5.   The Jenkins Committee Report of 1962 of the UK

This Report adopted a conservative philosophy in regard to annual accounts, stating that the primary purpose of the annual accounts of a business is to present information to the proprietors, showing how their funds have been utilized, and the profits derived from such use.[114]

7.2.4.6.   The Eggleston Committee Report of 1970

The Australian government established the Eggleston Committee[115] in 1967 to examine the disclosure regime following a number of corporate failures and public debate. Its Report was released in 1970 and stated that 'undoubtedly one of the most potent weapons available for the protection of investors is the compulsory disclosure of information as to the past performance of the company, coupled with the safeguard against misstatement provided by audit requirements'.[116] The Committee proposed a Companies Commission whose 'prime objective' would be 'to ensure adequate protection for the investing public'. The Report contended that the Commission's amendment of forms and the content of accounts should take account of developments in the accounting profession.[117]

7.2.4.7.   The Rae Report of 1974

Following the mining and share market booms of 1969 and 1970, a Senate Select Committee on Securities and Exchange was appointed to investigate the Australian securities markets and the 'desirability and feasibility of establishing a securities and exchange commission by the Commonwealth either alone or in cooperation with the Senates'.[118] It released a Report on Australian Securities Markets and Their Regulation in 1974, also known as the Rae Report.

In the Preface to this Report, the Committee stated that since its first meeting on 21 April 1970, the Committee had met on 176 occasions with evidence amounting to more than 12,000 pages of typed transcript, of which approximately 25% was heard *in camera*, which was taken at eighty-six meetings held primarily in Canberra, but also in Perth, Sydney, and Melbourne. According to the Preface, the 142 witnesses were drawn from all sections of financial and commercial life in Australia, including representatives of various regulatory bodies and government institutions related to the industry, university lecturers, stock exchange members and executives, stockbrokers, Companies Act Registrars, managers of mutual funds and other institutional investors, company directors, financial journalists,

---

114. Cited by Peter Little, *Report of the Company Law Committee*, 1962.
115. Company Law Advisory Committee to the Standing Committee of the Attorney-General.
116. The Eggleston Report, para. 7.
117. Cited by Peter Little, *The Eggleston Report*, para. 48.
118. The Rae Report (*Report from the Senate Select Committee on Securities and Exchange: Australian Securities Markets and their Regulation*), Part I vol. I (Canberra: The Government Printer of Australia, 1974), Preface, v.

accountants, company secretaries, geologists, engineers, representatives of life offices, and shareholders.[119]

The Rae Report had been strongly influenced by overseas experiences:

> to keep informing on current developments within the securities industry, the Committee sought and obtained extensive information from overseas countries, in particular, the United Kingdom, South Africa, the United States of America, Canada and Japan. Senator P.E. Rae, and the legal adviser, Professor D.E. Harding and the Secretary, Mr D.W. Whitebread, had been overseas in discussion with experts in securities industry.[120]

The report particularly expressed 'its gratitude for the ready co-operation given by various individuals and bodies, especially to officers of the United States Securities and Exchange Commission, to Professor Louis Loss, Professor of Law at Harvard University and to Mr James J. Needman, Chairman of the Board of the New York Stock Exchange'.[121]

The Committee detected a number of instances of improper behaviour by participants in the securities market. Among them there was an alarmingly frequent and serious failure to meet proper standards of full, accurate, and timely disclosure, whether through prospectuses, accounts submitted to the stock exchanges, or statements of the market.[122] The Report recommended legislative action on the grounds of 'fairness and commercial morality, and in the interests of economic efficiency'.[123] It also recommended the creation of a national market by uniform legislation to be supervised by a national securities commission.

It is noteworthy that during the period of the Inquiry, the Committee sought and obtained extensive information from other countries, in particular, the UK, South Africa, the USA, Canada, and Japan. Various reports of governmental and other inquiries overseas had been of considerable assistance to the Committee.[124] The Chairman and other members of the Committee had been overseas and had had valuable discussions with securities experts in countries such as the UK, the USA, South Africa, and Canada. They also visited stock exchanges in London, New York, Johannesburg, and other places.[125] It can be concluded that the corporations law amendments based on the suggestions of the Rae Report had been greatly influenced by foreign experiences.

It should also be noted that the Rae Report noticed the differences in the regulatory approaches in the USA and Australia. It pointed out that, 'In the United States the responsible authorities, both self-regulatory and governmental, have commissioned or ordered factual, in-depth studies on many matters concerning

119. *Ibid.*
120. *Ibid.*
121. *Ibid.*, viii.
122. The Rae Report, 471.
123. *Ibid.*
124. *Ibid.*, viii.
125. *Ibid.*

market activities,'[126] and that in addition 'these authorities have closely and objectively examined the arguments and considerations relevant to regulation'.[127] The Rae Report also criticized the Australian stock committees for failures not only in collecting the relevant statistics on various dubious practices, but also in discussions of the need for regulation of such practices.[128]

7.2.4.8.   The 1975 Corporations and Securities Industry Bill

The Australia Commonwealth Attorney-General's Department, in its submissions to the Senate Select Committee on the Corporations and Securities Bill (Cth) of 1975 (this Bill was first introduced in 1974[129]), set out the philosophy of disclosure to the effect that, 'The investing public cannot be protected unless they have access to adequate and reliable information concerning the financial and operating condition of the corporations to which their securities relate'.[130] Part VI of the Bill ensured that corporate accounts were kept and that financial statements would be properly prepared, audited, and presented. Unfortunately, this Bill lapsed with the dismissal of the Commonwealth government in November 1975.

7.2.4.9.   The 1983 Green Paper

A new cooperative scheme was established for uniform companies and securities legislation throughout Australia under an agreement made on 22 December 1978. It became effective after the Commonwealth and the states enacted uniform legislation. The National Companies and Securities Commission (NCSC) was established in 1979 as the national regulatory agency for administration of the companies and securities laws and for reviewing the regulation of the industry. The State Corporate Affairs Commissions continued to administer the application of the Commonwealth legislation under the delegated authority of the NCSC. In 1983, the Accounting Standards Review Board was established to develop accounting standards. This paved the way for a unified approach to financial disclosure in Australia.[131]

In 1983, the NCSC published a Green Paper entitled *Financial Reporting of the Companies Act and Codes*. This Green Paper also reflected the influence of American law on securities regulation. It endorsed the objectives of financial reporting applicable in the USA,[132] which has an economic rather than corporate law orientation.[133] It proposed amendments to state Companies Acts and their accompanying regulations. It recognized that it was necessary to articulate

---

126.   *Ibid.*, 474.
127.   *Ibid.*
128.   *Ibid.*
129.   The Griffiths Report of 1989, para. 2.1.10.
130.   Cited by P. Little, 97.
131.   *Ibid.*, 98.
132.   *Ibid.*, paras 2.11–2.13.
133.   Cited by Peter Little, 98.

'the essential assumptions and fundamental concepts' underlying financial reporting.[134] However, it rejected the proposal of the professional accounting bodies that their standards should enliven the minimum statutory requirements because of the fact that neither they nor users of financial statements in Australia had developed a conceptual framework capable of serving the information needs of the market.[135]

The NCSC also considered the statutory definition that constitutes a 'true and fair view' by reference to (i) the purposes of financial statements and (ii) the persons to be primarily served by those statements – or a wholly new requirement – might give more precise guidance to directors and auditors in discharging their responsibilities'.[136]

It is noteworthy that the financial reporting rules of Australia can be traced back to the UK Companies Act of 1844.[137] However, 'the first recommendations on accounting principles which were published by the Institute of Chartered Accountants in England and Wales in the 1940s were not substantially adopted by the Institute of Chartered Accountants in Australia until 1946'.[138]

7.2.4.10.   The Griffiths Report[139] of 1989

Corporate disclosure ensures that participants in the markets can access the market equally. One important aspect of the disclosure regime is to prevent insider trading. Prohibiting insider trading is based on the theories of fairness, fiduciary duty, economic efficiency, and corporate injury.[140] The earliest provisions on insider trading in Australia are in section 124 of the Uniform Companies Act of 1961, which prohibited company officers from using information acquired by their position to gain an advantage for themselves, or to cause detriment to the company.[141] The inquiry of the Rae Report in 1970 included an investigation of the powers of a Commonwealth securities commission to act speedily against manipulation of prices, insider trading, and other improper practices.[142] The first law in Australia specifically prohibiting insider trading was section 75 of the New South Wales Securities Industry Act of 1970.[143] Later on, section 128 of the

---

134. NCSC, *Financial Reporting Requirements of the Companies Act and Codes (the Green Paper of 1983)* (Canberra: AGPS, 1983), para. 2.7.
135. *Ibid.*, para. 2.9.
136. The Green Paper of 1983, para. 4.4.
137. *Ibid.*, para. 3.4.
138. *Ibid.*
139. The House of Representatives Standing Committee on Legal and Constitutional Affairs Report, *Fair Shares for All: Insider Trading in Australia*, 1989.
140. The Griffiths Report, para. 3.1.2.
141. *Ibid.*, para. 2.1.3.
142. *Ibid.*, para. 2.1.5.
143. *Ibid.*, para. 2.1.6.

Securities Industry legislation regulated insider trading under the cooperative scheme administered by the NCSC.[144]

On 8 February 1989, the then Attorney-General, the Honourable Lionel Bowen, requested that the House of Representatives Standing Committee on Legal and Constitutional Affairs conduct an inquiry into insider trading and other forms of market manipulation. The inquiry committee was chaired by Member of Parliament (MP) Alan Griffiths. It released the Griffiths Report, entitled *Fair Shares for All: Insider Trading in Australia* in October 1989. This inquiry arose as a result of evidence provided by the NCSC in July 1988 in the context of its inquiry into mergers, takeovers, and monopolies.[145] The NCSC indicated that proving insider trading cases under the existing legislation was extraordinarily difficult.[146] Another reason for the establishment of this inquiry was the release of a study into insider trading by Dr R.A. Tomasic and Mr. B.D. Pentony.[147] Tomasic and Pentony concluded in their study that, 'The law against insider trading is practically non-existent'.[148]

It is very import to note that the Griffiths Report reviewed and compared overseas experiences with Australian practices. It analysed the American approach of regulating insider trading and clearly pointed out that this approach did not suit Australia.[149] It also indicated that the Australian approach was closer to that of New Zealand and the UK.[150]

It is also worth mentioning that before conducting its inquiry in 1988, the NCSC retained Philip Anisman, then Professor of Law at Osgoode Hall Law School, York University of Canada, in 1986 to prepare an initial issues paper on insider trading. Although Professor Anisman could not finish his task because he left Australia, the NCSC published his recommendations as *Insider Trading Legislation for Australia: An Outline of the Issues and Alternatives* in 1986 for public debate.[151] From this perspective, Australian insider trading legislation might have been influenced by the Canadian experience as well.

7.2.4.11. The CASAC Report of 1991 and the Lavarch Committee Report of 1991

In 1989, the Commonwealth Parliament enacted the Corporations Act, the Australian Securities Commission Act, and related legislation, all of which were designed to nationally regulate the entire field of companies and securities law. The principal purpose of these acts was to establish a single national regulatory

---

144. P. Anisman, *Insider Trading Legislation for Australia: An Outline of the Issues and Alternatives* (Canberra: AGPS, 1986), vi.
145. The Griffiths Report of 1989, para. 1.2.1.
146. *Ibid.*
147. *Ibid.*, para. 1.2.2.
148. *Ibid.*, para. 1.2.4.
149. *Ibid.*, paras 2.2.4 and 2.2.5.
150. *Ibid.*, para. 2.2.7.
151. The Rae Report, Preface.

framework. The ASC, replacing the NCSC, was established as the supreme regulatory authority, and the state Corporate Affairs Commissions were abolished.
The ASC was formally responsible to the Commonwealth Attorney-General and
the Commonwealth Parliament. The Australian Accounting Standards Board
(AASB), taking the place of the Australian Accounting Review Board (AARB),
is responsible for the formulation and development of accounting standards.

The House of Representatives Standing Committee on Legal and
Constitutional Affairs (the LACA Committee) commenced its Inquiry into Corporate Practices and the Rights of Shareholders on 31 October 1989 at the request
of then Attorney-General Lionel Bowen. The Committee was re-established by the
new Parliament, and the new Inquiry was referred to the new Attorney-General,
Michael Duffy. The terms of the reference given the Committee remained
unchanged, and the Committee had access to the Inquiry evidence and records
of the previous Parliament.[152] The Inquiry was chaired by MP Michael Lavarch.
The Committee released the Lavarch Report in November 1991, entitled *Corporate Practices and the Rights of Shareholders.*

The LACA Committee had been formed to conduct the inquiry at a time when
several prominent business enterprises, such as Rothwells Limited, the Hooker
Corporation, and Qintex Australia Limited, had gone into receivership. There were
concerns about the practices of corporate executives and companies.[153] The
Lavarch Report considered that there were serious problems with the enforcement
of the LRs of the ASX. The LRs were drafted in 'discretionary' language rather
than precise statutory language.[154] One of the recommendations of the Lavarch
Report was that section 777 of the Corporations Law be changed to impose a
disclosure obligation on directors as well as companies to observe the LRs so as
to overcome the problem in the decision in *Hillhouse v. Gold Copper Exploration
NL* (1989) 14 ACLR 423. It was decided in that case that the LRs appeared to be
un-enforceable as they did not apply to directors but only to companies. This
recommendation was adopted by the Corporate Law Reform Act of 1994 (Cth).
The common law and statutory duties of directors drew heavily on forms of words
developed in case law around the turn of the century, with a view to ensuring that
directors were bound to act in the interests of shareholders. Many of the duties
under common law were codified into corporate legislation.

When the LACA Committee was making the Inquiry into Corporate Practices,
the Companies and Securities Advisory Committee (CASAC) was requested in
June 1991 by then Commonwealth Attorney-General Michael Duffy to examine
the need for a legislatively based continuous disclosure regime and the nature of
such a regime.[155] It recommended a continuous disclosure that went beyond what
was required in the USA. However, some people opposed this recommendation for

---

152. *The Lavarch Report: Corporate Practices and the Rights of Shareholders* (Canberra: AGPS,
     1991), 1.
153. *Ibid.,* 2.
154. *TNT Australia Pty Ltd v. Poseidon Ltd* (1989) 15 ACLR 80.
155. The Lavarch Report of 1991, 96.

the reasons that it imposed extra costs on companies with limited benefits that would be passed on to the consumers, that some of the information was not very useful, and that the relatively poorly funded NCSC needed additional resources to administer the recommended changes.[156]

In May 1991, Michael Duffy introduced the Corporations Legislation Amendment Bill to Parliament. He stated that in recent years there had been:

> widespread abuses of the existing company accounting and reporting requirements under which the true financial position of a group of companies has been able to be disguised by off-balance sheet reporting. This has enabled the financial statements of the company to be manipulated in such a way as to mislead investors and the market generally regarding the real level of liabilities or performance of a company or the group as a whole ... one of the consequences of these practices has been a significant loss of investor confidence, both amongst Australian and overseas investors, in the reality of corporate financial information in Australia.[157]

The Lavarch Report analysed the approaches of the LACA Committee and CASAC, which both advocated continuous disclosure. Different from the proposals of the LACA, CASAC proposed a further regulation under the Corporations Law and accepted proposals by the ASX to implement a regime of continuous disclosure through the Listing Rules.

In 1991, CASAC released its *Report on Reform of the Law Governing Corporate Financial Transactions*, proposing that the obligation to make disclosure be dealt with through the ASX Listing Rules. The ASX supported this legislative approach while noting that the proposals were complex and contained detailed requirements that would impose substantial burdens on corporations and their officers. The ASC also stated that the need for such provisions was the function of both the legalistic and technical approach adopted by the courts on some occasions and of the evident inability of self-regulatory mechanisms to maintain satisfactory standards of business ethics on a sufficiently comprehensive basis.[158]

However, some people advocated a non-legislative approach. Former Chairman of the NCSC Henry Bosch argued that:

- Legislation is too slow to enact, often taking two to three years where the issues are complex;
- The slow nature of the legislative process produces inflexibility and precludes a quick response to new loopholes;
- Legislation may provide a cover for the unscrupulous who may adhere to the letter of the law but defy its spirit;

---

156. R. Baxt, 'Opening Address to the 1992 National Corporate Law Teachers' Workshop', *Australian Journal of Corporate Law* 2, no. 1 (1992) 6–11 at 9.
157. House of Representatives, *Parliamentary Debates*, 29 May 1991, cited in the Lavarch Report of 1991, para. 4.5.1.
158. *Ibid.*, para. 4.5.8.

- Legislative prescriptions may impose onerous burdens on the honest majority of companies; and
- Alternations to the Corporations Law still require consultation with the states.[159]

Some practitioners criticized the legislation operating in the companies and securities field because of the prolixity and technicality of its drafting. John Green, then a partner with the law firm of Freehill, Hollingdale and Page, told the Lavarch Committee that:

> Disclosure is really one of the most important and underutilized defences to corporate crookery. Our disclosure mechanisms are not as good as we could have. For example the market might think twice about it if it knew that directors were trading in the shares, either buying or selling. That is something that the market would actually like to know.[160]

Malcolm McComas, Director of County NatWest Australia Ltd, suggested to the Lavarch Committee that the need for a higher standard of disclosure should be demanded through the Listing Rules of the ASX rather than through the legislation.[161] The Lavarch Committee favoured the non-legislative approach over the legislative approach proposed by CASAC. Its bases for this view were the following:

- CASAC proposals applied not only to the listed companies but also to non-listed companies. However, the requirement for disclosure should be imposed on the listed companies only at this stage.
- It was important not to increase the regulatory burden on companies, particularly smaller companies at a time when business enterprises were emerging from a recession.[162]

It can be seen that the Lavarch Report based its conclusion on economic as well as legal considerations. The Lavarch Report also recommended that a regime of 'continuous disclosure' by listed companies should be introduced, implemented, and enforced through the ASX LRs. Although the Larvarch Committee favoured disclosure regulation through the ASX LRs, it also made it clear that it would not support the ASX's new draft LRs as they were thought to be too extensive.[163]

In October 1990, the ASX issued a discussion paper entitled *Proposed Listing Reporting by Listed Companies*. It sought comments on the reporting measures, including upgraded half-yearly reports (e.g., whether to include cash flow statements, condensed balance sheets, etc.) and the introduction of a quarterly reporting requirement on all or large listed companies.

---

159. *Ibid.*, para. 4.5.9.
160. Cited in the Lavarch Report, para. 4.5.11.
161. *Ibid.*, para. 4.5.12.
162. *Ibid.*, 105.
163. *Ibid.*

In June 1991, the ASX issued an Exposure Draft entitled *Proposed Listing Rule Amendments to Become Effective Late 1991*. The ASX stated that it would not adopt the proposed quarterly reporting requirement (which is used in the USA) as it failed to gain enough support from respondents.[164] It also expressed concern regarding the costs to listed companies of maintaining such a system. This is another sign that although Australia has drawn upon experiences from other countries, it also considers the applicability of foreign experiences in Australia.

Henry Bosch pointed out that the LRs had a number of advantages compared to 'black-letter law', including that they had the force of law and were much more flexible.[165] Malcolm McComas stated that the Listing Rules were 'the appropriate way of regulating the quoted public company sector'. He advocated a greater use of the ASX Listing Rules to require disclosure. He also suggested that detailed changes were necessary to the rules. In doing so, Malcolm McComas drew attention to the listing requirements applicable to material transactions in the UK, where all transactions involving publicly listed companies were divided into classes according to the size of the deal and the relationship between the parties. Various classes of transactions require shareholders' approval in addition to the publication of a detailed information memorandum on the transaction for circulation to shareholders.[166]

The ASX in June 1991 released proposed Listing Rules amendments to become effective in January 1992. The new Listing Rule 3Y incorporated a number of old core ASX Listing Rules. It required listed companies to disclose significant transactions that are proposed to shareholders. This new Rule had been adopted from the listing requirements applicable to material transactions in the UK.[167] On 1 January 1992, the obligation under the ASX Listing Rule 3A(1) was expanded to encompass a similar definition to that used at that time in section 1022 of the Corporations Law, relating to prospectuses.

Malcolm McComas called for a quarterly report of profits and losses that would include revenue and profit details, a *pro forma* balance sheet, and a summary cash flow statement. He pointed out this was the accepted practice in North America.[168] However, this recommendation was not accepted.

The Lavarch Committee noted the numerous criticisms that had been made of the accounting and audit professions. As Malcolm McComas said:

> Public examinations undertaken by liquidators in recent months have revealed numerous cases of secret commissions, premature recognition of profits, inflated asset values and hidden management contracts that went undetected in the audit process. The failure to disclose the financial impact of material acquisitions, divestments and other financial arrangements ... has forced

---

164. <www.asx.com.au>, June 2003.
165. Cited in the Lavarch Report of 1991, para. 4.5.20.
166. *Ibid.*, 110.
167. *Ibid.*, 113.
168. *Ibid.*, 115.

analysts to spend considerable time recreating accounts to determine the true financial impact of a transaction to earnings and shareholder funds.[169]

Professor Robert Walker of the Department of Accountancy at the University of New South Wales, as then Chairman of the Australian Shareholders Association, made some recommendations to the Lavarch Committee:

> Some of the companies we have seen fail in recent years have in my view had very defective accounts and this was obvious to sophisticated readers. For example, Qintex adopted the very unusual practice of capitalizing trading losses. It was buried in the notes. Its accounts revealed that it had valued resorts among other assets at cost which included interest and trading losses during the development period and the development period of a resort can be four or five years. I do not believe those accounts were adequate. I do not believe they provided the true and fair view because they did not disclose the quantum of trading losses that were being capitalized.[170]

Professor Walker also noted that the same problem existed with the accounts of Bond Corporation Holdings Ltd.[171]

The Institute of Charted Accountants in Australia and the Australian Society of Accountants noted in a joint submission that problems in financial reporting had at times resulted from the non-application or misapplication of the accountancy standards.[172] The joint submission pointed out that the legislation's true and fair view requirement to be applied in accounting reports was paramount to the exclusion of the accountancy standards. This inconsistency might have led to the creation of opportunities to avoid the law. However, Henry Bosch held a different view on the true and fair view requirement:

> At the moment the law gives priority to true and fair and it is possible for companies to argue that a departure from an accounting standard has been done because it would be not true or not fair to adhere to the standards.[173]

The accountancy bodies suggested that the legislative provisions be amended so that the primary obligation was to observe the approved accounting standards. But Professor Robert Baxt stated that the problem with such a proposal was that the standards were neither settled nor comprehensive.[174] In this context, the ASC considered that the decision in the *Caparo* case[175] in the UK could be followed in Australia.[176] This is another example of Australia's having looked at other countries' disclosure standards.

---

169. *Ibid.*, 116.
170. *Ibid.*, 117.
171. *Ibid.*
172. *Ibid.*, 118.
173. *Ibid.*, 122.
174. R. Baxt, 'True and Fair Accounts: A Legal Anachronism', *ALJ* 44 (1970): 541 at 550.
175. *Caparo Industries PLC v. Dickman* (1990) BCC 164.
176. The Lavarch Report of 1991, 128.

The Lavarch Committee had studied the securities regulatory frameworks in the UK, the USA, and some other countries. It also looked into the submissions provided to it from a wide range of bodies and individuals. These submissions included those made by government departments (such as the Trade Practices Commission), professional bodies (such as the Australian Society of Certified Practising Accountants (ASCPA), and the Institute of Chartered Accountants), associations (such as the Australian Shareholders' Association), the ASX, companies, accounting firms, legal firms, banks, the Law Council of Australia, academics, and individuals. Therefore, the Lavarch Report, like other reports by previous special committees formed by the House of Representatives, represented a common view held by the public.

In addition to the general continuous disclosure requirement, the ASX had listed, for some time, detailed specific items that must be disclosed, such as the acquisition or disposal of non-current assets or investments; any calls to be made upon partly paid share capital of the company; and a change of the director, secretary, or auditors, under section 718 of the Corporations Law.[177] Clearly, Australia has focused on corporate disclosure for a long time.

In September 1991, CASAC issued its *Report on an Enhanced Statutory Disclosure System.* As CASAC stated, in preparing this report, it noted two ASX papers: 'Improved Reporting by Listed Companies' (October 1990) and 'Proposed Listing Rule Amendments to Become Operative Late 1991'.[178] CASAC also stated that it had reviewed continuous disclosure and interim reporting requirements in overseas jurisdictions, including the UK, the USA, and Canada.[179] One of the recommendations in this Report was to impose on directors an affirmative duty of timely disclosure of any material matter. CASAC favoured a statutory enhanced disclosure system. Disclosing entities are required not only to lodge half-yearly financial reports and annual financial reports, but also to 'make a timely disclosure of any "material matter" to the Australian Securities Commission'.[180]

From Annexure 2 of this CASAC Report, it is clear that CASAC had especially studied requirements for continuous disclosure and interim reporting in North America, but Australia did not simply follow the route of these countries. For instance, CASAC held the view that the Ontario system of 'sealed envelope' disclosure to its Stock Exchange and/or the Securities Commission was inappropriate for the Australian setting.[181] It also felt that when a system of continuous disclosure was operating effectively, the benefits associated with quarterly reporting might be substantially reduced because of the costs of the preparation.[182] Thus, the mandatory quarterly reporting required in the USA was another feature not adopted in Australia.

---

177. The ASX Listing Rules 3A, paras 4, 6, 10, and 14 and LR 16A.
178. CASAC, *Report on an Enhanced Statutory Disclosure System* (Canberra: AGPS, 1996), 1.
179. *Ibid.*, 2.
180. *Ibid.*, 6.
181. *Ibid.*, 11.
182. *Ibid.*, 27.

7.2.4.12.   The 1992 Cadbury Report of the UK

The UK experienced a number of corporate collapses of high-profile companies in the early 1990s, including the Bank of Commerce and Credit International (BCCI) and Maxwell Media. In response to this problem, the UK government set up the Cadbury Committee, the Committee on the Financial Aspects of Corporate Governance. This Committee submitted a Report commonly known as the Cadbury Report in 1992. In the preface to the Report, Sir Adrian Cadbury, the Chairman of the Committee, gave the reasons for the interest of corporate governance:

> The harsh economic climate is partly responsible, since it has exposed company reports and accounts to usually close scrutiny. It is, however, the continuing concern about standards of financial reporting and accountability, heightened by BCCI, Maxwell and the controversy over directors' pay, which has kept corporate governance in the public eye.[183]

The Cadbury Report recommended a Code of Best Practice, which primarily focused on financial reporting. This Code embraced important corporate governance principles, including the principle of disclosure:

> The principles on which the Code is based are those of openness, integrity and accountability: openness on the part of companies, within the limits set by their competitive position, is the basis for the confidence which needs to exist between business and all those who have a stake in its success. An open approach to the disclosure of information contributes to the efficient working of the market economy, prompts boards to take effective action and allows shareholders and others to scrutinize companies more thoroughly; integrity means both straightforward dealing and completeness. What is required of financial reporting is that it should be honest and that it should present a balanced picture of the state of the company's affairs. The integrity of the reports depends on the integrity of those who prepare and present them; boards of directors are accountable for their shareholders and both have to play their part in making that accountability affective. Boards of directors need to do so through the equality of the information which they provide to shareholders, and the shareholders through their willingness to exercise their responsibilities as owners.[184]

The Code of Best Practice later greatly influenced the development of corporate governance in Australia. The ASX's Corporate Governance Council released *Principles of Good Corporate Governance and Best Practice Recommendations* on 31 March 2003, which, to a large degree, followed the UK model. The ASX adopted a 'comply or explain' approach to particular corporate governance issues

---

183. The Committee on the Financial Aspects of Corporate Governance, *The Financial Aspects of Corporate Governance* (The Cadbury Report) (London: Gee and Co. Ltd, 1992), 9.
184. The Cadbury Report, paras 3.2, 3.3, and 3.4.

in its amended Listing Rules.[185] Under the amended LRs companies should require the chief executive officer and the chief finance officer to state in writing to the board of directors that the company's financial reports present a true and fair view and the company's financial conditions and results are all in accordance with relevant accounting standards. The principles stated in the Cadbury Report were also embraced by Australia's HIH Royal Commission Report, which was made 4 April 2003. The details about this will be discussed later.

7.2.4.13. The Ramsay Report of 2001

Following the collapses of a number of high-profile Australian companies, such as One-Tel, Harris Scarf, and HIH, during the first half of 2001, and especially after the collapses of large American companies such as Enron and WorldCom in the same year, great concerns were also raised in Australia as to corporate governance issues, in particular, audit independence. For the stability of the economy, the Senate appointed Professor Ian Ramsay to examine Australia's existing legislative and professional requirements on the independence of company auditors. The Ramsay Report was presented to the government in October 2001. In this Report, entitled *Independence of Australian Company Auditors: Review of Current Australian Requirements and Proposals for Reform*, seven major recommendations for amendments to the Corporations Act were made.[186] One of them was to enhance the disclosure requirement for non-audit services performed by auditing firms.

In the Ramsay Report, particular regard had been given to the following developments: the International Federation of Accountant's (IFAC's) proposals for changes to its ethical requirements on audit independence; the existing and proposed regulatory requirements of the EU; and the new regulatory requirements in the USA.[187] This review, again, is a demonstration that Australia studied foreign experiences empirically for its corporate law reform.

One of the recommendations made in the Ramsay Report related to the disclosure of non-audit services. It was recommended that an annual financial report must disclose the dollar amount of all non-audit services provided by the audit firm to the client, divided by categories of services, and with appropriate discussion of those services. It was also recommended that the financial report for the year must disclose whether the audit committee of the board of directors, or, if there were no such committee, then the board of directors, had considered whether the provision of non-audit services was compatible with maintaining the auditor's independence.[188]

---

185. ASX Listing Rule 4.10.3.
186. The Ramsay Report, *Independence of Australian Company Auditors: Review of Current Australian Requirements and Proposals for Reform*, October 2001, paras 3–6.
187. *Ibid.*, para. 3.02.
188. *Ibid.*, para. 5.94.

7.2.4.14. Principles of Good Corporate Governance and Best Practice Recommendations of the ASX Corporate Governance Council of 2003 and Its Amendments

The ASX set up the ASX Corporate Governance Council in August 2002 as a collaborative, industry-based body charged with the development of corporate governance recommendations for listed companies that reflected international practice.[189] It aimed to promote and restore investor confidence after a number of corporate failures at home and abroad.[190] According to the Council's *Principles of Good Corporate Governance and Best Practice Recommendations* (hereinafter Principles and Recommendations), which were released on 31 March 2003, the purpose of the Council was to develop recommendations that reflected international best practices.[191] In the mean time, in the Principles and Recommendations, the Council held the view that there was 'no single model of good corporate governance and best practice must evolve with developments both in Australia and overseas'.[192] The Council believed that there were about ten essential corporate governance principles, and it listed the fifth principle as 'making timely and balanced disclosure'. It made suggestions on how to ensure compliance with the disclosure requirements in ASX LRs.[193] These Principles and Recommendations were revised, and the Revised Corporate Governance Principles and Recommendations were released in August 2007 and adopted in 2008.[194] The fifth principle of the 2003 Principles of Good Corporate Governance and Best Practice Recommendations has been maintained as the fifth principle in the Revised Corporate Governance Principles and Recommendations. It is worth noting that the ASX corporate governance principles were recommendations only, although the ASX adopts an 'If not, why not?' approach which is also called 'comply or explain' approach.

7.2.4.15. The HIH Royal Commission Report of 2003

In August 2001, the Australian federal government set up the HIH Royal Commission and appointed Justice Owen to be the Commissioner to make an inquiry into the collapse of the HIH Insurance Company.[195] Justice Owen submitted his Report to the Governor-General in April 2003. According to Justice Owen, to achieve good corporate governance, Australia should not adopt a 'one-size-fits-all' approach, but disclosure must be a central feature of any corporate governance regime.[196]

---

189. <www.asx.com.au/ListingRules/guidance/gn09a_corporate_governance_principles.pdf>.
190. ASX Corporate Governance Council, *Principles of Good Corporate Governance and Best Practice Recommendations*, the ASX, March 2003, 4.
191. *Ibid.*
192. *Ibid.*, 3.
193. Recommendation 5.1 and 5.2.
194. The ASX, *Revised Corporate Governance Principles and Recommendations*, December 2007, <www.asx.com.au/ListingRules/guidance/gn09a_corporate_governance_principles.pdf>, 4 Feb. 2009.
195. The HIH Royal Commission, *The Failure of HIH Insurance*, vol. I, 2003, iv.
196. *Ibid.*, 133.

7.2.4.16. **The Corporate Law Economic Reform Program (Audit Reform and Corporate Disclosure) Act of 2004 (The CLERP 9 Act)**

The Corporate Law Economic Reform Program (CLERP) started in Australia in 1997 under the Howard administration.[197] Its main purposes were to improve market efficiency, reduce business costs, and enhance the competitiveness of Australian companies. The focus of the program was the key principles of market freedom, investor protection, and quality disclosure of relevant information to the market.[198] In response to the Ramsay Report, in a joint press statement on 27 June 2002, Treasurer Peter Costello and Parliamentary Secretary to the Treasurer Ian Campbell announced a process of further improvement in audits and a wider corporate disclosure framework as the next step of CLERP.[199] In September 2002, the Treasury released a CLERP 9 Discussion Paper entitled *Corporate Disclosure: Strengthening the Financial Reporting Framework*. The CLERP 9 Discussion Paper first stated that Australian corporate governance regulation and practices were recognized internationally as being of high quality and that the Australian disclosure regime provided timely and reliable information to the market.[200]

It also made it clear that its purpose was to ensure that Australia's corporate regulatory framework remained effective and helped define the world's best practices.[201] It reviewed issues such as the independence of auditors, accounting standards, continuous disclosure, enforcement, and shareholders' participation.[202] While reviewing these issues, a historical and comparative study was done. For example, in the review of the continuous disclosure regime, a study of the UK approach and the US approach had been conducted. In the following discussion, some details of this Paper will be examined. In the corporate governance legislation proposed by the federal government in September 2002, one of the key areas was corporate disclosure. These proposals included the following:

(i) an earlier disclosure of key executives' payment packages was required;
(ii) an expert panel would be set up to arbitrate accounting disputes between companies and ASIC;
(iii) the CEOs and CFOs would be required to certify the accuracy of financial statements to the board;
(iv) ASIC had the power to issue 'speeding fines' to companies for disclosure breaches.[203]

---

197. Treasury, *Corporate Disclosure: Strengthening the Financial Reporting Framework* (Canberra: Canprint Communications, 2002), iii.
198. *Ibid.*
199. *Ibid.*, 11.
200. *Ibid.*, iii.
201. *Ibid.*
202. *Ibid.*
203. F. Buffini, 'Disclosure Regime to Get Teeth', *Weekend Australian Financial Review*, 15–16 Mar. 2003, 5.

The requirement for CEOs and CFOs to certify the accuracy of financial statements to the board of directors came from the Sarbanes–Oxley Act[204] of the USA, which was approved by the US President on 30 July 2002. CLERP 9 clearly stated that the significant legislative reform in the area of corporate disclosure in the USA had been taken care of, as these American legislative changes had been made in response to the Enron Collapse and the overstatement of earnings by WorldCom and others.[205] It was believed that CLERP 9 would strengthen corporate disclosure in Australia and improve corporate governance. Most of the recommendations of the CLERP 9 Paper were incorporated into the CLERP 9 Act, which was passed by Parliament at the end of June 2004, with most sections of this Act entering into force on 1 July 2004.

7.2.5.   OVERVIEW OF THE FORMATION AND DEVELOPMENT OF AUSTRALIAN
            SECURITIES REGULATORY REGIME

As discussed above, the Australian securities market started relatively early as a result of colonization by the UK. The original disclosure framework was modelled on English laws. As the American securities market became the largest in the world, the American model had a great impact on the development of other securities markets, including those in Australia. This can be explained by the convergence theory. However, one of the reasons why the Australian securities regulatory regime is successful is that it did not simply mirror the practices of the UK and the USA. The Australian experience has also proved the theory of path dependence.

Based on its own needs for market development, Australia has established a market regulatory framework with a worldwide reputation. In the previous sections of this chapter, the reforms on corporate disclosure that were made in Australia and how Australia borrowed upon experiences from the UK, the USA, and other countries without simple copying them have been discussed. As stated in the CLERP 9 Discussion Paper, 'Australia is in line with or ahead of corporate disclosure',[206] but 'Australia cannot afford to be complacent'.[207] Therefore, it was timely to review Australia's corporate disclosure framework in view of overseas developments, in particular, in the USA.[208] As pointed out in the CLERP 9 Discussion Paper, Australia should not match the USA point for point, as recent US legislative reform tended to be prescriptive and rule-based, while Australia has traditionally relied on a principles-based approach employing a mix of regulation, co-regulation, and encouragement of industry best practices.[209]

---

204. The whole name of this Act is the Public Company Accounting Reform and Investor Protection Act.
205. The CLERP 9 Paper, 12, 13.
206. *Ibid.*, 13.
207. *Ibid.*
208. *Ibid.*
209. *Ibid.*

Different from the Australian and the US experiences, issuing shares in the PRC was first used by private enterprises and collective enterprises in the early 1980s to meet the capital needs that could not be met by state-owned banks. Soon after, share issuing was adopted by the government as a means to meet the capital needs of state-owned enterprises that could no longer get financial support from the state-owned banks. The re-emergence of the securities market and its development were driven by this need and were under the direct control of the government. Unlike the development of a free market economy, the economic reform in the PRC was designed and directed by the CPC and its Central Committee.

Policy-making on securities market regulation is under the strict and direct control of the central government, and the major players in the PRC securities market are the state-owned companies. When the CPC decided to adopt a 'socialist market economy' in late 1992, the securities market developed very quickly and without regulatory rules. Over-speculation caused great losses to investors. The securities regulators had to pass a number of rules to punish and prevent false disclosure and fraudulent conduct. As discussed in the previous chapters, the lack of regulatory experience forced PRC regulators to copy the US experience because of its influence on CSRC officials. Even if, theoretically, the PRC has relatively comprehensive disclosure rules, actual practice shows that its regulatory regime does not function properly. From the beginning of the establishment of the securities markets until now, cases of false disclosure constantly occur. Simply copying the American model is one of the major reasons why the PRC securities markets have been so vulnerable. Thus, the most important lesson that the PRC should have learnt is that it must not simply follow the American system, as this system mainly suits the American situation.

In contrast with the PRC securities markets, the Australian securities markets are more mature and more complicated. These markets can offer many experiences from which the PRC can learn. To precisely evaluate the Australian securities markets, it is necessary to make an empirical study of the history of these markets and the development of their corporate disclosure regulatory regime, as well as the driving forces behind this development.

7.3. THE ESTABLISHMENT AND DEVELOPMENT OF THE DISCLOSURE REGULATORY FRAMEWORK IN AUSTRALIA

Disclosure by listed companies not only includes financial information, but also their information that may have a material effect on securities' prices. However, corporate disclosure started from financial disclosure and centres on financial disclosure.

As Australia is a common law country, the corporate disclosure regulatory regime in Australia started from the rules in the courts' judgments and later developed through the reform of corporations legislation in Australia. In the 1990s, Australia formed a relatively complicated disclosure regulatory regime. In the past three years or so, this regime has been greatly improved and strengthened through the Australian government's CLERP reform. In the following parts of this chapter, the establishment and development of the Australian corporate disclosure regime will be reviewed. This development process confirms the rationales of both the convergence theory and the theory of path dependence. Because of the integration of the Australian economy into the world economy, Australia has adopted disclosure rules from the UK and the USA. Convergence has played an important role in the development of the Australian disclosure regime. However, with Australia's unique geographical location and historical connection with the UK, some of its disclosure rules are only recommended, which is different from the US mandatory approach.

In 1844, the House of Commons in the UK commissioned a Select Committee on Joint Stock Companies to deal with the regular abuses of fraudulent accounting and the payment of dividends out of capital.[210] The Commission recommended the implementation of a statutory regime that required honest financial disclosure by companies. It also recommended that the accounts of every company be available for inspection by members of the company.[211]

The Joint Stock Companies Act of 1844 required accounting records to be kept and a balance sheet to be prepared and presented to each ordinary meeting of shareholders; the balance sheet was normally to be sent to shareholders before shareholders' meeting. This Act for the first time allowed companies to be incorporated by registration. The prospectus became the only disclosure document of listed companies. The Joint Stock Companies Act of 1855 introduced the concept of limited liability but failed to improve the financial disclosure provisions. In 1856, when the two Companies Acts in 1844 and 1855 were consolidated, the compulsory reporting and auditing provisions were ignored. Instead, a table of model articles of association that included reporting and auditing provisions, as well as a standard form for balance sheets, was recommended.[212]

There were several attempts to re-introduce mandatory financial disclosure provisions. However, no changes were made until 1900, when the new Companies Act was passed. Even in this Act, there were no provisions for compulsory accounting and disclosure though an annual audit of accounting records, and the balance sheet was required for all companies.[213]

In the late 1980s, there were serious violations of corporate disclosure and corporate collapses in Australia. The CASAC),[214] which was commissioned by the Attorney-General of the Australian Commonwealth government and the Lavarch Committee, which was established by the Australian Commonwealth Parliament, reviewed the disclosure framework in Australia separately. Both Committees

---

210. First Report of the Select Committee on Joint Stock Companies, House of Commons, 1844, cited in Peter Little, 'Financial Disclosure by Corporations', *Australian Journal of Corporate Law* 1, no. 2 (1992): 87–106 at 88.
211. *Ibid.*
212. *Ibid.*
213. *Ibid.*
214. CASAC was later renamed CAMAC

stated the importance of having an enhanced disclosure regulatory framework. However, each Committee made different recommendations to resolve the violation of disclosure requirements in 1991. In 1994, a continuous disclosure regime was adopted by the Corporate Law Reform Act, which incorporated many recommendations of the Lavarch Report. In 1996, CASAC made new recommendations with regard to disclosure.[215] These recommendations had been incorporated into the corporate law reform.

In 2001, following the failure of big companies such as Enron and WorldCom in the USA, as well as One.Tel and HIH in Australia, many corporate governance issues again raised concerns in the Australian government. It enacted new laws to deal with these issues. One of these issues is further enhancement of corporate disclosure. The CLERP 9 Act of 2004 (Cth) contains the changes in this regard.

From the company law history of Australia, it can be concluded that a complicated Australian corporate disclosure regime was not really established until the late 1990s and that this regime was further improved in the early twenty-first century based on lessons from foreign experiences and its domestic situation.

7.3.1.   THE SOURCES OF CORPORATE DISCLOSURE RULES IN AUSTRALIA

Currently, corporate disclosure rules in Australia can be found in the Corporations Act of 2001 (Cth), the Listing Rules of the ASX, the rules of ASIC, and the accounting standards, as well as common law. This chapter focuses on the disclosure provisions in the Corporations Act and the Listing Rules.

As mentioned above, rules regarding corporate disclosure were first developed in the common law of the UK. They were subsequently incorporated into the Companies Act of the UK. Australia corporations legislation has clear disclosure rules. As discussed previously, under the Australia Constitution of the Commonwealth, the states and the Commonwealth have different legislative powers. For a long time, Australia had been a colony of the UK. Thus, each colony had its own corporation legislation, although each was based on the Companies Act of the UK.[216] However, with the development of interstate trade, states and the Commonwealth tried to unify the corporations legislation.[217] Beginning in the late 1950s, there were a number of trials to make a uniform company law in each state.[218] After the ASX was established in 1987, securities disclosure was subject to the state's Companies Act and the ASX Listing Rules.

---

215. See CASAC, *Report on Continuous Disclosure*, November 1996.
216. Tomasic, Bottomley & McQueen, *Corporations Law in Australia*, 15; R. Tomasic, J. Jackson & R. Woellner, *Corporations Law: Principles, Policy and Process*, 4th edn (Sydney: Butterworths, 2002), 16.
217. R.K. Yorston & S.R. Brown, *Company Law: A Concise Manual of the Principles and Practice of Company Law Incorporating the Legislation of New South Wales, Victoria and Queensland*, 2nd edn (Sydney: LBC, 1964), Preface, iii.
218. *Ibid.*

The third cooperative scheme, established in late 1989, was a relatively successful model.[219] Under this scheme, the Commonwealth Parliament enacted the Corporations Act for the Australian Capital Territory (ACT) with the power given by section 122 of the Constitution.[220] This Act became effective from 1 January 1991. Other states and territories, following their agreement with the Commonwealth, passed legislation taking the Corporations Act made for the ACT as their own law. While technically, the Corporations Act of each state is a state law, they were all treated for practical purposes as if they were a Commonwealth law rather than state laws.[221] Therefore, the companies were subject to the Corporations Law and the Listing Rules of the ASX with respect to corporate disclosure.

However, since the early days after the establishment of the Commonwealth, the High Court of Australia had held strict views on the Commonwealth's power to make laws governing the formation and regulation of companies, beginning with the case of *Huddart Parker & Co Pty Ltd v. Mooreland* (1909) 8 CLR 330.[222] The decision in the *Huddart* case was followed in the following High Court cases: *New South Wales v. Commonwealth* (1990) 8 ACLC 120, *Re Wakim* (1999) ACLC 1055, *Bond v. R* (2000) 169 ALR 607, and *R v. Hughes* (2000) 171 ALR 155.[223] In the *New South Wales* case, it was held that section 51(xx) of the Common Wealth Constitution did not empower the Commonwealth to make laws in relation to the incorporation of companies, including trading companies. Consequently, the provisions of the Corporations Act of 1989 (Cth), which provided for the incorporation of trading and financial corporations, were constitutionally invalid.

In 1990, the states' and Commonwealth Corporations Acts adopted cross-vesting provisions allowing the Federal Court of Australia to be the main court to hear corporations law cases, even if these cases were based on a state Corporations Act. However, in the *Wakim* case, it was held that cross-vesting provisions were unconstitutional and that the Federal Court did not have the power to decide matters that were exclusively within the jurisdiction of the states.[224] In 2000, the High Court again insisted in the *Bond* case that the Commonwealth Director of Public Prosecution (hereinafter DPP) did not have the power to appeal against sentences in corporations law cases, even if it had the power to initiate prosecutions.[225]

In the same year, the High Court in the *Hughes* case held that the Commonwealth DPP had the power to prosecute anyone under the Corporations Law

219. Tomasic, Jackson & Woellner, *Corporations Law*, 23.
220. *Ibid.*, 25.
221. EM to the Corporations Legislation Amendment Act 1990 (Cth) says that, 'The legislative framework . . . will enable Commonwealth and State laws regulating companies, securities and futures industries to operate to the greatest extent possible as national laws. By use of citation provisions, the law governing companies and securities in the States and Territories will be able to be referred to as simply the Corporations Law'.
222. Tomasic, Jackson & Woellner, *Corporations Law*, 27–29.
223. *Ibid.*
224. Tomasic, Bottomley & McQueen, *Corporations Law in Australia*, 28.
225. Lipton & Herzberg, *Understanding Company Law*, 9.

because Hughes invested money overseas.[226] The Commonwealth DPP has such power because section 51(i) and section 51(xxix) of the Constitution give the Commonwealth the power to legislate with respect to trade and commerce and the power to legislate with respect to external affairs.

The decisions in those cases cast doubts about the legitimacy of the Corporations Law. To avoid a crisis with the Corporations Law, the Commonwealth government and the states had to negotiate a solution. After a number of meetings, they reached an agreement of referral of powers based on section 51(xxxvii) of the Constitution. The Commonwealth Parliament was given the power to make corporations legislation referred to it by the states. By June 2001, all the states had referred their power to make and amend corporation law to the Commonwealth, with a sunset clause to allow a state to terminate the deferral after five years. On 15 July 2001, the Corporations Act of 2001 came into effect as a national law administered by a national regulatory body – ASIC.[227]

Since the Corporations Law was mirrored in the state's legislation in the early 1990s, the Commonwealth government conducted a number of corporation law simplification movements. However, the issue of appropriate securities disclosure was not directly addressed either in the Co-operative Scheme of the 1980s or the Corporations Law until 1994. Before 1994, the prospectus was the only disclosure document assuring that secondary trading would proceed between fully informed investors. The introduction of the Corporate Law Reform Act of 1994 distinguished between publicly traded securities and unlisted securities. In addition to the continuous disclosure requirements, the roles of the ASC and the ASX were clarified in the enforcement of the Listing Rules.

Since the introduction of continuous disclosure provisions, ASIC (and its predecessor, the Australian Securities Commission (ASC) has released several policies in this regard. ASIC policies consist of some of the disclosure rules. For example, in its Policy Statement of 1995 entitled *Relief from Continuous Disclosure Provisions*, the ASC indicated that although it had the power to relieve disclosing entities from continuous disclosure, its primary concern was to maintain the legislative purposes. It identified its objectives in this regard as follows:

  (i) to overcome the inability of general market forces to guarantee adequate and timely disclosure by disclosing entities;

  (ii) to ensure that equity and loan resources in the Australian market are more effectively channelled into appropriate investments, and that funds are withheld or withdrawn from poorly performing disclosing entities (to promote capital market efficiency);

  (iii) to assist investors in deciding whether to buy, sell, or hold securities, including the prospect of a change to alternative securities;

  (iv) to lessen the possible distorting effects of rumour on securities prices;

  (v) to minimize the opportunities for insider trading or similar market abuses;

---

226. Tomasic, Bottomley & McQueen, *Corporations Law in Australia*, 28.
227. Lipton & Herzberg, *Understanding Company Law*, 22.

(vi) to improve managerial performance and accountability by giving the market more timely indicators of performance;

(vii) to encourage the growth of information systems within disclosing entities to assist directors to make decisions and to comply with their fiduciary duties; and

(viii) to reduce the time and cost when preparing prospectuses.[228]

The ASX Listing Rules also contain disclosure rules. Different from Listing Rules of stock exchanges in the PRC, the ASX Listing Rules have been made legally enforceable by sections 674 and 678 of the Corporations Act of 2001 (Cth).

7.3.2. WHAT INFORMATION SHOULD BE DISCLOSED?

The information to be disclosed under the law is mainly reflected in the Corporations Act of 2001 and the Listing Rules of the ASX. The professional bodies, such as the Institute of Chartered Accountants and the Australian Society of Accountants, have also set the accounting standards and auditing standards that contain disclosure provisions. However, these disclosure requirements are not recognized by law and therefore will not be enforced by courts. However, they provide guidance for corporate disclosure. Some of the professional disclosure rules were adopted in the Corporations Act of 2001. For example, the 'true and fair view' requirement of the accounting records, the director's report, and auditors' report came from the professional requirements.[229]

Whether a director would be held in breach of duty to ensure that accounts were kept and financial statements prepared in a way such that a true and fair view of the relevant matters is obtained is determined by whether non-compliance with the standards affects the giving of a true and fair view of the profit or loss, or the state of affairs of the company.[230] In the following section, the major contents and forms of corporate disclosure will be examined so that the reader can compare them with those of the PRC.

7.3.2.1. Prospectus and Other Forms of Disclosure for Fundraising in the Primary Market

The most important aspect of financial disclosure is about fundraising. In the Corporations Act, there are numerous provisions in this regard. On 1 January 1992, the obligation under the ASX LR 3A(1) (now LR 3.1) was expanded. For public companies, the prospectus is the most common and important disclosure document. It was the only disclosure document in the primary securities market

---

228. The ASC Policy Statement 95.
229. The *Corporations Act 2001*, ss 297, 296, 303(3), 303(4), 304, 305, and 309.
230. P. Ickeringill, 'Statutory Responsibilities of Directors and Auditors in Relation to Company Accounts (including a Consideration of Approved Accounting Standards)', *C&SJL* 6, no. 1 (1988): 3 at 14.

until March 2000, when the CLERP Act of 1999 came into effect and introduced other, shorter forms of disclosure documents.

Apart from the prospectus,[231] there are other two forms of disclosure documents that may be used for share issuing: the offer and information statement[232] and the profile statement.[233] Companies have the flexibility to choose the disclosure documents that they will use according to their own situations. Simplification of disclosure requirements and various forms of disclosure documents have increased the efficiency of the Australian securities markets.

In the PRC, the prospectus is still the only form of disclosure document. The national law and the listing rules of the stock exchanges have detailed requirements and forms for the content of prospectuses. Compared with the flexibility provided to listed companies in Australia under Chapter 6D of the Corporations Act of 2001 (Cth), listed companies in the PRC have no flexibility in using disclosure documents. The inflexibility of disclosure documents to some degree led to the negative attitude towards corporate disclosure.[234]

7.3.2.2.   Periodic Disclosure in the Secondary Market

Financial information is usually found in the company's periodic disclosure: its annual financial report, half-yearly report, and quarterly report. Currently, the quarterly report is not mandatory under the Australian Corporations Act of 2001 (Cth). Section 292(1) requires listed companies to prepare a financial report, a director's report, and an auditor's report for each financial year. The financial report for a financial year consists of the financial statements for the year, the notes to the financial statements, and the director's declaration about the statements and notes under section 295(1). The director's report should contain both general information and specific information under sections 299 and 300.

Public companies must also prepare a half-yearly financial report, a director's report, and an auditor's report under section 302. The half-yearly financial report consists of the financial statements for the half-year, notes to the financial statements, and the director's declaration about the statements or notes under section 303(1). Both the annual financial report and the half-yearly financial report must be true and fair under sections 297 and 305.

A public company must make its annual financial reporting to the shareholders twenty-one days before the next annual general meeting (AGM) or four months after the end of the financial year.[235] This report must also be lodged with ASIC within three months after the end of the financial year.[236] The half-yearly financial

---

231. The *Australian Corporations Act 2001* (Cth), ss 9 and 709(1).
232. *Ibid.*, ss 709(4) and 715.
233. *Ibid.*, ss 709(2) and 714.
234. According to an interview of the author with members of a listed company in Shanghai in August 1998, some directors complained about the complexity of the requirements in the standard prospectus form of the CSRC.
235. Section 315(1).
236. Section 319(3).

report must be lodged with ASIC within seventy-five days after the end of the half-year.[237] Both financial reports are required to be audited.[238]

Before the collapse of Enron and WorldCom, the rules on periodic disclosure in Australia were very similar to those in most Western countries, except that the directors had to make a declaration about the reports' compliance with the disclosure standards.[239] For example, the US system, which had a great impact on Australia, did not impose this requirement on directors until the passage of the Sarbanes–Oxley Act in July 2002.[240] Of course, the Sarbanes–Oxley Act imposes this requirement not only on chief executive officers, but also on chief financial officers. In this regard, Australia provided a model for other countries.

Another difference is that, in the USA, quarterly reporting is required instead of half-yearly reporting. This approach was adopted because the USA does not have a continuous disclosure regime that is enforceable by courts, even though some markets such as the New York Stock Exchange require listed entities to continuously disclose price-sensitive information.[241] However, US issuers are also required to make ongoing disclosure in relation to a number of specified matters decided upon by the SEC. The US Congress passed the Sarbanes–Oxley Act in July 2002, which introduced tougher rules with regard to corporate disclosure. The SEC also broadened the list of matters in relation to ongoing disclosure. In Australia, for a long time only mining companies are required to prepare a quarterly report under the ASX Listing Rules, as CASAC held the clear view that the majority of listed disclosing entities were opposed to quarterly reporting.[242] Under the ASX Listing Rules, listed companies must also prepare an annual report and a half-yearly report.

Copies of all the periodic disclosure documents lodged with ASIC must also be given to the ASX at the same time.[243] Listed companies must complete Appendix 4B, an annual report, and a half-yearly report. The annual report of listed companies must be lodged with ASIC within three months after the end of the financial year and the half-yearly report within seventy-five days after the end of the accounting period.[244] Either the annual report or a concise report must be sent to those who are entitled to a notice of the annual general meeting at least twenty-one days before the annual meeting and no longer than four months after the end of the financial year. In practice, the annual report must be audited, while the half-yearly report may be either fully audited or the subject of a limited audit review.[245]

The ASX updates its Listing Rules from time to time. For instance, in October 1990, the ASX issued a discussion paper entitled *Improved Reporting by Listed*

---

237. Section 320(1).
238. Section 307.
239. Sections 295(4) and 303(4).
240. Sections 302(a) and 906.
241. The Treasury, CLERP 9 Paper of 2002, 136.
242. CASAC, *Report on Continuous Disclosure*, November 1996, para. 1.17.
243. The ASX Listing Rules, Ch. 4 Explanatory Note.
244. *Ibid.*, paras 4.1, 4.1.1, 4.2, and 4.2.1.
245. A. Greenwood, *International Securities Regulation: Australian Commentary* (New York: Oceana Publications, 2001), 22.

Companies, seeking comments on a variety of reporting measures, including upgrading half-yearly reporting and the introduction of a quarterly reporting requirement on all or large listed companies. In June 1991, the ASX issued an Exposure Draft entitled *Proposed Listing Rules Amendments to Become Effective Late 1991*. Since 1990, the ASX has amended its Listing Rules almost every year.

There was debate as to whether quarterly reports should be introduced into corporations legislation. To date, the Corporations Act does not have such a requirement. However, under the ASX's Listing Rules 1.3.2 and 4.7B that was introduced on 31 March 2000, if half or more of an entity's total tangible assets are cash or in a form readily convertible to cash, and the entity has commitments consistent with its business objectives to spend at least half of its cash, that entity must complete Appendix 4C, the quarterly cash flow report. A listed mining company must give the ASX, within one month after the end of each quarter, a report providing details of production, development, and exploration.[246]

7.3.2.3.   Continuous Disclosure

The term 'continuous disclosure' can be defined broadly or narrowly. In the broad sense, it includes regular and irregular reporting. A regular disclosure requirement provides for disclosure at fixed periods. This is also called periodic disclosure. It includes the annual financial report, the half-yearly report, and the quarterly report. Irregular disclosure is needed when some event or change of a company's affairs occurs.[247] In the narrow sense, continuous disclosure only refers to disclosure triggered by some event or change that may have a material effect on the securities market. Continuous disclosure in the narrow sense is different from periodic disclosure. The former requires companies to provide information that may have a material impact on securities' prices to the market once such information materializes. The latter refers to requirements whereby companies must provide information that may have a material impact on securities' prices at regular intervals.[248] 'Continuous disclosure' in this book is used in the narrow sense, as it is used in the Australian Corporations Act of 2001(Cth).

In the early 1990s, there was concern about whether an upgraded disclosure system should be incorporated in the Corporations Law and enforced by the ASC, or whether it should form part of listing agreements and be self-administered by the ASX.[249] Listing Rule 3.1 makes up the Australian continuous disclosure framework with Chapter 6CA of the Corporations Act of 2001 (Cth). Listing Rule 3.1 requires that an entity must immediately inform the ASX of any information once the entity is or becomes aware of information that a reasonable person would

---

246. The ASX Listing Rules, 5.1.
247. M. Blair, 'Australia's Continuous Disclosure Regime: Proposals for Change', *Australian Journal of Corporate Law* 2, no. 1 (1991): 54–68 at 56.
248. A. Neagle & N. Tyskin, *Please Explain: ASX Share Price Queries and the Australian Continuous Disclosure Regime* (Research Report of the Centre for Corporate Law and Securities Regulations, the University of Melbourne, 2001), 4.
249. *Ibid.*

expect to have a material effect on the price or value of the entity's securities. An entity becomes aware of information if a director or executive officer of the responsible entity has, or ought reasonably to have come into possession, of the information in the course of the performance of his or her duties as a director or executive officer of that entity.[250] Chapter 6CA sets out the obligations of listed disclosing entities to comply with the continuous disclosure provisions of the market listing rules in relation to that entity.[251] When these rules require disclosure of information not generally available to the market and that a reasonable person would expect to have a material effect on the price or value of enhanced disclosure (ED) securities[252] of the entity, the entity must notify the market operator of that information in accordance with the listing rules.[253] However, the obligation to comply with continuous disclosure provisions is subject to the following exceptions:

> 3.1A.1 A reasonable person would not expect the information to be disclosed.
> 3.1A.2 The information is confidential and ASX has not formed the view that the information has ceased to be confidential.
> 3.1A.3 One or more of the following applies:

> – It would be a breach of a law to disclose the information.
> – The information concerns an incomplete proposal or negotiation.
> – The information comprises matters of supposition or is insufficiently definite to warrant disclosure.
> – The information is generated for the internal management purposes of the entity;
> – The information is a trade secret.[254]

The continuous disclosure concept was first introduced in old Listing Rule 3A(1). This Rule was replaced by a completely revised set of the ASX Listing Rules, which came into effect on 1 July 1996.[255] LR 3A became LR 3.1., which imposes an obligation on a listed company to notify the home exchange of information likely to have a material effect on the price of shares and the immediate reporting of information necessary for investors and their advisers to appraise the position of the company to avoid false marketing of its shares. 'Material effect' is defined in section 677 of the Corporations Act of 2001 as 'the information that would or would likely influence persons who commonly invest in securities whether to acquire or dispose of the enhanced disclosing securities'.

---

250. ASX Guidance Note 8.
251. Section 674.
252. ED securities are securities if they are quoted on the ASX, or a disclosure document has been lodged, or they have been issued as consideration under a takeover bid, merger, or reconstruction.
253. Section 674(2).
254. Listing Rule 3.1A.
255. *Australian Corporations Law: Principles and Practice*, vol. 3 (Sydney: Butterworths, 2005), see 'Note to the Listing Rule'.

On 1 January 2003, the ASX again amended its LRs. Under the new Rule 3.1B, if the ASX considers that there is, or is likely to be, a false market in an entity's securities and asks the entity to give it information to correct or prevent a false market, the entity must give the ASX the information needed to correct or prevent the false market. The disclosure document must be given to the ASX immediately after it is lodged with ASIC.[256] Therefore, information must first be given to ASIC and then to the ASX. This requirement is confirmed in LR 15.7.

The disclosure provisions 'were designed to improve market fairness and market efficiency by requiring disclosing entities to publish price-sensitive information promptly, thereby assisting all investors to make properly informed decisions about the allocation of their investment funds'.[257] The timely disclosure provision allows securities, or more importantly their associated risk, to be priced accurately. Thus, it allows the appropriate distribution of capital throughout the economy.[258]

As discussed above, the Australian securities regulatory regime has learned a great deal from the American experience. However, the USA has not introduced continuous disclosure provisions into its legislation. US securities law provides for quarterly reports and the filing of current reports in addition to annual reports. A current report is required upon the occurrence of material events. It is generally regarded as including only those events specified in SEC Form 8-K. Events not specified in Form 8-K are generally not required to be disclosed.[259] In this regard, current reporting is different from continuous disclosure.

In 1991, CASAC was asked by the then Commonwealth Attorney-General to examine the need for a legislatively based continuous disclosure requirement and the nature of this requirement. CASAC issued its *Report on an Enhanced Statutory Disclosure System* in September 1991. One of the major recommendations of CASAC was the introduction of an affirmative obligation on directors to make a timely disclosure of any 'material matter' to the ASC, and when applicable, to the ASX. In relation to the form of disclosure, a two-step disclosure system was proposed. Under such a system, directors of a listed company, upon being warned of a 'material matter', should, as soon as practical and in any event within twenty-four hours, either lodge a completed statement with ASIC or issue and lodge a press release with ASIC (and the ASX if applicable) outlining the material matter. If directors choose the later option, they would subsequently be required to lodge a statement of 'material matter' with ASIC within two business days of the initial press release. Finally, ASIC should, within five business days of receiving a statement of material matter, make that statement available on its DOCIMAGE database.

---

256. The ASX LR 3.10.4.
257. CASAC, *Insider Trading: Discussion Paper* (June 2001), para. 2.63.
258. J. Coffee, 'Market Failure and the Economic Case for a Mandatory Disclosure System', *Virginia Law Review* 70, no. 4 (1984): 717–754 at 752.
259. <www.sec.com>, 1 Jun. 2002.

In November 1991, the Lavarch Report, entitled *Corporate Practice and the Rights of the Shareholders* was released. It recommended that an extensive continuous disclosure obligation be imposed on listed companies, and implemented and enforced through the LRs.[260] In relation to statutory recognition of the LRs, the Lavarch Report recommended that (then) section 777 of the Corporations Law be amended to extend the obligation in compliance with LRs to directors when they were only imposed on companies.[261] Furthermore, the Report argued that courts should be allowed to impose penalties on directors for non-compliance with the LRs when such non-compliance had resulted in a suspension of trading in the company's securities by the ASX.[262]

The CLERP 9 Paper, entitled *Corporate Disclosure: Strengthening the Financial Reporting Framework*, reviewed the Australian continuous disclosure regime in Chapter 8. It was of the view that 'Australia's current continuous disclosure regime is fundamentally sound'.[263] It also proposed some measures to further enhance the effectiveness of this regime. Thus, Australia has formed a relatively complicated disclosure regime. This regime has ensured the transparency and accountability of its securities market.

7.3.2.4. Specific Disclosure

7.3.2.4.1. Content of Specific Disclosure

'Specific disclosure' refers to disclosure of specific matters clearly required by legislation or the LRs. The most common form of specific disclosure is disclosure of takeover bids. Listing Rule 3.4 requires 'an entity or one of its child entities to inform the ASX' of information about a takeover bid within 10 business days after the end of offer period of a takeover bid. Section 661 B of the Corporations Act of 2001 requires a takeover bidder to prepare a notice in the prescribed form that informs the holders of the securities of that takeover bid and the compulsory acquisition procedure. Such notice must be lodged with ASIC and given to each holder of that class of securities and the relevant market operator. Section 670A(1) prohibits the release of the takeover documents if any of them contains a misleading or deceptive statement or misstatement. The principle of disclosure is also one of the cornerstones of the takeover legislation. This was enunciated by the Eggleston Committee, the Advisory Committee appointed by the Standing Committee of Attorney-Generals in 1969.

In the decisions of the *Cumberland* case[264] and the *ICAL* case,[265] the Supreme Courts of both Victoria and New South Wales made it clear that detailed care must

---

260. Paragraph 4.5.17.
261. Paragraph 4.5.25.
262. Paragraph 4.5.26.
263. CLERP 9 Paper, *Corporate Disclosure: Strengthening the Financial Reporting Framework* (Canprint Communications Pty Ltd, 2002), 129.
264. *Cumberland Credit Corporation Ltd v. TNT Australia Pty Ltd* (1988) 13 ACLR 371.
265. *ICAL Ltd v. County Natwest Securities Ltd and Transfield (Shipbuilding) Pty Ltd* (1988) 13 ACLR 129.

be given to ensure sufficient disclosure in takeover documents.[266] Under the Companies Codes, there was also a rule requiring the offeror to provide information to enable the shareholders in the target company to form a judgment on the merits of the proposal.[267] Disclosure under common law, such as the decision in the *Cumberland Credit* case, gives guidance as to what should be disclosed in takeover documents. It indicates that a summary of the alternative strategies considered by the offeror relating to the future of the target company should be disclosed to shareholders so that they may make an informed decision as to whether to accept the offeror's bid. If a final decision has been made, the decision should be disclosed; otherwise, the various alternatives need to be disclosed.[268] In the decision in the *ICAL* case, the Supreme Court of New South Wales considered the decision in the *Cumberland Credit* case and took a similar attitude in relation to 'future intentions'.[269] The court in the *ICAL* case held that even if the proposals were contingent and subject to further consideration and possible change, these intentions must be disclosed.[270] In conclusion, specific disclosure can be found in the legislation, the LRs, and case law.

7.3.2.4.2. *Disclosure of Corporate Governance Practices*

Under the ASX Listing Rules, listed companies must make a statement of the main corporate governance practices that it had in place in their annual report during the reporting period.[271] There are two readily available guides to best corporate practices developed in the Australian market. One is *Corporate Practices and Conduct*, issued by the Working Group on Corporate Practices and Conduct (known as the Bosch Committee) in November 1995. The other one is *Corporate Governance: A Guide for Investment Managers and Corporations*, issued by the Australian Investment Managers' Association in July 1997. In addition to these two guides, in March 2003, the ASX Corporate Governance Council released *Principles of Good Corporate Governance and Best Practice Recommendations*. In this document, the ASX applies the 'If not, why not?' approach, in which a listed company has the flexibility not to adopt the recommendation of disclosure of corporate governance practices, but this flexibility is tempered by the requirement to explain why.[272] On 2 August 2007, the ASX Corporate Governance Council released revised Corporate Governance Principles and Recommendations.

---

266. W. Kent, 'Implications for Disclosure in Takeover Documents after the ICAL and Cumberland Credit Decisions', *C&SLJ* 6, no. 4 (1988): 282–292 at 283.
267. Sections 59(1)(c) and 60(1)(c).
268. W. Kent, 'Implications for Disclosure in Takeover Documents after the ICAL and Cumberland Credit Decisions', *C&SLJ* 6, no. 4 (1988): 282–292 at 283.
269. *Ibid.*
270. *Ibid.*, 285.
271. ASX Listing Rule 4.10.3
272. The ASX Corporate Governance Council, *Principles and Recommendations*, March 2003, 5.

7.3.2.4.3. *Disclosure of Directors' Remuneration*

Directors' remuneration can be a big factor affecting the financial situation of a company. The CLERP 9 Act of 2004 embodied most of the recommendations made by the Ramsay Report and the CLERP 9 Discussion Paper. Members of both public and proprietary companies may obtain information about the remuneration paid to directors. Section 202B(1) provides that:

> A *company must* disclose the remuneration paid to each director of the company or a subsidiary (if any) by the company or by an entity controlled by the company if the company's directed to disclose the information by:
>
> (a) members with at least 5% of the votes that may be cast at a general meeting of the company; or
>
> (b) at least 100 members who are entitled to vote at a general meeting of the company.
>
> The company must disclose all remuneration paid to the director, regardless of whether it is paid to the director in relation to their capacity as director or another capacity.

It is also required that a remuneration report must be included in the annual directors' report.[273] Australian corporations legislation took the first step to enhance disclosure of directors' remuneration, although the following steps need to be adopted.

7.3.2.4.4. *Disclosure of Short Selling*

Soon after the global financial crisis started in 2008, short selling was thought to be an important reason for the collapse of five large investment banks on Wall Street. Major securities markets in the world started to limit short selling. Following the SEC's ban on short selling, ASIC also banned naked short selling of all securities on 21 September.[274] Although covered short sales were later permitted, short selling transactions had to be disclosed.[275]

At the end of 2008, the Corporations Amendment (Short Selling) Act of 2008 (Cth) was enacted. Sections 1020AA–1020AE set new requirements for the disclosure of short sales.

---

273. Section 300A(1A).
274. <www.asic.gov.au/asic/asic.nsf/byheadline/Requirements+for+disclosure+and+reporting+of+short+sales+from+19+November+2008?openDocument>, 28 Feb. 2009.
275. <www.asic.gov.au/asic/asic.nsf/byheadline/Short+selling?openDocument>, 10 Aug. 2009.

7.3.3.   THE ESTABLISHMENT OF A MANDATORY DISCLOSURE REGULATORY
              REGIME IN AUSTRALIA

Currently, Australia implements a scheme of self-regulation for securities markets.[276] The ASX assumes the role of co-regulator with ASIC to ensure that stock
markets are fair, well informed, and efficient.[277] The ASX takes primary responsibility for monitoring and enforcing compliance with the disclosure requirement
of the LRs.[278] ASIC has primary responsibility for enforcing section 674. When the
ASX believes that there has been a serious contravention or a possible contravention of the LRs or the Corporations Act, it may refer a matter to ASIC for further
investigation. ASIC may pursue a variety of remedies in such cases, including
possible civil or criminal actions.

The disclosure is made to the ASX by sending a form suitable for release to the
ASX's Company Announcements Platform (CAP) by fax or by other electronic
means. Under Listing Rule 15.7, information must not be disclosed to the market or
anyone else until the information has been given to the ASX; otherwise, there
would be a breach of Listing Rules 3.1 and 15.7. Rule 15.7 again gives the ASX
the status of the market regulator.

Following the corporate collapses that occurred in the USA in late 2001, the
SEC adopted new rules governing disclosure. These disclosure rules, again, have
had an impact on the revision of the Australian disclosure rules, as the Australian
economy to a large extent depends on the US economy. Following the US practice,
the ASX proposed the re-introduction of the requirement that listed companies
must respond to media speculation formally as of mid-2003.[279] The ASX indicated
that it reserved the right to force disclosure from a company when the market
appeared to be false, based on speculation that the company could clarify. It
claimed that disclosure would not be forced if information was confidential and
would not comprise an incomplete proposal or negotiation.[280] Breach of continuous disclosure is subject to criminal and civil liabilities.[281] However, Australia
again did not adopt the American approach to mandate quarterly reporting after the
empirical study of the US model[282] for the reasons that mandatory quarterly
reporting in Australia would add compliance costs for companies and that the
current unaudited quarterly reporting in the USA encourages a short-term focus
by companies.[283]

The intention of the introduction of mandatory continuous disclosure was first
indicated by the ASX in its discussion paper *The Role of the Australian Stock*

---

276. F. Donnan, 'Self-Regulation and the Demutualisation of the Australian Stock Exchange',
     Australian Journal of Corporate Law 10, no. 1 (1999): 1–33 at 11.
277. *Ibid.*
278. *Ibid.*
279. S. Kemp, 'Rumour Mill Rule under Fire', *The Age*, 2 Sep. 2002.
280. *Ibid.*
281. See fn. of ss 674 and 678 of the Corporations Act of 2001.
282. CLERP 9 Paper, 135.
283. *Ibid.*

Exchange and Its Listing Rules, released in October 1990. It stated that one of the policies underlying the Listing Rules was the 'market information' principle.[284] This principle is described as advising the market by timely disclosure of any information that may affect security values or influence investment decisions, or in which security holders, investors, and the exchange have a legitimate interest, or that is publicly disclosed elsewhere.

The then Attorney-General of the Commonwealth referred to the matter of introduction of continuous disclosure to CASAC in September 1991. CASAC consisted of members of the corporate sector and professional advisers. It recommended a statutory continuous disclosure regime by arguing that such a regime would promote investor confidence in the integrity of Australian capital markets and provide benefits to market participants and management in various interrelated ways.

In the debate on whether mandatory disclosure should be introduced, there were different arguments. Some people argued that these disclosure provisions are based on assumptions about the efficient market hypothesis (EMH):

> Modern economic theory recognises that in efficient capital markets information is quickly impounded in share prices and share prices generally reflect all generally available information. As such, a disclosure regime that recognises the operation of information in efficient markets and the investing habits of participants in the market is highly desirable. To the extent that information is already reflected in the market valuation and understanding of an issuer it would seem unnecessary to require a prospectus to then cover the same ground.[285]

CASAC recommendation was quickly acted upon by the ASX. It amended LR 3A(1), which came into effect on 1 January 1992 and clarified listed companies' obligation to report information in a timely fashion.

There was also debate on whether the ASX or the ASC should administer the Corporations Law. Then-Attorney-General Michael Duffy, rejecting the Lavarch Report recommendation that disclosure be made to the ASX, accepted the proposal by CASAC that the reporting should be made to the ASC, not the ASX. However, the subsequent legislative change following the federal election of 1993 gave the ASX the primary role of receiving disclosure made by listed companies when Michael Lavarch became the new Attorney-General of the Commonwealth government. The Corporate Law Reform Act received Royal Assent on 4 March 1994. The provisions dealing with enhanced disclosure came into effect in the second half of 1994. This Act recognized the enforceability of the Listing Rules of the ASX.

The prospectus is a traditional form of disclosure. However, with the purpose of improving market efficiency, a short-form prospectus has been allowed to be

---

284. Paragraph 22.
285. Cited by Herder, 'Corporate Finance Theory and the Australian Prospectus Legislation', *Corp & Bus LJ* 7 (1994): 181 at 182.

used since 1994. The rationale for this reform 'is that there is an externally determined market price for the securities based on disclosure, as well as ongoing scrutiny by market analysts and professional investors'.[286] This justification also came from the USA:

> Information is widely disseminated through the financial press, is publicly available for free or at nominal cost, and, for at least a certain set of issuers, is closely studied by financial analysts and other sophisticated market participants. Therefore, such public information should be reflected in the price of the issuer's securities. There is no reason to repeat such information.[287]

In comparison with Australia and the USA, the PRC has not simplified its disclosure document. As the content of disclosure required by the Securities Law is too general, the CSRC has to implement the disclosure principles by releasing administrative rules from time to time, even though the courts may not always recognize and enforce these rules. The enforceability of the LRs of the Shanghai and Shenzhen Stock Exchanges has not been clarified in the Securities Law. Thus, the authority of the LRs has been undermined. Although the Australian regulatory regime has been greatly influenced by US practices, its corporate law reform history shows that Australia always updates its laws after an empirical study of the US experience. However, as the history of the PRC's company and securities lawmaking is not formally available to the public, it is very hard to judge how the PRC lawmakers and rule makers draw upon lessons and experiences from foreign countries, such as the USA. If one examines the corporate disclosure rules released by the CSRC, many of them look similar to US rules, but when one examines the practices of the PRC, it is entirely different from that of the USA. When one examines the laws and rules of the PRC, most of the time, they are relatively well drafted, but they are often inappropriate for actual practice. One major reason that can explain this is that the PRC often simply copies foreign laws without first conducting an empirical study.

In Australia, the CASAC, in its *Report on an Enhanced Statutory Disclosure Scheme* in 1994, noted that:

> A statutory-based system of continuous disclosure will promote investor confidence in the integrity of Australian capital markets and provide benefits to market participants and management, in various interrelated ways.[288]

In addition to the market benefits, there are two specific benefits of disclosure to the shareholders foreseen by the CASAC:

(i) the improvement of managerial performance and accountability by providing the market with more timely indicators of corporate performance; and

---

286. Explanatory Memorandum, the Corporate Law Reform Act of 1994.
287. *Ibid.*
288. <www.asx.com.au>, 2 Jun. 2003.

(ii) the encouragement of 'the growth of information systems within disclosing entities thereby assisting directors in their decision making and compliance with their fiduciary duties'.[289]

Mark Blair pointed out another benefit of continuous disclosure:

An upgraded continuous disclosure regime might promote the growth of information systems within a reporting company. In the case of the irregular continuous disclosure proposals outlined above, directors would have to make continuous assessments of both aggregated and disaggregated financial information. ... The growth in management information systems brought about by such a requirement may well have benefits for managerial decision making (e.g., making them more quickly aware of profitable or adverse activities), with consequential improvements in company profits.[290]

The importance of disclosure by the board has long been recognized. In 1967, K.A. Aicken said:

It is both necessary and desirable that the directors and the directors alone, should have the powers to make decisions with regard to the actual conduct of the company's business, but it is neither desirable nor proper that the directors should conceal from the shareholders the manner in which they exercise their powers. I don't suggest that it's either usual or common for this to occur but it's not unknown. It is not easy to define in abstract terms what are permissible or legitimate questions from shareholders about the detailed conduct of the company's business, but if some improvement in the law in this field is thought desirable, then this is a point at which it would be convenient to start.[291]

However, there were also critical comments on the economical justifications of mandatory disclosure.[292] The theoretical debate on the need for mandatory disclosure will be discussed in the following parts. From the above discussion, it is clear that, in the debate on whether Australia should adopt a mandatory disclosure regime and what should be disclosed, US and other foreign experiences were studied carefully by the Australian legislators so as to establish a disclosure regime that suits its domestic environment.

---

289. *Ibid.*
290. Blair, M 'Australia's Continuous Disclosure Regime: Proposals for Change', *Australian Journal of Corporate Law* 2, no. 1 (1992): 54–68 at 64.
291. K.A. Aickin, 'Division of Power between Directors and General Meeting as a Matter of Law, and as a Matter of Fact and Policy', *Melbourne University Law Review* 5 (1967): 448–464 at 464.
292. See discussion in I. McEwin, 'Australia's Continuous Disclosure Regime: Some Comments', *Australian Journal of Corporate Law* 2, no. 1 (1992): 77–81.

7.3.4.   STANDARDS FOR DISCLOSURE

7.3.4.1.   Statutory Standards for Financial Reporting

Following the above discussion of the benefits of disclosure, we will next examine what standards of disclosure have been adopted in Australia. Under the Corporations Act of 2001 (Cth), the annual financial report[293] and the half-yearly financial report[294] are required to give a true and fair view of a company's financial state. These are the general standards for financial reporting. The detailed standards are reflected in the accounting standards. Different from PRC law, the Australian Corporations Act recognizes the enforceability of the accounting standards that were set by the professional accounting bodies prior to the enactment of the Corporations Act.[295] This approach is more realistic and more reasonable than the approach of the PRC.

The Accounting Standards Review Board (ASRB) required company accounts to give a true and fair view[296] as well as to be made out in accordance with applicable approved accounting standards.[297] The user-focused objectives of the US Financial Accounting Standards Board were also cited.[298] The ASRB was later replaced by the Australian Accounting Standards Board (AASB). The AASB inherited most of the ASRB standards. It also created the consolidated accounts in September 1991. The Corporations Act of 2001 recognizes professional accounting standards in sections 296 and 304. It goes further to clearly state the fundamental standards for financial reporting. Under sections 297 and 305, a financial statement must give a true and fair view of the financial position and performance of the company.

7.3.4.2.   Professional Standards for Disclosure

In 1990, the accounting profession in Australia adopted the concept of differential reporting and the preparation of accounts within a stated conceptual framework.[299] According to the differential reporting philosophy, the general-purpose financial reports 'are provided to users who are unable to command the preparation of reports so as to satisfy, specifically, all of their information needs'.[300]

The declared objectives of general-purpose financial reporting include several provisions to be noted. Firstly, 'accountability' was defined to mean 'the responsibility to provide information to enable users to make informed judgments about the performance, financial position, financing and investing, and compliance of the

---

293.   Section 297.
294.   Section 305.
295.   Sections 296(1) and 304.
296.   For instance, s. 169(1)(3), The Companies (Queensland) Code.
297.   *Ibid.*, s. 269(8A).
298.   Ford, *Principles of Company Law*, 101.
299.   *Ibid.*, 102.
300.   *Accounting Handbook 1991, Statement of Accounting Concepts*, para. 6.

reporting entity'. Secondly, information must be available so that, in the public interest, efficient choices can be made. Furthermore, such reporting provides a mechanism for management to discharge its accountability obligations to those who provide resources to the entity.[301]

7.3.4.3. The Disclosure Standards of ASIC

Before the ASC was established, the NCSC stated its objectives as the following:

> The Commission endeavours to exercise its functions and powers, both directly and indirectly through its Delegates, so that the market for securities functions efficiently in a manner facilitating the capital formation and allocation processes and regarded as an investment medium in which investors large and small can participate with confidence. It seeks to achieve this by:
>
> (i) promoting the supply of information that (a) is sufficiently accurate, complete and objectively comparable to permit rational investments decisions to be made with reasonable equal opportunity to deal and (b) is issued in a manner which is timely and restricts opportunity for exploitation by insiders;
> (ii) undertaking surveillance to detect and deal with manipulation and other malpractice and to encourage corporate controllers and managers and other market participants to act with integrity and with proper regard for the demands of accountability to existing and prospective investors.[302]

The NCSC published the 1984 Green Paper entitled *A True and Fair View and the Reporting Obligations of Directors and Auditors*, arguing that:

> S[ection] 331B(1) [of the Corporations Law] now relates compliance with true and fair behind primary compliance with applicable accounting standards, though it has been suggested that greater particularity is still required.

In summary, corporate disclosure must meet the standards as follows:

> (i) be true and fair;
> (ii) be timely;
> (iii) be relevant; and
> (iv) be accurate and complete.

The predecessor of ASIC, the ASC, said in its Policy Statement 1 that:

> The accounts, audit and director's report provisions of the Law are directed to attaining the objectives of the maintenance of investor confidence and the enhancement of market efficiency through the provision of relevant, reliable

---

301. *Ibid.*, paras 12–14.
302. NCSC Policy Statement 106, July 1981.

and timely financial and other information to market participants and in particular to share and debentures holders and present and prospective creditors.

Comparable with the Corporations Act of 2001, the ASIC Act of 2001 also recognizes the enforceability of the AASB's accounting standards.[303] In addition, it requires the AASB to adopt international accounting standards by taking account of the Australian legal or institutional environment and ensuring that any disclosure provisions in the standards are appropriate to the Australian legal and institutional environment.[304] It is noteworthy to point out that the Australian Corporations legislation has provisions requiring directors of companies to make a declaration that the disclosure has met the accounting standards and has formed a true and fair view.[305] A similar approach had not been adopted in the USA until July 2002, when the Sarbanes–Oxley Act was passed after the corporate collapses of Enron and WorldCom. This again demonstrates that Australian securities regulation is quite different from that of the USA, which some American corporate law scholars have recognized.[306]

7.3.5.   DUTY OF DISCLOSURE: DOES A COMPANY DIRECTOR OR THE COMPANY OWE SUCH A DUTY TO SHAREHOLDERS?

As in China, there was also a debate on to whom the directors' duty of information disclosure is owed in Australia. The common law tradition in this regard was found in the case *Percival v. Wright* (1902) 2 ChD 421. It was decided in this case that a director's fiduciary duty was owed to the company itself, and not to the shareholders. The decision in this case has been used by scholars, courts, and law commissions to argue that directors owe no duty to shareholders unless some special relationship exists, such as agency between director and shareholders, as occurred in the case of *Allen v. Hyatt* (1914) 30 TLR 444, in which the directors agreed to act as agents for individual shareholders in arranging sales of their shares.[307]

The Uniform Companies Act of Australia, which was passed in the 1960s, has a section that may be used to stop the conduct that occurred in the *Percival* case. Section 124(2) provides that, 'An officer of a company shall not make use of any information acquired by virtue of his position as an officer to gain directly or indirectly an improper advantage for himself or to cause detriment to the company'. However, it was unclear how far the court would use this particular section to overturn the decision in *Percival v. Wright.* It is clear that the plaintiff in

---

303. The ASIC Act of 2001 (Cth), s. 227(1).
304. *Ibid.*, s. 227(4).
305. The Australian Corporations Act of 2001, ss 295(4) and 303(4).
306. M.J. Roe, 'Corporate Law's Limits', *Journal of Legal Studies* 31 (2002) 233–271 at 252, 271.
307. CCH, *A Guide to Australian Securities Industry Law and Stock Exchange Control,* 702.

the *Percival* case could not use this section, as the remedies are only available to the company. The public cannot benefit from this section.

The problems with the decision in the *Percival* case and section 124 led to two reforms with respect to insider trading.[308] The first relates to disclosure by directors of substantial holdings in companies. The second requires companies to keep a register of substantial shareholders who each own 10% or more of the nominal value of the class of shares in a company. The persons who acquire such substantial holdings must notify the company of the particulars of his or her interest within twenty-one days of acquiring it.

To overcome the effect of the decision in the *Percival* case, the Eggleston Committee advocated a complete revision of section 124:

> The object of the proposed section 124A is to alter the law as declared in *Percival v. Wright* (1902) 2 ChD 421. It was decided in that case that the director's fiduciary duty is owed to the company itself and not to shareholders; and *a fortiori* not to outsiders. . . . On the whole we are of the opinion that the best course is to confine the proposed section 124A to cases in which the outsider is able to show that he suffered a loss by reason of a fall in value, leaving the other case to be deal with under section 124.

The Companies Act passed in the 1960s has a section that may be used to stop the conduct that occurred in the *Percival* case. Section 124(2) provides that, 'An officer of a company shall not make use of any information acquired by virtue of his position as an officer to gain directly or indirectly an improper advantage for himself or to cause detriment to the company'.[309]

The question of whether a statutory duty to give correct information to shareholders is imposed upon directors was raised again in the case *Hillhouse v. Gold Copper Exploration NL* (1989) 14 ACLR 423. In this case, the plaintiffs were minority shareholders of the company. The defendants were the listed company and its directors. The directors proposed a resolution to be posed at the company's annual general meeting in accordance with the LRs. The resolution was to approve the acquisition of certain shares from a vendor in circumstances in which a notice was required to be given to shareholders under the LRs. The plaintiffs sought relief against the company and the directors, including an injunction restraining the directors from making the resolution at the annual general meeting until the requirements of the LRs had been complied with. The directors argued that they should not be parties to the action on the basis that there was no duty imposed on directors under section 42(2) of the Securities Industry (QlD) Code. The relevant sections involved were as follows:

> S 42(1) [Court to order compliance with rules] Where any person who is under the obligation to comply with, observe, enforce or give effect to the business rules or listing rules of a securities exchange fails to comply with, observe,

---

308. *Ibid.*
309. *Ibid.*

enforce or give effect to any of those business rules or listing rules, as the case may be, on the application of the Commission, the securities exchange or a person aggrieved by the failure and after giving to the person against whom order is sought an opportunity of being heard, make an order giving directions to the last-mentioned person concerning the compliance with, observance or enforcement of, or the giving effect to, those business rules or listing rules.

S 42(2) [Person obliged to comply] for the purpose of sub-section (1), a person (in this sub-section referred to as the 'relevant person) being –

a body corporate that has, with its agreement, consent or acquiescence, been admitted to the official list of a securities exchange and has not been removed from that official list; or

a person associated with a body corporate that has, with its agreement, consent or acquiescence, been admitted to the official list of a securities exchange and has not been removed from that official list, shall be deemed to be under an obligation to comply with, observe and give effect to the listing rules of that securities exchange to the extent to which those rules purport to apply in relation to the relevant person.

The dissenting Macrossan J concluded that the plaintiffs could not rely on a deemed statutory duty because Listing Rules 3J(3)(a) and (b) did not require the directors or secretary to do anything.[310] Andrew CJ said that directors were not obliged to comply with the LRs that applied to the listed company.[311] It was held that section 42(2) did not give statutory recognition to the ASX Listing Rules that imposed on directors the duty to give the notice referred to. Although the company must act through its directors, they are not personally responsible as parties in legal proceedings without any specific statutory provisions placing an obligation directly upon them to comply with the LRs. The demurrer was allowed with costs.

Under this decision, Listing Rule 3A(1) did not purport to bind directors. Section 777 of the Corporations Law did not impose any criminal or civil liability on directors of the offending company in the event that Listing Rule 3A(1) was breached. However, it should be noted that a breach of the ASX Listing Rules might provide evidence of a breach of directors' duties in a derivative suit against directors.[312] The introduction of section 777(3) in 1994 overcame the effect of the decision in the *Hillhouse* case. Under section 777(3), the management and associates, such as directors of a listed company, must comply with the LRs, including the disclosure provisions.

The CASAC recommendations and the Lavarch Committee recommendations both emphasized the importance of disclosure of information. However, the former held that view that the ASC should play a key role in regulation, while the latter

---

310. *Hillhouse v. Gold Copper Exploration NL (No. 3)* ACLR 423 at 434.
311. *Ibid.*, 428.
312. *FAI Insurance Pty Ltd v. Pioneer Concrete Services Ltd* (1986) 10 ACLR 801; *Hillhouse v. Gold Copper Exploration NL (No. 3)* (1989) 14 ACLR 423.

held the view that the ASX should be the main player in regulation. The Lavarch Committee believed that the courts should be able to enforce the Listing Rules against the directors as well as the company. One of the recommendations it made on disclosure was 4.5.25 Recommendation 14:

> The Committee recommends that section 777 of the Corporations Law be amended to provide that where the Stock Exchange Listing Rules apply to a listed company, the directors of that company are deemed to be under an obligation to procure the company to comply with the Listing Rules and the directors can be subjected to orders of the court concerning compliance with the enforcement of those Listing Rules.[313]

7.3.6. THE THEORETICAL DEBATES OVER MANDATORY CORPORATE DISCLOSURE

Australia's approach to mandatory disclosure was not an invention of itself. The US approach was clearly a model for Australia in this regard.[314] The traditional pro-regulation view is that reporting requirements are necessary because managers lack sufficient incentives to disclose trustworthy information. Furthermore, it is widely held that managers will disclose material information only after they have exploited its value for their private gain by insider trading.[315] This section examines the major arguments or rationales for the adoption of mandatory disclosure:

(i) unequal possession of information among market participants;
(ii) monitoring of management;
(iii) reduction of social waste;
(iv) the public good hypothesis;
(v) public choice; and
(vi) efficient capital market hypothesis.[316]

Before further discussion of these rationales, it is worth noting that the Australian federal government supports mandatory disclosure rules on the grounds that such rules reduce fraud by managers and improve investment decisions by investors.[317] The disclosure rules in the USA were first introduced by the Securities Act of 1933, which regulates new issues of securities, and the Securities Exchange Act of 1934,

---

313. Parliament of the Commonwealth of Australia, *Corporate Practices and the Rights of Shareholders* (Canberra: AGPS, November 1991), para. 4.5.25.
314. CASAC, *Report on Enhanced Statutory Disclosure System*, 1991, 26.
315. Cox et al., *Securities Regulation*, 43; G. Coffee, 'Market Failure and the Economic Case for a Mandatory Disclosure System', *Va.L.Rev* 70 (1984): 717–754 at 722, 723.
316. See discussion in M. Blair & I. Ramsay, Chapter 3, 'Mandatory Corporate Disclosure Rules and Securities Regulation', in *Securities Regulation in Australia and New Zealand*, ed. G. Walker, B. Fisse & I. Ramsay, 2nd edn (Sydney: LBC, 1998).
317. Explanatory Memorandum to the Corporate Law Reform Act of 1994 (Cth), para. 254; the ASC Practice Note 63, 'Incorporation by Reference – s 1024F', June 1996.

which regulates ongoing disclosure. However, the USA to date has not adopted continuous disclosure requirements.

In Australia, a company had to disclose information that would be expected to have a material effect on the price or value of the company's securities according to Listing Rule 3.1. In 1994, the amendments to the continuous disclosure regime not only backed the Listing Rule 3.1 but also broadened the continuous disclosure obligation so that it applied to those companies and other entities that, although not listed on the stock exchange, raised funds from the public. There were criticisms of the impact of the continuous disclosure reform on the efficiency of the Australian share market and on the disclosure policies of listed companies.[318] Blair and Ramsay denied such an impact on the grounds that the reforms did not create any new disclosure obligations for listed companies but only introduced statutory criminal and civil liability for breaches of existing disclosure obligations.[319]

7.3.6.1. Unequal Possession of Information among Investors

In the securities markets, investors range from ill-informed to the well-informed. An early rationale for mandatory disclosure rules was that better-informed traders could reap 'unfair' profits from trading on their superior information[320] and that investors are adequately protected if all relevant aspects of the securities being marketed are 'fully and fairly disclosed'.[321] When a company is issuing shares, the people involved in the process of issuing know more about the company than any investor does. Thus, there exists an asymmetry of information between the two groups. Disclosure requirements are intended to close this gap by requiring initial disclosure of relevant information about the issuer in the prospectus. Proponents typically argue that, for reasons of fairness, a system of mandatory disclosure should do the following:

(i) ensure that all investors have equal access to company information; and
(ii) help simplify or standardize presentations so that information is more readily understood.[322]

Opponents of the equal possession rationale argue that:

(i) the market pricing mechanism already provides protection to ill-informed investors who are unaware, or have difficulties with the comprehension, of publicly released information;

---

318. Blair & Ramsay, 'Mandatory Corporate Disclosure Rules and Securities Regulation', in *Securities Regulation in Australia and New Zealand* (Auckland: Oxford University Press, 1994), 65.
319. *Ibid.*
320. *Ibid.*, 66.
321. S. Schwarcz, 'Rethinking the Disclosure Paradigm in a World of Complexity', *University of Illinois Law Review* 1 (2004): 1–38 at 11.
322. Blair & Ramsay, 'Mandatory Corporate Disclosure Rules and Securities Regulation', in *Securities Regulation in Australia and New Zealand* (Auckland: Oxford University Press, 1994), 66, 67.

(ii) mandatory disclosure understates the significance of several alternatives available to less-informed investors. First, all investors are free to access the services of financial intermediaries. Second, they can diversify their portfolios to reduce the probability that they will incur losses; and

(iii) asymmetric information between investors may simply reflect the differential costs and benefits that are associated with becoming informed.[323]

Equality and fairness are two fundamental principles of the securities market. Without implementation of these principles, it is hardly possible to maintain securities investors' confidence in the market. The arguments of the opponents of mandatory disclosure are not substantiated for the following reasons:

(i) market price does not always reflect the real value of securities; (ii) alternatives such as use of the services of financial intermediaries and diversity of investment portfolio are the means of self-protection by the investors, and they should be used as the major means of the market provider to protect investors; and (iii) asymmetry should be avoided without the hurdle of investors' capacity to cover the costs associated with acquiring information.[324]

However, after the corporate failure of Enron, there is one argument that in a world of complexity, disclosure alone will sometimes be insufficient to remedy the asymmetry of information between the originator and its investors.[325] Professor Schwarcz of Duke Law School argues that as some business structures are becoming so complex, most investors do not have the ability to evaluate structured transactions.[326] This complexity argument has not attracted much debate in Australia.

7.3.6.2.   Monitoring of Management

Some people argue that shareholders have incentives to monitor the costs of a company so as to reduce the possibility that managers may misappropriate company assets.[327] Periodic financial reporting by management plays an important role in this process. However, there are doubts about whether mandatory disclosure rules can enhance the monitoring process. Firstly, it is doubtful whether mandatory disclosure assists shareholders in detecting breaches of duties by managers.[328]

---

323. *Ibid.*
324. *Ibid.*, 67.
325. S. Schwarcz, 'Rethinking the Disclosure Paradigm in a World of Complexity', 16.
326. *Ibid.*, 12.
327. Blair & Ramsay, 'Mandatory Corporate Disclosure Rules and Securities Regulation', in *Securities Regulation in Australia and New Zealand* (Auckland: Oxford University Press, 1994), 69.
328. Weiss, 'Disclosure and Corporate Accountability', *Business Law* 34 (1979): 575 at 579.

A study by B. Black shows that shareholders usually chose not to exercise their right to vote.[329]

Although there are considerable doubts concerning whether mandatory disclosure can enhance shareholder monitoring of management, it is commonly recognized that mandatory disclosure rules may be necessary because 'managers have incentives to conceal information' that would be beneficial to investors in assessing a company's value and the performance of management.[330] This rationale for mandatory disclosure is referred to as the opportunistic reporting hypothesis and is based on two grounds: firstly, on the equity ground, proponents suggest that investors can be victimized systematically through managers failing to inform the market of material occurrences; and secondly, on the efficiency ground, proponents suggest that mandatory disclosure is needed to improve the accuracy of securities prices.[331]

Although not all investors will use the mechanisms provided by mandatory disclosure to protect their interests, mandatory disclosure at least provides the possibility for the protection of investors. It also prevents managers from being opportunistic in providing information to investors.

7.3.6.3.   The Social Waste Hypothesis

Duplication of research costs incurred by investors in the pursuit of trading gains merely results in the redistribution of wealth rather than creating additional wealth. From a social welfare perspective, such expenditure is wasteful and constitutes a so-called deadweight loss.[332] People supporting the social waste hypothesis argue that if a regulator requires comprehensive information on companies, this will reduce the incentives for private research and therefore reduce wasteful duplication. Furthermore, investors can analyse securities data more effectively through standardized reporting.

Opponents of mandatory disclosure argue that market forces work to reduce such wasteful expenditure. Investors valuing a company are likely to take into account the costs of obtaining relevant information.[333] However, this argument is subject to criticism. Homer Kripke, a member of the SEC's 1977 Advisory Committee on Corporate Disclosure, questioned the reality of this theory concerning securities information:

> Such an argument, based solely upon ordinary demand and supply conceptions, ignores the simple fact that an issuer must supply the information demands of the potential buyers of its securities, whether private places or

---

329. B. Black, 'Shareholder Passivity Re-examined', *Mic L. Rev* 89 (1990): 520, <www.heinonline. com>.
330. Blair & Ramsay, 'Mandatory Corporate Disclosure Rules and Securities Regulation', in *Securities Regulation in Australia and New Zealand* (Auckland: Oxford University Press, 1994),71.
331. *Ibid.*
332. *Ibid.*, 69.
333. *Ibid.*

underwriters; and firms desiring an active trading market in their securities must supply information sufficient to attract investor interest and to satisfy the needs of recommending brokers and analysts.[334]

One of the aims of modern securities markets is to enhance their efficiency and reduce the costs for investors. Mandatory disclosure well suits this aim.

7.3.6.4. The Public Good Hypothesis

Under this hypothesis, information is a 'public good'.[335] This theory has two characteristics:

(i) one person's use of information does not reduce the total supply of information available for others; and
(ii) owners or suppliers of information cannot exclude those who have not paid from using it.[336]

This theory has been used as a justification for government intervention in a number of contexts. One of the original rationales for this theory was to prevent fraud, because a mandatory disclosure system substantially limited firms' ability to remain silent.[337] Ramsay discussed the application of this theory.[338] Some other academics also asserted that disclosure of securities information had characteristics of the public good. Mendelson stated that:

> Information is now considered a public good in the sense that if A is provided with or sold information, the amount available to B is undiminished even though the value may be diminished. It is practically impossible to provide A with the exclusive use of the information. Similarly, it is not practical to confine information to stockholders. Hence stockholders cannot capture the entire value of the information.[339]

Professor Coffee stated that securities information displays the key characteristic of non-excludability because users have incentives to leak it. He concluded that

---

334. H. Kripke, *The SEC and Corporate Disclosure: Regulation in Search of A Purpose*, (new York: Law & Business Inc/Harcourt brace Jovanovich, 1979), 118.
335. F.H. Easterbrook & D.R. Fischel, 'Mandatory Disclosure and the Protection of Investors', *Virginia Law Review* 70 (1984): 669, Internet version at <www.lexis.com/research/ retrieve . . . k&-md5=014673f0a55071341b9b2e940b4137cc>.
336. Blair & Ramsay, 'Mandatory Corporate Disclosure Rules and Securities Regulation', in *Securities Regulation in Australia and New Zealand* (Auckland: Oxford University Press, 1994), 74.
337. Easterbrook & Fischel, 'Mandatory Disclosure and the Protection of Investors', *Virginia Law Review* 70 (1984): 669, Internet version at <www.lexis.com/research/retrieve . . . k&-md5=014673f0a55071341b9b2e940b4137cc>.
338. See Ramsay, 'Corporate Law and the Economics of Federalism', *Federal Law Review* 19 (1990): 169 at 171.
339. Mendelson, 'Economics and the Assessment of Disclosure Requirements', *J Comp Law & Sec Reg* 1 (1978): 49 at 53, 54

researchers would be unable to obtain the full economic recovery of a discovery.[340] Blair and Ramsay were very critical of social objectives provided by regulatory measures. They pointed out that it should not be taken at face value that regulatory measures were put forward to serve social objectives.[341] Although mandatory disclosure may protect the public good, this function is indirect and often works together with other factors. Therefore, the public good hypothesis is not a strong argument for mandatory disclosure.

7.3.6.5.   The Public Choice Theory

This theory suggests that mandatory disclosure rules may be implemented because of the influence of certain interest groups. According to this theory, the political process is viewed as a competition between individuals or groups, each seeking to impose their will upon others.[342] Three observations can be made about the public choice theory.[343] First, regulation reallocates resources, making some parties better off and others worse off. Secondly, society is characterized by a variety of interest groups. Finally, parties need a coalition of political support so as to get elected or remain in office.

With respect to mandatory disclosure, the public choice theory argues that the main beneficiaries of mandatory disclosure in the USA have been members of the professional trading companies.[344] It also argues that mandatory disclosure helps these traders acquire, process, and verify information cheaply.[345] Although mandatory disclosure is a result of public choice, it is not the only result of public choice. Politics is one of the many factors affecting the formation of a mandatory disclosure regime.

7.3.6.6.   The Efficient Capital Market Hypothesis

The efficient capital market theory is also called the efficient capital market hypothesis (ECMH). According to this theory, a capital market is said to be

---

340. J. Coffee, 'Market Failure and the Economic Case for a Mandatory Disclosure System', *Virginia Law Review* 70, no. 4 (1984): 717–754 at 727.

341. Blair & Ramsay, 'Mandatory Corporate Disclosure Rules and Securities Regulation', in *Securities Regulation in Australia and New Zealand* (Auckland: Oxford University Press, 1994), 75.

342. Blair & Ramsay, 'Mandatory Corporate Disclosure Rules and Securities Regulation', in *Securities Regulation in Australia and New Zealand* (Auckland: Oxford University Press, 1994),76; Cox, Hillman & Langevoort, *Securities Regulation: Cases and Materials*, 3rd edn. (New York: Aspen Law & Business, 1997), 13, 14.

343. S. Phillips & J.R. Zecher, *The SEC and the Public Interest* (Cambridge: The MIT Press, 1981). Cited by J. Cox, in *Securities Regulation: Case and Materials*, 14.

344. Blair & Ramsay, Mandatory Corporate Disclosure Rules and Securities Regulation', in *Securities Regulation in Australia and New Zealand* (Auckland: Oxford University Press, 1994), 77.

345. *Ibid.*

informationally efficient if price fully reflects available information. Fama classified the ECMH into three forms:

(i) weak form efficiency;
(ii) semi-strong form efficiency; and
(iii) strong form efficiency.[346]

In weak form efficiency, the information contained in the past sequence of prices of a security is not fully reflected in a security's current market price. In semi-strong efficiency, all publicly available information is fully reflected in the current market price. In strong form efficiency, all information, whether public or private, is fully reflected in the current price of a security.[347] According to Gilson and Kraakman, ECMH has served as the intellectual premise for a major revision of the administration of disclosure systems.[348]

The Australian share market is a semi-strong form, as new public information is quickly released and is incorporated into share prices in an unbiased manner.[349] There are three reasons why the Australian securities market is a semi-strong form. First, it may not be informationally efficient. Usually, the share prices of large companies may be more informationally efficient than those of smaller companies. One important reason for this is that institutional shareholders improve information efficiency by their information acquisition activities. Another reason is that the shares of large companies are more actively traded than those of smaller companies. The third reason is that there is mounting evidence that the market misprices securities.[350] If a securities price cannot represent the true value of the securities, such a market is not a strong efficient market.

The Australian government is quite clear about the importance of the efficiency of the financial systems that affect every business and individual.[351] It has established one of its reform priorities as shifting the focus of regulation more towards the conduct of market participants and disclosure of information.[352] Experiences in many countries have shown that semi-strong efficiency countries such as Australia must adopt a mandatory disclosure regime to reach strong market efficiency.

---

346. E. Fama, 'Efficient Capital Markets: A Review of Theory and Empirical Work', *Journal of Finance* 25 (1970): 383 at 385.
347. *Ibid.*
348. Gilson & Kraakman, 'The Mechanisms of Market Efficiency', *VA.L.Rev.* 79 (1984) 549–550 at 549.
349. Blair & Ramsay, 'Mandatory Corporate Disclosure Rules and Securities Regulation', in *Securities Regulation in Australia and New Zealand* (Auckland: Oxford University Press, 1994), 80.
350. *Ibid.*
351. The Final Wallis Report, 2.
352. *Ibid.*, 15.

7.3.7. OVERVIEW OF THE ESTABLISHMENT OF THE AUSTRALIAN SECURITIES
REGULATION FRAMEWORK

As the Australian legal system originated from the English legal system, it is usually presumed that the securities markets and their regulation in Australia are also copies of the UK. For example, until the 1960s, Australia's companies legislation was infused with a *laissez-faire* ethos borrowed from the UK.[353] However, a study of the history and development of the Australian securities markets and regulation of these markets, a different conclusion can be drawn. That is, the Australian securities market came into being mainly because of its economic needs. Although the experiences of other countries, in particular the UK and the USA, have had a great impact on Australia in the legislative process and securities rule-making process, the focus has been on its own domestic situation. This is the main reason why the Australian securities regulatory framework is successfully functioning, although there have been some cases involving false disclosure, such as the one involving One.Tel.

Some scholars argued that for a long time, the corporate governance practices in Australia had been ignored in the area of comparative corporate governance research.[354] However, legal academics recently have argued for a study of Australian corporate governance.[355] The Australian experience became extremely useful and significant after the collapses of Enron and WorldCom in the USA. Studying Australian securities regulation, especially the corporate disclosure regime, provides many useful lessons for transitional markets, such as that of the PRC. One of these lessons is how Australia adapted the laws and experiences from other countries to suit its own needs. For example, before the Lavarch Committee recommendations were made, 'short selling' and 'market stabilization' were restricted in Australia but permissible in the UK and the USA.

'Short selling' means that the selling of securities is not actually owned by the seller and is conducted at a future time. The sale is made in anticipation that the market will fall at a stage foreseen by the seller, when the seller will be able to sell the securities at a price lower than the buying price. When short selling was restricted for some time in Australia, if some securities were listed on the ASX as well as on an international stock exchange (such as that in London), short selling of these securities was allowed in London. There might have been price differences for the same securities traded in different stock exchanges. It would be difficult for the ASX to deal with such short selling except by cooperation with the London Stock Exchange. As the Corporations Law had been drafted without regard to questions of territorial scope, the ASX suggested that legislation be amended to

---

353. B.R. Cheffins, 'Comparative Corporate Governance and the Australian Experience', *Key Developments in Corporate Law and Trusts Law*, ed. I.M. Ramsay (Sydney: LexisNexis Butterworths, 2002), 27.
354. *Ibid.*, 13.
355. *Ibid.*, 14.

specify the degree of territorial connection with Australia that was necessary for Australian provisions to apply.[356]

'Market stabilization' is another area in which UK and US laws had an impact on Australia. These two countries both permit market stabilization. However, before 1991, section 997(7) of the Australian Corporations Law prohibited persons from taking part in two or more transactions that were likely to have the effect of maintaining or stabilizing the price of the securities with the intent to induce other people to subscribe for, to buy, or to sell securities. The Lavarch Committee recommended that the Attorney-General ask the CASAC to report on ways in which the market practices in Australia could be brought into harmony with practices in the USA and the UK, particularly in relation to short selling and market stabilization activities.[357] From these examples, again, it is clear that Australia does not simply copy foreign laws and practices. The history of the Australian experience might well be a good lesson for the PRC as it develops its own securities market.

7.4.	THE PARTICIPANTS OF SECURITIES REGULATION AND THEIR ROLES IN DISCLOSURE REGULATION

7.4.1.	THE HISTORY OF ASIC

ASIC is a government agency that was established by special legislation within the Department of Treasury. Its predecessor, the ASC, was established by the ASC Act of 1989 (Cth). Together with the securities market operator, the ASX, ASIC regulates the primary and secondary markets.

Before 1970, the stock exchanges in Australia were regulated by the rules of the AASE. In 1970, a Senate Committee on Securities and Exchange was formed to review the securities industry. It was initially chaired by Senator Cormick and then by Senator Rae. In 1974, Senator Rae submitted a Report (commonly known as the Rae Report) recommending that a commission similar to the SEC of the USA be established to oversee the regulation of the securities markets, since the interstate nature of the securities industry markets in Australia had made state regulation inappropriate.[358] The abuses and malpractices, as well as the breakdown of the securities industry, that occurred at the height of the mining boom were sufficient grounds according to the Rae Report for introducing national control in this area.

The Commonwealth, the states, and Northern Territory Ministers reached the historic Alice Spring Heads of Agreement for Future Corporate Regulation in June 1990. They first agreed that the ASC should be the sole administering authority for companies and securities regulation in Australia.[359] Secondly, the ASC should be

---

356. The Lavarch Report, 45.
357. *Ibid.*, 47.
358. Each state had its own Securities Industry Act.
359. Alice Spring Heads of Agreement, para. 1.1.

formally accountable to the Commonwealth Attorney-General and the Commonwealth Parliament.[360] Later, the ASC was made responsible to the Commonwealth Treasury. After the Alice Spring Agreement was reached, the funding issue was no longer a political football that the jurisdictions could toss between themselves. Securities regulation became the sole and direct responsibility of the Commonwealth government.[361]

However, for a long time, the ASC had a shortage in its budget. Even though it spent around AUD 471 million on 902 people to enforce the Act in 1992,[362] this was still not enough for the ASC to fulfil its responsibilities. Peter Costello, who was an MP then, made his point in 1992: 'I wholeheartedly agree that corporate crookery has abounded in Australia, and that one of the major problems was lack of resources devoted to enforcement agencies'.[363] In June 1998, the ASC was renamed as ASIC by the Company Law Review Act of 1998. ASIC not only inherited the powers of the ASC but is also vested with the power to regulate the financial services market. The functions of ASIC are being strengthened by giving it more and more powers through the continuing corporate law reform.

7.4.2.   Functions and Powers of ASIC

The functions and powers of ASIC can be found in the ASIC Act of 2001(Cth) and the Corporations Act of 2001 (Cth). ASIC has regional offices in each capital city of the states. It also runs business centres in the capital cities and some other big cities. It has the following functions and powers:

- to maintain, facilitate, and improve the performance of the financial system;
- to promote the confidence and informed participation of investors and consumers in the financial market;
- to administer the Corporations Act of 2001;
- to receive, process, and store efficiently and quickly the information given to it; and
- to ensure that information is available as soon as practicable for access by the public.[364]

ASIC is primarily an administrative organ, and it does not devote high priority to law reform, except that it may make submissions to the bodies that are involved in examining the proposals for changes of the law. Under the current regulatory framework, ASIC has two major roles. First, it ensures that market operators comply with their obligations under the Corporations Act. Second, it deals with

---

360. *Ibid.*, para. 9.1.
361. D. Edwards, 'Policy and Regulatory Responsibility', *Australian Journal of Corporate Law* 2 (1992): 20–28 at 27.
362. *Ibid.*
363. P. Costello, 'Is the Corporations Law Working?', *Australian Journal of Corporate Law* 2, no. 1 (1992): 12–19 at 16.
364. The ASIC Act of 2001, Art. 1(2).

contraventions of the disclosure provisions. In recent years, there have been discussions about whether ASIC should assume responsibility from market operators for the administration of the Listing Rules.[365]

ASIC is given a broad range of powers under the ASIC Act of 2001 to fulfil its role as the securities market regulator. Its major powers include the power of investigation,[366] the power to conduct hearings,[367] the power to summon witnesses and take advice,[368] and the power to initiate civil and criminal proceedings.[369] In the process of fundraising by securities issuing, ASIC has the power to make stop orders under section 739(1). The *Arcana Provident Limited* case is one example.[370] Arcana Provident Ltd (Arcana) is a derivative trading company. On 11 June 2002, it lodged a prospectus seeking to raise funds to provide working capital for the company. ASIC placed a stop order on the fundraising document on 28 June 2002 because it failed to disclose sufficient information in regard to a number of items, including past performance and investment strategy. On 5 August 2002, Arcana lodged a replacement prospectus addressing these concerns, following which ASIC revoked the stop order on 8 August 2002.

Section 713(1) of the Corporations Act of 2001 (Cth) includes the Reduced Prospectus Content Rule for continuously quoted securities. This Rule means that, so long as a prospectus of continuously quoted securities or options to acquire continuously quoted securities of a body meets section 713(2), (3), and (4), it satisfies the general content requirement under section 710. Section 713(6) gives ASIC the power to determine in writing that a body may not rely on section 713(1) if it is satisfied that, in the previous twelve months, any of a number of prescribed provisions was contravened. Such a determination must be published by ASIC in the *Gazette*. The *Stericorp* case is such an example.[371] ASIC was concerned that the financial forecast projections provided to the market in June 2001 with respect to the 2002, 2003, and 2004 financial years were no longer accurate, as internal forecasts materially differed from those provided to the market. ASIC was also concerned that the market had not been informed of a delay in the start-up of the operational status of its Argentinian investment, Medam B.A. ASIC determined that Stericorp Ltd failed to provide such information to the market and thus contravened the continuous disclosure requirements of the Corporations Act of 2001, and as a result, Stericorp might not rely upon section 713 until 29 April 2003.

ASIC has the power to determine in writing that a number of different bodies are closely related and that their transactions should be aggregated under section 740. Under section 741, ASIC also has the power to exempt a person from compliance with Chapter 6D, which has provisions on disclosure. The CLERP 9 Act of

---

365. The Treasury, *Corporate Disclosure: Strengthening the Financial Reporting Framework*, 2002, 137.
366. The ASCI Act of 2001, s. 13(1).
367. *Ibid.*, s. 51.
368. *Ibid.*, s. 58.
369. *Ibid.*, ss 50 and 49(2).
370. ASIC, Media and Information Release, 02/303, 20 Aug. 2002.
371. ASIC, Media and Information Releases, 02/320, 4 Sep. 2002.

2004 (Cth) has strengthened the continuous disclosure framework by enhancing ASIC's powers to penalize such contraventions: the maximum civil penalty has been increased from AUD 200,000 to AUD 1 million;[372] ASIC is empowered to seek civil penalties against individuals directly involved in civil contraventions;[373] and ASIC is also given the power to issue infringement notices to corporate bodies for contraventions that are less serious.[374]

Compared with ASIC, the securities regulator in the PRC – the CSRC – has a much weaker position. Although the CSRC is also a government agency established by a national law, it is not different from any other government ministry in terms of its organization. Ever since its establishment in 1992, the Chairman of the CSRC has been changed every two years. This has raised uncertainty in its rule making and enforcement.[375] The interference from the government, and even from the CPC, plays a key role in forming a 'policy market' in the PRC. The uncertainty of such a market has also contributed to the inefficiency of the regulation of such a market. As discussed in previous chapters, the CSRC has limited powers to enforce the laws and regulations. Lack of power and authority has limited the CSRC's ability to deal with the contraventions of securities regulation. To improve the regulation of the Chinese securities market, more statutory functions and powers should be given to the CSRC.

7.4.3.	FUNCTIONS OF THE ASX IN DISCLOSURE REGULATION

The ASX has a significant role to play in disclosure regulation. Its traditional role is regulating fundraising in the following aspects. First, the ASX makes the securities transferable on a centralized market, as there is a price attached to the securities. The price of a security is fixed by the operation of normal market forces, including the evaluation of information concerning the company in which the particular security is offered. Second, the ASX offers marketability of securities. The listed securities are more marketable than those that are not listed. In the 1980s, there was a demand for placement on the main board, and a second board was opened in each of the states of Australia. However, the economic recession discontinued trading on the second board on 30 June 1992, and all companies previously trading on those boards were re-listed on the main board on 2 January 1992. Third, the ASX plays an important part in allocating capital resources or savings to those who will make the best use of them. Fourth, the ASX helps ASIC enforce the Corporations Act while enforcing its LRs.

Regarding the securities market, the ASX has a dual function. On the one hand, it is given extensive powers as a market regulator established by statute. On the other hand, as a market operator, it charges fees from listed companies for

---

372. The Corporations Act of 2001, s. 1317G(1A).
373. *Ibid.*, ss 674–675.
374. *Ibid.*, s. 1317DAC.
375. Author's interview with a former deputy chairman of the CSRC in September 2002.

initial listing and continuous trading on this exchange as a commercial legal entity for the benefit of its shareholders. The ASX keeps an Official List and Quotation of the companies listed on its market. It has promulgated LRs governing the admission to its Official List. The LRs are aimed at promoting a fair, informed, and efficient market for quoted securities. The ASX has also promulgated business rules to regulate transactions on the market and the conduct of the participants on its exchange. As a market regulator, it enforces its listing rules, especially those relating to timely disclosure. It also enforces its business rules.[376]

Until the mid-1970s, listing rules of stock exchanges in Australia were private rules in nature imposed by private bodies.[377] Companies seeking listing had to enter into a contract or a listing agreement with a stock exchange. The ASX's ability to enforce LRs was derived from a private contract between the ASX and the listed company, and the statutory recognition given to the ASX rules under the Corporations Law.[378] Statutory recognition was first given to Australian listing rules in 1975.[379] Currently, the functions of the ASX are provided not only in the Corporations Act, but also in the ASX LRs.

The old section 777 of the Corporations Law granted courts the power to give directions with regard to compliance with, or enforcement of, the ASX LRs upon the application of the ASC, the ASX, or a person aggrieved by the failure to comply with or enforce the listing rules. Section 1114 allowed the courts to make such orders, as they thought fit on the application of the ASC or the ASX when there was a contravention of LRs.

The ASX published *the Role of the Australian Stock Exchange and its Listing Rules* in October 1990. It pointed out in this document that the Uniform Listing Rules introduced in 1964 were designed to ensure an adequately informed market. To date, the public trading of securities in Australia primarily occurs on the ASX, which became the world's ninth largest market at the end of June 2002.[380] Its number of entities with listed equities on 30 June 2002 was 1,510.[381]

As stated in its Annual Report of 2001/2002, the market run by the ASX 'is complex in operation, yet simple in philosophy'. The ASX believes that the markets 'should be fully informed and transparent at all times'. Australian listed companies have increasingly embraced a 'culture of disclosure', rather than targeting only compliance. The ASX believes in a principle-based system in preference to a prescriptive approach. In other words, the ASX wants investors to enter into their markets with fully informed confidence, rather than having a prescriptive form of disclosure that leads to a culture of compliance and a minimum standard of forced disclosure and information.[382]

---

376. P. Redmond, *Companies and Securities Law: Commentary and Materials*. 3rd edn. (Sydney: LBC, 2000), 71.
377. CCH, *A Guide to Australian Securities Industry Law and Stock Exchange Control*, 57.
378. The Corporations Law, ss 777 and 1114.
379. The Securities Industry Act (NSW) of 1975, s. 31.
380. *ASIC Annual Report 2001/2002*, <www.asx.com.au>, 15 Oct. 2002.
381. *Ibid.*
382. See *ASX's Annual Report 2001/2002.*

In the year between 1 July 2001 and 30 June 2002, listed companies made a total of 70,473 announcements, an average of 280 per day. This shows that the company announcement process and continuous disclosure standards are working. The ASX may have supervisory activities such as over trades, company announcements, alerts, price queries, and referrals to ASIC. In 1987, the ASX introduced the world's first fully electronic stock market, which connects brokers around Australia to a central pricing mechanism in real time. According to the Annual Report of 2001/2002 of the ASX, Global Securities Custodian Services ranks the ASX in the top four of the world for both efficiency and value. Its equities clearing and settlement system, CHESS, is rated the best in the world.

The ASX became a public company by shares in July 1998. It is listed on its own stock market. It is the first exchange in the world to de-mutualize.[383] It became a regulator of its market and a player in this market. There were some doubts about its independence in securities regulation. The solution to this is that ASIC and the ASX entered into an MOU under which the ASX's compliance with Listing Rules, including continuous disclosure provisions, is supervised by ASIC.[384]

The practices of the ASX since its de-mutualization in 1998 have shown that the ASX market is very developed and complicated in its regulation. This market has started to influence the practices of other leading markets. For example, the SEC of the USA requested a submission from the ASX explaining the philosophy, framework, and application of the Australian continuous disclosure policy.[385] In 2002, then Chairman of the SEC Harvey Pitt indicated his willingness to debate the merits of adopting a system that he described as 'current' disclosure.[386] It should also be noted that the ASX's Managing Director addressed the World Federation of Exchanges Annual Forum on the topic of continuous disclosure and current disclosure of information.[387]

Compared with the ASX, its counterparts in the PRC (the SSE and the SZSE) have lesspowers, and this has affected their functions. First, the SSE and the SZSE were formed by the government and are still controlled by the government. Lack of independence diminishes their regulatory role. Second, both stock exchanges use the same listing rules made by the CSRC, and this shows the inflexibility of Chinese securities regulation.

7.4.4.   FUNCTIONS OF CORPORATIONS AND MARKETS ADVISORY COMMITTEE

The Corporations and Markets Advisory Committee (CAMAC) is a corporate body established by Part 9 of the ASIC Act of 2001. Prior to 11 March 2002, CAMAC

---

383. *ASIC Annual Report 2001/2002*, <www.asx.com.au>, 15 Oct. 2002.
384. *Ibid.*
385. *Ibid.*
386. *Ibid.*
387. *Ibid.*

was known as CASAC, which was established by section 145 of the ASIC Act of 1989. CAMAC consists of part-time members as well as the Chairperson of ASIC.[388] The members must have professional skill either in business, financial markets, administration of companies, financial products and financial services, law, economics, or accounting.[389] The Governor of CAMAC is to be appointed by the Commonwealth Attorney-General in writing from members other than the Chairperson of ASIC.[390] Under section 148 of the ASIC Act of 2001, CAMAC's functions are, either on its own initiative or when requested by the Attorney-General, to make recommendations about any matter associated with the following:

(a) proposals to make corporations legislation, or to make amendments of the corporations legislation (other than the excluded provisions);
(b) the operation or administration of the corporations legislation;
(c) law reform in relation to the corporations legislation;
(d) companies or segmenst of the financial products and financial services industry; and
(e) proposals for improving the efficiency of the financial markets.

In the PRC, there is no special advisory body in securities regulation such as CAMAC, although it did form an international advisory committee in July 2004.[391] However, the members of this committee come from different countries around the world and were unable to provide advice on China's domestic environment. Most of the rules of the CSRC are formed through consultation and conciliation within government bodies. The rules made in this way do not always objectively reflect and assist the needs of the markets.

7.4.5. Quality of Disclosure in Australia

The quality of corporate disclosure in Australia is assessed as being very high. CASAC, in its review of disclosure provisions in November 1996, did a survey of listed disclosing entities and found that:

(i) respondents had no significant difficulty in applying the listed disclosing entity tests in Part 1.2A;
(ii) there was an increased use of formalized procedures to comply with the continuous disclosure requirements;
(iii) approximately one-third of respondents had significantly increased their level of disclosure since the introduction of continuous disclosure;
(iv) the arrangement for lodging documents with the ASX were satisfactory;

---

388. ASIC Act of 2001, s. 147(1)(2)
389. *Ibid.*, s. 147(4)
390. *Ibid.*, s. 147(3).
391. <www.csrc.gov.cn>, 30 Jul. 2005.

   (v) approximately one-third of respondents had sought some professional advice on continuous disclosure, though the continuing cost of compliance was comparatively low;

  (vi) approximately one-third of respondents had relied on the 'carve-outs' in the ASX Listing Rule 3.1, in particular, the exemption for incomplete proposals or negotiations;

 (vii) there was overwhelming support for the supervisory and enforcement role and powers of the ASX and the ASC in regard to continuous disclosure.[392]

Although the legislative and stock market based requirements for disclosure in Australia are well established, there is an increasing concern about compliance with the regime. The ASX has stated that it is concerned about the level of disclosure by the large number of new companies listed on the ASX, the directors of which often have limited experience in the management of listed companies.[393] ASIC identified the mining companies and newly listed technology companies as being most at risk of non-disclosure.[394]

The Neagle and Tyskin Report contains empirical research on whether particular behavioural or company characteristics may lead to systematic difficulties in compliance with the Australian continuous disclosure requirement. They drew samples of companies identified as having unexplained trading through the issuing of an ASX Price Query, known as a 'Please Explain', in the period from 1 January 1999 to 31 December 2000. They praised the current functions of the ASX but also identified areas for improvement.

In contrast, there has been no formal review of the quality of corporate disclosure in the PRC. However, the quality can be assessed through a large number of contraventions of disclosure rules exposed by the media in China. One researcher from the SSE summarized China's disclosure problems as follows: (a) disclosure was not timely, and this often led to insider trading; (b) listed companies treated disclosure as a burden, and passive disclosure caused the uncertainty of the means, contents, and timing of disclosure; (c) disclosure was not accurate or true; (d) the accounting standards of China lagged behind the international accounting standards; (e) internal supervision of disclosure needed to be improved; (f) some registered accountants had engaged in misconduct, and the quality of auditing was poor; and (g) disclosure was not complete, as listed companies conducted selective disclosure.[395]

---

392. Quoted in Neagle & Tyskin, *Please Explain*, 2.
393. *Ibid.*
394. ASIC Media Release, 00/379, *High Tech Disclosure Not What It Should Be*, 9 Apr. 2000.
395. Situ, Danian, 'Information Disclosure and Corporate Governance', in *Corporate Governance: International Experience and China's Practice* (in Chinese), ed. Tu, Guangshao & Congjiu Zhu (Beijing: People's Press, 2001), 342.

7.5.   THE AUSTRALIAN SECURITIES MARKET
           AND GLOBALIZATION

The International Accounting Standards Committee (IASC) recognizes that financial statements are 'a prime source of information for investors, employee groups, government agencies and many other bodies'. The accounting bodies in Australia have been working closely with the IASC to improve its domestic accounting standards. As a member of the IASC, Australia adopted IASC standards for financial reports in January 2005. The PRC is also a member of the IASC. The Ministry of Finance has an International Accounting Standards Committee in charge of compliance with the IASC standards. However, as the PRC for a long time had adopted accounting standards totally different from Western accounting standards, which are the foundation for IASC standards, it is not easy for the PRC to adopt the IASC standards in a short period of time.

7.6.   THE SECURITIES DISCLOSURE REGIME
           IN AUSTRALIA AND ITS ADOPTION OF
           FOREIGN EXPERIENCES

In 1974, the Rae Report stated that:

> Many of the promotional and manipulative techniques we observed have been well known and documented in other industralised countries and have long ago brought forth regulatory responses by governments. Some were known at the time of the 'South Sea Bubble' in Britain in the early eighteenth century. Many of them were described by the US Senate Committee on Banking and Currency's inquiry into the Stock Exchange Practices which followed the Wall Street Crash of 1929. Such evidence as is available about previous periods of high and rising activity in company securities. Australian markets suggest that similar patterns of abuse and shortcomings in disclosure have occurred before, though sometimes concentrated in other areas of the securities market. We have no doubt that, in the absence of an effective regulatory organisation, exploitation of the investor will continue, rising to serious levels whenever investor interest, conditions of liquidity and other circumstances occur and produce heightened stock market activity. Government in Australia would be irresponsible if it were not to upgrade substantially regulatory procedures so as to against repetition of fraud, abuse and incompetence on the scale of recent years.[396]

It can be clearly seen from this statement that the disclosure models in the UK and the USA have had a vital influence on the formation of the Australian disclosure regime. As discussed in the previous parts, foreign models continue to have an

---

396. The Rae Report, (*Australian Securities Markets and Their Regulation: Report from the Senate Select Committee on Securities and Exchanges*), Preface, vol. 1 (Canberra: AGPS, 1974).

impact on Australian regulation. This phenomenon is a reflection of the convergence theory. However, in the process of convergence, Australia strongly maintains its own features in terms of securities regulation, especially in corporate disclosure regulation. This persistence is explained by the theory of path dependence initiated by Bebchuk and Roe. This persistence will be further demonstrated in the following parts.

7.6.1.   THE INFLUENCE OF ENGLISH LAW

As former colonies of the UK, the states in Australia inherited the English Companies Act in the nineteenth century and continued to follow this Act until the early 1960s. The Uniform Companies Act of 1961, the Corporations Act of 1989, and the Australian Corporations Law of the 1990s all incorporated the IPO disclosure and periodic disclosure rules already found in the English Companies Act. The influence of UK laws and regulatory framework continues to exist. This can be seen in the reports of the government, such as the Ramsay Report of 2001 and the CLERP 9 Paper.[397] English laws will continue to influence Australian lawmaking, as London continues to be one of the international financial centres. However, English laws will no longer have an impact on Australia as imperial laws.

7.6.2.   THE INFLUENCE OF US LAW

The influence of US securities laws did not formally occur until Law Professor Louis Loss of the USA was invited by the Australian government to advise it on the Securities Industry Legislation in 1973. Professor Loss produced a working paper for the Attorney-General's Department.[398] The experience of the SEC was then conveyed to Australians by Professor Louis Loss.[399] Based on Professor Loss's advice, the Rae Report recommended that a national securities regulatory body with certain powers be established. Before this Report, Sir Richard Eggleston and his Committee in their First and Fifth Interim Reports to the Standing Committee of the Attorney-General already indicated that a National Companies Commission should be established with particular powers in relation to accounts and prospectuses. As for the use of the doctrine of restraint of trade in the regulation of the admission and suspension of members of the ASX, Professor Baxt suggested that the Trade Practice Act be applied, just as the Anti-trust laws (the equivalent of the Australian Trade Practice Act) had been applied in the USA to the stock exchange

---

397. CLERP 9 Paper, 137.
398. R. Baxt, *The Rae Repor: Quo Vadis?* (Sydney: Butterworths, 1974), 153.
399. *Ibid.*

industry by the Supreme Court in the case of *Silver v. The New York Stock Exchange.*[400]

Professor Baxt also favoured the establishment of a commission 'along the lines of the SEC in the US'.[401] He was influenced by the story of how insider trading was at least effectively controlled under sections 10 and 16 of the SEC Act. This story was told by American Professor Louis Loss during his Australian trip in 1973.[402] However, Australia did not simply borrow the US experience. For example, Professor Baxt argued that based on the US experience, the rules and guidelines should be made by the SEC, but he went on to note that:

> The Australian community, being in these terms more conservative than our US counterpart, might wish some safeguard against the overriding power of the regulatory body in the securities industry. The rules promulgated by the body might be placed before parliament with the possibility that these could be revoked. This could create certain complications, and might lead to problems, but these could be adequately covered.[403]

While recommending the establishment of an SEC-style national securities regulatory body, Professor Baxt was against the same level of power of the SEC, as it was dominated by lawyers. He argued that the dominance of lawyers could have a negative effect, as documentation might become too legalistic and formal.[404] In terms of securities regulation, Australia has been greatly influenced by the US model. As the Australian government chose US advisers to draft the Australian trade practices legislation, and as Professor Louis Loss and others associated with the securities industry in the USA visited Australia in 1973 and advised the government, in particular, about the securities industry, it can be assumed that the drafting of relevant legislation relied heavily on US 'precedent'. The latest developments of corporate disclosure in the Australian corporate law reform, as discussed above, have also shown US influences.

7.6.3.   THE CANADIAN INFLUENCE

The Canadian experience was also examined by the Australian legislators.[405] However, the Australian government realized that the changes of its laws must focus on its domestic situation. Soon after the Rae Report was issued, the financial world had to face the collapse of one of Australia's largest developers, Mainline Constructions Ltd. Afterwards, Cambridge Credit Corporation was placed into receivership.

---

400. *Ibid.*
401. *Ibid.*
402. *Ibid.*
403. *Ibid.,* 154.
404. *Ibid.,* 160.
405. *Ibid.,* 127.

At that time, the Ontario Securities Act provided for continuous disclosure, containing an exemption for 'sealed envelope' disclosures. A reporting issuer might file a form marked 'confidential' with the Securities Commission, stating the reasons for non-disclosure. If the issuer wanted the information to remain confidential, it must advise the Commission in writing every ten days from the date of the filing of the form. Arguably, this approach should not be adopted in the Australian context.[406]

On quarterly reporting, the ASX called for comments on this issue in October 1990 but rejected its implementation because of adverse comments by respondents, mainly listed companies.[407] CASAC also considered this issue. It stated that where a system of continuous disclosure was operating effectively, the benefits associated with mandated quarterly reporting might be substantially reduced relative to the costs of their preparation. It suggested that a quarterly reporting requirement might be a matter for future review once its proposed legislatively based continuous disclosure regime had been implemented and assessed. Countries such as the USA, Canada, France, Brazil, and the Philippines had quarterly reporting requirements. Most of the studies of the US quarterly reporting requirements suggested that they were used in investments decisions and helped investors predict annual results.[408]

Mark Blair, who worked as a deputy director of CASAC, suggested a US-style quarterly disclosure reporting system. However, to date, the Australian government is not in favour of mandatory quarterly reporting, as it worries that such a requirement in Australia would add to compliance costs for companies, and that the quarterly accounts would not be audited.[409]

7.7.   CONCLUSION

Historically Australia was a colony of the UK. The Australian legal system was based on the English model. Thus, the securities markets in Australia from the beginning had a sound legal environment to grow. The historical connection with the UK, the economic connection with the US, the similarity in terms of economic positions with Canada, provide the opportunities for Australia to easily establish its own securities regulatory regime. This is a reflection of the convergence hypothesis. But, the geographical isolation from the Europe and the growing economic relations with Asian countries has led to the persistence of some unique features of the Australian securities market and its regulation. The Australian practice supports the differentiation hypothesis. The current Australian corporate disclosure regulatory framework is such an example. The current co-regulation of the ASX and ASIC works well. It can provide experience to other transitional economies such as the PRC. The content of disclosure under the Australian information

---

406.   CASAC, *An Enhanced Statutory Disclosure System*, September 1991, 22.
407.   Blair, 66.
408.   *Ibid.*, 67.
409.   CLERP 9 Paper, 2002, 135.

disclosure regime, especially the continuous disclosure structure has even been studied and learnt by the US. It will also be of some help to the improvement of the disclosure regime for the PRC.

In conclusion, because the American securities market is the largest in the world the US securities regulatory regime has become a most commonly used model for most of the countries. Australia is no exception. In its process of establishing a national securities market and a national regulatory body the American influence is obvious. However, Australia does not simply copy the US model. As is clear from the above discussion, lessons and experience from the US were adopted after empirical study had been done by the relevant Committees/Commissions of the Australian government or by government advisory bodies. Australia has created a unique disclosure regulatory regime which demonstrates strong American influence on the one hand, whilst retaining apparent Australian characteristics on the other hand. As a relatively complicated market, Australia can provide helpful experience for other emerging securities markets, especially that of the PRC.

Chapter 8

Conclusions and Suggestions

8.1.   INTRODUCTION

The securities market in the PRC only re-emerged about two decades ago. Over the short period of time since then and now, the market has developed rapidly and dramatically. It has gone through many of the major processes that most securities markets in Western countries had passed through a period of more than a hundred years. The Chinese securities market has encountered problems and difficulties similar to those that were encountered by most Western securities markets. However, from the analysis presented throughout this book, it is clear that one of the major differences is that the PRC has had to solve a number of problems that have occurred suddenly and at much the same time. Another main difference is that the PRC government has very strong control of the securities market; in other words, China's securities market is a government-controlled and supported market. This book has examined the processes that the Chinese securities market has gone through, as well as the progress that the PRC has made. It has also illustrated that this market is still in a stage of transition, the regulatory regime still needs to be improved, and the quality of securities regulation still needs to be increased if it is to come close to developed securities markets in other countries.

National securities regulation regimes reflect each country's tradition, culture, economic structure, and policies.[1] This book has argued that because of its cultural, historical, political, and economic differences from those of other countries, the PRC has had to develop an approach to adopting foreign laws that suits the PRC's own circumstances in establishing a functioning securities regulatory regime. The fact that the PRC securities market emerged late in China's economic development has, of course, provided it with the opportunity to learn from the

---

1. A.N. Licht, 'Regulatory Arbitrage for Real: International Securities Regulation in a World of Interacting Securities Markets', *Virginia Journal of International Law* 38 (1998): 563 at 633.

experiences of established markets in Western countries. However, the emerging and volatile nature of the PRC market means that the PRC has to be careful when selecting models to learn from; it also has to be careful in adopting foreign models into its own practices, as there is no 'one size fits all' regulatory ideal.[2] Transplanting a system from one country into another has never been an easy task for any country, even if the borrowing country is keen to learn from other systems. While learning from other countries, the PRC has to consider its own history, culture, economy, and even its politics. Currently, the development of the PRC securities market demonstrates a strong influence of the divergence hypothesis, while the regulation – especially in the area of corporate disclosure – reflects a strong influence of the convergence hypothesis. The establishment and improvement of Australian securities regulation is a reflection of the differentiation hypothesis. This hypothesis seems also applicable to the improvement of PRC securities regulation. Therefore, the PRC should draw upon lessons from Australia. Only by learning from other countries has it been possible for the PRC to avoid the pitfalls that troubled Western countries and to fulfil its own goal of developing a securities market with high efficiency and low cost.

Unfortunately, in reality, the market designers, the legislators, and the rule makers in the PRC have not considered thoroughly enough how they should effectively learn from other markets. From the practices of the last two decades, it is clear that the PRC has encountered two major problems in learning from foreign experiences: first, the models that it has chosen have not always suited the PRC's situation; and second, it is apparent that the PRC has not done enough empirical study of foreign models. Some models may lead to bad results when they are transplanted into different environments. The simple reproduction of foreign models in a transitional market will almost inevitably lead to poor implementation of 'good laws'.

The inherent problems that arise in adopting foreign models in developing countries have produced significant challenges on how to effectively put theory into practice. Identifying a better approach for the PRC to draw upon foreign legal experiences has been the fundamental focus of this book from the beginning. This has been done by way of a close comparison with the securities laws of developed Western countries, particularly Australia.

The Australian model was chosen as the main basis for comparison for the reason that this model has been neglected by the PRC, not only in the process of developing the Chinese securities market, but also in the establishment and improvement of the securities regulatory regime. The importance of the Australian model not only lies in the complexity of its securities market, but also lies in its experience in adopting foreign models. This book has not purported to imply that the Australian model is better than other Western models; the fact that Australia reviews its regulatory regime, including its disclosure regime, from time to time

---

2. A. Cadbury & I.M. Millstein, *The New Agenda for ICGN*, discussion paper no. 1 for the ICGN Tenth Anniversary Conference, London, July 2005, 28.

demonstrates that this market also needs to be improved.[3] Rather, this book has argued that the practices of transplanting foreign laws into Australia can be very important and useful for the PRC. Although a number of issues have been raised in dealing with this theme, this book has focused on the aspect of corporate financial disclosure, as this is probably the fundamental building block of all advanced securities law regimes.

This book began with a brief introduction to the development of corporate disclosure and corporate governance in the PRC. Chapter 2 provided a big picture of the Chinese legal system, and a more detailed examination of this system was provided in Chapter 3. This book then examined the gatekeepers and their functions, and analysed the PRC securities regulatory regime from the aspect of corporate disclosure in Chapters 4 and 5. Some key problems arising under this regime were also identified in Chapter 5, especially from the perspective of how foreign models should be chosen and how foreign experiences should be drawn upon by a transitional market. By examining the disclosure regime, it was argued that the influence of the convergence hypothesis was evident. Chapter 6 reviewed the state of the securities market and demonstrated the application of the divergence hypothesis. It was pointed out that to develop a functional corporate disclosure regime, China should apply the differentiation hypothesis. Thus, China should selectively draw upon foreign experiences to suit its own domestic circumstances. Chapter 7 briefly reviewed the history of the Australian securities market and its regulation. It discussed the key features of the Australian securities market as making it a model of a relatively complex market. It closely analysed the ways in which foreign experiences were adopted by Australian authorities and concluded that Australia had many practical experiences to offer in solving developmental problems within the PRC. Two major problems with respect to disclosure laws in the PRC were identified and the reasons were analysed. Finally, Chapter 8 will emphasise that as the PRC seeks to incorporate foreign experiences in the context of its transitional securities market, it is necessary to look closely at the interactions among law, culture, politics, and economics. This issue is addressed below.

8.2. LAW AS CULTURE

As is well established, law does not exist outside a society.[4] A society has its particular culture and its laws reflect this particular culture. According to Professor Dean, some listed company directors and secretaries have stated that they need to

---

3. ASIC criticized the ASX's continuous disclosure regime focused on inconsistencies between the operation of state offices and each office's ability to obtain announcements from companies when demanded; see M. Moncrief, 'ASX Gets Pat on Back from ASIC', *The Age*, business page 2, 20 Jul. 2005.
4. K. Laster (ed.), *Law as Culture* (Sydney: The Federation Press, 1997), 1; L.M. Friedman, *Law and Society: An Introduction* (Upper Saddle River: Prentice-Hall Inc., 1977), 7; L.M. Friedman, *The Legal System: A Social Science Perspective* (New York: Russell Sage Foundation, 1975), 142.

operate and to be seen as operating in a way that is acceptable to society, not least because there has been a constant threat of yet more legislation; they regard paying attention to these issues as simple matters of 'common sense'.[5] Professor Laster sees law as a lens that reveals the dominant culture's values and the interests of a society and shows how these are preserved, challenged, and changed.[6] Friedman holds the view that cultural factors are an essential ingredient in turning a static structure and a static collection of norms into a body of living law.[7] On the question of the cultural influences on Asian legal systems, Pistor and Wellons conclude:

> Cultural factors may have played a role in the evolution of law and legal process. Our findings suggest that legal behaviour responded to changes in economic policies. Cultural factors may have determined the nuances of this response or even helped explain the change in policy, but they did not stop the legal system from adapting to changing economic strategy and environment.[8]

Pistor and Wellons also argue that although law is by no means static, legal evolution in each country is distinct and will produce vastly different outcomes as a result of cultural differences.[9] This is, of course, very evident when comparisons are made between legal change in the PRC and in Australia.

Research on the relationship between law and culture can be applied in the Chinese securities market and its regulation. The traditional Chinese approach of looking down on business and business people[10] is one of the factors that have slowed down the development of commercial law in China. In terms of the development of the securities market, people who showed interest in investing in this market were for a long time seen as speculators who only wanted to become rich overnight without doing hard work. Under this Chinese view, honest and decent people should not be speculators. This old view prevented the development of the PRC securities market, and the rules regulating the securities market in China reflected this cultural influence. Provisions reflecting such Chinese cultural influences can be found in the securities laws and rules. Obviously, those traditional ideas no longer suit a developed society. Thus, where there is any conflict between its traditions and the development of its securities market, the PRC is forced to make a choice.

---

5. J. Dean, *Directing Public Companies: Company Law & the Stakeholder Society* (London: Cavendish Publishing, 2001), 251.
6. K. Laster, (ed.), *Law as Culture*, 2nd edn (Sydney: The Federation Press, 2001), 1.
7. Friedman, *Law and Society*, 76.
8. K. Pistor & P. Wellons, *The Role of Law and Legal Institutions in Asian Economic Development 1960–1995* (New York: Oxford University Press, 1999), 15.
9. *Ibid.*, 35.
10. In ancient Chinese history, the rulers of different dynasties (starting from the Qin Dynasty) adopted the policy of *zhong nong yi shang* (Emphasize agriculture and resist commerce.). The businesspeople are customarily called *jian shang* (snobby business people). See Zeng, Xianyi (ed.), *The Legal History of China* (in Chinese), 84.

8.3.   LAW AS POLITICS

Professor Mark Roe has argued, in a wide range of published work, that the US system of ownership and control was not simply the product of market forces, but also a political and ideological contingent.[11] Different political systems have different impacts on their legal systems. The Western conception of law contrasts sharply from that used in the PRC. In the West, law defines rights and obligations, while in the PRC, lawmaking is now directed by the dominant state theory of Maxism-Leninism, Maozedong thoughts, Deng Xiaoping's theory, Jiang Zeming's Three Representations, and the scientific development theory.[12] This last theory sees law as the tool of a ruling class in the service of politics and rejects any sharp differentiation among judicial, legal, and administrative processes.[13] Chinese legal theorists divide the members of the society into the ruling class and the ruled class, and they also focus on the service function of law, but only for the purposes of the ruling class.[14]

The correlation of law with politics in the PRC is a result of the dominant role of the CCP. Under the PRC lawmaking procedures, the CCP (as the ruling party) can transform its policies into law as it wishes, and important lawmaking is therefore always under the direction of the CCP.[15] This practice causes the difficulty faced by the PRC in adopting the rule of law, as the policies of the CCP are often seen as superior to law. Some Chinese legal theorists even treat the needs of policies as a legal principle.[16] Because the PRC's policies can change very quickly and easily, this practice explains the conflicts and inconsistencies between laws and policies in China. To understand the Chinese legal system, the reader must consider the historical traditions and ways of thought that long predate the formation of the PRC and markedly differ from their Western counterparts.[17]

There has been great debate on the relationship between CCP policies and law. Although the Constitution of the PRC does not mention the status of CCP policies, only common sense is needed to understand that CCP policies have a higher status than the law. In China, the concept of the 'rule of law' has been confused with that of 'rule by law'.[18] Law is still seen in the PRC as a tool to implement CCP

---

11. See B.R. Cheffins, 'Law, Economic and the UK's Corporate Governance: Lessons from History', *Journal of Corporate Law Studies* 1, no. 1 (2001): 71–89 at 75.
12. Preamble, the PRC Constitution of 1982.
13. Lubman, *Bird in a Cage: Legal Reform in China after Mao* (Palo Alto: Stanford University Press, 1999), 88.
14. Zhang, Wenxian, *Jurisprudence* (in Chinese) (Beijing: Peking University Press and Higher Education Press, 1999), 46.
15. There is a department called Central Leading Group of Politics and Law under the Central Committee of the CCP. Its functions include giving directions to the draftspersons of bills on key issues.
16. Zhang, Wenxian, *Jurisprudence* (in Chinese), 75.
17. *Ibid.*, 11.
18. Zhang, Yujun et al., *Reform and Development of Chinese Stock Market in Transitional Period* (in Chinese) (Chengdu: Southwest Press of Finance and Economics, 2004), 10 of Introduction.

policies.[19] In terms of securities market regulation, CCP policies often decide the direction of change in CSRC's rules and directives. From time to time, the CSRC has been caught in the dilemma of whether or not to build a securities market suitable for a market economy in which the CSRC has to follow international trends and adopt rules that suit market economies but may not be accepted by ordinary Chinese people, or even by the senior officials. However, the volatile features of a transitional securities market can cause great turmoil (as did the Shenzhen incident that occurred in 1992),[20] threatening the rule of the CCP. Therefore, the CSRC has had to observe CCP policies when political needs surpass the need for a healthy securities market. This phenomenon has been given the name of a 'policy market' in China.[21] The decision to reduce state shareholdings in June 2001 and the subsequent decision to stop the reduction of state shareholdings in September 2001 is a typical example of such a policy market.[22] Another feature of a policy market is also evident in that share issuing is mainly used by the government to ease SOEs' capital shortages.[23]

The extent to which Chinese and Western political traditions have differed is also illustrated by noting that since the beginning of the twentieth century, every document of a constitutional nature proposed or adopted in China has consistently treated rights as contingent. In China, rights are granted by the state and can be changed by the state; government can limit rights by legislation and is not itself restrained by law.[24]

8.4.   LAW AND ITS ECONOMIC IMPLICATIONS

While economic development does not always keep pace with the development of economic law, for law to have a positive impact, it must be consistent with the prevailing economic policies. The change of the legal systems in Asia reflects such an implication. As some researchers pointed out:

> With the move towards market-oriented economic policies, the legal system in all countries became more market-allocative and more rule-based. Despite the overall trend towards a market-allocative legal system, the remaining

---

19. Gu, Angran, then Chairman of the Legislative Affairs Commission of the NPC Standing Committee of the PRC, *A Review of the Lawmaking in New China* (in Chinese) (Beijing: Law Press, 1995), 83.
20. Because of the high returns of share trading, the Shezhen Stock Exchange was surrounded by investors who were desperate to buy and trade shares on this market. The Shenzhen municipal government had to send police to maintain the order of the long queue.
21. Zhang, Wenxian, *Jurisprudence*, 2; Wang, Chunfeng, 'Chapter 2: The Political Impact: Is China's Stock Market a Policy-Driven Market?', in *Diagnosis and Treatment: Revealing the Stock Market of China* (in Chinese), ed. Cheng Siwei (Beijing: Economics Science Press, 2002).
22. *Ibid.*
23. Jin, Dehonge, *Contemporary Securities Market of China* (in Chinese), 30.
24. A. Nathan, *Chinese Democracy* (Berkeley: University of California Press, 1985), 113.

differences in legal process and institutions lead us to conclude that legal systems are partly converging, and partly diverging.[25]

In the PRC, whether the establishment of the securities market has speeded up economic reform is still a question. Issuing shares was first used in the countryside to meet the needs of raising capital by collective enterprises. It was not until the late 1980s that SOEs were allowed to issue shares as a major way of fundraising.[26] The first Company Law of the PRC, which was passed in 1993, should ideally have sought to accommodate the needs of all kinds of companies. However, the law's high capital requirement for establishing joint stock limited liability companies made it too difficult for joint stock companies to be set up by individuals.[27] Most private companies cannot issue shares to the public and cannot raise capital in a domestic securities market. Even though this high capital requirement has been eased by the PRC Company Law of 2005, it is still much higher than those required under laws of most Western countries.

From the history of the PRC securities market, one can draw the conclusion that the establishment of securities markets in the PRC was primarily intended to accommodate the capital needs of SOEs. Although in the following years, big private companies such as New Hope Corp Group and Yongyou Software Company were listed in a domestic stock exchange, SOEs have remained as the dominant participants in the Chinese securities market. Since the CSRC released its first administrative rule on disclosure by share issuing companies in 1993, numerous listed companies have violated these disclosure rules, most of which have been SOEs.

8.5. THE ESTABLISHMENT AND DEVELOPMENT OF THE PRC CORPORATE DISCLOSURE REGIME: WHAT HAS BEEN THE EFFECT?

The State Council's Interim Regulations of 1993 was the first administrative regulation involving corporate disclosure.[28] In the same year, the CSRC released the Implementing Rules Concerning Disclosure by Share Issue Companies (for Trial). This document was the first departmental administrative rule specifically dealing with corporate disclosure, although it only has a total of thirty-one articles. It lists all the major disclosure documents that a listed company must provide. Following

25. K. Pistor, & P. Wellons, *The Role of Law and Legal Institutions in Asia Economic Development 1960–1995*, 27.
26. In 1987, the State Council released the Regulation Concerning the Change of Administrative Scheme in SOEs, and the shareholding system was formally allowed to be used by SOEs.
27. Article 77 provides that a joint stock company can only be established with approval of a department designated by the State Council or by a provincial government. Art. 78 provides for the minimum for paid-up capital of CNY 10 million. These Articles constitute the basic structure of corporate disclosure in China.
28. Articles 16–19, 57–67 and 73–74. These Articles constitute the basic structure of corporate disclosure in China.

these Rules, the CSRC started releasing a number of administrative rules on the content and format of disclosure by listed companies. As the Chinese securities market has developed very quickly and continues to change, the CSRC has to update these Administrative Rules – mainly the rules on disclosure – from time to time. Although what the CSRC has done is to meet the requirements of market development, many market participants have not been happy with the constant changes that have been occurring, as they often are not given enough notice about when the rules will be changed.

Nevertheless, by the end of 2001, the PRC had formed a corporate disclosure regime that consisted of laws, administrative regulations, and administrative rules. But what is the function of this regime? Although the PRC's legislature and especially the CSRC have issued numerous rules regulating corporate disclosure, breaches of these laws and regulations continue to occur. Classic cases of false disclosure can be easily found. Cases such as *Shenzhen Yuanyie Corp, Qiongminyuan Corp, Chengdu Hongguang Corp, Shanxi Houwang Corp, Hubei Lantian Corp,* and *Yinguangxia Corp* became well-known after their breaches of disclosure regulations were exposed.[29] 2001 was named by the CSRC as 'the year of supervision'. There had been at least one case per month involving false disclosure exposed by the media in that year; most of these breaches were committed by state-owned companies. The reasons for the frequency of such breaches can be explained by internal and external factors. Of the internal factors, ignorance of corporate governance is a common problem within state-owned companies. Of the external factors, first, there is a lack of statutory punishment of some conduct involving false disclosure, and second, current levels of punishment are too lenient. For example, the directors of state-owned companies involving such misconduct rarely bear any personal liability to the shareholders who have suffered losses as a result of false disclosure, even though personal liabilities are provided under the Securities Law of 2005; these directors often are simply transferred to new positions. Another example of the lack of statutory punishment is that a lawyer who is involved in false disclosure may have his or her practicing certificate suspended for only a year. Even the maximum disqualification period is only ten years.

Recent practices show that although the disclosure regime has been formally established, it does not function properly, as the market is still developing. This market has not been fully transformed into a free market. For a variety of structural reasons, the rules necessary for a free market cannot be completely applied in the market of the PRC. The major participants in this market (state-owned companies) have not become free players. The regulator in this market (the CSRC) continues to exercise powers in the old way; over-regulation therefore becomes no regulation. To cure the problem of the epidemic of false disclosure, the PRC has to find appropriate foreign models to learn from and has to combine foreign experiences with China's practices.

---

29. 'Chapter 5: Major Securities Cases in China's Transitional Securities Market' in Zhang, Yujun et al. (eds), *Reform and Development of the Chinese Stock Market in the Transitional Period.*

8.6. THE CHOICE OF FOREIGN CORPORATE DISCLOSURE
MODELS AND ITS IMPACT ON THE PRC'S PRACTICES

The open-door policy adopted in the PRC in the late 1970s not only started the economic reform that we have seen, but also led to the establishment of a legal system in the PRC. Since the late 1980s, the Chinese legislature had been engaged in the 'borrowing' of foreign laws. Then-Chairman of the Standing Committee of the NPC Peng Zhen instructed the bill drafters that 'foreign experiences should be studied and borrowed, no matter whether they are from socialist or capitalist countries, no matter whether they are from the civil law system or the common law system'.[30] Since 1993, when the CCP decided to establish a socialist market economy, the legislature has been advocating 'more borrowing of foreign law into China'[31] so as to 'quickly make some laws with respect to the socialist market economy'.[32] However, this approach is too simplistic. Without doing empirical research into the background that led to a particular piece of legislation being introduced in a Western country, this 'borrowing' will not greatly help to establish a legal system that best suits the PRC. The borrowing of corporate disclosure rules is such an example. The US securities market has been developing for more than a hundred years. Although its system is relatively advanced, whether its experience suits China is by no means clear. Yet the US laws are always the first to be looked at by Chinese lawmakers and rule makers as models. However, with corporate collapses, such as those of Enron and WorldCom, the US model has been undermined. Hong Kong is always the easiest model for China to learn from, mainly for geographical and cultural reasons. As American culture and customs are much different from those of the PRC, ignorance of other Western models may not help China find a proper model to learn from; as most of the companies listed on the Hong Kong Stock Exchange are controlled by families, the Hong Kong model is not a sensible model for mainland China to follow either.

The Australian model has not raised much attention in the PRC. This situation results not only from the relatively small size of Australia in terms of population, but also from the lack of understanding of the Australian legal system. The Chinese consider the Australian legal system to be a mere copy of the English system. Very few Chinese have realized that English law has not directly applied in Australia for some time and that this was formalized by the passage of the Australia Act of 1986.

Chapter 5 of this book discussed the history and characteristics of the corporate disclosure regime in Australia. As a former colony of the UK, Australia established a legal system with a commitment to the rule of law. This system has laid the foundations for the healthy development of the Australian securities market. The Australian securities market is now a relatively sophisticated market

---

30. Cited by then Chairman of the Legislative Affairs Commission of the PRC NPC Standing Committee, Gu Angran, in his book *A Review of the Lawmaking of the New China*, (Beijing: Law Press, 1995) 70.
31. *Ibid.*, 70.
32. *Ibid.*, 29.

with an experienced regulatory body and experienced market participants. Its complexity is evidenced by the stability of the Australian securities market after the worldwide corporate crisis led by the failures of big companies in 2001 and during the global financial crisis that started in 2008. The Australian experience of how to learn from foreign experiences so as to improve its corporate disclosure regime has much in it that other countries like the PRC can learn from. It is certainly worth the attention of the PRC authorities who are so keen to learn from foreign experiences. The approach that the Australian government has used to adopt foreign legal experiences is extremely enlightening. During the 1990s, when the PRC government was reviewing its corporate disclosure regime, studies on foreign models were conducted. Many study reports were released for the improvement of legislation.[33] However, these reports were not very long, and all had less than ten pages. Compared with the Australian practice of using lengthy reports in lawmaking, the PRC legislature and rule makers should abandon their practice of using a flimsy four- or five-page-long 'research report' or 'investigation report'[34] as a basis for their lawmaking and rule-making activities and adopt more in-depth background research strategies.

8.7.   DIRECTORS' DUTIES OF DISCLOSURE

In Australian corporate history, there has been debate over whether company directors or the companies bear the duty of corporate disclosure.[35] Likewise, there was some uncertainty in this regard under PRC law. It is clear now in Australia that both the company and company directors bear such a duty under the law. However, Chinese law is still not quite clear on this important issue.[36] This ambiguity provides an excuse for irresponsible company directors and other controllers to evade disclosure rules. This is also a very important reason why many directors who have made false disclosure have not received any serious punishment and why breaches of disclosure rules continue to occur frequently in China.

8.8.   SHAREHOLDERS' REMEDIES

The Australian Corporations Act of 2001 (Cth) provides shareholders with relatively effective legal protection. The statutory derivative action[37] is one of the most

---

33. Liu, Shuqiang, *Annotation of the Securities Law*; see Part II 'The Instructions and Reports Regarding the Draft Securities Law'.
34. This is based on the author's experiences while working for the legislature of the PRC,.
35. *Percival v. Wright* [1902] 2 Ch. D 421; *Coleman v. Myers* [1977] 2 NZLR 225 at 267, 273.
36. The PRC Company Law of 1993 had vague articles on companies' duty to give true and complete information. The PRC Securities Law of 1998 only imposed criminal liability on directors and other controllers in breach of disclosure rules, but it did not impose civil liability on these directors and other controllers.
37. Sections 236–242.

important changes in legislation to protect shareholders, especially minority share-holders. Allowing courts to make a number of orders if the conduct or a resolution of a company or its directors is oppressive to, unfairly prejudicial to, or unfairly discriminatory against members of a company is another effective way to protect shareholders.[38] Enforcing orders made by the courts under section 461 and allowing courts to order an inspection of a company's books by its members also provide other means for protecting the interests of shareholders.

In contrast, although the PRC is a civil law country, its corporations legislation contains no clear provisions to protect the interests of shareholders. Since the early 1990s, there have been frequent breaches of disclosure requirements. However, because of a poor sense of individual rights among the Chinese, no one had sought to bring an action in court until 4 December 1998, when an individual investor sued Hognguang Industry Corp. and its senior staff in the Shanghai Pudong District Court.[39] As the Securities Law of 1998 and other laws did not have clear provisions for civil compensation, the Court dismissed this case for the reason that it could not establish that the losses suffered by investors was caused directly by the false disclosure of the defendants.

Lack of provisions for civil compensation remedies for investors has caused great anger and chaos in the Chinese securities market. The Supreme People's Court had to release judicial interpretations from time to time to solve the problems that were caused by this defect of the law. In early September 2001, some 176 individual investors in Yi'an Tech Corp were going to sue the company and its chairman of the board of directors.[40] Almost at the same time, twenty-eight individual investors brought an action against Yiguangxia Corp. and Zhongtianqin Accounting Firm. However, the Supreme People's Court released the Circular Concerning Non-Acceptance of Claims Involving Securities Civil Compensation on 21 September 2001. This judicial interpretation declared that courts did not have enough resources and ability to accept and hear securities cases involving false disclosure, insider trading, and market manipulation. Consequently, all the courts that had accepted such cases had to stop hearing them. The passive attitude of the courts has raised great concern and anger from the public.

On 1 January 2002, the CSRC and the State Commission of Economics and Trade jointly released the Code of Corporate Governance in Listed Companies. This Administrative Rule contains provisions on civil liability and civil compensation for false disclosure.[41] Following this step of the executive government, the Supreme People's Court released the Circular Concerning Several Issues Involving Civil Tortuous Disputes Caused by False Disclosure in the Securities Market on 15 January 2002. This Circular formally gives local courts the power to hear false disclosure cases on the condition that the conduct of false disclosure has to be first

---

38. Sections 232 and 235.
39. Zhang, Xiao, Long & Tang, 220.
40. *Ibid.*, 210.
41. Article 4.

dealt with by the CSRC.[42] Whether or not this condition is rational is worth debating. This Circular also allows plaintiffs to bring individual actions and joint actions, but no class action is allowed because of a lack of statutory basis.[43] Nevertheless, individuals can bring actions against a company and company directors or managers who breach disclosure requirements. On 9 January 2003, the People's Supreme Court issued the Several Provisions Concerning the Hearing of Civil Compensation Cases of False Disclosure in the Securities Market. Apart from the pre-requisite for a CSRC administrative decision, a previous criminal trial has been added as another pre-requisite for hearing such civil cases.[44]

It is noteworthy that although individual investors in the PRC now can bring an action against company directors and managers for breach of disclosure rules, such an action is not a derivative action. In the PRC, individual investors bring such an action on behalf of themselves, not on behalf of the company.[45]

| 8.9. | CONCLUSION AND SUGGESTIONS |

There has been a common acknowledgment that the first task of listed companies is to produce competitive returns for their shareholders. Some people continue to argue that there are two other things that listed companies must do if they want to thrive. The first of these is to satisfy its customers so as to produce returns for the companies; the second is to recruit and motivate excellent employees so as to achieve the goals of the company.[46] The unique features of the development of the securities market and securities regulations in the PRC, as well as the lack of empirical studies to be used by Chinese lawmakers, have provided the motives for this book on the Chinese securities market and its regulations, specifically, from the perspective of corporate disclosure.

There are several reasons why corporate disclosure by listed companies in the PRC was chosen to serve as the core theme of this book. Firstly, disclosure is the most important tool for ensuring that the principles of fairness, openness, and justice are achieved. On a securities market, investors in fact trade securities information. From this point of view, securities law is fundamentally about disclosure regulation. This means that a focus on disclosure should be central for the development of China's securities regulation. A comparison with parallel Australian corporate disclosure rules has provided a unique basis for the analysis of disclosure regulation in China that was developed in this book.

Secondly, reforms in corporate disclosure regimes in Western countries have provided models for China. From time to time, lawmakers and securities regulators in Western countries draw upon lessons learned from the effects of a bubble

---

42. Article 5.
43. Article 4.
44. Article 6.
45. The PRC Company Law of 1993, Art. 111.
46. Dean, *Directing Public Companies*, 251.

economy caused by false and misleading disclosure, and they have established clearly mandatory and timely disclosure requirements for public companies. The disclosure regulatory regimes that have originated in Western countries are viewed as being relatively comprehensive. Unfortunately, this does not always stop the misconduct of giving false or misleading information in Western securities markets. Following the corporate collapses of large corporations, such as Enron and Worldcom in the USA, Parmalat in Italy, and HIH and One-Tel in Australia around 2001, and Madoff, Sanford, and Saytam in India in 2008, the issues of reforming disclosure regulations and enhancing corporate governance have been constantly on the agenda of lawmakers and regulators in many countries. At this time, the reform of disclosure regimes that is intended to make them more effective and preventive has become a common task in both developed and complicated securities markets, such as those in the USA and Australia, and in emerging and transitional markets, such as that in the PRC. This movement toward reform of securities regulation around the world makes concerns raised in this book especially significant.

As the PRC had been relatively isolated for quite some time, Western countries could began to really know this country, with its ancient and unique civilization, after it adopted an open-door policy in the late 1970s. However, because China is a country that has traditionally respected authority instead of law, it is extremely hard for the PRC to establish a modern legal system. In the process of moving towards the rule of law, traditional legal concepts and rules still affect the lawmakers of the PRC. The lack of a doctrine of separation of powers has caused the poor record of enforcement of law, and the CCP's unchallengeable supreme authority has slowed down the move towards the rule of law.

Nevertheless, the PRC's economy is still developing very quickly, and its securities market is rapidly catching up with those in Western countries. Its securities regulatory regime has learned much from Western countries, and thus it has become a mixture of Western experiences and domestic practices. The establishment and development of corporate disclosure laws is one such example.

The first chapter of this book identified main disclosure issues with respect to corporate governance and was followed by an introduction to the Chinese securities market. To better understand the PRC securities disclosure regime, a basic knowledge of the PRC legal system was provided in Chapter 3, which also briefly reviewed the legal history of China. This book has sought to identify how this history has affected lawmaking in the PRC and has focused on lawmaking and enforcement in the PRC. An analysis of sources of law in the PRC has provided the reader with a broad picture of the structure of Chinese law and its differences from those of other countries. By examining the procedures for lawmaking and rule making in the PRC, one can trace the development of PRC corporate disclosure rules, and by reviewing the poor record of enforcement of law in the PRC, one can understand why there have been so many cases involving violations of disclosure rules.

Chapter 4 examined all kinds of participants in the PRC securities market. Examining their functions in and involvement with the securities market has identified disclosure problems in listed companies. Chapter 5 analysed the securities regulatory rules and provided a picture of the PRC regulatory regime. The discussion of the process of the making of disclosure rules has shown the problems that exist with the PRC's disclosure regime. Chapter 6 introduced the development of the Chinese securities market as well as false disclosure cases that have occurred in this market. This chapter also identified the problems with the current disclosure regulatory regime in the PRC. It showed the large gap that exists between PRC's disclosure rules and disclosure practices. Chapter 7 discussed key features of the Australian securities regulatory regime, with a detailed analysis of how Australia studied and adapted foreign laws to its corporate disclosure regime so as to improve it. The final chapter concluded that China's corporate disclosure laws should reflect its own cultural, economic, and political features, even though such laws had been heavily borrowed. The ineffectiveness of China's corporate disclosure laws is partly a result of the fact that China has not adopted an appropriate way to transplant foreign laws into its own unique environment. This chapter also suggested that the Australian experience be accepted as a model for China's transplanting of foreign laws.

In June 2002, Zhou Xiaochuan, then Chairman of the CSRC, said at the IOSCO Annual Meeting that, 'The capital market of the PRC is a new market and a transitional market'.[47] This was, in effect, an acknowledgment of the fragile and changing character of the Chinese securities market. This acknowledgment was not surprising, because the Chinese securities market has only a short history of about two decades. Compared with sophisticated securities markets, the PRC securities market is in a transitional stage in terms of market size, the quality of listed companies, supervision standards, corporate governance, and the securities regulatory system. One of the problems associated with this market is that the investors in the Chinese securities market are less influenced by the information disclosed by listed companies in their investment decision-making than are their counterparts in more sophisticated markets. There are many causes of this problem: the conduct of the participants in the market is often influenced by rumours and speculation; fraudulent and misleading conduct by listed companies occurs too often; securities regulatory rules are not comprehensive; the functions of the regulators are not effective; and compliance with disclosure laws by listed companies is very poor. These features of the Chinese securities market continue to result in high levels of speculation on the part of securities investors.

As a transitional economy, the PRC securities market is still strongly influenced by the plans and command of the state. The government's interference in the securities market is still very obvious.[48] As a result, state-owned shares play a dominant part in the shareholding structure in most listed companies, although this had been weakened by the divisions established by the state shareholding reform that started in 2005. The conduct of intermediaries in this market often does not

---

47. <www.cs.com.cn>, 19 Jun. 2002.
48. A typical example is the decision to reduce state-owned shares and then the decision to suspend reduction of state-owned shares in 2001.

comply with laws and rules. This transitional market produces inexperienced investors in the Chinese securities market who greatly lack sensibility in investment decision-making.

During this transitional period, the development of the securities market has to pass through a developing stage to a developed and sophisticated stage. Therefore, it is not practical to crudely evaluate this market with the standards used to evaluate a sophisticated market. By the same token, it is also wrong for China to simply copy the rules of complicated markets and impose them wholesale on the Chinese situation. This book has argued that to develop its securities market, the PRC has to learn selectively from foreign experiences. As the PRC is culturally, historically, and politically very different from Western countries, it should focus more on its domestic situation while still drawing upon lessons from sophisticated securities markets. Simple and uncritical borrowing of disclosure rules from sophisticated markets does not result in the expected effect. PRC legislators therefore have to change their misconceived idea that 'Bad law is better than no law' because the securities market has shown that bad law can be worse than no law.

In contrast with the Chinese securities market, the Australian securities market is certainly highly developed. This book has argued that the Australian experience, which has been acknowledged as being largely neglected in the Western corporate world,[49] should be used as one of the major foreign models in China's efforts to improve its securities regulation, especially in the area of corporate disclosure. The formation of the Australian disclosure regulatory regime, especially the continuous disclosure regime, offers good experiences for the PRC to relate to and learn from. Australia's diverse means of protection of shareholders can also provide useful lessons for the PRC. In particular, the way that Australian lawmakers have studied the corporate disclosure rules of other countries can provide valuable guidance for the improvement of China's securities regulatory regime.

---

49. Cheffins, B, 'Comparative Corporate Governance and the Australian Experience', in *Key Developments in Corporate Law and Trusts Law*, ed. I.M. Ramsay (Sydney: LexisNexis Butterworths, 2002), 13.

Bibliography

PART I   MATERIALS ON CHINA

A.   BOOKS AND BOOK CHAPTERS

Bian, Y.W. (ed.). *Basic Knowledge and Practice of Securities Law* (in Chinese). Beijing: Tongxin Press, 1999.

Bian, Y.W. (ed.). *American Law of Securities Transactions* (Chinese translation). Beijing: Law Publishing House, 1999.

Cai, J.W. *Declaration of Individual Investors* (in Chinese). Shenzhen: Haitian Publishing House, 2000.

Cao, F.Q. *Development and Standardization of Chinese Securities Markets & Internationalization* (in Chinese). Beijing: China Finance Press, 1998.

Cecil, R.D., Y.C. Zhang & M.J. Ma. *The Chinese Financial System*. Westport: Greenwood Press, 1994.

Chen, D.G. 'Chapter 6: The Regulation of Secured Transactions in Emerging Chinese Stock Markets'. In *Commercial Laws in the People's Republic of China: Regulation and Reform Affecting the Market*, edited by B. Bacher & H.L. Fu. Singapore: Butterworths Asia, 1995.

Chen, G., S.Y. Zhou & X.Q. Wu. *Securities Issue and Trade* (in Chinese). Beijing: China People University Press, 1998.

Chen, H.W. (ed.). *Securities Markets and the Supervision of Accounting* (in Chinese). Beijing: China Finance and Economics Press, 2001.

Chen, J.F. *Chinese Law: Towards an Understanding of Chinese Law, Its Nature and Development*. The Hague: Kluwer Law International, 1999.

Chen, J.F., Y.W. Li & J.M. Otto (eds). *Implementation of Law in the People's Republic of China*. The Hague: Kluwer Law International, 2002.

Cheng, S.W. (ed.). *Diagnosis and Treatment: Revealing the Stock Market of China*. Beijing: Economic Science Press, 2002.

China Securities Regulatory Commission (ed.). *Collection of Essays and Articles from the International Symposium on Securities Law Bill* (in Chinese and English). Beijing: Law Press, 1997.

China Securities Regulatory Commission (ed.). *Disclosure Requirements of China Securities Market 2001* (in Chinese). Beijing: China Finance and Economics Publishing House, 2001.

China Securities Regulatory Commission. *China Capital Markets Development Report* (in Chinese). Beijing: China Finance Press, 2008.

Dong, H. *On Judicial Interpretation* (in Chinese). Beijing: China University of Politics and Law Press, 1999.

Dong, S.P. *China's Securities Policies and Securities Trading* (in Chinese). Beijing: Economy and Management Publishing House, 1997.

Drafting Group of the PRC Securities Law. *Annotation of the PRC Securities Law* (in Chinese). Beijing: China Finance Press, 1999.

Economy and Technology Publishing House. *Year Book of the Shenzhen Stock Exchange 1996* (in Chinese). Beijing: Economy and Technology Publishing House, 1996.

Gan, P. & L. Jianbo (eds). *Studies on Corporate Governance.* Beijing: Peking University Press, 2009.

Gao, R.X. & M.X. Wang. *American Securities Law* (Chinese translation). Beijing: Law Publishing House, 2000.

Gao, S.Q. & F.L. Chi (ed.). *The Chinese Securities Market.* Beijing: Foreign Languages Press, 1996.

Gao, X.M. (ed.). *The Secrets of Listed Companies* (in Chinese). Beijing: World Publishing Corp., 2001.

Gao, Y. & P.J. Yi (ed.). *Understanding and Application of Securities Law and Comments on Securities Cases* (in Chinese). Beijing: People's Court Press, 1997.

Guo, F. *China Securities Regulation and Legislation* (in Chinese). Beijing: Law Press, 2000.

Harrison, M. *Asia Pacific Securities Markets.* Hong Kong: Law & Tax Asia Pacific, 1997.

Hong, W.L. *Securities Regulation: Theory and Practice* (in Chinese). Shanghai: Shanghai Finance and Economics University Press, 2000.

Hu, J.Y. & W.L. Li. *An Analysis of Securities Cases* (in Chinese). Jinan: Shandong University Press, 2000.

Hu, Y.Z. *Legal Regulation of the Securities Market* (in Chinese). Beijing: China Legal System Press, 1999.

Hua, S. *An Economic Analysis of China's Securities Market* (in Chinese). Beijing: Economic Science Press, 2004.

Huang, P.C.C. *Code, Custom, and Legal Practice in China: The Qing and the Republic Compared.* Palo Alto: Stanford University Press, 2001.

Huang, R.J. *Securities Legal Theory and Practice* (in Chinese). Beijing: Publishing House of Law, 1997.

Jiang, Ping. *To Shout Is My Duty* (in Chinese). Beijing: Law Press, 2007.

Jin, D.H. *Contemporary Securities Market of China* (in Chinese). Shanghai: Shanghai Finance and Economics University Press, 1999.

Lang, L.H.P. *Corporate Governance* (in Chinese). Beijing: Social and Scientific Publishing, 2004.

Lees, F.A. & K. Liaw. *Foreign Participation in China's Banking and Securities Markets*. Westport: Quorum Books, 1994.

Leng, Jing. *Corporate Governance and Financial Reform in China's Transition Economy*. Hong Kong: Hong Kong University Press, 2009.

Li, J. *Legal System History of China* (in Chinese). Beijing: University of International Business and Economics Press, 2007.

Li, Z.Z. *Report on the Development of the Chinese Securities Market* (in Chinese). Beijing: World Knowledge Press, 2000.

Liu, S.Q. *Annotation of Securities Law* (in Chinese). Beijing: People's Court Press, 1999.

Lu, F.Q. *A Legal Perspective of Information Disclosure* (in Chinese). Beijing: People's Court Press, 2000.

Lubman, S. *Bird in a Cage: Legal Reform in China after Mao*. Palo Alto: Stanford University Press, 1999.

Nie, Q.P. 'Chapter 7: Legal Structure of the Securities Market in China'. In Wang CG and XC Zhang (eds) *Commercial Laws in the People's Republic of China: Regulation and Reform Affecting the Market*. Singapore: Butterworths Asia, 1995.

Otto, J.M., et al. *Law Making in the People's Republic of China*. The Hague: Kluwer Law International, 2000.

Peerenboom, R. *China's Long March toward Rule of Law*. Cambridge: Cambridge University Press, 2002.

Qi, B. *Information Disclosure Regulations on the Stock Market* (in Chinese). Beijing: Law Publishing House, 2000.

Qiao, X.Y. (ed.). *Lectures on the Law on Law Making*. Beijing: China Democracy and Legal System Press, 2000.

Ratner, D. *Securities Regulation*. Beijing: Law Press and West Group, 1999.

Ren, J.L. *The Implementing Rules for the Chinese Securities Law: An Analysis and Comment on Classic Cases*. Beijing: China Procurator Publishing House, 2000.

Securities Times (ed.). *Collection of Securities Economic Essays* (in Chinese). Beijing: China Economy Press, 1997.

Securities Times (ed.). *Transparency of Securities Phenomena* (in Chinese). Beijing: China Economy Press, 1997.

Shanghai Stock Exchange. *Practical Guidelines for the Listed Companies*. Shanghai: Shanghai Stock Exchange, 1997.

Shanghai Stock Exchange. *China Corporate Governance Report 2003*. Shanghai: Fudan University Press, 2003.

Shanghai Stock Exchange. *China Corporate Governance Report 2004: Independence and Effectiveness of Boards of Directors* (in Chinese). Shanghai: Fudan University Press, 2004.

Shanghai Stock Exchange. *China Corporate Governance Report 2005: Corproate Governance of Listed Private Holding Companies* (in Chinese). Shanghai: Fudan University Press, 2005.

Shanghai Stock Exchange. *China Corporate Governance Report 2006: Corporate Governance of State Holding Listed Companies* (in Chinese). Shanghai: Fudan University Press, 2006.

Shanghai Stock Exchange. *Markets Quality Report 2009 of the Shanghai Stock Exchange*. Shanghai: Shanghai Stock Exchange, 2009.

Shi, T.T. *Research on Legal Issues in Related Parties*. Beijing: Law Publishing House, 1998.

Shi, T.T. *Annotation and Comments of Securities Law* (in Chinese). Beijing: Industry and Commerce Press, 1999.

Song, Y.N. & S.Q. Liu. *Textbook on China's Company Law* (in Chinese). Beijing: University Press of the Central Committee of the Chinese Communist Party, 1994.

Tam, O.K. *The Development of Corporate Governance in China*. Cheltenham: Edward Elgar Publishing Limited, 1999.

The NPC Drafting Group of the Securities Law. *Annotation of the PRC Securities Law*. Beijing: China Financial Press, 1999.

Tokley, I.A. & T. Ravn. *Company and Securities Law in China*. Hong Kong: Sweet & Maxwell Asia, 1998.

Tong, D.C. *The Heart of Economic Reform: China's Banking Reform and State Enterprise Restructuring*. Burlington: Ashgate, 2002.

Tu, G. & C. Zhu (eds). *Corproate Governance: International Experience and Chinese Practice* (in Chinese). Beijing: People's Press, 2001.

Walter, C.E. & F.J.T. Howie. *'To Get Rich Is Glorious!' China's Stock Markets in the '80s and '90s*. Hong Kong: Palgrave, 2001.

Walter, C.E. & F.J.T. Howie. *Privatizing China: The Stock Markets and Their Role in Corporate Reform*. Singapore: John Wiley & Sons (Asia) Pte Ltd, 2003.

Wang, B.S. *Information Disclosure of Listed Companies and the Protection of the Investors* (in Chinese). In *Collection of Commercial Law Theses*, vol. 1. Beijing: Law Press, 1997, 279–280.

Wang, B.S. (ed.). *Chinese Commercial Law* (in Chinese). Beijing: People's Court Press, 1996.

Wang, H.B. (ed.). *Chinese Shareholders: What You Can Get from Securities Law* (in Chinese). Beijing: Dragon Gate Press, 1999.

Wang, J.C.F. *Contemporary Chinese Politics: An Introduction*. 7th edn. Upper Saddle River: Prentice Hall, 2002.

Wang, J.L. *Textbook of Securities Cases* (in Chinese). Beijing: Economic Management Press, 2000.

Wang, K.G. *A Thought of Cross-Century Development of the Chinese Securities Markets* (in Chinese). Shanghai: Shanghai Finance and Economics University Press, 1999.

Wang, L.Z. & C. Li (eds). *Uneasy Securities Law* (in Chinese). Shanghai: Shanghai Sanlian Bookshop Press, 2000.

Wang, W.G. & R. Tomasic (eds). *Reform of PRC Securities and Insolvency Law.* Beijing: China University of Politics and Law Press, 1999.

Wang, Y.M. & A. Jiang. *The Economic Law Perspective of State-Owned Enterprises Reform* (in Chinese). Beijing: China University of People's Public Security Press, 2001.

Wen, C.Y. & H.Q. Leng. *Securitization of Ownership and Second Board Capital Raising* (in Chinese). Beijing: China Finance Press, 2000.

Wu, J.L. *Ten-Year History of Share Markets* (in Chinese). Shanghai: Shanghai Far East Press, 2001.

Wu, J.L. *Reform: Now at a Critical Point* (in Chinese). Beijing: Sanlian Bookshop, 2002.

Wu, Z.P. & J.J. Bai (eds). *Law and Practice of Securities Transactions* (in Chinese). Beijing: China University of Politics and Law Press, 2000.

Xu, Z.H. & H. Zheng (eds). *Analysis of Selective Securities Law* (in Chinese). Shanghai: Oriental Publishing Centre, 2001.

Yang, M.X. & L. Xin. *A Collection of Most Recent Shareholding Cases* (in Chinese), Beijing: China Metropolitan Press, 1998.

Yang, Z.H. *Research on the Securities Legal System.* Beijing: University Press of China, University of Politics and Law, 1995.

Yao, G. (ed.). *The Risks and Their Prevention in the Chinese Securities Markets* (in Chinese). Guangzhou: Guangdong Economics Press, 2000.

Ye, L. *Securities Law of China* (in Chinese). Beijing: China Auditing Press, 1999.

Yu, G.H. & M.K. Gu. *Laws Affecting Business Transactions in the PRC.* The Hague: Kluwer Law International, 2001.

Zhang, Youyu. *Select Essays of Zhang Youyu* (in Chinese), vols 1 and 2. Beijing: Law Press, 1997.

Zheng, S.Y. *Law and Practice of Misconduct in the Securities Market* (in Chinese). Beijing: China University of Politics and Law Press, 2000.

Zheng, Z.L. *Comparative Study of Securities Markets in Different Countries* (in Chinese). Beijing: China Development Press, 1996.

Zheng, Z.L. *A Brief History of the Chinese Securities Development* (in Chinese). Beijing: Economic Science Press, 2000.

Zhu, S.Z. *Securities Regulation in China.* Ardsley, NY: Transnational Publishers, 2000.

Zhu, S.Z. *Securities Dispute Resolution in China.* Surrey: Ashgate, 2007.

Zhou, Y.S. *On Securities Law* (in Chinese). Chengdu: Sichuan People's Press, 1999.

Zhou, Z.Q. *Guiding Theories of Securities Markets.* Beijing: China Finance Press, 1998.

Zhou, Z.Q. *Textbook on Securities Knowledge.* Beijing: China Finance Press, 1998.

Zhu, W.Y. *An Analysis of American Company Law Cases.* Beijing: China Legal System Press, 2000.

B.   Aʀᴛɪᴄʟᴇs

Art, R.C. & M.K. Gu. 'China Incorporated: The First Corporation Law of the People's Republic of China'. *Yale Journal of International Law* 20 (1995): 273.

Bergman, M.S., R. Borisoff & N.C. Howson. 'First Direct Listing for Chinese Company in New York'. *International Financial Law Review* 13, no. 12 (1994): 41–44.

Brink, D.J. & L.L. Xiao. 'A Legal and Practical Overview of Direct Investment and Joint Ventures in the New China'. *Journal of Marshall Law Review* 28 (1995): 567.

Chan, C. 'New Law to Scrap A-Shares Classes'. *South China Morning Post*, 10 December 1993.

Chan, C. 'One A-Share: Many Gains, but Several Headaches'. *South China Morning Post*, 21 December 1993.

Chen, J.F. 'Securitization of State-Owned Enterprises and the Ownership Controversy in the PRC'. *The Sydney Law Review* 15 (1993): 59–85.

Chen, K. 'China to Establish Regional Exchanges'. *South China Morning Post*, 26 November 1993.

Chen, K. 'Legislators Press on with Securities Law'. *South China Morning Post*, 6 August 1993.

Chen, K. 'Share Trading Rules to Be Revealed Soon'. *South China Morning Post*, 3 May 1993.

Chen, S. & M.Y. Lu. 'On the Basic Principles of Information Disclosure of Listed Companies' (in Chinese). Copied Newspaper and Journal Articles by the People's University. *Economic Law and Labour Law* 6 (1998): 21–28.

Daly, B. 'Of Shares, Securities and Stakes: The China Insider Trading Law and the Stakeholder Theory of Legal Analysis'. *The American University Journal of International Law and Policy* 11 (1996): 971–1026.

Fang, L.F. 'China's Corporatization Experiment'. *Duke Journal of Comparative and International Law* 5 (1995): 149–174.

Fu, J. 'Information Disclosure and Corporate Governance in Listed Companies in China: From Yinguangxia to Enron'. *Australian Journal of Corporate Law* 17, no. 1 (2004): 48–70.

Fu, J. 'Information Disclosure and Investor Protection in China's Securities Markets'. *Australian Journal of Corporate Law* 9, no. 2 (1998): 194–220.

Fu, J. 'The Enterprise Concept in Chinese Law and Its Application in PRC Company Law'. *Australian Journal of Corporate Law* 8, no. 3 (1998): 266–299.

Fung, N. 'Commonwealth Influence Reform'. *South China Morning Post*, 20 September 1995.

Gao, X.Q. 'The Perceived Unreasonable Man: A Response to Fang Liufang'. *Duke Journal of Comparative & International Law* 5 (1995): 271–288.

Gao, X.Q. 'Developments in Securities and Investment Law in China'. *Australian Journal of Corporate Law* 6 (1996): 228–247.

Gao, X.Q. 'The Theoretical Bases for the System of Compulsory Information Disclosure in Securities Markets' (in Chinese). *The Shenzhen Securities Market Directory*, 4 October 1996, 17.

Gao, X.Q. 'Compulsory Disclosure and the Effectiveness of Securities Market'. *Shanghai Securities Daily*, 25 February 1997, 9, 10.

Gao, X.Q. 'The Art of Working with Four Sets of Laws in One Country'. *The National Business Review*, 12 December 1997, 14.

Gu, M.K. & R. Art. 'Securitization of State Ownership: Chinese Securities Law'. *Michigan Journal of International Law* 18 (Fall, 1996): 115–139.

Guo, F. (ed.). 'What Values the Judiciary Should Hold: Beginning with the Difficult Acceptance of Securities Civil Compensation Cases by the Courts'. *Securities Law Review* 3 (2003): 319–326.

He, M. 'Several Questions to Be Corrected in the Approval and Information Disclosure of Listed Companies' (in Chinese). *People's Daily*, 18 June 1997.

Hu, J. 'A Research on the System of False Information Disclosure in the Securities Law' (in Chinese). *Civil and Commercial Law Review* 3 (1998): 607–697.

Hsu, P.S.P. & L.S. Liu. 'The Transformation of the Securities Market in Taiwan, the People's Republic of China'. *Columbia Journal of Transnational Law* 27 (1988): 169–194.

International Securities Regulation Report. 'Discrepancies with Provisional Rules Delays Passage of New Securities Law'. *International Securities Regulation Report*, 19 October 1993.

Johns, D.K. 'Reforming the State-Enterprise Property Relationship in the People's Republic of China: The Corporatization of State-Owned Enterprises'. *Michigan Journal of International Law* 16 (1995): 911.

Lai, R. 'New Law Fails on Overseas Listings'. *South China Morning Post*, 18 March 1994, 5.

Latimer, M.D. 'Gilding the Iron Rice Bowl: The Illusion of Shareholder Rights in China'. *Washington Law Review* 69 (1994): 1097–1119.

Leung, C.Y. '"Red Chips" Face Quotas under the New Rules'. *China Law and Practice* 11, no. 6 (1997): 47.

Li, B.S. 'The Characteristics and Lessons of the Securities Legislation in Contemporary China' (in Chinese). *Science of Law* 3 (1996): 20.

Li, Y.N. 'Shenzhen Must Be Prepared for Shanghai Threat'. *South China Morning Post*, 13 December 1993.

Li, Y.N. 'Standardization Needed for Balance'. *South China Morning Post*, 14 February 1994.

Li, Y.N. 'Viewpoint: Proposed Securities Law Faces Major Difficulties'. *South China Morning Post*, 18 April 1994, 4.

Lin, G.C. & L. Peng. 'The Effectiveness of Chinese Securities Markets and the Standardization of Disclosure of Listed Companies'. *Financial Theory and Practice*, 1997, 45.

Liu, L.S. & P. Potter. 'Foreign Access to Securities Markets in Taiwan and the People's Republic of China'. *Melbourne University Law Review* 19 (1993): 330–351.

Montagnon, P. 'China Blames Two Firms for Bonds Scandal'. *Financial Times*, 22 September 1995.

Nottle, R. 'The Development of Securities Markets in China in the 1990s'. *Company and Securities Law Journal* 11 (1993): 503–523.

Potter, P.B. 'The Legal Framework for Securities Markets in China: The Challenge of Maintaining State Control and Inducing Investor Confidence'. *China Law Reporter* 7 (1992): 59–94.

Qian, A.X. 'Riding Two Horses: Corporatizing Enterprises and the Emerging Securities Regulatory Regime in China'. *UCLA Pacific Basin Law Journal* 12 (Fall, 1993): 62–97.

Qian, A.X. 'Why Does Not the Rising Water Lift the Boat? Internationalization of the Stock Exchange Market and the Securities Regulatory Regime'. *The International Lawyer* 29 (Fall, 1995): 615–632.

Reuter Textline. 'China: Securities Law Expected This Year'. *Shanghai Star*, 14 April 1995.

Roll, S. 'What Does the Future Hold for B and H Shares'. *China Law and Practice* 10 (1996): 17.

Shen Z.L. 'On Legal Transplant and Comparative Law'. *Comparative Law in China* 1 (2001): 67–77.

Shinkle, J.T. 'Observations on Capital Market Regulation: Hong Kong and the People's Republic of China'. *University of Pennsylvania Journal of International Economic Law* 18 (Spring, 1997): 255–296.

Solomon, M.K. 'Securities Markets and China's International Integration'. *Journal of International Affairs* 49 (1996): 525.

South China Morning Post. 'Shanghai Futures to Trade on Monday'. *South China Morning Post*, 2 October 1993.

South China Morning Post. 'Amendments to Law Should Challenge Market'. *South China Morning Post*, 11 April 1994, 3.

South China Morning Post. 'Overseas Share Listing Controls to Be Published'. *South China Morning Post*, 7 June 1994, 5.

South China Morning Post. 'China: Rule Change to Clean up Bond Market'. *South China Morning Post*, 2 February 1995.

South China Morning Post. 'China Bond Issues Set to Double'. *South China Morning Post*, 1 November 1996.

Tarbutton, B.R. 'China: A National Regulatory Framework for the PRC's Stock Markets Begins to Merge'. *Ga. J. Int'l and Comp. L.* 24 (1994): 411–420.

The Reuter Asia-Pacific Business Report. 'China Promises Securities Law Soon'. *BC Cycle*, 15 September 1994.

Tobert, P.M. 'Broadening the Scope of Investment'. *The China Business Review* 21, no. 3 (1994): 48.

Wang, G.W. 'Out of the Weak Market with an Incomplete Structure'. *Shanghai Securities*, 20 February 1997, 3.

Wong, K.M. 'Securities Regulation in China and Their Corporate Finance Implications on State Enterprise Reform'. *Fordham Law Review* 65 (1996): 1221–1245.

Xi, X.M. & W. Jia. 'The Civil Compensation System on False Disclosure in the Securities Market: An Analysis of the *Several Provisions on the Civil Compensation Cases of False Disclosure in the Securities Market*. Released by the Supreme Peoples' Court on 1 January 2003'. In *Securities Law Review*, edited by F. Guo. 3 (2003): 33–75.

Yang, M.Y. 'A Study on the Civil Liability for False Statement in Securities Issue'. *Securities Law Review* 1 (2001): 123–170.

Yi, C.Z. & D. Yu. 'China's Emerging Securities Market'. *Columbia Journal of World Business* 29 (1994): 113.

Zhang, J.Z. 'Securities Markets and Securities Regulation in China'. *The North Carolina Journal of International Law and Commercial Regulation* 22 (Winter, 1997): 557–630.

Zhang, Y.P. 'Pay Attention to the Market Risks Caused by Improper Disclosure'. *Shanghai Securities*, 19 January 1997, 3.

Zheng, H.R. 'Business Organisation and Securities Law of the People's Republic of China'. *The Business Lawyer* 43 (1988): 549–619.

Zhou, W.X. 'Analysis of the Shortcomings of the CSRC's Interim Provisions on the *Jinru* System in the Securities Market' (in Chinese). Copied Newspaper and Journal Articles by People's University: *Economic Law and Labour Law* 8 (1998): 50–52.

Zhou, Z.Q. 'The Amendment to the Securities Law Is Good for a Long Term'. *China Securities Daily*, 27 April 2005, 3.

C.   Relevant Laws and Regulations

Laws by the National People's Congress of the PRC or Its Standing Committee

The PRC Company Law of 2005.
The PRC Securities Law of 2005.
The PRC Company Law of 1993.
The PRC Securities Law of 1998.
The PRC Criminal Law of 1979 and the Amendments.
Decision of the Standing Committee of the National People's Congress Concerning Punishment of Crimes against the Company Law (28 February 1995).
Law on the People's Bank of China of 1995.
Law on Commercial Banks of 1995.
Arbitration Law of 1995.
Decision of the Standing Committee of the National People's Congress on Punishment of Crimes of Disrupting Financial Order (30 June 1995).
Law on Negotiable Instruments of 1995.
Law on Administrative Penalty of 1996.
Securities Law (29 December 1998).
Law on Law-making of 2000.
The Constitution of 1982 and its Amendments in 2004.

Administrative Regulations (by the State Council or its General Office) and Departmental Administrative Rules (by the Ministries)

The Provisional Regulations on the Administration of Share Issue and Trading (22 April 1993).

Regulations on State Treasury Bonds (18 May 1992).

The Administrative Regulations on Enterprise Debentures (2 August 1993).

The Urgent Circular of the General Office of the State Council on Stopping Issuing of Domestic Staff Shares (3 April 1993).

The Circular of the General Office of the State Council on the Implementation of the Standard Opinions on the Joint Stock Companies (15 May 1993).

The Administrative Regulations on Foreign-Invested Financial Institutions (25 February 1994).

The Administrative Regulations on Company Registration (24 June 1994).

Special Regulations of the State Council on the Joint Stock Companies Offering Shares and Seeking A Listing Overseas (4 August 1994).

The Administrative Measures on the Establishment of Chinese Industrial Investment Funds outside China (6 September 1995).

The Regulations of the State Council on the Listing of the Foreign Shares inside China by the Joint Stock Companies (25 December 1995).

The Circular of the State Council on the Standardization of the Old Limited Liability Companies and the Joint Stock Companies in Accordance with the Company Law (3 July 1995).

The Circular of the General Office of the State Council on Transmitting the Instructions Regarding the Suspension of the Assignment of the State Shares and the Legal Entity Shares to Foreign Business persons (23 September 1995).

Departmental Administrative Rules (by Government Departments)

The Measures on the Testing of Joint Stock Enterprise (15 May 1992).

Standard Opinions on the Joint Stock Limited Liability Companies (15 May 1992).

Standard Opinions on the Limited Liability Companies (15 May 1992).

The Provisional Administrative Regulations on the State Assets of the State-Owned Joint Stock Testing Enterprises (27 July 1992).

The Administrative Measures of the State Assets Administration and the Ministry of Finance on the Collecting of the Interests of the Shares of the Joint Stock Testing State-Owned Enterprises (1992).

The Provisional Administrative Measures on the Stock Exchanges (7 July 1993).

The Provisional Measures on the Prohibition of Securities Frauds (2 September 1993).

The Report of the CSRC on the Problems Regarding the Issuing and Listing of Domestic Enterprises' Shares outside China (9 April 1993).

The Circular of the State Council's Securities Commission Regarding the Authorization of the CSRC to Investigate and Punish the Conduct Violating the Relevant Securities Laws and Regulations (17 August 1993).

The Circular of the CSRC on the Required Materials by the Enterprises Publicly Issuing Shares (3 June 1993).

Appendix 1: Standard Form for the Required Materials by the Enterprises Applying for Publicly Issuing Shares (Provisional).

Appendix 2: Rule No. 1 of the Rules on the Content and Format of Information Disclosure by the Enterprises Publicly Issuing Shares: Instructions on the Format and Content of the Prospectus.

The Circular of the CSRC on the Enactment of Implementing Rules on Information Disclosure by the Enterprises Publicly Issuing Shares (Provisional) (10 June 1993).

Appendix: The Implementing Rules on Information Disclosure by the Enterprises Publicly Issuing Shares.

The Circular of the CSRC on Strengthening the Function of the Securities Underwriters and Professional Intermediaries in the Process of Share Issue (24 June 1993).

The Provisional Regulations of the CSRC on the Share Allocation by the Listed Companies (17 December 1993).

The Circular of the State Commission for Restructuring the Economic System Regarding the Compulsory Provisions of the Memorandum of the Enterprises Applying for Being Listed in Hong Kong (10 June 1993).

The Administrative Regulations of the State Commission for Restructuring the Economic System on the Domestic Staff Shares Issued to Certain People by the Joint Stock Limited Companies (1 July 1993).

The Circular of the State Commission for Restructuring the Economic System on Standardization (*qing li*) of the Non-standard Conduct in Staff Shareholding of the Joint Stock Limited Companies (5 July 1993).

The Circular of the State Council's Securities Commission and the State Commission for Restructuring the Economic System on the Enforcement of the Compulsory Provisions in the Memorandum of the Companies Listing Overseas (27 August 1994).

Appendix: The Compulsory Provisions in the Memorandum of the Companies Listing Overseas.

The Circular of the CSRC on the Notice of Rule No. 2 on the Content and Form of Information Disclosure by the Publicly Share-Issuing Companies: Content and Format of Annual Report (Provisional) (10 January 1994).

Appendix: The Instructions on Rule No. 2 on the Content and Form of Information Disclosure by the Publicly Share-Issuing Companies: Content and Format of Annual Report.

The Letter of the CSRC on the Collecting and Administration of the Shares of the Companies Listed in the Shanghai Stock Exchange by the Shanghai Securities Central Registration and Clearing Company (16 August 1994).

The Letter of the CSRC on the Collecting and Administration of the Shares of the Companies Listed in the Shenzhen Stock Exchange by the Shenzhen Securities Registration Ltd. Co. (16 August 1994).

The Circular of the CSRC on the Notice of Rule No. 3 on the Content and Form of Information Disclosure by the Publicly Share-Issuing Companies: Content and Format of Half-Year Report (Provisional) (23 June 1994).

Appendix: Instructions on Rule No. 3 on the Content and Format of Information Disclosure by the Publicly Share-Issuing Companies: Content and Format of Half-Year Report.

The Circular of the CSRC on the Enforcement of the Company Law and the Standardization of Listing and Share Allocation (28 September 1994).

The Circular of the CSRC on the Notice of Rule No. 6 on the Content and Format of Information Disclosure (28 October 1994).

Appendix: Rule No. 6 on the Content and Format of Information Disclosure by the Publicly Share-Issuing Companies.

The Circular of the CSRC on the Notice of the Detailed Regulations on the Share Allocation (*pei gu*) Application and Information Disclosure by the Listed Companies (27 October 1994).

Appendix 1: The Detailed Regulations on the Share Allocation and Information Disclosure by the Listed Companies.

Appendix 2: Instructions on Rule No. 4 on the Content and Format of Information Disclosure by the Listed Companies.

Appendix 3: Instructions on Rule No. 5 on the Content and Format of Information Disclosure by Listed Companies.

The Supplementation of the State Commission for Restructuring the Economic System and the State Securities Commission on the Allocation and Sale of Shares to Their Staff by the Publicly Listed Companies (1 February 1994).

The Circular of the State Commission for Restructuring the Economic System on the Immediate Stop to Approve the Joint Stock Companies Issuing Certain Shares and to Issue Domestic Staff Shares (19 June 1994).

The Provisional Measures of the State Assets Administration and the State Commission for Restructuring the Economic System on the Administration of State-Owned Shares in the Joint Stock Companies (3 November 1994).

The Circular of the State Council's Securities Commission and the State Commission for Reconstructing the Economic System on the 1995 Shareholders' General Meeting and the Amendment of the Memorandum of the Companies Listed Overseas (29 March 1995).

The Circular of the State Securities Commission on the Distribution of the Provisional Regulations on the Qualification Administration of the Securities Professionals (18 April 1995).

Appendix: The Provisional Regulations on the Qualification Administration of the Securities Professionals.

The Circular of the CSRC on Several Issues on the Share-Allocation Application Materials by the Listed Companies (19 January 1995).

The Circular of the CSRC on the Distribution of the Opinions on the Measures for Share Issue and Trading (20 October 1995).

Appendix: Measures for Share Issue and Trading.

The Circular of the CSRC on the Distribution of the Several Provisions on the Mass Media Administration about Information Disclosure of the Shanghai Securities Market (13 November 1995).

Appendix: Several Provisions on the Mass Media Administration about Information Disclosure of the Shanghai Securities Market.

The Circular of the CSRC on the Enforcement of the Company Law and Standardization of Information Disclosure of Listed Companies (21 December 1995).

Appendix: The Instructions on Rule No. 2 on the Content and Format for Information Disclosure: Content and Format of Annual Reports (Revised).

The Circular of the State Securities Commission on the Notice of the Implementation Provisions for the Regulations on the Joint Stock Companies Listing Foreign-Owned Shares inside China (3 March 1996).

Appendix: The Implementation Provisions for the Regulations on the Joint Stock Companies Listing Foreign-Owned Shares inside China.

The Circular of the State Council's Securities Commission on the Distribution of the Business Administrative Measures of the Securities Trading Institutions Underwriting Shares (17 June 1996).

Appendix: The Business Administrative Measures of the Securities Trading Institutions Underwriting Shares.

The Circular of the State Council's Securities Commission on the Notice of the Administrative Measures on the Stock Exchanges (21 August 1996).

Appendix: The Administrative Measures on the Stock Exchanges.

The Circular of the CSRC on the Share Allocation of Listed Companies in 1996 (24 January 1996).

Appendix: The Standard Format for the Application Materials of Listed Companies (Provisional).

The Circular of the CSRC on the Prohibition of Undue Conduct in the Process of Share Issue (25 January 1996).

The Circular of the CSRC on the Standardization of the Shareholders' General Meetings of the Listed Companies (10 February 1996).

The Circular of the CSRC on the Authorization to the Local Securities and Futures Regulatory Departments Enforcing Part of its Regulatory Powers (21 May 1996).

The Circular of the CSRC on the Standardization of the Enterprises Debentures Listed and Traded on the Stock Exchanges (5 June 1996).

The Circular of the CSRC on the Administration of the Directors, Supervisors and Managers Holding Company Shares (22 April 1996).

The Circular of the CSRC on the Strengthening of Local Newspapers and Other Mass Media about the Information about the Securities and Futures Market (29 May 1996).

The Circular of the CSRC on the Notice of Rule No. 3 on the Content and Format of Information Disclosure by the Publicly Share-Issuing Companies: Content and Format of the Half-Yearly Report (Revised) (20 June 1996).

Appendix: Content and Format of the Half-Yearly Report (Revised).

The Circular of the CSRC on the Strict Administration of the Account Opening of B Shares (28 June 1996).

The Circular of CSRC on the Opinions on the Problems in the Process of B Share Issue (17 July 1996).

The Circular of CSRC on the Standardization of Some Company Conduct (24 July 1996).

The Circular of CSRC on the Strict Prohibition of the Manipulation of the Securities Market (31 October 1996).

The Circular of CSRC on the Provisional Regulations on the Forms of Share Issue and Share Trading (26 December 1996).

The Circular of CSRC on Auditing and Reporting in 1998 of Securities Companies (27 January 1999).

The Circular of CSRC on Further Strengthening Supervision of Securities Companies (16 May 1999).

The Circular of CSRC on the Work of Share Allotment (*pei gu*) by Listed Companies (17 March 1999).

CSRC. Rules on Content and Format of Disclosure – Share Allotment (Revision) (17 March 1999).

CSRC. Circular on Strengthening Administration of Consulting and Disclosure by Securities Institution (21 September 1999).

The Circular of CSRC on Distribution of Standard Form for B Shares Issue Application (25 May 1999).

CSRC. Rule No. 6 on Content Format of Disclosure by Listed Companies – Content and Format of Legal Opinions (Revision) (15 June 1999).

CSRC. Regulations on Securities Issue Examination Commission (16 September 1999).

The Circular of CSRC on Improvement of the Quality of Financial Disclosure by Listed Companies (10 October 1999).

The Circular of CSRC on Supplementary Disclosure of Year 2000 Computer Problems by Companies Applying for Share Issue (21 October 1999).

CSRC. Rules on Content and Format of Annual Reports of Securities Companies (19 November 1999).

The Circular of CSRC on the Establishment of Internal Examination Group on Securities Issue (2 December 1999).

The Circular of CSRC on Establishment of System of Examination of Share Issue Application Materials by Main Underwriters (6 December 1999).

The Circular of the CSRC on the Work of Year 1999 Annual Reports by Listed Companies (8 December 1999).

CSRC. Interim Measures for Supervision of Share Issue and Listing (16 March 2000).

CSRC. The Procedures for Approval of Share Issue (16 March 2000).

CSRC. Standard Opinions on Shareholders' General Meeting of Listed Companies (Revised on 18 March 2000).

The Circular of the CSRC on Strengthening Supervision of Disclosure by ST and PT Companies (7 June 2000).

The Circular of the CSRC on Some Issues on Share Issue Quotas for 1997 (7 June 2000).

The Circular of the CSRC on the Arrangement of Share Listing (9 June 2000).

CSRC. Rule No. 3 on the Format and Content of Disclosure by Share Issue Companies (Revised in 2000).

CSRC. Rules on Disclosure Reports of Companies Issuing Securities (No. 1–6) (2 November 2000).

CSRC. Standard Opinions on Improvement of Disclosure of Companies Issuing Shares to the Public (23 December 2000).

The Circular of the CSRC on Issues in the Annual Reports in 2000 of Listed Companies (27 November 2000).

CSRC. Rules on Disclosure Reports of Companies Issuing Shares (Nos 7–8) (21 December 2000).

Ministry of Finance. Accounting Rules for Enterprises: Disclosure of Related Parties and Their Transactions (22 March 1997).

CSRC. Rules No. 1–24 Concerning Content and Format of Disclosure by Listed Companies.

CSRC and State Economics and Trade Commission. Code of Corporate Governance in Listed Companies (7 January 2002).

CSRC. Administrative Measures Concerning Changes of Shareholding by Shareholders in Listed Company (28 September 2002).

CSRC. Several Provisions Concerning Strengthening the Protection of Public Individual Shareholders (12 July 2004).

Ministry of Finance. Accounting Rules for Enterprises – Disclosure of Related Parties and Their Transactions (22 May 1997).

PBOC. Interim Measures Concerning Disclosure by Commercial Banks (15 May 2002).

Judicial Interpretations

Supreme People's Court. Circular Concerning Acceptance of Civil Tort Cases Caused by False Disclosure in the Securities Market (15 January 2002).

Supreme People's Court. Circular Concerning Hearing of Civil Compensation Cases Caused by False Disclosure in the Securities Market (1 September 2003).

The Shanghai Stock Exchange, Listing Rules (1998, 2001, 2004, 2006).

The Shenzhen Stock Exchange, Listing Rules (1998, 2001, 2004, 2006).

PART II   MATERIALS ON AUSTRALIAN AND OTHER
           SECURITIES MARKETS

A.   BOOKS AND BOOK CHAPTERS

Adamson, G. *A Century of Change: The First Hundred Years of the Stock Exchange of Melbourne.* Sydney: Currey O'Neil Ross Pty Ltd, 1984.

Adamson, G. *Miners and Millionaires: The First One Hundred Years of the People, Markets and Companies of the Stock Exchange of Perth, 1889–1989.* Perth: Australian stock Exchange (Perth) Limited, 1989.

Anisman, P. *Insider Trading Legislation for Australia: An Outline of Issues and Alternatives.* Canberra: AGPS, 1986.

ASC. *Commonwealth of Australia Gazette.* Australian Government Public Service, 1992.

Austin, R. & I. Ramsay. *Ford's Principles of Corporations Law.* 12th edn. Sydney: LexisNexis Butterworths, 2005.

Australia National Companies and Securities Commission. *Reforming the Law Relating to Offers of Securities: An Interview Report*, 1988.

Australia Stock Exchange. *Memorandum and Articles of Association and Business Rules.* Sydney: ASX, 1994.

Australian Companies and Securities Advisory Committee. *Netting in Financial Markets Transactions: Financial Report.* Sydney: Australian Companies and Securities Advisory Committee, 1997.

Australian Corporations & Securities Reports. Sydney: Butterworths, 1990.

Australian Parliament House of Representatives Standing Committee on Legal and Constitutional Affairs. *Report on Continuous Disclosure*, 1996.

Australian Parliament House of Representatives Standing Committee on Legal and Constitutional Affairs. *Corporate Practices and the Rights of Shareholders: Report of the House of Representatives Standing Committee on Legal and Constitutional Affairs.* Canberra: Australia Government Service, 1991.

Baxt, R., H.A.J. Ford & A.J. Black. *Securities Industry Law.* Sydney: Butterworths, 1996.

Beaver. 'The Nature of Mandated Disclosure'. In *Economics of Corporations Law and Securities Regulation*, edited by Poster & Scott. New York: Aspen Publishers, 1980.

Blair, M. & I.M. Ramsay. 'Mandatory Corporate Disclosure Rules and Securities Regulation'. In G. Walker (ed.) *Securities Regulation in Australia and New Zealand.* Auckland: Oxford University Press, 1994.

Brandeis, L. *Other People's Money and How the Banks Use It.* Chevy Chase: National Home Library Foundation, 1933.

Cadbury, A. & I.M. Millstein. *The New Agenda for ICGN.* Discussion Paper No. 1 for the ICGN 10th Anniversary Conference, London, July 2005.

Campbell, E., P.Y. Lee & J. Tooher. *Legal Research Materials and Methods.* 4th edn. Sydney: LBC, 1996.

Castan, M. & S. Joseph. *Federal Constitutional Law: A Contemporary View.* Sydney: Law Book Co., 2001.

Cheffins, B.R. 'Comparative Corporate Governance and the Australian Experience'. In *Key Developments in Corporate Law and Trusts Law: Essays in Honour of Professor Harold Ford*, edited by I.M. Ramsay. Chatswood: LexisNexis Butterworths, 2002.

Coffee, J.C., et al. (eds). *Knights, Raiders and Targets: The Impact of the Hostile Takeover.* New York: Oxford University Press, 1988.

Corporate Law Economic Reform Program. *Takeovers: Corporations Law Bulletin.* North Ryde: Butterworths, 1991.

Davies, A. *Best Practice in Corporate Governance: Building Reputation and Sustainable Success.* Aldershot: Gower Publishing Limited, 2006.

Davies, P.L. *Gower's Principles of Modern Company Law.* 6th edn. London: Sweet & Maxwell, 1997.

Davis, P.L. *Gower and Davies' Principles of Modern Company Law.* 7th edn. London: Thomson Sweet & Maxwell, 2003.

Dean, J. *Directing Public Companies: Company Law and the Stockholder Society.* London: Cavendish Publishing, 2001.

Dun & Bradstreet Marketing Pty. *Jobson's Year Book of Public Companies.* Sydney: Dun & Bradstreet Marketing Pty, 1996.

Earp, M.K. & G.M. McGrath. *Listed Companies: Law and Market Practice.* Sydney: LBC Information Services, 1996.

Easterbrook F. & D. Fischel. *The Economic Structure of Corporate Law.* Cambridge: Harvard University Press, 1991.

Farrar, J. *Corporate Governance: Theories, Principles, and Practice.* 2nd edn. Melbourne: Oxford University Press, 2005.

Fisse, B. & J. Braithwaite. *Corporations, Crime and Accountability.* Cambridge: Cambridge University Press, 1993.

Flom, J. *Disclosure Requirements of Public Companies and Insiders.* New York: Practicing Law Institute, 1970.

Ford, H., R. Austin & I.M. Ramsay. *Ford's Principles of Corporations Law.* 12th edn. North Ryde: Butterworths, 2005.

Gibbs, R.M. *Bull, Bears and Wildcats: A Centenary History of the Stock Exchange of Adelaide.* Norwood: Peacock Publications, 1988.

Goodrich, P. *Reading the Law: A Critical Introduction to Legal Method and Techniques.* Oxford: Blackwell, 1986.

Gower, L.C.B. *Principles of Modern Company Law.* 5th edn. London: Sweet & Maxwell, 1992.

Greig, J. & B. Horrigan. *Enforcing Securities.* Sydney: LBC, 1994.

Hall, A.R. *The Stock Exchange of Melbourne and the Victoria Economy 1852–1900.* Canberra: ANU Press, 1968.

Hazen, T.L. *The Law of Securities Regulation.* St Paul: West Publishing Co., 1985.

Hong Kong International Securities Consultancy. *The Capital Guide to China's Securities Markets.* Hong Kong: Hong Kong International Securities Institute, 1994.

Jordan, C. *International Survey of Corporate Law in Asia, Europe, North American and the Commonwealth*. Melbourne: Melbourne University Press, 1997.

Kent, W. 'Implications for Disclosure in Takeover Documents after the ICAL and Cumberland Decisions'. *C&SLJ* 6, no. 4 (1988): 282–292.

Kripke, H. *The SEC and Corporate Disclosure: Regulation in Search of a Purpose.* New York: Law & Business Inc./Harcourt Brace Jovanovich, 1979.

Laster, K. *Law as Culture*. 2nd edn. Sydney: The Federation Press, 2001.

Legal and Constitutional Committee. *Investigatory Powers of the Australia Securities Commission's Report.* Canberra: Legal and Constitutional Committee, 1995.

Levy, R. *Takeovers: Law and Strategy.* Sydney: LBC, 1996.

Little, P. *Law of Company Takeovers.* Sydney: LBC, 1997.

Loss, L. *Fundamentals of Securities Regulation.* Boston: Little Brown & Co., 1988.

Lougheed, A.L. *The Brisbane Stock Exchange 1884–1984.* Brisbane: Boolarong Publications, 1984.

Lubman, S.B. *Bird in a Cage: Legal Reform in China after Mao.* Palo Alto: Stanford University Press, 1999.

Lyon, G. & J.J. du Plessis. *The Law of Insider Trading in Australia.* Lchhardt: The Federation Press, 2005.

Marshman, P. & P. Davies. 'The Role of the Stock Exchange and the Financial Characteristics of Australian Companies'. In *Handbook of Australian Corporate Finance*, edited by R. Bruce et al. 3rd edn. Sydney: Butterworths, 1989, 68–70.

Miller, R.V. *Annotated Trade Practices Act.* Sydney: LBC, 1997.

Nathan, A. *Chinese Democracy.* Berkeley: University of California Press, 1985.

Nathan A.J. & Tianjian Shi. 'Left and Right in Deng's China'. In *China's Transition*, edited by A. Nathan. New York: Columbia University Press, 1997, 174–197.

Neagle, A.M. & N. Tyskin. *'Please Explain': ASX Share Price Queries and the Australian Continuous Disclosure Regime.* The University of Melbourne, Centre for Corporate Law and Securities Regulation, 2001.

Oditah, F. (ed.). *The Future for the Global Securities Market: Legal and Regulatory Aspects.* New York: Clarendon Press, 1996.

Pistor, K. & P. Wellons. *The Role of Law and Legal Institutions in Asian Economic Development 1960–1995.* New York: Oxford University Press, 1999.

Podgorecki, A. *Law and Society.* London: Routledge & Kegan Paul, 1974.

Poser, N.S. *International Securities Regulation.* Boston: Little Brown & Co., 1991.

Ramsay, I. *Independence of Australian Company Auditors: Review of Current Australian Requirements and Proposals for Reform.* Canberra: The Commonwealth of Australia, 2001.

Redmond, P. *Companies and Securities Law: Commentary and Materials.* 3rd edn. Sydney: LBC, 2000.

Romano, R. *Foundations of Corporate Law: Interdisciplinary Readers in Law.* New York: Oxford University Press, 1993.

Salisbury, S. & K. Sweeney. *The Bull, the Bear and the Kangaroo: The History of the Sydney Stock Exchange.* Sydney: Allen & Unwin, 1988.

Senate Economics References Committee. *Inquiry into the Framework for the Market Supervision of Australia's Stock Exchanges.* Canberra: The Senate Printing Unit, 2002.

Senate Select Committee on Securities and Exchanges. *Australian Securities Markets and Their Regulation* (the Rae Report). Canberra: AGPS, 1974.

Stevensen, R.B. *Corporations and Information: Secrecy, Access and Disclosure.* Baltimore: John Hopkins University Press, 1980.

Tokley, I.A. *Company Securities: Disclosure of Interests.* Singapore: Butterworths Asia, 1995.

Tomasic, R. & B. Pentony. *Casino: Capitalism: Insider Trading in Australia.* Canberra: Australian Institute of Criminology, 1991.

Tomasic, R., J. Jackson & R. Woellner. *Corporations Law: Principles, Policy and Process.* 4th edn. North Ryde: Butterworths, 2001.

Tomasic, R., S. Bottomley & R. McQueen. *Corporations Law in Australia.* 2nd edn. Sydney: The Federation Press, 2002.

Tomasic, R. & S. Bottomley. *Directing the Top 500: Corporate Governance and Accountability in Australian Companies.* Sydney: Allen & Unwin, 1993.

Tomasic, R. *The Sociology of Law.* London: Sage, 1985.

Van Den Berghe, L. *Corporate Governance in a Globalising World: Convergence or Divergence? A European's Perspective.* The Hague: Kluwer Academic Publishers, 2002.

Walker, G. (ed.). *Securities Regulation in Australia and New Zealand.* 2nd edn. Sydney: LBC, 1998.

B. ARTICLES

Acquaah-Gaisie, G. 'Toward More Effective Corporate Governance Mechanisms'. *Australian Journal of Corporate Law* 18, no. 1 (2005): 1–47.

Agnew, R. 'Reforming Collective Investments'. *Australian Accountant* 63, no. 11 (1993): 12.

Anderson, R. & M. Epstein. 'The Usefulness of Annual Reports'. *Australian Accountant* (1995): 28.

Andrews, N. 'Management Buyouts: An Un-Australian Activity?'. *Australian Journal of Corporate Law* 5 (1995): 100.

Andrews, N., et al. 'The Death of Privilege for the Privileged'. *Australian Journal of Corporate Law* 5 (1995): 106.

Bartholomeusz, S. 'Carve-Out Rule Shifts Line for Disclosure'. *The Age*, 25 September 2001.

Baxt, R. 'The Achilles Heel of the Disclosure Debate'. *Australian Business Law Review* 19 (1991): 365.

Baxt, R. 'The Full Federal Court Indorses Higher Standards of Disclosure on Directors'. *Company and Securities Law Journal* 11 (1993): 1172.

Benston. 'The Value of the SEC's Accounting Disclosure Requirements'. *Accounting Review* 44 (1969): 515.

Benston, G. 'Required Disclosure and the Stock Market: An Evaluation of the Securities Exchange Act of 1934'. *American Economic Review* 63 (1973): 132.

Bianchi, C. & J. Rosengren. 'Accessing the Capital Markets in the United States'. *New Law Journal* 145 (1995): 865.

Black, J.M. 'An Economic Analysis of Regulation: One View of the Cathedral'. *Oxford Journal of Legal Students* 16, no. 4 (1996): 699.

Blair, M. 'Australia's Continuous Disclosure Regime: Proposals for Change'. *Australian Journal of Corporate Law* 2 (1992): 54.

Blair, M. 'The Debate over Mandatory Corporate Disclosure Rules'. *UNSW Law Journal* 15 (1992): 177.

Breeden, R.C. 'Giving It Away: Observations on the Role of the SEC in Corporate Governance and Corporate Charity'. *New York Law School Law Review* 41 (1997): 1179.

Brown, M. & S. MacLachlan. 'When Worlds Collide: The Reconciliation of Conflicting Requirements in Cross-Border Acquisitions'. *Securities Regulation Law Journal* 19 (1991): 99.

Burgoyne, T. 'Annual Disclosure in Canada: The Final Word?'. *International Financial Law Review* 9 (1990): 26.

Butler, A. 'Interview with Tony Hartnell'. *Commercial Law Quarterly* 6, no. 4 (1992): 11.

Cato, S. 'The World's Best and Worst Annual Reports'. *Chief Executive* 107 (1995): 32–39.

Cassidy, A. & L. Chapple. 'Australia's Corporate Disclosure Regime: Lessons from the US Model'. *Australian Journal of Corporate Law* 15, no. 2 (2003): 81–104.

Cheffins, B.R. 'Law, Economics and the UK's System of Corporate Governance: Lessons from History'. *The Journal of Corporate Law Studies* 1, no. 1 (2001): 77–89.

Cheffins, B.R. 'Corporate Law and Ownership Structure: A Darwinian Link?'. *UNSWLJ* 25, no. 2 (2002): 346–378.

Cheffins, B.R. 'Corporate Governance Convergence: Lessons from Australia'. *The Transitional Lawyer* 16, no. 1 (2002): 13–43.

Clark, F. & G. Dean. 'Chaos in the Counting-House: Accounting under Scrutiny'. *Australian Journal of Corporate Law* 2, no. 2 (1992): 177–201.

Coffee, J.C. 'Market Failure and the Economic Case for a Mandatory Disclosure System'. *Virginia Law Review* 70 (1984): 717.

Company and Securities Advisory Committee. *Report on an Enhanced Statutory Disclosure System*, 1991.

Corbett, A. 'A Proposal for a More Responsive Approach to the Regulation of Corporate Governance'. *Australian Federal Law Review* 23, no. 2 (1995): 277.

Corporate Practices and the Rights of Shareholders. Report of the House of Representatives Standing Committee of Legal and Constitutional Affairs. Canberra: AGPS, November, 1991.

Corporate Practices and the Rights of Shareholders. Submissions to the House of Representatives Standing Committee of Legal and Constitutional Affairs. Canberra: AGPS, 1991.

Courtis, J. 'Readability of Annual Reports: Western Versus Asian Evidence'. *Accounting, Auditing and Accountability Journal* 8, no. 2 (1995).

Cox, J.D. 'The ALI Institutionalization and Disclosure: The Quest for the Outside Director''s Spine'. *Gorge Washington Law Review* 61 (1993): 1233.

Craig, R.J. & F.L. Clarke. 'Phases in Australian Accounting Standards Setting: Control, Capture, Co-existence and Coercion'. *Australian Journal of Corporate Law* 3, no. 1 (1993): 50–64.

Cunningham, N. 'Capital Market Theory, Mandatory Disclosure, and Price Discovery'. *Wash & Lee Law Review* 51 (1994): 843.

Diamond, E. 'Outside Investors: A New Breed of Insider Traders?'. *Fordham Law Review* 60 (1992): 319.

Doty, J. 'The Role of the Securities and Exchange Commission in an Internationalized Marketplace'. *Fordham Law Review* 60 (1992): 77.

Duffy, M. 'Corporate Law Reform'. *Canberra Survey* 45, no. 6 (1992).

Easterbrook, F. & D. Fischel. 'Mandatory Disclosure and the Protection of Investors'. *Virginia Law Review* 70 (1984): 669, Internet edition at <www.lexis.com.research/retrive . . . k&-md5=014673f0a55071341b9b2e940b4137cc>.

Estreicher, A.G. 'Securities Regulation and the First Amendment'. *Georgia Law Review* 24 (1990): 97.

Explanatory Memorandum, Corporate Law Reform Act of 1994, Australia.

Fanto, J.A. 'Investor Education, Securities Disclosure, and the Creation and Enforcement of Corporate Governance and Firm Norms'. *The Catholic University Law Review* 48 (Fall, 1998): 15.

Fanto, J.A. 'The Absence of Cross-Cultural Communication: SEC Mandatory Disclosure and Foreign Corporate Governance'. *Northwestern School of Law Journal of International Law & Business* 17 (Fall, 1996): 1.

Fanto, J.A. 'We're All Capitalism Now: The Importance, Nature, Provision and Regulation of Investor Education'. *Case Western Reserve Law Review* 49 (Fall, 1998): 49.

Feller, R.H. 'Environmental Disclosure and the Securities Laws'. *Boston Environmental College Environmental Affairs Law Review* 22 (1995): 225.

Fife, K.S. 'Mandatory Disclosure of Soft Information in the Market for Corporate Control'. *Emory Law Journal* 35 (1986): 213.

Fox, M.B. 'Securities Disclosure in a Globalizing Market: Who Should Regulate Whom'. *Michigan Law Review* 95 (1997): 2498.

Fox, M.B. 'The Political Economy of Statutory Reach: U.S. Disclosure Rules in a Globalizing Market for Securities'. *Michigan Law Review* 22 (1998): 696.

Geiger, U. 'Harmonization of Securities Disclosure Rules in the Global Market: A Proposal'. *Fordham Law Review* 66 (1998): 1785.

Geiger, U. 'Special Symposium Issue: The Case for the Harmonization of Securities Disclosure Rules in the Global Market'. *Columbia Business Law Review* 241 (1997): 241.

Georgakopoulos, N. 'Why Should Disclosure Rules Subsidize Informed Traders?'. *International Review of Law and Economics* 16 (1996): 417.

Gillen, M. 'Capital Market Efficiency Assumptions: An Analytical Framework with an Application to Disclosure Laws'. *Canadian Business Law Journal* 23 (1994): 346.

Gilson, R.J. & R.H. Kraakman. 'The Mechanisms of Market Efficiency'. *Virginia Law Review* 70 (1984): 549, Internet edition at <www.lexis.com/research/ retrive . . . k&-m5=c6e4364641a15998eb98a1436661b5d0>.

Golding, G. & N. Kalfus. 'The Continuous Evolution of Australia's Continuous Disclosure Laws'. *Companies and Securities Law Journal* 22, no. 6 (2004): 385–425

Green, E., D. Braverman & S. Sperber. 'Hegemony or Deference: U.S. Disclosure Requirements in the International Capital Markets'. *Business Lawyer* 50 (1995): 413.

Guttman, S., S. Dunlop & J. Mackie. 'Corporate Governance, Timely Disclosure Policy and Liability for Corporate Disclosures'. In Fraser Beatty, <www. fraserbeatty.ca/fbhome/publications/SecuritiesUpdate_Feb96.html>.

Hammond, I. 'Interview: Accounting Standards and the High Cost of Compliance'. *Company Director* 10, no. 3 (1994): 19.

Hazen L.T. 'Commentary: Symposium on Securities Market Regulation'. *The Catholic University Law Review* 36 (Summer, 1987).

Herder, G. 'Corporate Finance Theory and the Australian Prospectus Legislation'. *Corporate and Business Law Journal* 7 (1995): 181.

Hewitt, J. 'Developing Concepts of Materiality and Disclosure'. *Business Lawyer* 32 (1977): 887.

Ickeringill, P. 'Statutory Responsibilities of Directors and Auditors in Relation to Company Accounts'. *C&SLJ* 6, no. 1 (1988): 2–26.

Jennings, M., P. Reckers & D. Kneer. 'Concepts of Materiality and Disclosure: Can the Disciplines and Practitioners Agree?'. *Securities Regulation Law Journal* 12 (1985): 337.

Jones, M.J. 'Readability of Annual Reports: Western versus Asian Evidence: A Comment to Contextualize'. *Accounting, Auditing and Accountability Journal* 9, no. 2 (1996).

Jones, M.J. 'Whatever Happened to the Corporate Report'. *Management Accounting* 73, no. 7 (1995): 53.

Jordan, C. 'Regulation of Canadian Capital Markets in the 1990's: The United States in the Driver''s Seat'. *Pacific Rim Law & Policy Journal* 4 (1995): 577.

Kehoe, J. 'Exporting Insider Trading Laws: The Enforcement of U.S. Insider Trading Laws Internationally'. *Emory International Law Review* 9 (1995): 345.

Kitch, E. 'The Theory and Practice of Securities Disclosure'. *Brooklyn Law Review* 61 (1995): 763.

Knauss R.L. 'A Reappraisal of the Role of Disclosure'. *Michigan Law Review* 62 (1964): 607.

Koeck, W. & I. Ramsay. 'Continuous Disclosure: A Critical Review'. *Australian Corporate Lawyer* 3 (1993): 6.

Koeck, W. 'Continuous Disclosure'. *Company and Securities Law Journal* 13 (1995): 485.

Landau, D. 'SEC Proposals to Facilitate Multinational Securities Offerings: Disclosure Requirements in the United States and the United Kingdom'. *International Law and Politics* 19 (1987): 457.

Langevoort, D.M. 'Information Technology and the Structure of Securities Regulation'. *Harvard Law Review* 98 (1985): 747.

Lavarch, M. 'Interview: A Fresh Look at Corporations Law'. *Company Director* 9, no. 9 (1993): 20.

Lavarch, M. 'The Government's Approach to Corporate Law Reform'. *Australian Journal of Corporate Law* 4 (1994): 1–19.

Leftwich, R.W., R.L. Watts & J.L. Zimmerman. 'Voluntary Corporate Disclosure: The Case of Interim Reporting'. *Supp J Acc Rev* 19 (1981): 50.

Levy, P. 'Internationalisation of the Securities Market: Jurisdiction and Enforcement Issues'. *C&SLJ* 6, no. 2 (1988): 75–95.

Licht, A.N. 'Regulatory Arbitrage for Real: International Securities Regulation in a World of Interacting Securities Markets'. *Virginia Journal of International Law* 38 (1998): 563.

Little, P. 'The Policy Underlying Financial Disclosure by Corporations and Its Effect upon Legal Liability'. *Australian Journal of Corporate Law* 1 (1991): 97.

Loewenstein, M.J. 'The SEC and the Future of Corporate Governance'. *Alabama Law Review* 45 (Spring, 1994): 783.

Longstreth, B. 'A Look at the SEC's Adaptation to Global Market Pressures'. *Columbia Journal of Transnational* 33 (1995): 319.

Lorne, S. 'Current Trends in International Securities Regulation'. *Cornell International Law Journal* 28 (1995): 453.

Lowenstein, L. 'Financial Transparency and Corporate Governance: You Manage What You Measure'. *Columbia Law Review* 96 (1996): 1335.

Macey, J. & H. Kanda. 'The Stock Exchange as a Firm: The Emergence of Close Substitutes for the New York and Tokyo Stock Exchanges'. *Cornell Law Review* 75 (1990): 1007.

Mahoney, P. 'Mandatory Disclosure as a Solution to Agency Problems'. *University of Chicago Law Review* 62 (1995): 1047.

Mahoney, P.G. 'Mandatory Disclosure as a Solution to Agency Problems'. *University of Chicago Law Review* 62 (Winter, 1995): 187.

Mahoney, P.G. 'Securities Regulation by Enforcement: An International Perspective'. *Yale J. on Reg.* 7 (1990): 305.

Malloy, M. 'Bumper Cars: Themes of Convergence in International Regulation'. *Fordham Law Review* 60 (1992): 1.

Maughan, C.W. & S.F. Copp. 'Company Law Reform and Economic Methodology Revisited'. *Company Law* 21 (2000): 14.

McDonald, M. 'Confidentiality and Takeovers'. *Company and Securities Law Journal* 11 (1993): 173.

McGreger, W. 'True and Fair View: An Accounting Anachronism'. *Australian Accountant* 62 (1992): 68.

McQueen, R. 'Corporate Law and Historical Methodology: A Critical Perspective'. *Canberra Law Review* 3 (1996): 7.

McQueen, R. 'The Corporate Image: The Regulation of Annual Reports in Australia'. *Macquarie Law Journal* 1, no. 1 (2001): 93–128.

Meier-Shatz, C.J. 'Objectives of Financial Disclosure Regulation'. *J Comp Bus & Cap Market Law* 8 (1986): 219.

Mitchell, S. 'ASC Chief Calls for Disclosure Regime'. *The Australian Financial Review*, 29 May 1991.

Morris, R.D. 'Corporate Disclosure in a Substantially Unregulated Environment'. *Abacus* 20 (1984): 52.

Morris, M.S. 'The Securities Enforcement Remedies and Penny Stock Reform Act of 1990: By Keeping up with the Joneses, the SEC's Enforcement Arsenal Is Modernize'. *Admin. L. J. Am. U.* 7 (Summer, 1993): 151.

Ng, E.J. & H.C. Koh. 'An Agency Theory and Profit Analytic Approach to Corporate Non-mandatory Disclosure Compliance'. *Asia-Pacific J of Accounting* 1 (1994): 29.

Nicoll, G. 'Lost Opportunities for Improved Disclosure within the Corporate Law Reform Bill (No. 2) 1992'. *Australian Journal of Corporate Law* 3 (1993): 27.

Nicoll, G. 'The Changing Face of the Company as a Whole and Directors' Responsibilities to Members in the Exercise of Management Powers'. *Australian Journal of Corporate Law* 4 (1993): 287.

Ogus, A.I. 'Regulatory Appraisal: A Neglected Opportunity for Law and Economics'. *European Journal of Law and Economics* 6 (1998): 53.

Opinion. 'Getting Closure on Disclosure'. *Australian Financial Review*, 17 September 2001, 74.

Painter, R.W. 'Disclosure of Environmental Legal Proceedings under the Securities Laws: A Potential Step Backward'. *University of Oregon Journal of Environmental Law and Litigation* 11 (1996): 91.

Pinto, A.R. 'Section III: Corporate Governance: Monitoring the Board of Directors in American Corporations'. *The American Society of Comparative Law* 46 (1998): 317.

Ragsdale, M.E. 'Executive Composition: Will the New SEC Disclosure Rules Control "Executive" Pay at the Top?'. *Curators of the University of Missouri at Kansas City Law Review* 61 (1993): 537.

Ramsay, I.M. 'Law and Economics as an Approach to Corporate Law Research'. *Canberra Law Review* 3 (1996): 48.

Rifkind, N.C. 'Should Uninformed Shareholders Be a Threat Justifying Defensive Action by Target Directors in Delaware: "Just Say No" after *Moore v. Wallace*'. *Boston University Law Review* 78 (1998): 105.

Roberts, R. 'The Constantly Involving Nature of Federal Securities Law: An Introduction to the Symposium'. *Alabama Law Review* 45 (Spring, 1994): 729.

Roberts, R. Remarks at New York Society of Security Analysts Conference on Current Issues in the Derivatives Markets, <www.gsionline.com/speech/SPCH040TXT>, 1995.

Rodier, R. 'The Efficient Capital Market Hypothesis, Economic Theory and the Regulation of the Securities Industry'. *Stanford Law Review* 29 (1977): 1031.

Rogers, A. 'What Are We Trying to Achieve by the Corporations Law?'. *Commercial Law Quarterly* 6, no. 4 (1992): 15.

Romano, R. 'Empowering Investors: A Market Approach to Securities Regulation'. *Yale Law Journal* 107 (1998): 2359.

Ruder, D.S. 'Reconciling U.S. Disclosure Policy with International Accounting and Disclosure Standards'. *Northwestern School of Law Journal of International Law & Business* 17 (Fall, 1996): 119.

Sargent, M.A. 'State Disclosure Regulation and the Allocation of Regulatory Responsibilities'. *Maryland Law Review* 46 (1987): 240.

Schwarcz, S. 'Rethinking the Disclosure Paradigm in a World of Complexity'. *Illinois Law Review* 1 (2004): 1–37.

Sealy, L.S. 'The "Disclosure Philosophy" and Company Law Reform'. *Company Lawyer* 2 (1981): 51.

'SEC Considers Disclosure Simplification Task Force Recommendations'. *AIMR Advocacy Bulletin* (1996), <www.aimr.com/aimr/advocacy/ad_bulletin_mar.html>.

Securities Exchange Commission. Municipal Securities Disclosure, Release No. 34-34961, <www.sec.gov/rules/final/adpt6.txt>, 1994.

Securities Industry Association. Press Release, Rapid Advances in Technology, Globalisation and Markets Create Pressing Need for Prompt Reforms, <www.sia.com/sia04zq.htm>, 1996.

Seligan. 'The History Need for a Mandatory Disclosure Regime'. *Journal of Corporate Law* 9 (1983): 1.

Seligman, J. 'The Mandatory Disclosure System and Foreign Firms'. *Pacific Rim Law & Policy Journal* 4 (1995): 807.

Singh, B. & O. Seiler. 'Shareholder Participation in Corporate Decision-Making under German Law: A Comparative Analysis'. *Brooklyn Journal of International Law* 24 (1998): 493.

Stapledon, G.P. & J. Lawrence. 'Board Composition, Structure and Independence in Australia's Largest Listed Companies'. *Melbourne University Law Review* 21 (1997): 150.

Stapleton, G. & J. Webster. 'Putting the Spills of Litigation into the Shareholders' Pockets: When Can Shareholders Bring A Personal Action against the

Directors of Their Company'. *Companies and Securities Law Journal* 22, no. 8 (2004): 535–544.

Steinberg, M.I. 'Some Thoughts on Regulation of Tender Offers'. *Maryland Law Review* 43 (1984): 240.

Stigler, G.J. 'Public Regulation of the Securities Market'. *Journal of Business* 37 (1964): 117.

Thomson, S.C. 'The Merger and Acquisition Provisions of the ALI Corporate Governance Project as Applied to the Three Steps in the Time-Warner Acquisition'. *Columbia Business Law Review* 2 (1996): 145.

Thornton, G. 'Improving the Disclosure Process and Access to Capital Markets: Highlights of the Securities and Exchange Commission's Report on the Task Force on Disclosure Simplification', <www.gt.com/gtonline/assurance/accestoc.html>.

Tomasic, R. 'Reform and Enforcement of Australian Stock Exchange Rules and the New Continuous Disclosure Laws'. *Asia Pacific Law Review* 4 (1995): 21.

Tomasic, R. 'Using Social Science Research Methods in the Study of Corporate Law'. *Canberra Law Review* 3 (1996): 24.

Treasury. Submissions to Financial System Inquiry (Wallis Inquiry), <www.treasury.gov.au/fsi/FSI_info.html>.

Verrecchia, R.E. 'Discretionary Disclosure'. *J Acc & Econ* 5 (1983): 179.

Villiers, C. 'Disclosure Obligations in Company Law: Bringing Communication Theory into the Fold'. *The Journal of Corporate Law Studies* 1 (2001): 181–210.

Walker, I. 'ASC Is Suggesting a Whole New Regime of Disclosure Demands'. *New Accountant*, March 1991, 16.

Wallace, C. 'Control through Disclosure Legislation: Foreign Multinational Enterprises in Industrialized States'. *International and Comparative Law Quarterly* 32 (1983): 141.

Webster, J. 'The NRMA Case: Implications for Directors'. *Company and Securities Law Journal* 13 (1995): 281.

Weiss, E. 'Disclosure and Corporate Accountability'. *Business Lawyer*, 1979, 575.

C.   Legislation

The Australian Securities and Investments Commission Act of 2001 (Commonwealth).

The Corporations Act of 2001 (Commonwealth).

Corporations Amendment (Short Selling) Act of 2008 (Cth).

Listing Rules of the Australian Securities Exchange.

Index